Love UNDER FIRE

W9-BOF-472

Pacific Press® Publishing Association
Nampa, Idaho
Oshawa, Ontario, Canada
www.pacificpress.com

Cover design by Doug Church
Cover illustration by Eric Joyner © Pacific Press® Publishing Association
Inside design by Aaron Troia

Additional copies of this book are available by
calling toll-free 1-800-765-6955 or
online at www.adventistbookcenter.com.

ISBN 13: 978-0-8163-2627-3
ISBN 10: 0-8163-2627-4

11 12 13 14 15 • 5 4 3 2 1

Contents

Foreword..5
Lifting the Veil on the Future 7
  1. A Forecast of the World's Destiny 13
  2. The First Christians—Loyal and True 20
  3. Spiritual Darkness in the Early Church 24
  4. The Waldenses Defend the Faith 30
  5. The Light Breaks in England 37
  6. Two Heroes Face Death 44
  7. Luther, a Man for His Time 54
  8. A Champion of Truth 64
  9. Light Kindled in Switzerland 75
 10. Progress in Germany 80
 11. The Protest of the Princes 85
 12. Daybreak in France 90
 13. The Netherlands and Scandinavia 101
 14. Truth Advances in Britain 105
 15. France's Reign of Terror: Its True Cause 113
 16. Seeking Freedom in a New World 123
 17. Promises of Christ's Return 127
 18. New Light in the New World 134
 19. Why the Great Disappointment? 145
 20. Love for Christ's Coming 149
 21. Reaping the Whirlwind 157
 22. Prophecies Fulfilled 163
 23. The Open Mystery of the Sanctuary 169
 24. What Is Christ Doing Now? 175
 25. God's Law Unchangeable 179
 26. Champions for Truth 187
 27. How Successful Are Modern Revivals? 190
 28. Facing Our Life Record 197
 29. Why Was Sin Permitted? 203
 30. Satan and Humanity at War 208
 31. Evil Spirits 210

32. How to Defeat Satan 213
33. What Happens After Death? 218
34. Who Are the "Spirits" in Spiritualism? 225
35. Liberty of Conscience Threatened 230
36. The Approaching Conflict 237
37. Our Only Safeguard 241
38. God's Final Message 244
39. The Time of Trouble 248
40. God's People Delivered 256
41. The Earth in Ruins 263
42. Eternal Peace: The Controversy Ended 267
Appendix... 274

Foreword

What is happening to our world? Storms, earthquakes, and tsunamis devastate large areas, with a huge toll of death and injury, loss of property, and ongoing suffering. War and conflict, not only between nations but between ideologies and ethnic groups, seem more and more common and unsolvable. Economic setbacks, even in the richest nations, threaten the security of people everywhere. A decline in morality and—worse yet—a lack of moral awareness seems at the root of an increase of crime and of much social deterioration. Are we on the verge of a global upheaval?

Love Under Fire outlines the grand sweep of events that have brought us to this point and will usher in this world's final events. In doing so it emphasizes the authority of the Bible while presenting the underlying cause of the evils we see around us— the ongoing conflict that Satan has waged against Christ. Throughout the history of this earth, Satan has misrepresented God's character of love. He has put "love under fire," especially in the person of Christ, who is love, but also in Christ's true followers. This conflict has affected the whole world. *Love Under Fire* picks up the story where the New Testament leaves it,

tracing the startling account of what has happened to the Christian faith since Bible times and what will soon develop in the great controversy between Christ and Satan. How did we get where we are today? And where are events leading us? Despite difficult days ahead, the book points us to a glorious future, grander than we can imagine.

Love Under Fire is an adaptation of *From Here to Forever*, a 1982 condensed edition of Ellen G. White's classic volume, *The Great Controversy*. The condensed volume included all the chapters of the original, using only the author's own words but shortening the account.

The current adaptation goes a step beyond this, using some words, expressions, and sentence constructions more familiar to twenty-first century readers. It does this not only in the portions written by Ellen G. White, but also in the quotations she included from others and in the Appendix material, to enhance readability. Occasionally, it restores a sentence or clause left out of the original condensation. Most of the Bible quotations come from the New King James Version, which closely resembles the King James Version that Ellen White commonly used. It is hoped that readers who are new to her writings will enjoy this adaptation and that it will encourage them to read the original editions of her works.

This volume presents insights into Bible prophecy, highlighting significant prophecies that have already met their fulfillment and showing what the Bible says is soon to happen. It places these events of the past, present, and future into their larger framework, so that the reader can understand the meaning of history and the purpose for what is yet to come.

Ellen G. White wrote five powerful volumes that together comprise the Conflict of the Ages series, tracing the conflict between Christ and Satan from its origin in heaven, through the major events of Bible times, and finally in post-Bible times down to the end of the conflict. *Love Under Fire* was condensed and adapted from the last of the five volumes. That many more readers may be drawn to God through these books and their presentation of Bible themes is the hope and prayer of

Lifting the Veil on the Future*

Before sin entered this world, Adam and Even enjoyed open fellowship with their Maker. But since our first parents separated themselves from God by disobedience, the human race has been cut off from this great privilege. The plan of redemption, however, opened a way for those living on the earth still to have a connection with heaven. God has communicated with human beings by His Spirit by giving divine light to the world through revelations to His chosen servants. "Holy men of God spoke as they were moved by the Holy Spirit" (2 Peter 1:21).

During the first twenty-five hundred years of human history, there was no written message from God. Those whom God had instructed communicated their knowledge to others, and it was handed down from father to son over many generations. The recording of such things in writing began in the time of Moses. Inspired revelations were then put together in an Inspired Book. This work continued during the long period of sixteen hundred years— from Moses, the historian of creation and the law, to John, the recorder of the grandest truths of the gospel.

The Bible points to God as its author, yet it was written by human hands, and in the varied style of its different books it reflects the characteristics of the individual writers. The truths revealed are all "given by inspiration of God" (2 Timothy 3:16), yet they are expressed in human words. By His Holy Spirit the Infinite One has brought light into the minds and hearts of His servants. He has given dreams and visions, symbols and illustrations; and those to whom He revealed these truths have themselves put the thought into human language.

Written in different ages, by men who differed widely in social status and occupation and in their mental and spiritual abilities, the books of the Bible present a wide contrast in style as well as a diversity in the kinds of subjects they treat. The various writers use different forms of expression. Often one will present the same truth more strikingly than another. And as several writers present a subject in different ways and from different perspectives, readers who are superficial, careless, or prejudiced may think they see a discrepancy or contradiction, where the thoughtful, reverent student, with

---

*Author's Introduction.

clearer insight, recognizes the underlying harmony.

The different authors bring out the truth in its varied aspects. One writer is more strongly impressed with one phase of the subject, and he grasps the points that relate to his experience or to his ability to understand and appreciate them. Another relates to a different phase. Under the guidance of the Holy Spirit, each presents what most strongly impresses his own mind—a different aspect of the truth in each, but a perfect harmony through them all. And the truths revealed in this way unite to form a perfect whole, adapted to meet human needs in all the circumstances and experiences of life.

God has chosen to communicate His truth to the world by human agencies. He Himself, by His Holy Spirit, qualified these men and women and enabled them to do this work. He guided their minds in selecting what to speak and write. God entrusted the treasure to earthen vessels, yet it is still from Heaven. The message comes through the imperfect expression of human language, yet it is the testimony of God. The obedient, believing child of God sees in this message the glory of a divine power, full of grace and truth.

In His Word, God has committed to us the knowledge we need for salvation. We are to accept the Holy Scriptures as an authoritative, infallible revelation of His will. They are the standard of character, the revealer of doctrines, and the test of Christian experience. "All Scripture is given by inspiration of God, and is profitable for doctrine, for reproof, for correction, for instruction in righteousness, that the man of God may be complete, thoroughly equipped for every good work" (2 Timothy 3:16, 17).

Yet the fact that God has revealed His will to humanity through His Word does not make the continued presence and guiding of the Holy Spirit unnecessary. On the contrary, our Savior promised to give the Spirit to open the Word to His servants, to illuminate and apply its teachings. And since it was the Spirit of God who inspired the Bible, it is impossible for the teaching of the Spirit ever to be contrary to that of God's Word.

The Spirit was not given—and never will be given—to replace the Bible, because the Scriptures explicitly say that the Word of God is the standard by which we must test all teaching and experience. The apostle John says, "Do not believe every spirit, but test the spirits, whether they are of God; because many false prophets have gone out into the world" (1 John 4:1). And Isaiah declares, "To the law and to the testimony! If they do not speak according to this word, it is because there is no light in them" (Isaiah 8:20).

The work of the Holy Spirit has been blamed for the errors of people who claim to be enlightened by the Spirit and then say that they no longer need the Word of God to guide them. They are governed by impressions that they think are the voice of God in the heart. But the spirit that controls them is not the Spirit of God. This following of impressions while neglecting the Scriptures can only lead to confusion, to deception and ruin. It serves only to aid the plans of the evil one. Since the ministry of the Holy Spirit is vitally important to the church of Christ, it is one of Satan's schemes to use the errors of extremists and fanatics to discredit the work of the Spirit and cause the people of God to neglect this source of strength that our Lord Himself has provided.

In harmony with the Word of God, His Spirit was to continue working throughout the gospel era. During the ages while the Scriptures of both the Old and the New Testament were being given, the Holy Spirit did not stop communicating light to individual minds, even apart from the revelations that were to be included in the books of the Bible. The Bible itself tells how people received warning, reproof, counsel, and instruction through the Holy Spirit in matters unrelated to the giving of the Scriptures. And it mentions prophets in different ages whose messages are not recorded. In the same way, after the Bible was complete, the Holy Spirit was still to continue working, to enlighten, warn, and comfort the children of God.

Jesus promised His disciples, "The Helper, the Holy Spirit, whom the Father will send in My name, He will teach you all things, and bring to your remembrance all things that I said to you." "When He, the Spirit of truth, has come, He will guide you into all truth; . . . and He will tell you things to come." (John 14:26; 16:13.) Scripture plainly teaches that these promises, instead of just being limited to the days of the apostles, extend to Christ's church in all ages. The Savior assures His followers, "I am with you always, even to the end of the age" (Matthew 28:20). And Paul declares that the gifts and workings of the Spirit were given to the church "for the equipping of the saints for the work of ministry, for the edifying of the body of Christ, till we all come to the unity of the faith and of the knowledge of the Son of God, to a perfect man, to the measure of the stature of the fullness of Christ" (Ephesians 4:12, 13).

For the believers at Ephesus the apostle prayed "that the God of our Lord Jesus Christ, the Father of glory, may give to you the *spirit of wisdom and revelation* in the knowledge of Him, *the eyes of your understanding being enlightened;* that you may know what is the hope of His calling . . . and what is the *exceeding greatness* of His power toward us who believe" (Ephesians 1:17–19). The ministry of the divine Spirit to enlighten the understanding and open to the mind the deep things of God's Holy Word was the blessing that Paul was seeking for the Ephesian church.

After the wonderful outpouring of the Holy Spirit on the Day of Pentecost, Peter urged the people to repent and be baptized in the name of Christ for the forgiveness of their sins, and he said: "You shall receive the gift of the Holy Spirit. For the promise is to you and to your children, and to all who are afar off, as many as the Lord our God will call" (Acts 2:38, 39).

Directly connected with the scenes of the great day of God, through the prophet Joel the Lord has promised a special manifestation of His Spirit (Joel 2:28). This prophecy received a partial fulfillment in the outpouring of the Spirit on the Day of Pentecost. But it will be completely fulfilled in the display of divine grace that will accompany the closing work of the gospel.

The great controversy between good and evil will become more and more intense to the very end of time. In all ages Satan has shown his anger against the church of Christ, and God has given His grace and Spirit to His people to strengthen them to stand against the power of the evil one. When the apostles of Christ were to carry His gospel to the world and to record it for all future ages, they were especially given the enlightenment of the Spirit. But as the church approaches its final deliverance, Satan will work with greater power. He comes down "having great wrath, because he knows that he has a short time" (Revelation 12:12). He will work "with all power, signs, and lying wonders" (2 Thessalonians 2:9). For six thousand years that mastermind that once was highest among the angels of God has given all of his energy to the work of deception and ruin. And all the subtle depths of satanic skill he has acquired, all the cruelty he has developed during these struggles of the ages, he will bring against God's people in the final conflict. And in this time of danger the followers of Christ are to carry to the world the warning of the Lord's second advent. Their testimony is to help prepare a people to stand before Him at His coming, "without spot and blameless" (2 Peter 3:14). At this time the church needs the special gift of divine grace and power at least as much as in the days of the apostles.

Through the illumination of the Holy Spirit, the scenes of the long-running conflict between good and evil have been opened to the writer of these pages. From time to time I have been permitted to see the working, in different ages, of the great controversy between Christ, the Prince of life, the Author of our salvation, and Satan, the prince of evil, the author of sin, the first transgressor of God's holy law. Satan's malice against Christ has been directed against His followers. In all the history of the past we may trace the same hatred of the principles of God's law, the same policy of deception, by which Satan has tried to make error appear as truth, substitute human laws for the law of God, and lead people to worship the creature rather than the Creator. In all ages Satan has tried continually to misrepresent the character of God, to lead people to cling to a false concept of the Creator, and then to regard Him with fear and hate rather than with love. He has tried to set aside the divine law, leading people to think they are free from its requirements. And he has persecuted those who dare to resist his deceptions. We can see these things in the history of patriarchs, prophets, and apostles, of martyrs and Reformers.

In the great final conflict, Satan will use the same approaches, reveal the same spirit, and work for the same goal as in all the preceding ages. What has been will be, except that the coming struggle will be marked with a terrible intensity such as the world has never seen before. Satan's deceptions will be more subtle, his attacks more determined. If it were possible, he would lead astray those whom God is saving (Mark 13:22).

As the Spirit of God has opened to my mind the great truths of His Word and the scenes of the past and the future, I have been told to make known to others what has been revealed in this way—to trace the history of the controversy in past ages, and especially to present it in a way that will shed light on the fast-approaching struggle of the future. In doing this, I have tried to select and group together events in the history of the church in such a way as to show the unfolding of the great testing truths that have been given to the world at different times, that have stirred up the anger of Satan and the hatred of a world-loving church, and that have been preserved by the witness of those who "did not love their lives to the death" (Revelation 12:11).

In these records we may see a preview of the conflict ahead of us. Looking at them in the light of God's Word and with the illumination of His Spirit, we may see Satan's deceptions revealed and the dangers we must shun if we want to be found "without fault" before the Lord at His coming (Revelation 14:5).

The great events that have marked the progress of reform in past ages are matters of history, well known and universally acknowledged by the Protestant world. They are facts that no one can refute. This history I have presented briefly, in keeping with the scope of the book and the need to condense the facts into as little space as possible while still giving a proper understanding of their meaning for us.

In some cases where a historian has grouped events together in a way to give a brief yet comprehensive view of the subject, or has summarized details in a convenient manner, his words have been quoted. But for some of these no specific credit has been given, since the quotations are not given for the purpose of citing that writer as authority, but because his statement offers a convenient and forcible presentation of the subject. In telling about the experience and views of those carrying forward the work of reform in our own time, I have made similar use of their published works.

This book is intended not so much to present new truths about the struggles of times past as to bring out facts and principles that relate to coming events. Yet when we view them as a part of the controversy between the forces of light and darkness, we see all these records of the past with a new significance. Through them a light shines on the future, illuminating the pathway of those who, like the reformers of past ages, will be called, even at the risk of losing everything that this world offers, to witness "for the word of God and for the testimony of Jesus Christ" (Revelation 1:9).

The purpose of this book is to unfold the scenes of the great controversy between truth and error, to reveal Satan's deceptions and the means by which we may successfully resist him, to present a satisfactory solution to the great problem of evil, shedding light on the origin and the final end of sin in a way that reveals fully the justice and goodness of God in all His dealings with His creatures, and to show the holy, unchanging nature of His law. It is my earnest prayer that through the influence of this book, people may be delivered from the power of darkness and become "partakers of the inheri- tance of the saints in the light" (Colossians 1:12), to the praise of Him who loved us and gave Himself for us.

E.G.W.

A Forecast of the World's Destiny

From the crest of the Mount of Olives, Jesus looked at Jerusalem. The magnificent buildings of the temple were in full view. The setting sun lighted up its snowy white marble walls and gleamed from the golden tower and pinnacle. What child of Israel could gaze on that scene without a thrill of joy and admiration! But other thoughts occupied Jesus' mind. "As He drew near, He saw the city and wept over it" (Luke 19:41).

Jesus' tears were not for Himself, even though ahead of Him lay Gethsemane, the scene of His approaching agony, and Calvary, the place of crucifixion, was not far away. Yet it was not these scenes that cast the shadow over Him in this time of gladness. He wept for the thousands of doomed people in Jerusalem.

Jesus saw the history of more than a thousand years of God's special favor and guardian care for the chosen people. God had honored Jerusalem above all the earth. The Lord had "chosen Zion . . . for His dwelling place" (Psalm 132:13). For ages, holy prophets had given their messages of warning. Daily the priests had offered the blood of lambs, pointing to the Lamb of God.

If Israel as a nation had preserved her loyalty to Heaven, Jerusalem would have stood forever as God's chosen city. But the history of the people God had favored was a record of backsliding and rebellion. With more than a father's tender love, God had "compassion on His people and on His dwelling place" (2 Chronicles 36:15). When appeals and rebuke had failed, He sent the best gift of heaven, the Son of God Himself, to plead with the unrepentant city.

For three years the Lord of light and glory had been among His people, "doing good and healing all who were oppressed by the devil," setting free those who were bound, restoring sight to the blind, causing the lame to walk and the deaf to hear, cleansing lepers, raising the dead, and preaching the gospel to the poor (see Acts 10:38; Luke 4:18; Matthew 11:5).

Jesus lived as a homeless wanderer to minister to people's needs and their troubles, to plead with them to accept the gift of life. The waves of mercy, beaten back by those stubborn hearts, returned in a stronger tide of sympathetic, inexpressible love. But Israel had turned from her best Friend and only Helper, despising the pleadings of His love.

The time of hope and pardon was

quickly passing. The cloud that had been building through ages of apostasy and rebellion was about to burst upon a guilty people. They had scorned, abused, and rejected the only One who could save them from their approaching fate, and they would soon crucify Him.

As Christ looked at Jerusalem, He saw before Him the doom of a whole city and a whole nation. He saw the destroying angel with sword uplifted against the city that had been God's dwelling place for so long. From the very spot that Titus and his army later occupied, He looked across the valley at the sacred courtyards and covered walkways of the temple. With tear-filled eyes He saw foreign forces surrounding the walls. He heard the tread of armies marshaling for war, the voice of mothers and children crying for food in the besieged city. He saw Jerusalem's holy house, her palaces and towers, given to the flames, a heap of smoldering ruins.

Looking down the ages, He saw the covenant people scattered in every land, "like wrecks on a desert shore." Divine pity and yearning love found a voice in the mournful words: "O Jerusalem, Jerusalem, the one who kills the prophets and stones those who are sent to her! How often I wanted to gather your children together, as a hen gathers her chicks under her wings, but you were not willing!" (Matthew 23:37).

Christ saw Jerusalem as a symbol of the world hardened in unbelief and rebellion, hurrying on to meet the judgments of God. His heart was moved with pity for the afflicted and suffering ones of earth. He longed to relieve them all. He was willing to give His last measure of life to bring salvation within their reach.

The Majesty of heaven in tears! That scene shows how hard it is to save the guilty from the results of violating the law of God. Jesus saw the world involved in deception similar to that which caused Jerusalem's destruction. The great sin of the Jews was their rejection of Christ; the great sin of the world would be their rejection of God's law, the foundation of His government in heaven and earth. Millions in slavery to sin, doomed to suffer the second death, would refuse to listen to words of truth in their day of opportunity.

Magnificent Temple Doomed

Two days before the Passover, Christ went again with His disciples to the Mount of Olives overlooking the city. Once more He gazed on the temple in its dazzling splendor, a crown of beauty. Solomon, the wisest of Israel's rulers, had completed the first temple, the most magnificent building the world ever saw. After Nebuchadnezzar destroyed it, it was rebuilt about five hundred years before the birth of Christ.

But the second temple was not as magnificent as the first. No cloud of glory, no fire from heaven, descended on its altar. The ark, the mercy seat, and the tablets of the law were not to be found there. No voice from heaven made known to the priest the will of God. The second temple was not honored with the cloud of God's glory, but with the living presence of One who was God Himself revealed in the flesh. The "Desire of all nations" had come to His temple when the Man of Nazareth taught and healed in its sacred courts. But Israel had refused that Gift from heaven. When the humble Teacher went out from its golden gate that day, the glory had forever departed from the temple. Already the Savior's words were fulfilled: "Your house is left to you desolate" (Matthew 23:38).

The disciples had been amazed at Christ's prediction of the overthrow of the temple, and they wanted to understand what His words meant. Herod the Great had lavished both Roman and Jewish treasure on the temple. Massive blocks of white marble, shipped from Rome, formed part of its structure. The disciples had called the attention of their Master to these, saying, "See what manner of stones and what buildings are here!" (Mark 13:1).

Jesus made the solemn and startling reply, "Assuredly, I say to you, not one stone shall be left here upon another, that shall not be thrown down" (Matthew 24:2). The Lord had told the disciples that He would come the second time. So when He mentioned judgments on Jerusalem, their minds went to that coming, and they asked: "When will these things be? And what will be the sign of Your coming, and of the end of the age?" (Matthew 24:3).

Christ presented to them an outline of important events before the close of time. The prophecy He spoke had two meanings. While foreshadowing the destruction of Jerusalem, it also predicted the terrors of the last great day.

Judgments were to fall on Israel for rejecting and crucifying the Messiah. " 'Therefore when you see the "abomination of desolation," spoken of by Daniel the prophet, standing in the holy place' (whoever reads, let him understand), 'then let those who are in Judea flee to the mountains' " (Matthew 24:15, 16; see also Luke 21:20, 21). When the pagan banners of the Romans would be set up in the holy ground outside the city walls, then the followers of Christ were to run for safety. To escape, they must not allow any delay. Because of her sins, God had decreed judgment against Jerusalem. Her stubborn unbelief made her doom certain.

The inhabitants of Jerusalem accused Christ of being the cause of all the troubles that had come upon them because of their sins. Though they knew that He was sinless, they declared that His death was necessary for their safety as a nation. They agreed with the decision of their high priest that it would be better for one man to die than for the whole nation to perish (see John 11:47–53).

While they killed their Savior because He condemned their sins, they thought of themselves as God's favored people and expected the Lord to deliver them from their enemies!

God's Long-suffering

For nearly forty years the Lord delayed His judgments. There were still many Jews who were ignorant of Christ's character and work. And the children had not had the light that their parents had rejected. God would cause light to shine on them through the apostles' preaching. They would see how prophecy had been fulfilled not only in Christ's birth and life, but in His death and resurrection. God did not condemn the children for the sins of the parents, but when the children rejected the additional light He gave them, they became partakers of the parents' sins and filled up the cup of their iniquity.

In their stubborn refusal to repent, the Jews rejected the last offer of mercy. Then God withdrew His protection from them. The nation was left to the control of the leader it had chosen. Satan stirred up the fiercest and lowest passions of the heart. People were beyond reason—controlled by impulse and blind rage, and satanic in their cruelty. Friends and relatives betrayed one another. Parents killed their children, and children their parents. Rulers had no power to rule themselves. Uncontrolled passions made them tyrants. The Jews had accepted false testimony to condemn the innocent Son of God. Now false accusations made their lives uncertain. The fear of God no longer disturbed them. Satan was at the head of the nation.

Leaders of opposing groups attacked each other's forces and slaughtered without mercy. Even the sacredness of the temple could not restrain their fierce fighting. The sanctuary was polluted with the bodies of the dead. Yet the leaders behind this hellish work declared that they had no fear that Jerusalem would be destroyed, for it was God's own city! Even while Roman legions surrounded the temple, many Jews still strongly believed that the Most High would step in to defeat their enemies. But Israel had turned her back on God's protection, and now they had no defense.

Omens of Disaster

All the predictions Christ had given about Jerusalem's destruction were fulfilled to the letter. Signs and wonders appeared. For seven years a man continued to go up and down the streets of Jerusalem, announcing disasters to come. This strange man was imprisoned and whipped, but in the face of insult and abuse he answered only, "Woe, woe to Jerusalem!" He was killed in the siege he foretold.[1]

Not one Christian died in the destruction of Jerusalem. After the Romans under their leader Cestius had surrounded the city, they abandoned the siege unexpectedly when everything seemed ready for the attack. The Roman general withdrew his forces for no apparent reason. The waiting Christians recognized the promised sign (Luke 21:20, 21).

God so overruled events that neither Jews nor Romans would prevent the Christians' escape. When Cestius retreated, the Jews pursued, and while both forces were fully engaged, the Christians throughout the land were able to make their escape without interference to a place of safety, the city of Pella.

The Jewish forces pursued Cestius and his army and attacked the fleeing forces from behind. Only with great difficulty did the Romans succeed in making their retreat. The Jews returned to Jerusalem in triumph with their spoils. Yet this apparent success brought them only evil. It inspired their spirit of stubborn resistance to the Romans, which soon brought indescribable suffering on the doomed city.

Terrible were the disasters that fell on Jerusalem when Titus resumed the siege. The city was surrounded at the time of the Passover, when millions of Jews were assembled within its walls. Supplies of food had previously been destroyed through the revenge of the warring factions. Now the inhabitants experienced all the horrors of starvation. People gnawed the leather of their belts and sandals and the covering of their shields. Great numbers slipped out at night to gather wild plants growing outside the city walls, though the Romans put many to death with cruel torture. Often those who returned in safety were robbed of what they had found. Husbands robbed their wives, and wives their husbands. Children snatched the food from the mouths of their aged parents.

The Roman leaders made efforts to strike terror to the Jews and so cause them to surrender. Prisoners who resisted capture were scourged, tortured, and crucified before the wall of the city. Along the Valley of Jehoshaphat and at Calvary, the Romans erected crosses in great numbers. There was scarcely room to move among them. These things fulfilled that awful curse spoken before Pilate's judgment seat: "His blood be on us and on our children" (Matthew 27:25).

Titus was filled with horror as he saw bodies lying in heaps in the valleys. Like someone under a spell, he looked at the magnificent temple and gave a command that not one stone of it was to be touched. He made an earnest appeal to the Jewish leaders not to force him to defile the sacred place with blood. If they would fight in any other place, no Roman would violate the sacredness of the temple! Josephus himself begged them to surrender, to save themselves, their city, and their place of worship. But with bitter curses, they hurled darts at him, their last human mediator. Titus's efforts to save the temple were in vain. Someone greater than he had declared that not one stone was to be left on another.

Titus finally decided to take the temple by storm, determined if possible to save it from destruction. But the troops disregarded his commands. A soldier threw a flaming torch through an opening in the porch, and immediately the cedar-lined rooms around the holy house were in a blaze. Titus rushed to the place and commanded the soldiers to put out the flames. His words went unheeded. In their fury the soldiers hurled blazing torches into the rooms attached to the temple and then slaughtered those who had found shelter there. Blood flowed down the temple steps like water.

After the temple was destroyed, the whole city fell to the Romans. The leaders of the Jews abandoned their unconquerable towers. Titus declared that God had given them into his hands, for no war machines, however powerful, could have won against those stupendous defenses. Both the city and the temple were destroyed to their foundations, and the ground on which the holy house had stood was "plowed like a field" (see Jeremiah 26:18). More than a million people died. The survivors were carried away as captives, sold as slaves, dragged to Rome, thrown to wild beasts in the amphitheaters, or scattered as homeless wanderers throughout the earth.

The Jews had filled for themselves the cup of vengeance. In all the troubles that followed in their scattering, they were reaping the harvest that their own hands had sown. "O Israel, thou has destroyed thyself"; "for thou hast fallen by thine iniquity." (Hosea 13:9; 14:1, KJV.) People often say that the Jews' sufferings were a punishment by the direct decree of God. This is the way the great deceiver tries to conceal his own work. By stubbornly rejecting divine love and mercy, the Jews had caused God's protection to be withdrawn from them.

We cannot know how much we owe to Christ for the peace and protection we enjoy. The restraining power of God prevents mankind from coming fully under the control of Satan. The disobedient and unthankful have every reason to be grateful for God's mercy. But when people pass the limits of God's patient appeals, restraint is removed. God does not act as an executioner of the sentence against transgression. He leaves the rejectors of His mercy to reap what they have sown. Every ray of light rejected is a seed sown, and it yields its unfailing harvest. The Spirit of God, persistently resisted, is finally withdrawn. Then there is no power left to control the evil desires of the heart, no protection from the malice and hatred of Satan.

Danger of Resisting God's Call

The destruction of Jerusalem is a solemn warning to everyone who is resisting the pleadings of God's mercy. The Savior's prophecy of judgments on Jerusalem is to have another fulfillment. In the fate of that chosen city we can see the doom of a world that has rejected God's mercy and trampled on His law. Dark are the records of human misery that the earth has witnessed. Terrible have been the results of rejecting Heaven's authority. But a scene still darker is presented in the revelations of the future. When the restraining Spirit of God will be completely withdrawn, no longer holding back the outburst of human passion and satanic anger, the world will see the results of Satan's rule like it has never seen them before.

In that day, as when Jerusalem was destroyed, God's people will be delivered. Christ will come the second time to gather His faithful ones to Himself. "Then all the tribes of the earth will mourn, and they will see the Son of Man coming on the clouds of heaven with power and great glory. And He will send His angels with a great sound of a trumpet, and they will gather together His elect from the four winds, from one end of heaven to the other" (Matthew 24:30, 31).

People should be careful not to neglect the words of Christ. As He warned His disciples about Jerusalem's destruction so that they could escape, so He has warned the world of the day of final destruction. All who choose may flee from the wrath to come. "There will be signs in the sun, in the moon, and in the stars; and on the earth distress of nations" (Luke 21:25; see also Matthew 24:29; Mark 13:24–26; Revelation 6:12–17). "Watch therefore," are Christ's words of counsel (Mark 13:35). Those who obey the warning will not be left in darkness.

The world is no more ready to believe the message for this time than the Jews were to receive the Savior's warning about Jerusalem. No matter when it comes, the day of God will come as a surprise to the ungodly.

When life is going on in its usual way, when people are absorbed in pleasure, in business, in money-making, when religious leaders are praising the world's progress, and people are lulled in a false security— then, as the midnight thief slips into the unguarded home, so shall sudden destruction come upon the careless and ungodly, "and they shall not escape" (see 1 Thessalonians 5:2–5).

---

1. Henry Hart Milman, *History of the Jews*, bk. 13.

The First Christians—
Loyal and True

Jesus revealed to His disciples the experience of His people from the time when He would be taken from them to His return in power and glory. Seeing deep into the future, His eye detected the fierce storms that were to beat upon His followers in coming ages of persecution (see Matthew 24:9, 21, 22). The followers of Christ must walk the same path of condemnation and suffering that their Master walked. The hatred that the world's Redeemer had borne would be displayed against all who would believe on His name.

Paganism foresaw that if the gospel triumphed, her own temples and altars would be swept away. For this reason she summoned her forces to light the fires of persecution. Christians had their possessions taken away and were driven from their homes. Great numbers of people—noble and slave, rich and poor, educated and ignorant—were killed without mercy.

Persecutions began under Nero and continued for centuries. Christians were falsely declared to be the cause of famines, epidemics, and earthquakes. For money, informers stood ready to betray the innocent as rebels and pests to society. Large numbers of Christians were thrown to wild beasts or burned alive in amphitheaters. Some were crucified; others were covered with skins of wild animals and shoved into the arena to be torn apart by dogs. At public festivals vast crowds assembled to enjoy the sight and greet the Christians' dying agonies with laughter and applause.

The followers of Christ were forced into hiding in lonely places. Beneath the hills outside the city of Rome, long corridors had been tunneled through earth and rock for miles beyond the city walls. In these underground refuges the followers of Christ buried their dead. Here also, when they were outlawed, they found a home. Many remembered the words of their Master, that when persecuted for Christ's sake, they were to be very glad. Great would be their reward in heaven, for they were persecuted in the same way as the prophets were before them (see Matthew 5:11, 12).

Songs of triumph went up from the midst of crackling flames. By faith the martyrs saw Christ and angels gazing on them with the deepest interest and approving of their firmness. A voice came from the throne of God, "Be faithful until death, and I will give you the crown of life" (Revelation 2:10).

Satan's efforts to destroy the church of Christ by violence were in vain. He could kill God's workmen, but the gospel continued to spread and its followers increased. A Christian said, "The more often you mow us down, the more we grow in number; the blood of Christians is seed."[1]

For this reason Satan made plans to war more successfully against God by planting his banner in the Christian church, to gain by deception what he failed to get by force. Persecution ended. In its place came the attractions of worldly prosperity and honor. Idol worshipers began to receive a part of the Christian faith, while they rejected essential truths. They professed to accept Jesus, but they had no conviction of sin and felt no need of repentance or change of heart. With some concessions on their part they proposed that Christians should also make concessions, so that they all could unite on the platform of "belief in Christ."

Now the church was in terrible danger. Prison, torture, fire, and sword were blessings in comparison with this! Some Christians stood firm. Others were in favor of modifying their faith. Under a cloak of pretended Christianity, Satan found his way into the church to corrupt their faith.

In the end, most Christians consented to lower the standard. They formed a union between Christianity and paganism. Although the idol worshipers professed to unite with the church, they still clung to their idolatry. They simply changed the objects of their worship to images of Jesus and even of Mary and the saints. False doctrines, superstitious rites, and idol-

atrous ceremonies became a part of the church's faith and worship. The Christian religion was corrupted, and the church lost her purity and power. Some, however, were not misled. They still remained faithful to the Author of truth.

Two Classes in the Church

There have always been two classes among those who claim to follow Christ. While some people study the Savior's life and earnestly try to correct their defects and conform to the Pattern, the others shun the plain, practical truths that expose their errors. Even in her best state the church did not consist of only the true and sincere. Judas was connected with the disciples, that through Christ's instruction and example he could be led to see his errors. But by indulging in sin he invited Satan's temptations. He became angry when Jesus reproved his faults, and so he came to betray his Master (see Mark 14:10, 11).

Ananias and Sapphira pretended to make an entire sacrifice for God while they covetously withheld a portion for themselves. The Spirit of truth revealed to the apostles the real character of these pretenders, and the judgments of God rid the church of the foul stain on its purity. (See Acts 5:1–11.) As persecution came to Christ's followers, only those who were willing to forsake everything for the truth wanted to become His disciples. But when persecution ended, the church added converts who were less sincere, and the way was open for Satan to find a foothold.

When Christians agreed to unite

with those who were half converted from paganism, Satan celebrated. He then inspired them to persecute those who remained true to God. These apostate Christians, uniting with half-pagan companions, turned their warfare against the most essential features of Christ's teachings. It required a desperate struggle to stand firm against the deceptions and evils introduced into the church. The church no longer accepted the Bible as the standard of faith. It called the doctrine of religious freedom a heresy, and it condemned those who upheld this teaching.

After long conflict, the faithful saw that separation was absolutely necessary. They did not dare to tolerate errors that would be fatal to their own souls and would endanger the faith of their children and grandchildren. They felt that peace would be too costly if they had to buy it with the sacrifice of principle. If they could obtain unity only by compromising truth, then let there be difference, and even war.

The early Christians were truly a distinct people. Few in numbers, without wealth, position, or titles of honor, they were hated by the wicked, even as Abel was hated by Cain (see Genesis 4:1–10). From the days of Christ until now His faithful disciples have roused the hatred and opposition of those who love sin.

How, then, can the gospel be called a message of peace? Angels sang above the plains of Bethlehem, "Glory to God in the highest, and on earth peace, goodwill toward men!" (Luke 2:14). There appears to be a contradiction between these prophetic declarations and the words of Christ,

"I did not come to bring peace but a sword" (Matthew 10:34). Rightly understood, though, the two are in perfect harmony. The gospel is a message of peace. The religion of Christ, if received and obeyed, would spread peace and happiness throughout the earth. It was the mission of Jesus to reconcile us to God and so to one another. But the world at large is under the control of Satan, Christ's bitterest enemy. The gospel presents principles of life completely opposite to people's habits and desires, and they rise up against it. They hate the purity that condemns sin, and they persecute those who urge its holy claims on them. It is in this sense that the gospel is called a sword.

Many who are weak in faith are ready to throw away their confidence in God because He allows evil people to prosper, while the best and purest are tormented by their cruel power. How can One who is just and merciful and infinite in power tolerate such injustice? God has given us enough evidence of His love. We are not to doubt His goodness because we cannot understand His workings. The Savior said: "Remember the word that I said to you, 'A servant is not greater than his master.' If they persecuted Me, they will also persecute you" (John 15:20). Those who are called to endure torture and martyrdom are only following in the steps of God's dear Son.

The righteous are placed in the furnace of affliction so that they themselves may be purified, their example may convince others of the reality of faith and godliness, and their consistent lives may condemn the ungodly and unbelieving. God permits the wicked to prosper and to reveal their hatred against Him so that all may see His justice and mercy in their complete destruction. God will punish every act of cruelty toward His faithful ones as though it had been done to Christ Himself.

Paul states that "all who desire to live godly in Christ Jesus will suffer persecution" (2 Timothy 3:12). Why is it, then, that persecution seems to sleep? The only reason is that the church has conformed to the world's standard, and so it awakens no opposition. Religion in our day is not the pure and holy faith of Christ and His apostles. Because people are indifferent to the truths of the Word of God, because there is so little vital godliness in the church, Christianity is popular with the world. Let there be a revival of the early church's faith, and the fires of persecution will be lit again.

---

1. Tertullian, *Apology,* par. 50.

Spiritual Darkness in the Early Church

The apostle Paul wrote that the day of Christ would not come "unless the falling away comes first, and the man of sin is revealed, the son of perdition, who opposes and exalts himself above all that is called God or that is worshiped, so that he sits as God in the temple of God, showing himself that he is God." And furthermore, "the mystery of lawlessness is already at work." (2 Thessalonians 2:3, 4, 7.) Even at that early date the apostle saw errors creeping in that would prepare the way for the papacy.

Little by little, "the mystery of lawlessness" carried on its deceptive work. The customs of heathenism found their way into the Christian church, held back for a time by fierce persecutions under paganism. But as persecution ended, Christianity turned away from the humble simplicity of Christ and adopted the pomp of pagan priests and rulers. The emperor Constantine's professed conversion caused great rejoicing. But now the work of corruption progressed rapidly. Paganism, which seemed to have been conquered, became the conqueror. Its doctrines and superstitions were merged into the faith of those who claimed to be followers of Christ.

This compromise between paganism and Christianity resulted in "the man of sin" that prophecy had foretold. That false religion is a masterpiece of Satan, a monument to his effort to seat himself on the throne to rule the earth according to his will.

It is one of Rome's leading doctrines that God has given the pope supreme authority over bishops and pastors in all the world. More than this, the pope has been called "Lord God the Pope" and declared infallible (see Appendix). The same claim that Satan urged in the wilderness of temptation he still urges through the Church of Rome, and vast numbers give him worship.

But those who reverence God meet the papacy's false claim as Christ met Satan: "You shall worship the LORD your God, and Him only you shall serve" (Luke 4:8). God has never appointed any man head of the church. Papal supremacy is opposed to the Scriptures. The pope can have no power over Christ's church except by claiming it falsely. The Roman Catholic Church charges Protestants with willfully separating from the true church, but she is the one that departed from "the faith which was once for all delivered to the saints" (Jude 3).

Satan knew very well that it was

the Holy Scriptures that enabled the Savior to resist his attacks. At every assault, Christ presented the shield of eternal truth, saying, "It is written." In order for Satan to maintain his control over people and establish the authority of the papal usurper, he must keep them ignorant of the Bible. He must conceal and suppress its sacred truths. For hundreds of years the Roman Church prohibited the circulation of the Bible. The people were forbidden to read it. Priests and leaders interpreted its teachings to support their boastful claims. In this way the pope came to be acknowledged by almost everyone as God's appointed ruler on earth.

How the Sabbath Was "Changed"

Prophecy declared that the papacy would "intend to change times and law" (Daniel 7:25). As a substitute for idol worship, the adoration of images and relics was gradually introduced into Christian worship. The decree of a general council (see Appendix) finally established this idolatry. Rome dared to remove from the law of God the second commandment, which forbids image worship, and to divide the tenth commandment into two in order to preserve the number at ten.

Unconsecrated leaders of the church also tampered with the fourth commandment, to set aside the ancient Sabbath, the day that God had blessed and sanctified (Genesis 2:2, 3). In its place they exalted the festival the heathen observed as "the venerable day of the sun." In the first centuries all Christians had kept the true Sabbath, but Satan worked to bring about

his will. The church made Sunday a festival in honor of the resurrection of Christ. Religious services were held on it, yet it was thought of as a day of recreation. In addition, the true Sabbath was still being sacredly observed.

Before Christ came to earth, Satan had led the Jews to load the Sabbath with rigorous rules, making it a burden. Now, taking advantage of the false light in which he had placed it, Satan caused people to despise it as a "Jewish" institution. While Christians generally continued to observe Sunday as a joyous festival, he led them to make the Sabbath a day of sadness and gloom in order to show their hatred for Judaism.

The emperor Constantine issued a decree making Sunday a public festival throughout the Roman Empire (see Appendix). The day of the sun was reverenced by his pagan subjects and honored by Christians. The bishops of the church urged him to do this. Thirsting for power, they recognized that if both Christians and heathen observed the same day, it would advance the power and glory of the church. But while many God-fearing Christians gradually came to think of Sunday as having some degree of sacredness, they still held the true Sabbath and observed it in obedience to the fourth commandment.

The archdeceiver had not completed his work. He was determined to exercise his power through his appointed ruler, the proud pontiff who claimed to represent Christ. Vast councils were held to which dignitaries came from all the world. Nearly every council pressed the Sabbath down a little lower while exalting Sunday. This is how the pagan festival finally came to be honored as a divine institution, while people declared the Bible Sabbath a relic of Judaism and pronounced a curse on its observance.

The great apostate had succeeded in exalting himself "above all that is called God or that is worshiped" (2 Thessalonians 2:4). He had dared to change the only commandment in the divine law that points to the true and living God. The fourth commandment reveals God as the Creator. To commemorate the work of creation, God sanctified the seventh day as a rest day for mankind. It was designed to keep the living God always before people's minds as the object of worship. Satan works to turn people from obedience to God's law. To accomplish this, he directs his efforts especially against the one commandment that points to God as the Creator.

Protestants now claim that Christ's resurrection on Sunday made it the Christian Sabbath. But neither Christ nor His apostles gave any such honor to the day. Sunday observance had its origin in that "mystery of lawlessness" (2 Thessalonians 2:7) that had begun its work even in Paul's day. What reason can anyone give for a change that the Scriptures do not authorize?

In the sixth century, the bishop of Rome was declared to be the head over the entire church. Paganism was replaced by the papacy. The dragon had given the beast "his power, his throne, and great authority" (Revelation 13:2).

Now began the 1,260 years of papal oppression that the prophecies of Daniel and the Revelation had foretold (Daniel 7:25; Revelation 13:5–7; see Appendix). Christians were forced to choose: either yield their integrity and accept the papal ceremonies and worship, or wear away their lives in dungeons or suffer death. Now the words of Jesus were fulfilled: "You will be betrayed even by parents and brothers, relatives and friends; and they will put some of you to death. And you will be hated by all for My name's sake" (Luke 21:16, 17).

The world became a huge battlefield. For hundreds of years the church of Christ found shelter in hiding and obscurity. "The woman fled into the wilderness, where she has a place prepared by God, that they should feed her there one thousand two hundred and sixty days" (Revelation 12:6).

The Roman Catholic Church's rise to power marked the beginning of the Dark Ages. People transferred their faith from Christ to the pope of Rome. Instead of trusting in the Son of God for forgiveness of sins and for eternal salvation, they looked to the pope and to the priests to whom he gave authority. The pope was their earthly mediator. He stood in the place of God to them. To turn aside even a little from his requirements was reason enough for severe punishment. In this way the minds of the people were turned away from God to fallible and cruel men—more than that, to the prince of darkness himself who exercised his power through them. When human beings suppress the Scriptures and come to regard themselves as supreme, we can expect only fraud, deception, and degrading evil.

Dangerous Days for the Church

God's faithful believers were few. At times it seemed that error would triumph completely, and true religion would be banished from the earth. People lost sight of the gospel, and they were burdened with difficult requirements. The church taught them to trust to their own works to atone for sin. Long pilgrimages, acts of penance, the worship of relics, the building of churches, shrines, and altars, the payment of large sums to the church treasury—the church required them to do these things in order to appease God's wrath or to gain His favor.

About the close of the eighth century, those who supported the pope claimed that in the first ages of the church the bishops of Rome had possessed the same spiritual power which they now said they had. Monks forged ancient writings. Decrees of councils that no one had heard of before were discovered, establishing the universal supremacy of the pope from the earliest times. (See Appendix.)

These developments perplexed the few faithful ones who were building on the sure foundation of Christ (1 Corinthians 3:10, 11). Growing tired from the constant struggle against persecution, fraud, and every other obstacle that Satan could invent, some who had been faithful became discouraged. To gain peace and security for their property and their lives, they turned away from the sure foundation. Others were not swayed by the opposition of their enemies.

Image worship became widespread. People burned candles in front of images and offered prayers to them. The most senseless customs prevailed. Reason itself seemed to have lost its power. When even the priests and bishops were pleasure-loving and corrupt, it is no wonder that the people who looked to them for guidance were sunken in ignorance and vice.

In the eleventh century, Pope Gregory VII proclaimed that the church had never erred, nor would it ever err, according to the Scriptures. But he offered no Scripture proofs to accompany his assertion. The proud pontiff also claimed power to remove emperors. This promoter of infallibility showed his character as a tyrant by his treatment of the German emperor, Henry IV. For daring to disregard the pope's authority, this monarch was expelled from the church and dethroned. The pope's decree encouraged Henry's own princes to rebel against him.

Henry felt the importance of making peace with Rome. With his wife and faithful servant he crossed the Alps in the middle of winter, so that he could humble himself before the pope. When he reached Gregory's castle, he was taken into an outer court. There, in the severe cold of winter, with uncovered head and bare feet, he waited for the pope's permission to come into his presence. Not until he had spent three days fasting and making confession, did the pope grant him pardon. Even then it was only on condition that the emperor would wait for the permission of the pope before again taking the symbols of royalty or exercising its power. Gregory was elated by his triumph. He boasted that it was his duty to pull down the pride of kings.

What a sharp contrast between this haughty pope and Christ, who portrays Himself as pleading at the door of the heart to be let in. He taught His disciples, "Whoever desires to become great among you, let him be your servant" (Matthew 20:26).

Even before the papacy was established, the teachings of heathen philosophers had exerted an influence in the church. Many still clung to the beliefs of pagan philosophy and urged others to study it as a means of extending their influence among the heathen. Serious errors came into the Christian faith this way.

How False Doctrines Came In

One such major teaching was the belief that we are immortal by nature and are conscious in death. This doctrine laid the foundation for Rome to establish prayer to the saints and the adoration of the Virgin Mary. From this sprang also the heresy of eternal torment for those who refuse to repent. This belief became part of the papal faith in the church's early years.

This opened the way for still another invention of paganism—purgatory, which the church used to terrify the superstitious people. This heresy claimed that a place of torment existed in which souls of those who do not deserve eternal damnation suffer punishment for their sins, and from which, when they are freed from impurity, they are admitted to heaven. (See Appendix.)

Rome needed still another lie to be able to profit from the fears and vices

of her followers: the doctrine of indulgences. The church promised full remission of sins past, present, and future to all who would enlist in the pope's wars to punish his enemies or to exterminate those who dared to deny his spiritual supremacy. By paying money to the church, people could free themselves from sin and also release the souls of friends who had died and were being kept in the tormenting flames. In ways like these Rome filled her treasuries and sustained the magnificence, luxury, and vice of the pretended representatives of Jesus, who had nowhere to lay His head. (See Appendix.)

The Lord's Supper had been replaced by the idolatrous sacrifice of the mass. Papal priests pretended to convert the simple bread and wine into the actual "body and blood of Christ."[1] With blasphemous presumption, they openly claimed the power of creating God, the Creator of all things. Christians were required to confess their faith in this Heaven-insulting heresy or face death.

In the thirteenth century, the church established the most terrible weapon of the papacy—the Inquisition. In its secret councils Satan and his angels controlled the minds of evil men. Unseen in the midst of them stood an angel of God, taking the dreadful record of their evil decrees and writing the history of deeds too horrible for human eyes to see. "BABYLON THE GREAT" was "drunk with the blood of the saints" (see Revelation 17:5, 6). The mangled bodies of millions of martyrs cried to God for vengeance on that apostate power.

The papacy had become the world's despot. Kings and emperors bowed to the decrees of the Roman pontiff. For hundreds of years people accepted the doctrines of Rome without question. They honored her clergy and sustained them liberally. Never since has the Catholic Church attained to greater dignity, magnificence, or power.

But "the noon of the papacy was the midnight of the world."[2] The Scriptures were almost unknown. The papal leaders hated the light that would reveal their sins. Because God's law, the standard of righteousness, had been removed, they practiced vice without restraint. The palaces of popes and other church leaders were scenes of vile immorality. Some of the popes were guilty of crimes so revolting that secular rulers tried to depose them as monsters too evil to be tolerated. For centuries Europe made no progress in learning, arts, or civilization. A moral and intellectual paralysis had fallen on Christendom.

Such conditions were the results of banishing the Word of God!

---

1. Cardinal Wiseman's Lectures on "The Real Presence," lecture 8, sec. 3, par. 26.

2. James A. Wylie, *History of Protestantism,* bk. 1, ch. 4.

The Waldenses Defend the Faith

During the long period of the popes' supremacy, there were witnesses for God who cherished faith in Christ as the only mediator between God and man. They took the Bible as the only rule of life, and they kept the true Sabbath. The church branded them as heretics and suppressed, misrepresented, or mutilated their writings. But they still stood firm.

There is almost no mention of them in human records, except in the accusations of their persecutors. Rome sought to destroy everything "heretical," whether persons or writings. The church also tried to destroy every record of its cruelty toward those who disagreed with it. Before the invention of printing, books were few in number, and so there was little to prevent Rome's forces from carrying out their plans. No sooner had the papacy obtained power than it stretched out its arms to crush all who refused to acknowledge its authority.

In Great Britain, simple Christianity had taken root early, uncorrupted by the Roman apostasy. Persecution from pagan emperors was the only gift the first churches of Britain received from Rome. Many Christians fleeing persecution in England found safety in Scotland. From there, believers carried truth to Ireland, and people in these countries received it gladly.

When the Saxons invaded Britain, heathenism gained control, and the Christians were forced to retreat to the mountains. In Scotland, a century later, the light shone out to far-distant lands. From Ireland came Columba and his co-workers, who made the lonely island of Iona the center of their missionary work. Among these evangelists was one who kept the Bible Sabbath, and he introduced this truth among the people. A school was established at Iona, and missionaries went out from it to Scotland, England, Germany, Switzerland, and even Italy.

Rome Meets Bible Religion

But Rome was determined to bring Britain under its rule. In the sixth century, Catholic missionaries worked to convert the heathen Saxons. As the work progressed, the pope's leaders came up against the simple Christians—humble and scriptural in their character, doctrine, and manners. Rome's representatives exhibited the superstition, pomp, and arrogance of the papal system. Rome demanded that these Christian churches acknowledge the pope as their ruler. The Britons replied that the pope was not entitled to supremacy in the church, and they could give him only the submission that is due to every follower of Christ. They knew no other master than Christ.

Now the true spirit of the papacy was revealed. The leader from Rome said, "If you will not receive brethren who bring you peace, you will receive enemies who will bring you war."[1] Rome used war and deception against these witnesses for Bible faith, until the churches of Britain were destroyed or forced to submit to the pope.

In lands beyond the rule of Rome, Christian groups remained almost entirely free from papal corruption for centuries. They continued to take the Bible as their only rule of faith. These Christians believed in the permanence of the law of God and observed the Sabbath of the fourth commandment. Churches that held to this faith and practice existed in Central Africa and among the Armenians of Asia.

Of all who resisted the papal power during that time, the Waldenses are the most significant. In the very land where the papal system had established its headquarters, the churches of Piedmont kept their independence. But the time came when Rome insisted that they submit. Some, however, refused to yield to pope or bishop and were determined to preserve the purity and simplicity of their faith. A separation took place. Those who held to the ancient faith now left their homes. Some, leaving behind their native Alps, raised the banner of truth in foreign lands. Others retreated to the rocky strongholds of the mountains and there preserved their freedom to worship God.

Their religious belief was established on the written Word of God. Those humble peasants, shut away from the world, had not arrived at truth all by themselves in opposition to the teachings of the apostate church. They had inherited their religious belief from their ancestors. In conflict, they upheld the faith of the apostolic church. "The church in the wilderness," and not the proud hierarchy on the throne in the world's great capital, was the true church of Christ, the guardian of the treasures of truth that God committed to His people to give to the world.

Among the main reasons leading the true church to separate from Rome was Rome's hatred toward the Bible Sabbath. As prophecy had foretold, the papal power trampled the law of God in the dust. Churches under the papacy were forced to honor Sunday. Surrounded by widespread error, many of the true people of God became so bewildered that while they observed the Sabbath, they also did no work on Sunday. But this did not satisfy the papal leaders. They demanded that the people must trample on the Sabbath, and they denounced those who dared to honor it.

Hundreds of years before the Reformation the Waldenses had the Bible in their native language. This made them the special focus of persecution. They declared that Rome was the apostate Babylon of the book of Revelation. At the risk of their lives they stood up to resist her corruptions. Through ages of apostasy there were Waldenses who denied Rome's supremacy, rejected image worship as idolatry, and kept the true Sabbath (see Appendix).

Behind the high walls of the mountains the Waldenses found a hiding place. Those faithful exiles pointed their children to the heights towering above them in majesty and spoke of Him whose word endures like the everlasting hills. God had set the mountains securely in place. No arm but God's could move them. In the same way He had established His law. Human power could just as likely uproot the mountains and hurl them into the sea as change one command of God's law. Those pilgrims did not complain because their lives were hard. They were never lonely in the mountains' isolation. They rejoiced in their freedom to worship. From many a high cliff they chanted praise, and the armies of Rome could not silence their songs of thanksgiving.

Valued Principles of Truth

They valued principles of truth more than houses and lands, friends, family, and even life itself. They taught the youth from earliest childhood to consider the claims of God's law as sacred. Copies of the Bible were rare, so they committed its precious words to memory. Many were able to repeat large portions of both the Old and the New Testament.

They were educated from childhood to endure hardship and to think and act for themselves. They were taught to bear responsibilities, to guard their words, and to understand the wisdom of silence. One careless word in the hearing of their enemies might endanger the lives of hundreds of believers, for like wolves hunting prey, the enemies of truth pursued those who dared to claim freedom of religious faith.

The Waldenses worked for their living with unwavering patience. Every spot of tillable land among the mountains they carefully improved. They taught their children to practice economy and self-denial. The work was hard but wholesome, just what fallen human beings need. The youth were taught that all their powers belonged to God, to be developed for His service.

The Vaudois* churches resembled the church in the time of the apostles. Rejecting the supremacy of popes and bishops, they taught that the Bible is the only infallible authority. Their pastors, unlike the lordly priests of Rome, fed the flock of God, leading them to the green pastures and living fountains of His Holy Word. The people gathered, not in magnificent churches or grand cathedrals, but in the Alpine valleys, or, in time of danger, in some rocky stronghold, to listen to the words of truth from the servants of Christ. The pastors not only preached the gospel, they visited the sick and worked to promote harmony and brotherly love. Like Paul the tentmaker, each learned some trade so that he could provide for his own support if necessary.

The youth received instruction from their pastors. The Bible was their chief study. They committed the Gos-

---

* *Vaudois [vo-DWAH] is the French word for the Waldenses and is often used for them.*

pels of Matthew and
as well as many of th

With persistent (
in the dark caverns o
light of torches, they
cred Scriptures, ver
gels from heaven s
faithful workers.

Satan had urg
priests and bishops t
of truth beneath the
and superstition. But
way it was preserv
through all the ages (
the ark on the rolling
of God outrides the s
en it with destruction.
has rich veins of gold
beneath the surface,
tures have treasures (
the humble, prayerful seeker will find.

were coarse and travel-stained, these are the faith
missionaries passed through great cit-
ies and even reached distant lands.
Churches sprang up in their path, and
the blood of martyrs witnessed for t
truth. Veiled and silent, the Wo
God was meeting a glad welc
many homes and hearts.

The Waldenses belie
end of all things was
they studied the Bi
ly impressed wit
its saving tr
They found
in believ
their
sp

God designed the Bible to be a lessonbook to all mankind as a revelation of Himself. Every truth that we see is a fresh disclosure of its Author's character.

Some youth were sent from their schools in the mountains to institutions of learning in France or Italy, where there was a wider field for study and observation than in their native Alps. These youth were exposed to temptation. They encountered Satan's agents who urged subtle heresies and dangerous deceptions on them. But their education from childhood prepared them for this.

In the schools where they went they were not to confide in anyone. Their clothes were designed specifically to conceal their greatest treasure—the Scriptures. Whenever they could they cautiously placed some

ficult times. The youth saw before them, not earthly wealth and glory, but hard work and danger and possibly a martyr's death. The missionaries went out two by two, as Jesus had sent His disciples.

To reveal their mission would have ensured its defeat. Every minister possessed a knowledge of some trade or profession, and the missionaries carried out their work under cover of a secular trade, usually as merchants or peddlers. "They carried silks, jewelry, and other articles, . . . and were welcomed as merchants where they would have been spurned as missionaries."[2] They secretly carried copies of the Bible, either the entire book or parts of it. Often they were able to interest someone in reading God's Word, and they left some part with those who wanted it.

With bare feet and clothes that

... e
... d of
... ome in

... ved that the
... ot far away. As
... e they were deep-
... their duty to make
... ths known to others.
... comfort, hope, and peace
... ng in Jesus. As the light made
... own hearts glad, they longed to
... ead its beams to those in the darkness of Rome's errors.

Under the guidance of pope and priest, most people were taught to trust in their good works to save them. They were always looking to themselves, their minds dwelling on their sinful condition, afflicting soul and body, yet finding no relief. Thousands spent their lives in convent cells. By frequent fasts and whippings, by midnight vigils, by lying on cold, damp stones, by long pilgrimages—haunted with the fear of God's avenging wrath—many suffered on, until exhausted nature gave way. Without one ray of hope they sank into the grave.

Sinners Pointed to Christ

The Waldenses longed to bring these starving souls messages of peace in the promises of God and to point them to Christ as their only hope of salvation. They knew that the doctrine that good works can atone for sin was based on falsehood. The merits of a crucified and risen Savior

... foundation of the Christian
... . We must depend on Christ as
... osely as an arm is attached to the body or a branch to the vine.

The teachings of popes and priests had led people to consider God and even Christ as stern and frightful, with so little sympathy that sinners must have the mediation of priests and saints. Those whose minds had received the light longed to clear away the obstructions that Satan had piled up, so that people could come directly to God, confess their sins, and find pardon and peace.

Invading the Kingdom of Satan

The Vaudois missionaries cautiously produced the carefully written portions of the Holy Scriptures. The light of truth penetrated many a darkened mind, until the Sun of Righteousness shone healing beams into the heart. Often the hearer asked for some portion of Scripture to be repeated, as if to be sure that he had heard it correctly.

Many saw how useless it is for human beings to mediate in behalf of the sinner. With joy they exclaimed, "Christ is my priest; His blood is my sacrifice; His altar is my confessional." The flood of light shining on them was so great that they seemed to be in heaven. All fear of death was gone. They could now even look forward to prison if that would honor their Redeemer.

In secret places the Waldenses brought out the Word of God and read it, sometimes to a single soul, sometimes to a little company longing for light. Often they spent the entire night in reading God's Word to others. People often asked questions like, "Will God accept *my* offering? Will He smile upon *me*? Will He pardon *me*?" They heard the answer read from Scripture, "Come to Me, all you who labor and are heavy laden, and I will give you rest" (Matthew 11:28).

Those happy people returned to their homes to spread the light, to repeat to others, as well as they could, their new experience. They had found the true and living way! Scripture spoke to the hearts of those who were longing for truth.

The Waldensian messenger of truth went on his way. In many instances his hearers had not asked where he came from or where he was going. They had been so overwhelmed that they had not thought to question him. Now they asked each other, Could he have been an angel from heaven?

In many cases the messenger of truth had made his way to other lands or was slowly dying in some dungeon, or perhaps his bones were whitening where he had witnessed for the truth. But the words he had left behind were doing their work.

The papal leaders saw danger from the work of these humble travelers. The light of truth would sweep away the heavy clouds of error that enveloped the people; it would direct minds to God alone and eventually destroy the supremacy of Rome.

These people, holding the faith of the ancient church, were a constant testimony to Rome's apostasy and therefore were hated and persecuted. Their refusal to give up the Scriptures was an offense that Rome could not tolerate.

Rome Determines to Destroy the Waldenses

Now began the most terrible crusades against God's people in their mountain homes. Harsh investigators were put upon their track. Again and again Rome's forces ruined their fertile lands and swept away their homes and chapels. No charge could be brought against the moral character of these outlawed people. Their biggest offense was that they would not worship God according to the will of the pope. Because they were seen as guilty of this "crime," every insult and torture that men or devils could invent was heaped on them.

When Rome determined to exterminate the hated group, the pope issued a bull [edict] condemning them as heretics and ordering their slaughter (see Appendix). They were not accused as lazy, or dishonest, or disorderly, but it was declared that they had an appearance of piety and sanctity that seduced "the sheep of the true fold." This edict called all members of the church to join the crusade against the heretics. As an incentive it "released all who joined the crusade from any oaths they might have taken; it legitimated their title to any property they might have illegally acquired, and promised forgiveness of all their sins to those who would kill any heretic. It cancelled all contracts made in favor of Vaudois, forbade all persons to give them any aid whatever, and empowered all persons to take possession of their property."[3] This document clearly reveals the roar of the dragon and not the voice of Christ. The same spirit that crucified Christ and killed the apostles, that moved the bloodthirsty Nero against the faithful Christians in his day, was at work to rid the earth of those who were beloved by God.

In spite of the crusades against them and the inhuman butchery they suffered, this God-fearing people continued to send out missionaries to scatter the precious truth. They were hunted to the death, yet their blood watered the seed they sowed, and it yielded fruit.

In this way the Waldenses witnessed for God centuries before Luther. They planted the seeds of the Reformation that began in the time of Wycliffe, grew broad and deep in the days of Luther, and is to be carried forward to the close of time.

1. J. H. Merle D'Aubigné, *History of the Reformation of the Sixteenth Century,* bk. 17, ch. 2.

2. James A. Wylie, *History of Protestantism,* bk. 1, ch. 7.

3. Ibid., bk. 16, ch. 1.

The Light Breaks in England

God had not allowed His Word to be totally destroyed. In different countries of Europe the Spirit of God moved people to search for truth as for hidden treasure. He guided them to the Holy Scriptures, and they were willing to accept light at any cost to themselves. Though they did not see everything clearly, the Spirit helped them to grasp many long-buried truths.

The time had come for the Scriptures to be given to the people in their own language. The world had passed its midnight. In many lands, signs of the coming dawn appeared.

In the fourteenth century, the "morning star of the Reformation" arose in England. John Wycliffe was noted at college for his fervent spirituality as well as his sound scholarship. Educated in scholastic philosophy, the laws of the church, and civil law, he was prepared to take up the great struggle for civil and religious liberty. He had acquired the intellectual discipline of the schools, and he understood the tactics of the scholars. The extent and thoroughness of his knowledge commanded the respect of both friends and foes. His enemies were not able to discredit the cause of reform by exposing the ignorance or

weakness of its spokesman.

While Wycliffe was still at college, he began to study the Scriptures. Before this, he had felt a great lack, which neither his scholastic studies nor the teaching of the church could satisfy. In the Word of God he found what he had been looking for. Here he saw Christ presented as our only advocate. He determined to proclaim the truths he had discovered.

When he began his work, Wycliffe did not set himself in opposition to Rome. But the more clearly he recognized the errors of the papacy, the more earnestly he presented the teaching of the Bible. He saw that Rome had abandoned the Word of God for human tradition. He fearlessly accused the priesthood of having banished the Scriptures, and he demanded that the Bible be restored to the people and that its authority be established in the church again. He was a skilled and eloquent preacher, and his daily life demonstrated the truths he preached. His knowledge of the Scriptures, the purity of his life, and his courage and integrity won widespread respect. Many saw the evils in the Roman Church. They welcomed with unconcealed joy the truths Wycliffe brought to view. But the papal leaders were filled with rage; this Reformer was gaining an influence greater than their own.

A Sharp Detector of Error

Wycliffe was a sharp detector of error and struck fearlessly against abuses that Rome approved. While chaplain for the king, he took a bold stand against payment of tribute that the pope claimed from the English king. Papal claims of authority over secular rulers were contrary to both reason and revelation. The demands of the pope had stirred up resentment, and Wycliffe's teachings influenced the leading minds of the nation. The king and the nobles united in refusing to pay the tribute.

Begging friars swarmed over England, eroding the greatness and prosperity of the nation. The monks' lives of idleness and beggary were not only a drain on the resources of the people, they brought contempt on useful labor. Youth were demoralized and corrupted. Many were persuaded to devote themselves to a monastic life not only without the consent of their parents, but even without their knowledge and against their commands. By this "monstrous inhumanity," as Luther later called it, "savoring more of the wolf and the tyrant than of the Christian and the man," the hearts of children were steeled against their parents.[1]

The monks deceived even students in the universities and got them to join their orders. Once caught in the snare, it was impossible to break free. Many parents refused to send their sons to the universities. The schools declined, and ignorance prevailed.

The pope had empowered these monks to hear confessions and grant pardon—a source of great evil. The friars, eager for money, were so ready to grant forgiveness that criminals turned to them, and the worst vices rapidly increased. Gifts that should have helped the sick and the poor went to the monks. The wealth of the friars was constantly increasing, and their magnificent buildings and luxurious tables made the growing poverty of the nation more obvious. Yet the friars continued to keep their hold on the superstitious people and led them to believe that all religious duty consisted of acknowledging the supremacy of the pope, adoring the saints, and making gifts to the monks. This was enough to secure a place in heaven!

Wycliffe, with clear insight, struck at the root of the evil, declaring that the system itself was false and should be abolished. His efforts awakened discussion and inquiry. Many began to question whether they should not seek pardon from God rather than from the pope of Rome (see Appendix). "The monks and priests of Rome," they said, "are eating us away like a cancer. God must deliver us, or the people will perish."[2] Begging monks claimed they were following the Savior's example, saying that Jesus and His disciples had been supported by the gifts of the people. This claim led many to the Bible to learn the truth for themselves.

Wycliffe began to write and publish tracts against the friars, to call the people to the teachings of the Bible and its Author. There was no more effective way that he could have used to overthrow that mammoth system that the pope had erected, in which millions were held captive.

To defend the rights of the English crown against the encroachments of Rome, Wycliffe was appointed a royal ambassador to the Netherlands. Here he came into contact with churchmen from France, Italy, and Spain, and had opportunity to look behind the scenes and learn many things that had been hidden from him in England. In these representatives from the papal court he read the true character of the church's leadership. He returned to England to repeat his earlier teachings with greater zeal, declaring that pride and deception were the gods of Rome.

After Wycliffe returned to England, the king appointed him to the rectory of Lutterworth. This assured him that his plain speaking had not displeased the king. Wycliffe's influence helped to mold the belief of the nation.

The pope was soon hurling thunders against him, dispatching three edicts ("bulls") that commanded immediate action to silence the teacher of "heresy."[3]

The arrival of the papal bulls put all England under a command to imprison the heretic (see Appendix). It appeared certain that Wycliffe must soon fall to Rome's vengeance. But the same God who declared to Abram, "Do not be afraid. . . . I am your shield" (Genesis 15:1), stretched out His hand to protect His servant. Death came, not to the Reformer, but to the pope who had ordered his destruction.

The death of Gregory XI was followed by the election of two rival popes (see Appendix). Each called for the faithful to make war on the other, enforcing his demands by terrible curses against his enemies and promises of rewards in heaven for his supporters. The rival factions had all they could do to attack each other, and for a while Wycliffe had rest.

This division, with all the strife and corruption it caused, prepared the way for the Reformation by letting people see what the papacy really was. Wycliffe called the people to consider whether these two popes were not speaking the truth in condemning each other as the antichrist.

Determined to have the light carried to every part of England, Wycliffe organized a group of preachers—simple, devout men who loved the truth and wanted to spread it. These men, teaching in market places, in the streets of the great cities, and in country lanes, went looking for the old, the sick, and the poor, and opened to them the good news of God's grace.

At Oxford, Wycliffe preached the Word of God at the university. He received the title of "the Gospel Doctor." But the greatest work of his life was to be the translation of the Scriptures into English, so that everyone in England could read the wonderful works of God.

Attacked by Dangerous Illness

But suddenly his labors came to a stop. Though he was not yet sixty, constant work, study, and the attacks of enemies had sapped his strength and made him prematurely old. He was struck with a dangerous illness.

The friars thought he would repent of the evil he had done the church, and they hurried to his room to listen to his confession. "You have death on your lips," they said. "Be touched by your faults, and retract in our presence all that you have said against us."

The Reformer listened in silence. Then he asked his attendant to raise him in his bed. Gazing steadily on them, he said in the firm, strong voice that had so often made them tremble, "I shall not die, but live; and again declare the evil deeds of the friars."[4] Astonished and humiliated, the monks hurried from the room.

Wycliffe lived to give his countrymen the most powerful of all weapons against Rome—the Bible, the Heaven-appointed agent to liberate, enlighten, and evangelize the people. Wycliffe knew that he had only a few years left to work. He saw the opposition he must meet, but encouraged by the promises of God's Word, he went forward. In the full strength of his intellectual powers, rich in experience, he had been prepared by God's hand for this, the greatest of his labors. In his parsonage at Lutterworth, paying no attention to the storm that raged around him, the Reformer applied himself to his chosen task.

Finally the work was completed—the first English translation of the Bible. Wycliffe had placed in the hands of the English people a light that would never be put out. He had done more to break the chains of ignorance and to liberate and elevate his country than any victory on the battlefield ever achieved.

Copies of the Bible could only be made by tiresome labor. So many people wanted to have the book that copyists could scarcely keep up with the demand. Wealthy purchasers wanted the whole Bible. Others bought only a portion. In many cases, families joined together to buy a copy. Wycliffe's Bible soon found its way to the homes of the people.

Wycliffe now taught the distinctive doctrines of Protestantism—salvation through faith in Christ and that the Bible alone is infallible. Nearly one half of the people of England accepted the new faith.

Church authorities were dismayed to find the Scriptures available. At this time there was no law in England prohibiting the Bible, since it had never before been published in the language of the people. Later, such laws were enacted and rigorously enforced.

Again Rome's leaders plotted to silence the Reformer's voice. First, a synod of bishops declared his writings heretical. They won the young king, Richard II, to their side and obtained a royal decree condemning to prison all who held the condemned doctrines.

Wycliffe appealed the synod's decision to Parliament. He fearlessly accused the hierarchy before the national council and demanded reform of the enormous abuses that the church approved. His enemies were brought to confusion. Everyone had expected that the Reformer, in his old age, alone and friendless, would yield to the authority of the crown. But instead, Parliament was moved by Wycliffe's stirring appeals. It repealed the persecuting edict, and the Reformer was free again.

He was brought to trial a third time, and now it was before the highest church court in the kingdom. Here at last the Reformer's work would be stopped, the pope's followers thought. If they could accomplish their aim, Wycliffe would leave the court only for the flames.

Wycliffe Refuses to Retract

But Wycliffe did not retract. He fearlessly defended his teachings and repelled the accusations of his persecutors. He summoned his hearers before the divine court and weighed their false reasonings and deceptions in the balances of eternal truth. The power of the Holy Spirit came over the hearers. The Reformer's words pierced their hearts like arrows from the Lord's quiver. He threw back on them the charge of heresy that they had brought against him.

"With whom do you think you are dealing?" he said. "With an old man on the brink of the grave? No! with Truth—Truth that is stronger than you and will overcome you."[5] After saying this, he left the hall, and not one of his opponents tried to prevent him.

Wycliffe's work was almost done, but once more he was to bear witness for the gospel. He was summoned for trial before the papal court at Rome, which had so often shed the blood of God's people. A stroke made it impossible for him to go. But though he could not personally be heard at Rome, he could speak by letter. The Reformer wrote the pope a letter that was respectful and Christian in spirit but was a sharp rebuke to the papacy's pomp and pride.

Wycliffe demonstrated the meekness and humility of Christ to the pope and his cardinals, showing not only them but all Christendom the contrast between those leaders and the Master whom they claimed to represent.

Wycliffe fully expected that he would pay for his fidelity with his life. The king, the pope, and the bishops were united to destroy him, and it seemed certain that in a few months at most he would be burned at the stake. But his courage was unshaken.

Having stood boldly his whole life in defense of the truth, Wycliffe would not fall a victim of the hatred of its enemies. The Lord had been his protector, and now, when Wycliffe's opponents felt sure that he was in their grasp, God's hand removed him beyond their reach. In his church at Lutterworth, as he was about to serve the communion, he had a stroke and in a short time died.

First Spokesman of a New Era

God had put the word of truth in Wycliffe's mouth and had protected his life and prolonged his work until he had laid a foundation for the Reformation. There was no one before Wycliffe whose work could help him shape his system of reform. He was the first spokesman of a new era. Yet in the truth he presented there was a unity and completeness that later Reformers did not exceed and that some did not reach. The framework was so firm and true that those who followed him did not need to redo it.

The great movement that Wycliffe began—to set free the nations so long tied to Rome—had its origin in the

Bible. Here was the source of the stream of blessing that has flowed down the ages since the fourteenth century. Though Wycliffe had been educated to consider Rome the infallible authority and to accept her thousand-year-old teachings and customs with unquestioning reverence, he turned away from all these to listen to God's Holy Word. He declared that the only true authority was not the church speaking through the pope, but the voice of God speaking through His Word. And he taught that the Holy Spirit is its only interpreter.

Wycliffe was one of the greatest of the Reformers. Few who came after him equaled him. Purity of life, constant diligence in study and labor, incorruptible integrity, and Christlike love characterized the first of the Reformers.

It was the Bible that made him what he was. The study of the Bible will make noble every thought, feeling, and ambition as no other study can. It gives firmness of purpose, courage, and strength. An earnest, reverent study of the Scriptures would give the world people of stronger intellect and of nobler principle than has ever resulted from the best training available from human philosophy.

Wycliffe's followers, known as Wycliffites and Lollards, scattered to other lands and carried the gospel with them. Now that their leader was gone, the preachers worked with even more zeal than before. Many people flocked to listen. Some of the nobility, and even the wife of the king, were among the converts. In many places the people removed Rome's idolatrous symbols from the churches.

But soon relentless persecution burst on those who had dared to accept the Bible as their guide. For the first time in the history of England, the law condemned the disciples of the gospel to the stake. Martyrdom followed martyrdom. Those who preached the truth were hunted as enemies of the church and traitors to the kingdom, yet they continued to preach in secret places. They found shelter in the humble homes of the poor and often hid even in dens and caves.

A calm, patient protest against the corruption of religious faith continued for centuries. The Christians of that early time had learned to love God's Word and patiently suffered for its sake. Many sacrificed their earthly possessions for Christ. Those who were allowed to live in their homes gladly sheltered their banished fellow believers. Then when they too were driven out, they cheerfully accepted the role of the outcast. Many bore fearless testimony to the truth in dungeon cells and in torture and flames, rejoicing that they were counted worthy to know "the fellowship of his sufferings."

The hatred of the pope's advocates could not be satisfied while Wycliffe's body rested in the grave. More than forty years after his death, they dug up his bones. They then burned them publicly and threw the ashes into a nearby brook. "This brook," says an old writer, "conveyed his ashes into the Avon River, the Avon into the Severn, the Severn into the narrow seas, and the seas into the main ocean. And so the ashes of

Wycliffe are a symbol of his doctrine, which now is dispersed all over the world."[6]

Through the writings of Wycliffe, John Huss of Bohemia came to renounce many of the Catholic Church's errors. From Bohemia the work went out to other lands. A divine hand was preparing the way for the Great Reformation.

---

1. Barnas Sears, *The Life of Luther,* pp. 70, 69.

2. J. H. Merle D'Aubigné, *History of the Reformation of the Sixteenth Century,* bk. 17, ch. 7.

3. Augustus Neander, *General History of the Christian Religion and Church,* period 6, sec. 2, pt. 1, par. 8. See also Appendix.

4. D'Aubigné, bk. 17, ch. 7.

5. James A. Wylie, *History of Protestantism,* bk. 2, ch. 13.

6. Thomas Fuller, *Church History of Britain,* bk. 4, sec. 2, par. 54.

Two Heroes Face Death

As early as the ninth century the people of Bohemia* had the Bible in their language and conducted public worship in their language. But Gregory VII was intent on enslaving the people, and the papacy issued an edict forbidding public worship in the Bohemian tongue. The pope declared that "it was pleasing to God that His worship be celebrated in an unknown language."[1] But Heaven had provided agencies to preserve the church. Many Waldenses and Albigenses, driven by persecution, came to Bohemia. They worked earnestly in secret. In this way they preserved the true faith.

Before the days of Huss there were people in Bohemia who condemned the corruption in the church. This stirred the fears of the hierarchy, and they began to persecute those who taught the gospel. After a time there was a decree that all who strayed from Rome's way of worship would be burned. But the Christians looked forward to the victory of their cause. As he died, one of them declared, "Someone will arise from among the common people, without sword or authority, and they will not be able to prevail against him."[2] Already there

was one coming to prominence, whose testimony against Rome would stir the nations.

John Huss was born into a humble home. The death of his father left him an orphan at an early age. His pious mother, who believed that education and the fear of God were the most valuable possessions, made efforts to provide this heritage for her son. Huss studied at the provincial school, then left for the university at Prague, where he was admitted as a charity scholar.

At the university, Huss soon drew attention by his rapid progress. His gentle, winning conduct made everyone admire him. He was a sincere follower of the Roman Church who sought earnestly for the spiritual blessings it claims to give. After completing his college course, he entered the priesthood. Quickly gaining prominence, he became attached to the court of the king. He was also made professor and later rector [dean] of the university. The humble charity scholar had become the pride of his country, his name honored throughout Europe.

Jerome, who later became associated with Huss, had brought with him from England the writings of Wycliffe.

---

* Now part of the Czech Republic.

The queen of England, a convert to Wycliffe's teachings, was a Bohemian princess. Through her influence the Reformer's works circulated widely in her native country. Huss was inclined to look favorably on Wycliffe's reforms. Already, though he did not know it, he had started on a path that would lead him far away from Rome.

Two Pictures Impress Huss

About this time, two strangers from England, men of learning, had received the light and had come to spread it in Prague. They were soon silenced, but because they were unwilling to give up their plans, they resorted to other measures. Being artists as well as preachers, they drew two pictures in a place where the public could see them. One represented Christ's entry into Jerusalem, "lowly, and sitting on a donkey" (Matthew 21:5) and followed by His disciples in travel-worn clothes and bare feet. The other picture showed a high church procession—the pope in his rich robes and triple crown, riding on a magnificently decorated horse, with trumpeters in front of him and cardinals and officials following in dazzling array.

Crowds came to gaze at the drawings. No one could miss the moral. A great commotion arose in Prague, and the strangers found it necessary to leave. But the pictures made a deep impression on Huss and led him to a closer study of the Bible and of Wycliffe's writings.

Though he was not ready yet to accept all the reforms that Wycliffe ad-vocated, he saw the true character of the papacy, and he denounced the pride, ambition, and corruption of the hierarchy.

Prague Placed Under Censure

News about these things reached Rome, and Huss was ordered to appear before the pope. To obey would bring certain death. The king and queen of Bohemia, the university, members of the nobility, and officers of the government united in appealing to the pontiff to allow Huss to remain at Prague and answer by a representative. Instead, the pope proceeded to put Huss on trial and condemn him, and he declared the city of Prague under interdict.[*]

In that age this sentence caused great alarm. The people thought the pope was the representative of God, holding the keys of heaven and hell and possessing power to bring God's judgment on them. They believed that until the pope removed the ban, the dead were shut out from heaven. All religious services were suspended. The churches were closed. Marriages were performed outside in the churchyard. The dead were buried in ditches or fields without funerals.

Prague was filled with commotion. Many people denounced Huss and demanded that he be given up to Rome. To quiet the storm, the Reformer went away for a time to his home village. He did not stop his work, but traveled through the country preaching to eager crowds. When the excitement in Prague died down, Huss returned to

---

[*] *Interdict: A Roman Catholic ecclesiastical censure, withdrawing most sacraments and Christian burial from a person or district.*

continue preaching the Word of God. His enemies were powerful, but the queen and many nobles were his friends, and great numbers of the people sided with him.

Huss had stood alone in his work. Now Jerome joined in the reform. From then on the lives of the two were united, and in death they were not to be divided. In those qualities that make for real strength of character, Huss was the greater. Jerome, with true humility, recognized his worth and yielded to his counsels. Under their labors together, the reform spread rapidly.

God permitted great light to shine on the minds of these chosen men, revealing to them many of Rome's errors, but they did not receive all the light that God had for the world. God was leading the people out of the darkness of Romanism, and He led them on, step by step, as they could bear it. Like the full glory of the noonday sun to those who have been in the dark a long time, all the light would have caused them to turn away. So God revealed it little by little, as the people could receive it.

The split in the church continued. Three popes were now competing for supremacy. Their strife filled the whole Christian world with confusion. Not content with hurling condemnation at each other, each set about to buy weapons and obtain soldiers. Of course they needed money for this. To get it, they offered the gifts, offices, and blessing of the church for sale. (See Appendix.)

With increasing boldness Huss thundered against the terrible abuses that were tolerated in the name of religion. The people openly accused Rome as the cause of the miseries that overwhelmed the Christian world.

Again Prague seemed on the edge of a bloody war. As in past ages, God's servant was accused of being the "troubler of Israel" (1 Kings 18:17). Rome again placed the city under interdict, and Huss left for his native village. He was to speak from a wider platform, to all Christianity, before laying down his life as a witness for truth.

A general council was called to meet at Constance [in southwestern Germany]. The emperor Sigismund wanted to have such a council, so one of the three rival popes, John XXIII, called it. Pope John, whose character and policy would not look good under investigation, dared not oppose Sigismund's will. (See Appendix.) The main things to be accomplished were to heal the split in the church and to root out "heresy." The two antipopes were summoned to appear, as well as John Huss. The rival popes were represented by their delegates. Pope John came with many misgivings. He was afraid he would have to answer for his vices that had disgraced the papal crown as well as for the crimes he had committed to secure it. Yet he made his entry into the city of Constance with great pomp, accompanied by high church officials and a procession of other attendants. Above his head was a golden canopy, held by four of the chief magistrates. The communion wafer for the mass was carried before him, and the rich dress of the cardinals and nobles made an impressive display.

Meanwhile another traveler was approaching Constance. Huss said goodbye to his friends as if he would never see them again, feeling that his journey was leading him to the stake. He had obtained a safe-conduct from the king of Bohemia and one also from Emperor Sigismund. But he made all his arrangements with the fact in mind that he would probably die.

Safe Conduct From the King

In a letter to his friends he said: "My brethren, . . . I am departing with a safe-conduct from the king to meet my many mortal enemies. . . . Jesus Christ suffered for His well-beloved; and therefore should we be astonished that He has left us His example? . . . Therefore, beloved, if my death will contribute to His glory, pray that it may come quickly, and that He may enable me to bear all my calamities faithfully. . . . Let us pray to God . . . that I may not suppress one speck of the truth of the gospel, in order to leave my brethren an excellent example to follow."[3]

In another letter, Huss spoke with humility of his own errors, accusing himself "of having felt pleasure in wearing rich clothing and of having wasted hours on trivial things." He then added, "May the glory of God and the salvation of souls occupy your mind, and not the possession of wealth and property. Beware of adorning your house more than your soul; and, above all, pay attention to spiritual things. Be pious and humble

with the poor, and don't spend your resources on feasting."[4]

At Constance, Huss was given full liberty. He received not only the emperor's safe-conduct, but also a personal assurance of protection by the pope. But in spite of these repeated declarations, in a short time the Reformer was arrested on orders from the pope and cardinals and thrown into a miserable dungeon. Later he was taken to a strong castle across the Rhine to be kept as a prisoner. Soon after, the pope himself was committed to the same prison.[5] He had been proven guilty of the lowest crimes, besides murder, simony,* and adultery, "sins not fit to be named." He was finally deprived of the crown. The antipopes also were deposed, and a new pontiff was chosen.

Though the pope himself had been guilty of greater crimes than those with which Huss had charged the priests, yet the same council that removed the pontiff went on to crush the Reformer. The imprisonment of Huss stirred up great resentment in Bohemia. The emperor, who did not want to violate a safe-conduct, opposed the proceedings against Huss. But the Reformer's enemies argued that "faith should not be kept with heretics, nor persons suspected of heresy, even when they are given safe-conducts from the emperor and kings."[6]

Weak from illness—the damp dungeon brought on a fever that nearly ended his life—Huss was finally brought before the council. Loaded with chains he stood in the presence

---

* Simony: Selling high positions in the church for money.

of the emperor, who had pledged to protect him. He firmly presented the truth and solemnly protested against the corruptions of the hierarchy. When the council required him to choose whether he would recant his doctrines or be put to death, he accepted the martyr's fate.

The grace of God sustained him. During the weeks of suffering before his final sentence, heaven's peace filled his soul. "I write this letter," he said to a friend, "in my prison, and with my chained hand, expecting my sentence of death tomorrow. . . . When, with the assistance of Jesus Christ, we meet again in the delicious peace of the future life, you will learn how merciful God has been toward me, how well He has supported me in my temptations and trials."[7]

Triumph Foreseen

In his dungeon he could see that the true faith would triumph in the future. In his dreams he saw the pope and bishops leaving no trace of the pictures of Christ that he had painted on the walls of the chapel at Prague. "This vision distressed him: but on the next day he saw many painters occupied in restoring these pictures in greater number and in brighter colors. . . . The painters, . . . surrounded by an immense crowd, exclaimed, 'Now let the popes and bishops come; they will never remove them again!' " The Reformer said, "The image of Christ will never be erased. They wanted to destroy it, but it will be painted afresh in all hearts by much better preachers than myself."[8]

For the last time, Huss was brought before the council, a huge and brilliant assembly—emperor, princes of the empire, royal deputies, cardinals, bishops, priests, and an immense crowd. When those presiding asked him for his final decision, Huss refused to renounce his views. Looking intently at the monarch who had so shamelessly violated his pledged word, he declared, "I decided, of my own free will, to appear before this council, under the public protection and faith of the emperor here present."[9] A deep blush reddened the face of Sigismund as all eyes turned to him.

After sentence was pronounced, the ceremony of degradation began. Again urged to retract, Huss replied, turning toward the people: "With what face, then, could I look to heaven? How should I look on those multitudes of people to whom I have preached the pure gospel? No; I consider their salvation more valuable than this poor body, now condemned to death." Huss's priestly vestments were removed one by one, each bishop pronouncing a curse as he performed his part of the ceremony. Finally, "they put on his head a cap or pyramid-shaped miter of paper, on which were painted frightful figures of demons, with the word 'Archheretic' prominent in front. 'Most joyfully,' Huss said, 'will I wear this crown of shame for Your sake, O Jesus, who wore a crown of thorns for me.' "[10]

Huss Dies at the Stake

Huss was now led away. An immense procession followed. When everything was ready for the fire to be lighted, the martyr was urged once more to save himself by renouncing his errors. "What errors shall I renounce?" said Huss. "I know that I am guilty of none. I call God to witness that everything I have written and preached has been for the purpose of rescuing souls from sin and destruction. Therefore, most joyfully will I confirm with my blood the truth that I have written and preached."[11]

When the flames started to burn around him, he began to sing, "Jesus, Thou Son of David, have mercy on me," and continued to sing till his voice was silenced forever. A zealous Catholic described the martyrdom of Huss, and of Jerome, who died soon after, this way: "They prepared for the fire as if they were going to a marriage feast. They uttered no cry of pain. When the flames rose, they began to sing hymns, and the intensity of the fire could scarcely stop their singing."[12]

When the body of Huss had been consumed, his ashes were gathered up and thrown into the Rhine and were carried onward to the ocean to be like seed scattered in all the countries of the world. In lands unknown at the time, it would later yield abundant fruit in witnesses for the truth. The voice in the council hall of Constance echoed through all the coming ages. His example would encourage a great many others to stand firm in the face of torture and death. His execution had shown to the world the treacherous cruelty of Rome. The enemies of truth had been helping the cause they were trying to destroy!

Yet the blood of still another witness must testify for the truth. Jerome had urged Huss to be courageous and firm, saying that if Huss fell into danger, he would rush to his aid. When he heard of the Reformer's imprisonment, the faithful disciple prepared to fulfill his promise. Without a safe-conduct he set out for Constance. On arriving, he became convinced that he had only exposed himself to danger without the possibility of doing anything for Huss. He fled but was arrested and brought back, loaded with chains. At his first appearance before the council his attempts to reply were met with shouts, "To the flames with him!"[13] He was thrown into a dungeon and fed on bread and water. The cruelties of his imprisonment made him sick and threatened his life. His enemies, fearing he might escape them, treated him less harshly, though he remained in prison one year.

Jerome Submits to the Council

The violation of Huss's safe-conduct had created a storm of anger. So the council decided that, instead of burning Jerome, they would force him to retract. He was offered the choice to recant or to die at the stake. Weakened by illness, by the harshness of prison, and by the torture of anxiety and suspense, separated from friends, and crushed by the death of Huss, Jerome gave in. He pledged himself to cling to the Catholic faith and accepted the action of the council in condemning Wycliffe and Huss, except, however, for the "holy truths"[14] they had taught.

But alone in his dungeon, he saw clearly what he had done. He thought of the courage and faithfulness of Huss and pondered his own denial of the truth. He thought of the divine Master who endured the cross for his sake. Before his retraction, even in his sufferings he had found comfort in the assurance of God's favor. Now remorse and doubt tortured his soul. He knew that he would have to make many other retractions before he could be at peace with Rome. The path upon which he was starting down could only end in complete apostasy.

Jerome Finds Repentance and New Courage

Soon he was brought before the council again. His submission had not satisfied the judges. Only by complete surrender of truth could Jerome preserve his life. But he had decided to proclaim his faith and follow his brother martyr to the flames.

He renounced his earlier recanting and, as a dying man, solemnly claimed the right to make his defense. The church officials insisted that he simply affirm or deny the charges brought against him. Jerome protested against such cruel injustice. "You have held me shut up three hundred and forty days in a frightful prison," he said. "You then bring me out before you, and listening to my mortal enemies, you refuse to hear me. . . . Be careful not to sin against justice. As for me, I am only a feeble mortal; my life is of little importance; and when I urge you not to deliver an unjust sentence, I speak less for myself than for you."[15]

His request was finally granted. In the presence of his judges, Jerome knelt down and prayed that the divine Spirit would control his thoughts so that he would say nothing contrary to truth or unworthy of his Master. That

day the promise was fulfilled to him, "When they deliver you up, do not worry about how or what you should speak. For it will be given to you in that hour what you shall speak; for it is not you who speak, but the Spirit of your Father who speaks in you" (Matthew 10:19, 20).

For a whole year Jerome had been in a dungeon, unable to read or even see. Yet he presented his arguments with as much clearness and power as if he had had undisturbed opportunity for study. He pointed his hearers to the long line of holy men condemned by unjust judges. In almost every generation those seeking to elevate the people of their time had been cast out. Christ Himself was condemned as a felon at an unrighteous trial.

Jerome now stated his repentance and testified to the innocence and holiness of the martyr Huss. "I knew him from his childhood," he said. "He was a most excellent man, just and holy; he was condemned, even though he was innocent. . . . I am ready to die. I will not turn away in the face of the torments that my enemies and false witnesses have prepared for me. One day they will have to give an account for their deceptions before the great God, whom nothing can deceive."

Jerome continued: "Of all the sins that I have committed since my youth, none weigh so heavily on my mind and cause me such keen remorse as the one I committed in this fatal place, when I approved of the evil sentence rendered against Wycliffe, and against the holy martyr, John Huss, my teacher and my friend. Yes! I confess it from my heart and declare with horror that

I disgracefully gave in to fear when, through a dread of death, I condemned their doctrines. I therefore beg . . . Almighty God to stoop to pardon me my sins, and this one in particular, the most terrible of all."

Pointing to his judges, he said firmly, "You condemned Wycliffe and John Huss. . . . The things that they affirmed, and which are irrefutable, I also think and declare, like them."

His words were interrupted. The church officials, trembling with rage, cried out: "What need is there of further proof? We see with our own eyes the most stubborn of heretics!"

Unmoved by this storm, Jerome exclaimed: "What! do you suppose that I am afraid to die? You have held me for a whole year in a frightful dungeon, more horrible than death itself. . . . I cannot help expressing my astonishment at such inhuman treatment toward a Christian."[16]

Assigned to Prison and Death

Again the storm of rage burst out, and Jerome was hurried away to prison. Yet his words had made a deep impression on some, and they wanted to save his life. These dignitaries visited him and urged him to submit to the council. They presented bright prospects as reward.

"Prove to me from the Holy Writings that I am in error," he said, "and I will renounce it."

"The Holy Writings!" exclaimed one of his tempters. "Is everything then to be judged by them? Who can understand them till the church has interpreted them?"

"Are the traditions of men more worthy of faith than the gospel of our Savior?" Jerome replied.

"Heretic!" was the response. "I repent having pleaded so long with you. I see that you are urged on by the devil."[17]

Before long Jerome was led out to the same spot on which Huss had yielded up his life. He went singing on his way, his face lighted up with joy and peace. To him death had lost its terrors. When the executioner stepped behind him to light the wood, the martyr exclaimed, "Apply the fire before my face. If I had been afraid, I would not be here."

His last words were a prayer: "Lord, Almighty Father, have pity on me, and pardon me my sins, for You know that I have always loved Your truth."[18] The ashes of the martyr were gathered up and, like those of Huss, thrown into the Rhine. So perished God's faithful light-bearers.

The execution of Huss had lit a flame of indignation and horror in Bohemia. The whole nation declared that he had been a faithful teacher of the truth. The people accused the council of murder. Huss's doctrines attracted greater attention than before, and many came to accept the reformed faith. The pope and the emperor united to crush the movement, and the armies of Sigismund were hurled against Bohemia.

But God raised up a deliverer. Ziska, one of the ablest generals of his age, was the leader of the Bohemians. Trusting in the help of God, the Bohemian people withstood the mightiest armies that could be brought against them. Again and again the emperor invaded Bohemia, only to be repulsed. The Hussites rose above the fear of death, and nothing could stand against them. The brave Ziska died, but his place was filled by Procopius, who in some respects was a more capable leader.

The pope proclaimed a crusade against the Hussites. An immense force descended on Bohemia, only to suffer terrible defeat. Another crusade was called. In all the papal countries of Europe men, money, and munitions of war were raised. Great numbers flocked to the papal banner.

The vast force entered Bohemia. The people rallied to repel them. The two armies approached each other until only a river lay between them. "The crusaders had the greatly superior force, but instead of dashing across the stream and engaging in battle with the Hussites whom they had come so far to meet, they stood gazing silently at those warriors."[19]

Suddenly a mysterious terror fell on the army. Without striking a blow, that mighty force broke and scattered as if dispelled by an unseen power. The Hussite army pursued them, and immense plunder fell into the hands of the victors. The war, instead of impoverishing the Bohemians, enriched them.

A few years later, under a new pope, still another crusade was launched. A vast army entered Bohemia. The Hussite forces fell back before them, drawing the invaders farther into the country, leading them to think they had already won the victory.

At last the army of Procopius advanced to give them battle. As the invaders heard the sound of the approaching force, even before the Hussites were in sight, a panic again fell on them. Princes, generals, and common soldiers fled in all directions, throwing away their armor. Their defeat was complete, and again an immense amount of plunder fell into the hands of the victors.

So for the second time a great army of warlike men, trained for battle, fled without a blow before the defenders of a small and feeble nation. The invaders were struck with a supernatural terror. The same God who scattered the armies of Midian before Gideon and his three hundred had again stretched out His hand (see Judges 7:19–25; Psalm 53:5).

Betrayed by Diplomacy

The papal leaders finally resorted to diplomacy. They struck a compromise with the Bohemians that betrayed them into the power of Rome. The Bohemians had specified four points as the condition of peace with Rome: (1) the free preaching of the Bible; (2) the right of the whole church to both the bread and the wine in the communion and the use of the mother tongue in divine worship; (3) the exclusion of the clergy from all secular offices and authority; and, (4) in cases of crime, the jurisdiction of the civil courts over clergy and laity alike. The papal authorities agreed to accept the four articles but said "that the right of explaining them . . . should belong to the council—in other words, to the pope and the emperor."[20] So they signed a treaty, and Rome gained by deceit and fraud what she had failed to gain by conflict. Placing her own interpretation on the Hussite articles, as she had on the Bible, she could twist their meaning to suit her purposes.

Many people in Bohemia could not consent to the treaty, recognizing that it betrayed their liberties. Disagreements arose, leading to strife among themselves. The noble Procopius fell, and the liberties of Bohemia died.

Again foreign armies invaded Bohemia, and those who remained faithful to the gospel met with bloody persecution. Yet their firmness was unshaken. Forced to find refuge in caves, they still met to read God's Word and unite in His worship. Through messengers secretly sent to different countries they learned "that amid the mountains of the Alps was an ancient church, resting on the foundations of Scripture and protesting against the idol-worshiping corruptions of Rome."[21] With great joy, they opened correspondence with the Waldensian Christians.

Faithful to the gospel, the Bohemians waited through the night of their persecution. In the darkest hour they still turned their eyes toward the horizon like people watching for the morning.

1. James A. Wylie, *History of Protestantism,* bk. 3, ch. 1.
2. Ibid.
3. François P. E. B. de Bonnechose, *The Reformers Before the Reformation,* vol. 1, pp. 147, 148.
4. Ibid., vol. 1, pp. 148, 149.
5. Ibid., vol. 1, p. 247.
6. Jacques Lenfant, *History of the Council of Constance,* vol. 1, p. 516.
7. Bonnechose, vol. 2, p. 67.
8. J. H. Merle D'Aubigné, *History of the Reformation of the Sixteenth Century,* bk. 1, ch. 6.

9. Bonnechose, vol. 2, p. 84.
10. Wylie, bk. 3, ch. 7.
11. Ibid.
12. Ibid.
13. Bonnechose, vol. 1, p. 234.
14. Ibid., vol. 2, p. 141.
15. Ibid., vol. 2, pp. 146, 147.
16. Bonnechose, vol. 2, pp. 151, 153.
17. Wylie, bk. 3, ch. 10.
18. Bonnechose, vol. 2, p. 168.
19. Wylie, bk. 3, ch. 17.
20. Ibid., bk. 3, ch. 18.
21. Ibid., bk. 3, ch. 19.

Luther, a Man for His Time

Among those called to lead the church from Rome's darkness into the light of a purer faith, Martin Luther is chief. Having no fear but the fear of God, and acknowledging no foundation for faith but the Holy Scriptures, Luther was the man for his time.

Luther spent his early years in the humble home of a German peasant. His father wanted him to become a lawyer, but God intended to make him a builder in the great temple that was rising slowly through the centuries. Hardship, poverty, and severe discipline were the school in which Infinite Wisdom prepared Luther for his life mission.

Luther's father was a man of active mind. His unfailingly good sense led him to distrust the monastic system. He was unhappy when Luther entered a monastery without his permission. It took two years before the father reconciled with his son, and even then his opinions remained the same.

Luther's parents tried to instruct their children in the knowledge of God. Earnestly and constantly they worked to prepare their children to live useful lives. Sometimes they were too strict, but the Reformer himself found more to approve than to condemn in their discipline.

At school Luther was treated harshly and even with violence. He often suffered from hunger. That era's gloomy, superstitious ideas of religion filled him with fear. He would lie down at night with a heavy heart, constantly terrified at the thought of God as a cruel tyrant rather than a kind heavenly Father.

When he entered the University of Erfurt, the future looked brighter than in his earlier years. By thrift and hard work his parents had become well-to-do, and they were able to give him all the help he needed. And wise, caring friends to some extent reduced the gloomy effects of his earlier training. With good influences, his mind developed rapidly. Consistent attention to his studies soon placed him in the top rank among his associates.

Luther did not fail to begin each day with prayer; his heart continually breathed a request for guidance. "To pray well," he often said, "is the better half of study."[1]

One day in the library of the university he discovered a book he had never seen—a Latin Bible. He had heard portions of the Gospels and Epistles, and he had thought that these were the entire Bible. Now, for the first time, he was looking at the whole of God's Word. With awe and wonder he turned the sacred pages and read for himself the words of life, pausing to exclaim, "O that God would give me such a book for myself!"[2] Angels were by his side. Rays of light from God revealed treasures of truth to his understanding. Like never before, the deep conviction that he was a sinner took hold of him.

Peace With God

A desire to find peace with God led him to devote himself to a monk's life. As part of this, he was required to do the lowest jobs and to beg from house to house. He patiently endured this humiliation, believing it was necessary because of his sins.

Luther loved to study God's Word. He had found a Bible chained to the convent wall, and he often went to it there, robbing himself of sleep and grudging even the time he spent at his meager meals.

He led a very strict life, trying to subdue the evils of his nature by fasting, vigils, and whippings. Later he said, "If ever a monk could gain heaven by his monkish works, I would certainly have been entitled to it. . . . If it had continued much longer, I would have carried my self-denial even to death."[3] With all his efforts, his burdened heart found no relief. Finally he was driven nearly to despair.

When it seemed that all hope was gone, God raised up a friend for him. Staupitz opened the Word of God to Luther's mind and urged him to look away from self and look to Jesus. "Instead of torturing yourself because of

your sins, throw yourself into the Redeemer's arms. Trust in Him, in the righteousness of His life, in the atonement of His death. . . . The Son of God . . . became man to give you the assurance of God's favor. . . . Love Him who first loved you."[4] His words made a deep impression on Luther's mind. Peace came to his troubled heart.

After being ordained a priest, Luther was called to a professorship in the University of Wittenberg. He began to lecture on the Psalms, the Gospels, and the Epistles to crowds of delighted listeners. Staupitz, his supervisor, urged him to go into the pulpit and preach. But Luther felt that he was unworthy to speak to the people in Christ's place. It was only after a long struggle that he yielded to the request of his friends. He was mighty in the Scriptures, and the grace of God rested on him. He presented the truth with a clearness and power that convinced their understanding, and his earnest appeals touched their hearts.

Luther was still a true son of the papal church, and he had no thought that he would ever be anything else. Led to visit Rome, he made the journey on foot, spending the night at monasteries along the way. He was amazed at the magnificence and luxury that he saw. The monks lived in elegant apartments, dressed in costly robes, and feasted on rich food. Luther's mind was becoming perplexed.

Finally in the distance he saw the seven-hilled city. He stretched himself face down on the earth, exclaiming: "Holy Rome, I salute you!"[5] He visited the churches, listened to the priests and monks tell their fantastic tales, and performed all the required ceremonies. Everywhere, what he saw filled him with astonishment—evils among the clergy, indecent jokes from church officials. He was filled with horror by their foul language even during mass. He met intemperance and immorality. "No one can imagine," he wrote, "what sins and shameful actions are committed in Rome. . . . They are in the habit of saying, 'If there is a hell, Rome is built over it.'"[6]

Truth on Pilate's Staircase

The pope had promised an indulgence to everyone who would climb on their knees up "Pilate's staircase," which was said to have been miraculously brought from Jerusalem to Rome. One day, as Luther was climbing these steps, a voice like thunder seemed to say, "The just shall live by faith" (Romans 1:17). He jumped to his feet in shame and horror. At that moment, he saw more clearly than ever before how wrong it was to trust in human works for salvation. He turned his face from Rome. Beginning then, the separation grew until he cut all connection with the papal church.

After he returned from Rome, Luther received the degree of doctor of divinity. Now he was free to devote himself to the Scriptures that he loved. He had taken a solemn vow to be faithful in preaching the Word of God, not the doctrines of the popes. He was no longer just a monk, but the authorized herald of the Bible, called as a shepherd to feed the flock of God that were hungering and thirsting for truth. He firmly declared that Chris-

tians should receive no other doctrines than those that are based on the authority of the Sacred Scriptures.

Eager crowds listened to him intently. The good news of a Savior's love, the assurance of pardon and peace through His atoning blood, made their hearts rejoice. At Wittenberg a light began to shine whose rays would become brighter and brighter to the close of time.

But there is always conflict between truth and error. Our Savior Himself declared, "I did not come to bring peace but a sword" (Matthew 10:34). A few years after the start of the Reformation, Luther said: "God . . . pushes me forward. . . . I want to live in peace, but I am thrown into the middle of uprisings and revolutions."[7]

Indulgences for Sale

The Roman Church put the grace of God up for sale. Under the pressure of raising funds to build St. Peter's at Rome, the church offered to sell indulgences for sin under authority of the pope. A temple was to be built for God's worship, paid for by the price of crime. This is what stirred up the papacy's most successful enemies and led to the battle that shook the papal throne and the triple crown on the pope's head.

Tetzel was the official appointed to sell indulgences in Germany. He had been convicted of shameful offenses against society and the law of God, but he was hired to carry out the fundraising projects of the pope in Germany. He told glaring lies and marvelous tales to deceive an ignorant and superstitious people. If they had possessed the Word of God, they would not have been deceived. But the church had kept the Bible from them.[8]

As Tetzel entered a town, a messenger went ahead, announcing, "The grace of God and of the holy father is at your gates."[9] The people welcomed the blasphemous deceiver as if he were God Himself. From the pulpit in the church, Tetzel glorified indulgences as the most precious gift of God. He declared that by means of his certificates of pardon, all the sins that the buyer would *afterward* desire to commit would be forgiven him, and "not even repentance is necessary."[10] He assured his hearers that his indulgences had power to save the dead; the very moment the money would clink against the bottom of his case, the soul for whom it had been paid would escape from purgatory and make its way to heaven.[11]

Gold and silver flowed into Tetzel's treasury. A salvation bought with money was easier to get than one that requires repentance, faith, and diligent effort to resist and overcome sin. (See Appendix.)

Luther was horrified. Many of his own congregation had bought certificates of pardon. They soon began to come to their pastor, confessing sins and expecting forgiveness, not because they were sorry and wanted to reform, but on the basis of the indulgence. Luther refused, and he warned them that unless they repented and reformed, they must die in their sins. They went back to Tetzel complaining that their confessor had refused his certificates, and some boldly demanded their money back. In a rage, the friar uttered terrible curses, caused

fires to be lighted in the public squares, and declared that he "had received an order from the pope to burn all heretics who dared to oppose his most holy indulgences."[12]

Luther's Work Begins

Luther spoke from the pulpit in solemn warning. He told the people how offensive sin is to God and how impossible it is for anyone by his own works to reduce its guilt or avoid its punishment. Nothing but repentance toward God and faith in Christ can save the sinner. The grace of Christ cannot be purchased—it is a free gift. He counseled the people not to buy indulgences but to look in faith to a crucified Redeemer. He told about his own painful experience and assured his hearers that it was by believing in Christ that he found peace and joy.

As Tetzel continued making his ungodly claims, Luther decided on a more effective protest. The castle church of Wittenberg possessed relics that were exhibited to the people on certain holy days. All who visited the church on those days and made confession were granted full remission of sins. On the day before one of the most important of these occasions, the festival of All Saints, Luther joined the crowds already making their way to the church and on its door posted ninety-five propositions against the doctrine of indulgences.

His challenges attracted everyone's attention. They were read and repeated in every direction, creating great excitement in the whole city. These theses showed that God had never committed to the pope or any man the power to pardon sin and to remove its penalty. They clearly showed that God bestows His grace freely on all who seek it by repentance and faith.

Luther's theses spread through all Germany and in a few weeks had echoed throughout Europe. Many devoted Roman Catholics read them with joy, recognizing the voice of God in them. They felt that the Lord had begun to act to stop the rising tide of corruption issuing from Rome. Princes and magistrates secretly rejoiced that a limit was to be put on the arrogant power that denied the right to appeal from its decisions.

Crafty church leaders were enraged to see their profits endangered. The Reformer had bitter accusers to meet. "Who does not know," he responded, "that it is rare for someone to suggest any new idea without . . . being accused of stirring up quarrels? . . . Why were Christ and all the martyrs put to death? Because . . . they advanced novelties without having first humbly taken counsel of the established religious leaders."[13]

The accusations of Luther's enemies, their misrepresentation of his intentions, and their hate-filled assaults on his character swept over him like a flood. He had felt confident that the leaders would gladly unite with him in reform. Looking forward, he had seen a brighter day dawning for the church.

But encouragement from some leaders had changed to criticism. Many officials of church and state soon saw that the acceptance of these truths would effectively undermine

Rome's authority, stop thousands of streams now flowing into her treasury, and so restrict the luxury of the papal leaders. To teach the people to look to Christ alone for salvation would overthrow the pope's throne and eventually destroy their own authority. So they set themselves against Christ and the truth by opposing the man He sent to enlighten them.

Luther trembled as he looked at himself—one man opposed to the mighty powers of earth. "Who was I," he wrote, "to oppose the majesty of the pope, before whom . . . the kings of the earth and the whole world trembled? . . . No one can know what my heart suffered during these first two years and into what sadness, even what despair, I had sunk."[14] But when human support failed, he looked to God alone. He could safely lean on that all-powerful arm.

Luther wrote to a friend: "Your first duty is to begin by prayer. . . . Hope for nothing from your own labors, from your own understanding. Trust in God alone and in the influence of His Spirit."[15] Here is an important lesson for those who feel that God has called them to present to others the vital truths for this time. Going against the powers of evil requires something more than intellect and human wisdom.

Luther Appealed Only to the Bible

When enemies appealed to custom and tradition, Luther met them with the Bible only. Here were arguments they could not answer. From his sermons and writings came beams of light that awakened and illuminated thousands. The Word of God was like a two-edged sword, cutting its way to the hearts of the people. The eyes of the people, so long directed to human ceremonies and earthly priests, were now turning in faith to Christ and Him crucified.

This widespread interest stirred the fears of the papal authorities. Luther received a summons to appear at Rome to answer the charge of heresy. His friends knew very well the danger that threatened him in that corrupt city, already drunk with the blood of the martyrs of Jesus. They requested that he receive his examination in Germany.

This was arranged, and the pope's representative, or legate, was appointed to hear the case. The instructions to this official stated that Luther had already been declared a heretic. The legate was therefore "to prosecute and restrain him without any delay." The legate was empowered "to ban him in every part of Germany; to banish, curse, and excommunicate all those who are attached to him," to excommunicate all, no matter their rank in church or state, except the emperor, who would neglect to seize Luther and his followers and deliver them to the vengeance of Rome.[16]

The document reveals not a trace of Christian principle or even common justice. Luther had had no opportunity to explain or defend his position, yet he was pronounced a heretic and in the same day counseled, accused, judged, and condemned.

When Luther so much needed the advice of a true friend, God sent Melanchthon to Wittenberg. Melanch-

thon's sound judgment, combined with a pure and upright character, won everyone's admiration. He soon became Luther's most trusted friend. His gentleness, caution, and exactness helped to supplement Luther's courage and energy.

The trial was to take place at Augsburg, and the Reformer set out on foot. There had been threats that he would be murdered on the way, and his friends begged him not to go. But he said, "I am like Jeremiah, a man of strife and contention; but the more their threats increase, the more my joy is multiplied. . . . They have already destroyed my honor and my reputation. . . . As for my soul, they cannot take that. Whoever wants to proclaim the word of Christ to the world must expect death at every moment."[17]

The news of Luther's arrival at Augsburg gave great satisfaction to the pope's representative. The troublesome heretic who had caught the world's attention seemed now to be in Rome's power, and he would not escape. The representative intended to force Luther to retract, or if this failed, to send him to Rome to share the fate of Huss and Jerome. So through his agents he tried to get Luther to appear without a safe-conduct and trust himself to his mercy. But the Reformer declined to do this. Not until he had received the document pledging the emperor's protection did he appear in the presence of the pope's ambassador.

As a strategy, the pope's delegates decided to win Luther by seeming to treat him gently. The ambassador professed great friendliness, but he demanded that Luther submit completely to the church and yield every point without argument or question. In his reply, Luther expressed his regard for the church, his desire for truth, and his readiness to answer all objections to what he had taught and to submit his doctrines to the decision of leading universities. But he protested against the cardinal's requiring him to retract without having proved him to be in error.

The only response was, "Retract, retract!" The Reformer showed that his position was supported by Scripture. He could not renounce truth. The ambassador, unable to refute Luther's arguments, overwhelmed him with a storm of accusations, attacks, flattery, quotations from tradition, and the sayings of the church fathers, giving the Reformer no opportunity to speak. Luther finally received a reluctant permission to present his answer in writing.

In writing to a friend, he said, "What is written may be submitted to the judgment of others; and second, one has a better chance of working on the fears, if not on the conscience, of an arrogant and babbling despot, who would otherwise overpower by his haughty language."[18]

At the next interview, Luther gave a clear, concise, and forcible presentation of his views, supported by Scripture. After reading this paper aloud, he handed it to the cardinal, who threw it aside, dismissing it as a mass of idle words and irrelevant quotations. Luther now met the haughty official on his own ground—the traditions and teaching of the church—and

completely overthrew his claims.

The official lost all self-control. In a rage he cried out, "Retract! or I will send you to Rome." And he finally declared, in a haughty and angry tone, "Retract, or return no more."[19]

The Reformer promptly left with his friends, indicating plainly that the ambassador could expect no retraction from him. This was not what the cardinal had intended. Now, left alone with his supporters, he looked from one to another in chagrin at the unexpected failure of his schemes.

The large assembly who were there had opportunity to compare the two men and to judge for themselves the spirit each had shown, as well as the strength and truthfulness of their positions. The Reformer was simple, humble, and firm, having truth on his side. The pope's representative was self-important, haughty, unreasonable, and without a single argument from the Scriptures, yet loudly demanding, "Retract, or be sent to Rome."

Escape From Augsburg

Luther's friends argued that since it was useless for him to stay, he should return to Wittenberg immediately, and that he should exercise the greatest caution. So he left Augsburg before daybreak on horseback, accompanied only by a guide that the magistrate provided. He made his way secretly through the dark streets of the city. Enemies, watchful and cruel, were plotting to destroy him. Those were moments of anxiety and earnest prayer. He reached a small gate in the wall of the city. It was opened for him, and he and his guide passed through.

Before Rome's representative learned that Luther was gone, he was beyond the reach of his persecutors.

The news of Luther's escape overwhelmed the representative with surprise and anger. He had expected to receive great honor for his firmness in dealing with this disturber of the church. In a letter to Frederick, the elector of Saxony, he bitterly denounced Luther, demanding that Frederick send the Reformer to Rome or banish him from Saxony.

Up to this point, the elector had little knowledge of the reformed doctrines, but he was deeply impressed by the force and clearness of Luther's words. Until someone proved that the Reformer was in error, Frederick determined to stand as his protector. In reply to the official he wrote: "Since Doctor Martin has appeared before you at Augsburg, you should be satisfied. We did not expect that you would try to make him retract without first convincing him of his errors. None of the learned men in our territory have informed me that Martin's doctrine is sacrilegious, antichristian, or heretical."[20] The elector saw that the church needed a work of reform. He secretly rejoiced that a better influence was arising in the church.

Only a year had passed since the Reformer posted his theses on the castle church, yet his writings had sparked a new interest in the Holy Scriptures everywhere. Students flocked to the university not only from all parts of Germany, but from other lands. Seeing Wittenberg for the first time, young men "raised their hands to heaven and praised God for having caused the light of truth to shine out from this city."[21]

At this time Luther was only partially converted from Rome's errors. But, he wrote, "I am reading the decrees of the pontiffs, and . . . I do not know whether the pope is antichrist himself, or his apostle, since Christ is so greatly misrepresented and crucified in them."[22]

Rome became more and more angry over Luther's attacks. Fanatical opponents, even doctors in the church's universities, declared that whoever killed the monk would be without sin. But God was his defense. His doctrines were heard everywhere—"in cottages and convents, . . . in the castles of the nobles, in the universities, and in the palaces of kings."[23]

About this time Luther found that the Bohemian Reformer, Huss, had held the great truth of justification by faith before him. Luther said, "We have all—Paul, Augustine, and I— been Hussites without knowing it!" "The truth was preached . . . a century ago, and burned!"[24]

Regarding the universities, Luther wrote: "I fear that the universities will prove to be the great gates of hell, unless they work diligently to explain the Holy Scriptures and engrave them in the hearts of youth. . . . Every institution that does not engage people constantly with the word of God must become corrupt."[25]

This appeal circulated throughout Germany. It stirred the whole nation. Luther's opponents urged the pope to take decisive action against him. A decree was issued that his doctrines must be condemned immediately. If the Reformer and his followers did not recant, they were all to be excommunicated.

A Terrible Crisis

That was a terrible crisis for the Reformation. Luther was not blind to the storm that was about to burst, but he trusted in Christ to support and shield him. "What is about to happen I do not know, nor do I care to know. . . . Not even a leaf falls without the will of our Father. How much more will He care for us! It is a light thing to die for the Word, since the Word that was made flesh has Himself died."[26]

When the papal decree reached Luther, he said: "I despise and attack it as ungodly and false. . . . It is *Christ* Himself who is condemned in it. Already I feel greater liberty in my heart; for at last I know that the pope is antichrist, and that his throne is that of Satan himself."[27]

Yet the demands of Rome were not without effect. The weak and superstitious trembled before the decree of the pope, and many felt that life was too precious to be risked. Was the Reformer's work about to close?

Luther was still fearless. With terrible power he flung the sentence of condemnation back on Rome herself. In the presence of a crowd of people from all levels of society, Luther burned the pope's edict. He said, "A serious struggle has just begun. Up to now I have been only playing with the pope. I began this work in God's name; it will be ended without me, and by His might. . . . Who knows if God has not chosen and called me, and if they shouldn't be afraid that,

by despising me, they despise God Himself? . . .

"God never selected as a prophet either the high priest or any other great person, but ordinarily He chose low and despised people, once even the shepherd Amos. In every age, God's people have had to reprove the great—kings, princes, priests, and wise men—at the peril of their lives. . . . I do not say that I am a prophet, but I say that they ought to fear precisely because I am alone and they are many. I am sure of this, that the word of God is with me, and that it is not with them."[28]

Yet Luther had a terrible struggle with himself before deciding finally to separate from the church: "Oh, how much pain it has caused me, though I had the Scriptures on my side, to justify it to myself that I should dare to make a stand alone against the pope and identify him as antichrist! How many times have I not asked myself with bitterness that question which was so frequent on the lips of the pope's loyalists: 'Are you alone wise? Can everyone else be mistaken? How will it be if, after all, it is you who is wrong and who is involving in your error so many souls who will then be eternally damned?' That is how I fought with myself and with Satan, till Christ, by His own infallible word, fortified my heart against these doubts."[29]

A new edict appeared, declaring the Reformer's final separation from the Roman Church, denouncing him as cursed by Heaven, and including in the same condemnation anyone else who received his doctrines.

Everyone whom God uses to present

truths that apply especially to their time will face opposition. There was a present truth in the days of Luther; there is present truth for the church today. But the majority today want truth no more than Luther's opponents did. Those who present the truth for this time should not expect to be received more favorably than the earlier Reformers were. The great controversy between truth and error, between Christ and Satan, is to increase to the close of this world's history. (See John 15:19, 20; Luke 6:26.)

1. J. H. Merle D'Aubigné, *History of the Reformation of the Sixteenth Century,* bk. 2, ch. 2.

2. Ibid.

3. Ibid., bk. 2, ch. 3.

4. Ibid., bk. 2, ch. 4.

5. Ibid., bk. 2, ch. 6.

6. Ibid.

7. Ibid., bk. 5, ch. 2.

8. See John C. L. Giesler, *A Compendium of Ecclesiastical History,* period 4, sec. 1, par. 5.

9. D'Aubigné, bk. 3, ch. 1.

10. Ibid.

11. See K. R. Hagenbach, *History of the Reformation,* vol. 1, p. 96.

12. D'Aubigné, bk. 3, ch. 4.

13. Ibid., bk. 3, ch. 6.

14. Ibid.

15. Ibid., bk. 3, ch. 7.

16. Ibid., bk. 4, ch. 2.

17. Ibid., bk. 4, ch. 4.

18. W. Carlos Martyn, *The Life and Times of Martin Luther,* pp. 271, 272.

19. D'Aubigné, London ed., bk. 4, ch. 8.

20. D'Aubigné, bk. 4, ch. 10.

21. Ibid.

22. Ibid., bk. 5, ch. 1.

23. Ibid., bk. 6, ch. 2.

24. James A. Wylie, *History of Protestantism,* bk. 6, ch. 1.

25. D'Aubigné, bk. 6, ch. 3.

26. D'Aubigné, 3rd London ed., Walther, 1840, bk. 6, ch. 9.

27. D'Aubigné, bk. 6, ch. 9.

28. Ibid., bk. 6, ch. 10.

29. Martyn, pp. 372, 373.

A Champion of Truth

A new emperor, Charles V, came to the throne of Germany. The elector of Saxony, who was largely responsible for putting Charles on the throne, urged him to take no action against Luther before granting him a hearing. This placed the emperor in a perplexing and embarrassing position. The pope's followers would be satisfied with nothing short of Luther's death. The elector had declared "that Dr. Luther should be furnished with a safe-conduct, so that he might appear before a tribunal of learned, pious, and impartial judges."[1]

The assembly met at the city of Worms. For the first time the princes of Germany were to meet their young monarch in assembly. Officials of church and state and ambassadors from foreign lands all gathered at Worms. Yet the subject that stirred the deepest interest was the Reformer. Charles had instructed the elector to bring Luther with him, assuring protection and promising free discussion of the disputed questions. Luther wrote the elector: "If the emperor calls me, I cannot doubt that it is the call of God Himself. If they intend to use violence against me, . . . I place the matter in the Lord's hands. . . . If He will not save me, my life is of little impor-

tance. . . . You may expect everything from me . . . except to run away or to recant. Flee I cannot, and still less retract."[2]

As the news circulated that Luther would appear before the assembly, a general excitement arose. Aleander, the pope's representative, was alarmed and enraged. To take up a case in which the pope had already pronounced sentence of condemnation would show contempt for the pope's authority. Furthermore, the powerful arguments of this man might turn many of the princes from the pope. Aleander urged Charles not to allow Luther to appear at Worms, and he persuaded the emperor to yield.

Not content with this victory, Aleander worked to have Luther condemned, accusing the Reformer of "sedition, rebellion, impiety, and blasphemy." But his strong language revealed the spirit driving him. "He is moved by hatred and vengeance," was the general opinion.[3]

With fresh zeal Aleander urged the emperor to carry out the pope's rulings. Worn down by this insistence, Charles invited him to present his case to the assembly. Those who favored the Reformer were uneasy about what Aleander would say. The elector of

Saxony was not present, but some of his councilors took notes of Aleander's speech.

Luther Accused of Heresy

With learning and eloquence, Aleander set himself to overthrow Luther as an enemy of the church and the state. "In Luther's errors there is enough," he declared, to justify the burning of "a hundred thousand heretics."

"What are all these Lutherans? A crew of insolent teachers, corrupt priests, immoral monks, ignorant lawyers, and degraded nobles. . . . How far superior to them is the Catholic party in number, ability, and power! A unanimous decree from this illustrious assembly will enlighten the ignorant, warn the reckless, decide the waverers, and give strength to the weak."[4]

People still make the same arguments against all who dare to present the plain teachings of God's Word. "Who are these preachers of new doctrines? They are uneducated, few in numbers, and from the poorer class. Yet they claim to have the truth and to be the chosen people of God. They are ignorant and deceived. How greatly superior in numbers and influence is our church!" These arguments are no more valid now than they were in the days of the Reformer.

Luther was not there to vanquish the papal champion with the clear and convincing truths of God's Word. Most of the assembly was inclined not only to condemn him and the doctrines he taught, but if possible to uproot the heresy. All that Rome could say in her own defense had been said. From here on, the contrast between

truth and error would become clearer as the open warfare developed.

Now the Lord moved upon a member of the assembly to give a true account of the effects of papal tyranny. Duke George of Saxony stood up in that princely gathering and specified with terrible precision the church's deceptions and abominations:

"Abuses . . . cry out against Rome. All shame has been put aside, and their only interest is . . . money, money, money, . . . so that the preachers who should teach the truth speak nothing but falsehoods. They are not only tolerated, but rewarded, because the greater their lies, the greater their gain. It is from this foul spring that such tainted waters flow. Indecency stretches out the hand to greed. . . . Sad to say, it is the scandal caused by the clergy that hurls so many poor souls into eternal condemnation. We must bring about a general reform."[5] The fact that the speaker was a determined enemy of the Reformer gave greater influence to his words.

Angels of God sent beams of light into the darkness of error and opened hearts to truth. The power of the God of truth controlled even the enemies of the Reformation and prepared the way for the great work about to take place. The voice of One who was greater than Luther had been heard in that assembly.

A committee was appointed to prepare a list of papal oppressions that weighed heavily on the German people. This list was presented to the emperor, with a request that he take measures to correct these abuses. The request said, "It is our duty to prevent the ruin and dishonor of our people. For this reason we most humbly but most urgently ask you to order a general reformation and use your power to accomplish it."[6]

Luther Summoned to Appear

The council now demanded that Luther appear before them. The emperor finally consented, and Luther was summoned. With the summons he was granted a safe-conduct. A herald took these to Wittenberg, with instructions to bring Luther to Worms.

Knowing the prejudice and hatred against him, Luther's friends feared that his safe-conduct would not be honored. He replied: "Christ will give me His Spirit to overcome these ministers of error. I despise them during my life; I will triumph over them by my death. They are busy at Worms to force me to retract, and this will be my retraction: I said before that the pope was Christ's vicar, but now I assert that he is the Lord's adversary and the devil's apostle."[7]

Besides the imperial messenger, three friends determined to go with Luther. Melanchthon's heart was knit to Luther's, and he wanted to follow him. But Luther denied his pleas. The Reformer told him: "If I do not return, and my enemies put me to death, continue to teach, and stand firmly in the truth. Labor in my place. . . . If you survive, my death will be of little importance."[8]

Gloomy forebodings filled the minds of the people. They learned that Luther's writings had been condemned at Worms. The herald, afraid for Luther's safety at the council,

asked if he still wanted to go forward. He answered, "Although condemned in every city, I shall go on."[9]

At Erfurt, Luther passed through the streets he had often walked, visited his convent cell, and thought about the struggles that had brought to his heart the light now flooding Germany. People urged him to preach. He had been forbidden to do so, but the herald gave him permission, and the friar who had once slaved at the worst duties of the convent now entered the pulpit.

The people listened as if spellbound. Luther broke the bread of life to those starving souls. He lifted up Christ before them as higher than popes, church officials, emperors, and kings. Luther made no reference to his own dangerous position. In Christ he had lost sight of self. He hid behind the Man of Calvary, seeking only to present Jesus as the sinner's Redeemer.

The Courage of a Martyr

As the Reformer went on his way, an eager crowd surged around him, and friendly voices warned him of the Catholic authorities. "They will burn you," said some, "and reduce your body to ashes, as they did with John Huss." Luther answered, "Even if they lit a fire all the way from Worms to Wittenberg, . . . I would walk through it in the name of the Lord. I would appear before them, . . . confessing the Lord Jesus Christ."[10]

Luther's approach to Worms stirred up great commotion. Friends trembled for his safety, and enemies feared for their cause. The pope's followers arranged for some to urge him to go to the castle of a friendly knight, where, they declared, all difficulties could be resolved with goodwill. Friends described the dangers that threatened him. Luther, still unshaken, declared: "Even if there were as many devils in Worms as tiles on the housetops, still I would enter it."[11]

When he arrived at Worms, a vast crowd flocked to the gates to welcome him. The excitement was intense. "God will be my defense," said Luther as he stepped from his carriage. His arrival filled Rome's supporters with dismay. The emperor summoned his councilors. What course should they follow? A rigid Catholic declared: "We have consulted on this matter a long time already. Let your imperial majesty get rid of this man at once. Did not Sigismund cause John Huss to be burnt? We are not obligated either to give or to honor the safe-conduct of a heretic." "No," said the emperor, "we must keep our promise."[12] They decided that the Reformer should be heard.

Everyone in the city was eager to see this remarkable man. Luther, tired from the journey, needed quiet and rest. But he had enjoyed only a few hours' relief when noblemen, knights, priests, and citizens gathered eagerly around him. Among these were nobles who had boldly demanded that the emperor reform the church's abuses. Enemies as well as friends came to see the fearless monk. His bearing was firm and courageous. His pale, thin face wore a kindly and even joyous expression. The deep earnestness of his words carried a power that even his enemies could not completely resist.

Some were convinced that a divine influence was with him. Others declared, as the Pharisees had about Christ, "He has a demon" (John 10:20).

On the following day an imperial officer was sent to bring Luther to the assembly hall. Every street was crowded with spectators eager to see the monk who had dared to resist the pope. An old general, the hero of many battles, said to him kindly: "Poor monk, you are now going to make a nobler stand than I or any other captains have ever made in the bloodiest of our battles. But if your cause is just, . . . go forward in God's name, and fear nothing. God will not forsake you."[13]

Luther Stands Before the Council

The emperor sat on his throne, surrounded by the most important people in the empire. Martin Luther was now to answer for his faith. "This appearance was itself a clear victory over the papacy. The pope had condemned the man, and he was now standing before a tribunal which, by this very act, set itself above the pope. The pope had placed him under a ban and cut him off from all human society, and yet he was summoned in respectful language and was received before the most distinguished assembly in the world. . . . Rome was already descending from her throne, and it was the voice of a monk that caused this humiliation."[14]

The lowly born Reformer seemed awed and embarrassed. Several princes approached him, and one whispered: "Do not fear those who kill the body but cannot kill the soul." Another said: "When you are brought before governors and kings for My sake, it will be given you, by the Spirit of your Father, what you shall say." (See Matthew 10:28, 18–20.)

A deep silence fell on the crowded assembly. Then an imperial officer arose and, pointing to Luther's writings, demanded that the Reformer answer two questions—whether he acknowledged them as his, and whether he intended to retract the opinions they advanced. After the titles of the books were read, Luther answered the first question, acknowledging that the books were his. "As to the second," he said, "I would act rashly if I replied without reflection. I might affirm less than the occasion demands, or more than truth requires. For this reason I ask your imperial majesty, with all humility, to allow me time, that I may answer without offending against the word of God."[15]

Luther's reply convinced the assembly that he did not act from passion or impulse. Such calmness and self-command, unexpected in someone so bold and uncompromising, enabled him to answer later with wisdom and dignity that surprised his opponents and rebuked their haughty arrogance.

The next day Luther was to give his final answer. For a time his heart sank. His enemies seemed about to triumph. Clouds gathered around him and seemed to separate him from God. In anguish of spirit he poured out those broken, heart-rending cries, which no one but God can fully understand.

"O almighty and everlasting God," he pleaded, "if it is only in the strength of this world that I must put my trust, everything is over. . . . My last hour has come, my condemnation has been pronounced. . . . O God, do help me against all the wisdom of the world. . . . The cause is Yours, . . . and it is a righteous and eternal cause. O Lord, help me! Faithful and unchangeable God, in no man do I place my trust. . . . You have chosen me for this work. . . . Stand at my side, for the sake of Your well-beloved Jesus Christ, who is my defense, my shield, and my strong tower."[16]

Yet it was not the fear of personal suffering, torture, or death that overwhelmed him with terror. He felt his inadequacy. Through his weakness the cause of truth might suffer loss. He wrestled with God, not for his own safety, but for the triumph of the gospel. In his complete helplessness he fastened his faith on Christ, the mighty Deliverer. He would not appear before the council alone. Peace returned to his heart, and he rejoiced that he was permitted to lift up the Word of God before the rulers of the nations.

Luther thought about his answer, examined passages in his writings, and drew from Scripture suitable proofs to uphold his positions. Then, laying his left hand on the Sacred Volume, he lifted his right hand to heaven and vowed "to remain faithful to the gospel and freely to confess his faith, even if he would seal his testimony with his blood."[17]

Luther Before the Assembly Again

When Luther was again ushered

into the assembly, he was calm and peaceful, yet brave and noble, as God's witness among the great ones of earth. The imperial officer now demanded his decision. Did he desire to retract? Luther made his answer in a humble tone, without violence or passion. His demeanor was modest and respectful, yet he showed a confidence and joy that surprised the assembly.

"Most serene emperor, illustrious princes, gracious lords," said Luther, "I appear before you this day to comply with the order given me yesterday. If, through ignorance, I might violate the customs and forms of courts, I ask you to pardon me, for I was not brought up in the palaces of kings, but in the seclusion of a convent."[18]

Then he stated that in some of his published works he had written of faith and good works, and even his enemies said they were beneficial. To retract these would condemn truths that all accepted. The second class consisted of writings exposing the corruptions and abuses of the papacy. To revoke these would strengthen the tyranny of Rome and open a wider door to great sacrilege. In the third class he had attacked individuals who defended existing evils. Concerning these he freely admitted that he had been more violent than was proper. But even these books he could not revoke, for the enemies of truth would then take the opportunity to curse God's people with still greater cruelty.

He continued, "I will defend myself as Christ did: 'If I have spoken evil, bear witness of the evil.' . . . By the mercy of God, I appeal to you, most serene emperor, and you, most illustrious princes, and all men of every degree, to prove from the writings of the prophets and apostles that I have been wrong. As soon as I am convinced of this, I will retract every error and be the first to lay hold of my books and throw them into the fire. . . .

"Far from being dismayed, I rejoice to see that the gospel is now, as in former times, a cause of trouble and dissension. This is the character, this is the destiny, of the word of God. 'I came not to send peace on earth, but a sword,' said Jesus Christ. . . . Beware lest, by presuming to put a stop to dissensions, you persecute the holy word of God and draw down on yourselves a frightful flood of insurmountable dangers, of present disasters, and eternal desolation."[19]

Luther had spoken in German; he was now requested to repeat the same words in Latin. He again delivered his speech with the same clearness as before. God's guidance directed in this. Error and superstition had so blinded many of the princes that at first they did not see the force of Luther's reasoning, but the repetition enabled them to understand clearly the points he presented.

Those who stubbornly closed their eyes to the light were enraged over the power of Luther's words. The spokesman of the assembly said angrily: "You have not answered the question put to you. . . . You are required to give a clear and precise answer. . . . Will you, or will you not, retract?"

The Reformer answered: "Since your most serene majesty and your high mightinesses require from me a clear, simple, and precise answer, I will give you one, and it is this: I cannot submit my faith either to the pope or the councils, because it is clear as the day that they have frequently erred and contradicted each other. Unless therefore I am convinced by the testimony of the Scripture. . . . *I cannot and I will not retract,* for it is unsafe for a Christian to speak against his conscience. Here I stand. I can do no other. May God help me. Amen."[20]

Thus stood this righteous man. His greatness and purity of character, his peace and joy of heart, were clear to all as he witnessed to the superiority of the faith that overcomes the world.

At his first answer Luther had spoken with a respectful, almost submissive bearing. The pope's followers thought the request for delay was just the first step toward recanting his faith. Charles himself, noting with some contempt the monk's worn body, his plain clothing, and the simplicity of his speech, had declared, "This monk will never make a heretic of me." The courage and firmness that he now displayed, the power of his reasoning, filled everyone with surprise. The emperor exclaimed in admiration, "This monk speaks with a brave heart and unshaken courage."

The supporters of Rome had lost the controversy. They tried to maintain their power, not by appealing to Scripture, but by threats—Rome's unfailing argument. The spokesman of the assembly said, "If you do not retract, the emperor and the states of the empire will consult what course to adopt against an unreformable heretic."

Luther said calmly, "May God be my helper, for I can retract nothing."[21]

He was told to step out while the princes consulted together. Luther's persistent refusal to submit could affect the history of the church for ages. They decided to give him one more opportunity to retract. Again the question came to him: Would he renounce his doctrines? "I have no other reply to make," he said, "than the one I have already made."

The papal leaders were chagrined that their power did not intimidate a humble monk. Luther had spoken to all with Christian dignity and calmness, and his words were free from passion and misrepresentation. He had lost sight of himself and felt only that he was in the presence of One infinitely superior to popes, kings, and emperors. The Spirit of God had been present, impressing the hearts of the chiefs of the empire.

Several princes boldly acknowledged that Luther's cause was just. Another group did not express their convictions then, but at a future time they became fearless supporters of the Reformation.

The elector Frederick had listened to Luther's speech with deep emotion. With joy and pride he witnessed the doctor's courage and calmness, and he determined to stand more firmly in Luther's defense. He saw that the power of truth had defeated the wisdom of popes, kings, and church dignitaries.

As the pope's representative saw the effect that Luther's speech produced, he resolved to use every means at his command to bring about the Reformer's overthrow. With eloquence and diplomatic skill he presented to the young emperor the danger of sacrificing the friendship and support of Rome for the cause of an insignificant monk.

The day after Luther's answer, Charles announced to the assembly his determination to uphold and protect the Catholic religion. He intended to use vigorous measures against Luther and the heresies he taught: "I will sacrifice my kingdoms, my treasures, my friends, my body, my blood, my soul, and my life. . . . I will . . . proceed against him and his followers as obstinate heretics, by excommunication, by official ban, and by every means calculated to destroy them."[22] Nevertheless, the emperor declared, Luther's safe-conduct must be respected. He must be allowed to reach his home safely.

Luther's Safe-conduct in Jeopardy

The pope's representatives again demanded that the emperor disregard the Reformer's safe-conduct. "The Rhine should receive his ashes, as it received those of John Huss a century ago."[23] But princes of Germany, though sworn enemies of Luther, protested such a violation of public faith. They pointed to the disasters that had followed the death of Huss. They did not dare to bring upon Germany a repetition of those terrible evils.

In answer to the disgraceful proposal, Charles said, "Though honor and faith were banished from all the world, they ought to find a refuge in the hearts of princes."[24] Luther's papal enemies continued to urge him to deal with the Reformer as Sigismund had dealt with Huss. But remembering the scene when in public assembly Huss

had pointed to his chains and reminded the monarch of his pledges of safe-conduct, Charles V declared, "I would not like to blush like Sigismund."[25]

Yet Charles deliberately rejected the truths that Luther presented. He would not step out of the path of custom to walk in the ways of truth and righteousness. Because his fathers did, he also would uphold the papacy. In this way he refused to accept light that went beyond what his fathers had received.

Many today cling to the traditions of their ancestors. When the Lord sends additional light, they refuse to accept it because their fathers had not received it. God will not approve us if we look to our fathers to decide our duty instead of searching the Word of Truth for ourselves. We are accountable for the additional light that now shines on us from the Word of God.

Through Luther, divine power had spoken to the emperor and princes of Germany. God's Spirit pleaded for the last time with many in that assembly. As Pilate had done centuries before, so Charles V yielded to worldly pride and decided to reject the light of truth.

The threats against Luther circulated widely, stirring up excitement throughout the city. Knowing the deceitful cruelty of Rome, many friends resolved to prevent the Reformer from being sacrificed. Hundreds of nobles pledged to protect him. Signs were posted on the gates of houses and in public places, some condemning Luther and others defending him. One of them carried the significant words, "Woe to you, O land, when your king is a child" (Ecclesiastes 10:16). Popular enthusiasm in Luther's favor convinced the emperor and the assembly that any injustice to him would endanger the peace of the empire and the stability of the throne.

Efforts for Compromise With Rome

Frederick of Saxony carefully concealed his real feelings toward the Reformer. At the same time he guarded Luther with constant vigilance, watching his movements and those of his enemies. But many others did not try to hide their sympathy with Luther. "The doctor's little room," wrote Spalatin, "could not contain all the visitors who presented themselves."[26] Even those who had no faith in his doctrines could not help admiring the integrity that led him to risk death rather than violate his conscience.

Some tried earnestly to get Luther to agree to a compromise with Rome. Nobles and princes told him that if he set up his own judgment against the church and the councils, he would be banished from the empire and have no defense. They again urged him to submit to the emperor's judgment. Then he would have nothing to fear. In reply he said: "I consent with all my heart that the emperor, the princes, and even the meanest Christian, should examine and judge my works; but on one condition, that they take the word of God for their standard. Humanity has nothing to do but to obey it."

To another appeal he said: "I consent to renounce my safe-conduct. I place my person and my life in the emperor's hands, but the word of God—never!"[27] He said he was willing to submit to a general council, but only if the council were required to decide according to the Scriptures. "In what concerns the word of God and the faith, every Christian is as good a judge as the pope, even if a million councils side with the pope."[28] Both friends and enemies were finally convinced that further effort to reconcile the two sides would be useless.

If the Reformer had given in on a single point, Satan and his angels would have gained the victory. But his unwavering firmness was the means of freeing the church. The influence of this one man who dared to think and act for himself was to affect the church and the world, not only in his own time, but in all future generations.

The emperor soon commanded Luther to return home. His condemnation would quickly follow. Threatening clouds hung over his path, but as he left Worms, his heart was full of joy and praise.

After he left, Luther wanted to make it clear that his firmness was not rebellion. He wrote to the emperor: "I am ready most earnestly to obey your majesty, in honor or in dishonor, in life or in death, and with no exception but the word of God, by which man lives. . . . When eternal interests are involved, God does not want one person to submit to another. This is because such submission in spiritual matters is a real worship, and it ought to be given only to the Creator."[29]

On the journey from Worms, princely church leaders welcomed the excommunicated monk, and civil rulers honored the man whom the emperor had denounced. They urged him to preach, and, despite the imperial ban, he again entered the pulpit. "I never pledged myself to chain up the word of God," he said, "nor will I."[30]

He had not been away from Worms very long when Catholic leaders got the emperor to issue an edict against him. Luther was denounced as "Satan himself under the form of a man and dressed in a monk's clothing."[31] As soon as his safe-conduct expired, everyone was forbidden to shelter him, give him food or drink, or help him by word or act. He was to be delivered to the authorities, his followers also to be imprisoned and their property taken. His writings were to be destroyed, and finally, anyone who dared to act contrary to this decree was included in its condemnation. The elector of Saxony and the princes most friendly to Luther had left Worms soon after Luther, and the emperor's decree received approval from the assembly that remained. The supporters of Rome were overjoyed. They thought the fate of the Reformation was sealed.

God Uses Frederick of Saxony

A vigilant eye had followed Luther's movements, and a true and noble heart had resolved to rescue him. God gave Frederick of Saxony a plan to save the Reformer's life. On his trip homeward Luther was separated from his attendants and was quickly taken through the forest to the castle of Wartburg, an isolated mountain fortress. His hiding place was such a closely guarded secret that even Frederick himself did not know where he had been taken. This ignorance was planned; as long as the elector knew nothing, he could reveal nothing. Satisfied that the Reformer was safe, he was content.

Spring, summer, and autumn passed, and winter came, and Luther still remained a prisoner. Aleander and his followers boasted of their success. The light of the gospel seemed about to be extinguished. But the Reformer's light was to shine out even more brightly.

Security at Wartburg

In the friendly security of the Wartburg castle, Luther rejoiced to be free from the heat and turmoil of battle. But he was used to a life of activity and hard conflict, and he could hardly stand to remain inactive. In those lonely days the condition of the church rose up before him. He feared being called a coward for withdrawing from the contest. Then he scolded himself for being idle and self-indulgent.

Yet at the same time, every day he was accomplishing more than it seemed possible for one man to do. His pen was never still. His enemies were astonished and confused by tangible proof that he was still active. A great many tracts from his pen circulated throughout Germany. He also translated the New Testament into the German language. From his rocky Patmos he continued for nearly a whole year to proclaim the gospel and rebuke the errors of the times.

God had taken His servant away from the stage of public life. In the quiet isolation of his mountain retreat, Luther was removed from earthly supports and shut out from human praise.

This saved him from the pride and self-confidence that success so often brings.

As people rejoice in the freedom that the truth brings them, Satan tries to turn their thoughts and affections from God and to fasten them on human agencies, to honor the instrument and to ignore the Hand that directs the events God chooses. Too often religious leaders who are praised like this begin to trust in themselves. The people tend to look to them for guidance instead of to God's Word. God wanted to guard the Reformation from this danger. Human eyes had looked to Luther as the expounder of the truth. He was removed so that all eyes could be directed to the eternal Author of truth.

---

1. J. H. Merle D'Aubigné, *History of the Reformation of the Sixteenth Century,* bk. 6, ch. 11.
2. Ibid., bk. 7, ch. 1.
3. Ibid.
4. Ibid., bk. 7, ch. 3.
5. Ibid., bk. 7, ch. 4.
6. Ibid.
7. Ibid., bk. 7, ch. 6.
8. Ibid., bk. 7, ch. 7.
9. Ibid.
10. Ibid.
11. Ibid.
12. Ibid., bk. 7, ch. 8.
13. Ibid.
14. Ibid.
15. Ibid.
16. Ibid.
17. Ibid.
18. Ibid.
19. Ibid.
20. Ibid.
21. Ibid.
22. Ibid., bk. 7, ch. 9.
23. Ibid.
24. Ibid.
25. Jacques Lenfant, *History of the Council of Constance,* vol. 1, p. 422.
26. W. Carlos Martyn, *The Life and Times of Martin Luther,* vol. 1, p. 404.
27. D'Aubigné, bk. 7, ch. 10.
28. Martyn, vol. 1, p. 410.
29. D'Aubigné, bk. 7, ch. 11.
30. Martyn, vol. 1, p. 420.
31. D'Aubigné, bk. 7, ch. 11.

Light Kindled in Switzerland

A few weeks after Luther was born in a miner's cabin in Saxony, Ulric Zwingli was born in a herdsman's cottage among the Alps. Brought up among scenes of nature's grandeur, even in childhood his mind was impressed with the majesty of God. At the side of his grandmother he listened to the few precious Bible stories she had learned among the legends and traditions of the church.

At the age of thirteen Zwingli went to Bern, which at the time possessed the best school in Switzerland. Here, however, a danger arose. The friars made determined efforts to lure him into a monastery. Through God's intervention, his father received information about the friars' plans. He recognized that his son's future usefulness was at stake, and he instructed him to return home.

Zwingli obeyed the command, but he could not be content very long to remain in his native valley, and he soon resumed his studies, traveling, after a time, to Basel. Here Zwingli first heard the gospel of God's free grace. Wittembach, a teacher of ancient languages, had been led to the Holy Scriptures while studying Greek and Hebrew, and so rays of divine light fell on the minds of the students under his instruction. He taught that the death of Christ is the sinner's only ransom. To Zwingli these words were like the first ray of light that precedes the dawn.

Zwingli was soon called away from Basel to begin his lifework. His first assignment was in a parish in the Alps. Ordained as a priest, he "devoted himself with his whole heart to the search for divine truth."[1]

The more he searched the Scriptures, the more clearly he saw the contrast between truth and the false teachings of Rome. He submitted himself to the Bible as the Word of God, the only sufficient, infallible rule. He saw that the Bible must be its own interpreter. He pursued every aid to obtaining a correct understanding of its meaning, and he asked for the help of the Holy Spirit. "I began to ask God for His light," he wrote later, "and the Scriptures began to be much easier for me."[2]

The doctrine Zwingli preached had not come from Luther. It was the doctrine of Christ. "If Luther preaches Christ," Zwingli said, "he does what I am doing. . . . I have not written one single word to Luther, nor Luther to me. And why? . . . To demonstrate how much the Spirit of God is in unison with itself, since both of us, without any collusion, teach the doctrine of Christ with such uniformity."[3]

In 1516, Zwingli was invited to preach in the convent at Einsiedeln. Here he would exert an influence as a Reformer that would extend far beyond his native Alps.

Among the chief attractions of Einsiedeln was an image of the Virgin Mary. People said it had the power to work miracles. Above the convent's gateway was the inscription, "Here a complete remission of sins may be obtained."[4] Crowds came to the shrine of the Virgin from all parts of Switzerland and even from France and Germany. Zwingli took the opportunity to proclaim liberty through the gospel to these slaves of superstition.

He said, "Do not imagine that God is in this temple more than in any other part of creation. . . . Can useless works, long pilgrimages, offerings, images, or appeals to the Virgin or the saints obtain for you the grace of God? . . . How can a glossy cowl, a smooth-shorn head, a long and flowing robe, or gold-embroidered slippers be any help at all in forgiving sins?" "Christ," he said, "who was once offered on the cross, is the sacrifice and victim that paid the debt for the sins of believers to all eternity."[5]

To many it was a bitter disappointment to be told that their difficult journey had been in vain. They could not comprehend pardon that was freely offered through Christ. They were satisfied with the way that Rome had directed them. It was easier to trust their salvation to the priests and pope than to seek purity of heart.

But other people gladly received the good news of redemption through Christ, and in faith they accepted the Savior's blood as their atonement. They went home and told others about the precious light they had received. In this way the truth traveled from town to town, and the number of pilgrims to the Virgin's shrine greatly decreased. The offerings were reduced, and so was Zwingli's salary, which came from them. But this only made him rejoice as he saw that the power of superstition was being broken. The truth was gaining hold of people's hearts.

Zwingli Called to Zurich

After three years Zwingli was called to preach in the cathedral at Zurich, the most important town in the Swiss confederacy. The influence he exerted here would be widely felt. The churchmen proceeded to instruct him about his duties:

"You will make every effort to collect the revenues of the chapter without overlooking the least of them. . . . You will be diligent in increasing the income arising from the sick, from masses, and in general from every church function." "As for the administration of the sacraments, the preaching, and the care of the flock, . . . you may employ a substitute, especially in preaching."[6]

Zwingli listened in silence to this instruction and said in reply, "The life of Christ has been hidden from the people for too long. I will preach on the whole of the Gospel of St. Matthew. . . . I will consecrate my ministry to God's glory, to the praise of His Son, to the real salvation of souls, and to their growth in the true faith."

The people flocked in great numbers to listen to his preaching. He began his ministry by opening the Gospels and explaining the life, teachings, and death of Christ. "It is to Christ," he said, "that I desire to lead you—to Christ, the true source of salvation." Statesmen, scholars, craftsmen, and peasants listened to his words. He fearlessly rebuked the evils and corruptions of the times. Many returned from the cathedral praising God. "This man," they said, "is a preacher of the truth. He will be our Moses, to lead us out from this Egyptian darkness."[7]

After a time opposition arose. The monks heckled him and sneered at him; others resorted to insults and threats. But Zwingli bore it all patiently.

When God is preparing to break the chains of ignorance and superstition, Satan exerts his greatest power to keep people in darkness and to fasten their shackles more firmly. Rome worked with renewed energy to open her market throughout the Christian world, offering pardon for money. Every sin had its price, and the church gave people free license for crime if it would keep the treasury of the church well filled. So the two movements advanced— Rome licensing sin and making it her source of income, and the Reformers condemning sin and pointing to Christ as the sacrifice and deliverer.

Sale of Indulgences in Switzerland

In Germany the infamous Tetzel conducted the sale of indulgences. In Switzerland the church put sales under the control of Samson, an Italian monk. Samson had already raised huge sums from Germany and Switzerland to fill the papal treasury. Now he traveled throughout Switzerland, draining the poor peasants of their meager earnings and demanding rich gifts from the wealthy. When he arrived with his wares at a town near Einseideln, Zwingli immediately set out to oppose him. Zwingli was so successful in exposing the friar's lies that Samson had to leave for other towns. Later, Zwingli preached zealously in Zurich against those who tried to sell God's forgiveness. When Samson approached the place, he used a clever maneuver to gain entrance. But when the people there sent him away without the sale of a single pardon, he soon left Switzerland.

The plague, or Great Death, swept over Switzerland in the year 1519. Many came to feel how useless and worthless were the pardons they had bought. They longed for a surer foundation for their faith. At Zurich Zwingli came down with the plague, and the report circulated widely that he was dead. In that awful hour he looked in faith to the cross of Calvary, trusting in the all-sufficient sacrifice for sin. When he came back from the gates of death, he preached the gospel with greater intensity than ever before. The people themselves had come from caring for the sick and the dying, and they felt the value of the gospel as never before.

Zwingli had come to a clearer understanding of the gospel's truths and had more fully experienced its renewing power in himself. "Christ," he said, ". . . has purchased for us a never-ending redemption. . . . His suffering is . . . an eternal sacrifice, and it has eternal power to heal. It satisfies the divine justice forever for all who rely on it with firm and unshaken faith. . . . Wherever there is faith in God, there is also a zeal urging and driving people to good works."[8]

Step by step the Reformation gained ground in Zurich. In alarm its enemies arose to oppose it openly. They made repeated attacks on Zwingli, trying to silence the teacher of heresy. The bishop of Constance sent three deputies to the Council of Zurich, accusing Zwingli of endangering the peace and order of society. If the authority of the church were set aside, he urged, complete anarchy would result.

The council declined to take action against Zwingli, and Rome prepared for a fresh attack. The Reformer exclaimed: "Let them come on. I fear them like the rocky cliff fears the waves that thunder at its feet."[9] The efforts of the church officials only helped the cause that they were trying to overthrow. The truth continued to spread. In Germany its followers, discouraged by Luther's disappearance, took heart again as they saw the progress of the gospel in Switzerland. As the Reformation became established in Zurich, its fruits were more fully seen in the reduction of crime and the promotion of order.

Debate With Rome's Representatives

When they saw how little persecution had accomplished in suppressing Luther's work in Germany, the representatives of Rome decided they would hold a debate with Zwingli. They would make sure of victory by choosing not only the place of combat but the judges that would decide between the two sides. And if they could just get Zwingli in their power, they would see to it that he did not escape. This intention, however, they carefully concealed.

The debate was scheduled to be held at Baden. But the Council of Zurich, suspecting the plans of Rome's representatives and warned by the fires lit in the papal cantons to burn those who accepted the gospel, forbade their pastor to venture into such a dangerous situation. To go to Baden, where the blood of martyrs for the truth had just been shed, was to go to certain death. Oecolampadius and Haller were chosen to represent the Reformers, while the famous Dr. Eck, supported by a great many scholars and church officials, was the champion of Rome.

The Roman side chose all the secretaries, and everyone else was forbidden to take notes, on pain of death. Even so, a student attending the debate made a record each evening of the arguments presented that day. Two other students undertook to deliver these papers to Zwingli at Zurich, with the daily letters of Oecolampadius. Zwingli answered, giving counsel. To avoid being caught by the guard at the city gates, these messengers brought baskets of poultry on their heads and were permitted to pass without trouble.

Myconius said that Zwingli "has labored more by his deep thoughts, his sleepless nights, and the advice that he transmitted to Baden, than he would have done by discussing in person surrounded by his enemies."[10]

Rome's representatives had come to Baden in their richest robes and glittering with jewels. They ate luxuriously from tables spread with costly delicacies and choice wines. In contrast to this, the Reformers had simple, inexpensive food that kept them only a short time at the table. Oecolampadius's landlord sometimes watched him in his room. Finding him always studying or praying he reported that the heretic was at least "very pious."

At the conference, "Eck haughtily ascended a pulpit splendidly decorated, while the humble Oecolampadius, poorly clothed, was forced to take his seat in front of his opponent on a crudely carved stool." Eck's loud voice and limitless assurance never failed him. As the defender of the faith, he was to be rewarded by a handsome fee. When he didn't have better arguments, he resorted to insults and even swearing.

Oecolampadius, modest and self-distrustful, did not relish the combat. Yet although he was gentle and courteous in conduct, he proved himself capable and unflinching. He held firmly to the Scriptures. "Custom," he said, "has no force in our Switzerland, unless it agrees with the constitution. Now, in matters of faith, the Bible is our constitution."[11]

The calm, clear reasoning of the Reformer, presented so gently and modestly, appealed to minds that turned in disgust from Eck's boastful claims.

The discussion continued eighteen days. Rome's representatives claimed the victory. Most of the delegates sided with Rome, and the council pronounced the Reformers defeated and declared that they and Zwingli were cut off from the church. But the contest resulted in new energy for the Protestant cause. Not long afterward, the important cities of Bern and Basel declared for the Reformation.

---

1. James A. Wylie, *History of Protestantism,* bk. 8, ch. 5.

2. Ibid., bk. 8, ch. 6.

3. J. H. Merle D'Aubigné, *History of the Reformation of the Sixteenth Century,* bk. 8, ch. 9.

4. Ibid., bk. 8, ch. 5.

5. Ibid.

6. Ibid., bk. 8, ch. 6.

7. Ibid.

8. Ibid., bk. 8, ch. 9.

9. Wylie, bk. 8, ch. 11.

10. D'Aubigné, bk. 11, ch. 13.

11. Ibid.

Progress in Germany

Luther's mysterious disappearance upset all of Germany. Wild rumors circulated, and many people believed he had been murdered. There was great mourning, and many took solemn vows to avenge his death.

At first Luther's enemies rejoiced at his supposed death, but they were filled with fear when they learned that he had become a captive. "The only remaining way to save ourselves," one of them said, "is to light torches and hunt for Luther through the whole world, to restore him to the nation that is calling for him."[1] The news that he was safe, though a prisoner, calmed the people, while they read his writings more eagerly than ever before. Increasing numbers took sides with the heroic man who had defended the Word of God.

The seed Luther had sown sprang up everywhere. His absence accomplished a work that his presence would have failed to do. Now that their great leader was removed, other laborers stepped forward so that the work that had begun so nobly would not be held back.

Satan now tried to deceive and destroy the people by palming off on them a counterfeit in place of the true work. Just as there were false christs in the first century, so there arose false prophets in the sixteenth.

A few men imagined that they had received special revelations from Heaven and that God had commissioned them to carry forward the Reformation which, they claimed, Luther had only feebly begun. Actually, they were undoing the work that he had accomplished. They rejected the principle of the Reformation—that the Word of God is the all-sufficient rule of faith and practice. In place of that unerring guide, they substituted the uncertain standard of their own feelings and impressions.

People who were naturally inclined to fanaticism united with them. The deeds of these extremists created considerable excitement. Luther had stirred the people to feel the need of reform, and now some really honest persons were misled by the false claims of the new "prophets."

The leaders of the movement urged their claims on Melanchthon: "God has sent us to instruct the people. We have held direct conversations with the Lord; we know what will happen. In a word, we are apostles and prophets, and we appeal to Dr. Luther."

The Reformers were perplexed.

Melanchthon said: "There are indeed extraordinary spirits in these men; but what spirits? . . . On the one hand, let us beware of quenching the Spirit of God, and on the other, of being led astray by the spirit of Satan."[2]

The Fruit of the New Teaching Becomes Visible

The false prophets led the people to neglect the Bible or to cast it aside completely. Students, throwing off all restraint, left their studies and withdrew from the university. The men who thought that they were fit to revive and control the work of the Reformation succeeded only in bringing it nearly to ruin. Rome's supporters now regained their confidence and exclaimed triumphantly, "One last struggle, and all will be ours."

At the Wartburg castle, Luther heard about what had happened. He said with deep concern, "I always expected that Satan would send us this plague."[3] He recognized the true character of those pretended "prophets." The opposition of the pope and the emperor had not caused such great perplexity and distress as these developments had. The professed "friends" of the Reformation had become its worst enemies, stirring up strife and creating confusion.

The Spirit of God had urged Luther forward and had carried him beyond himself. Yet he often trembled over the results his work might have: "If I knew that my doctrine injured one person, one single person, however lowly and obscure—which it cannot, for it is the gospel itself—I would rather die ten times than not retract it."[4]

Wittenberg itself was falling under the power of fanaticism and lawlessness, and all over Germany Luther's enemies were blaming him for it. In bitter anguish he asked, "Is this, then, going to be the end of this great work of the Reformation?" But as he wrestled with God in prayer, peace flowed into his heart. "The work is not mine, but Yours," he said. But he determined to return to Wittenberg.

He was under the empire's condemnation. Enemies were free to kill him, friends forbidden to shelter him. But he saw that the work of the gospel was in danger, and he went out fearlessly in the name of the Lord to battle for truth. In a letter to the elector, Luther wrote: "I am going to Wittenberg under a protection far higher than that of princes and electors. I am not asking for your highness's support, and far from wanting your protection, I would rather protect you myself. . . . There is no sword that can help this cause along. God alone must do everything." In a second letter, Luther added: "I am ready to receive the displeasure of your highness and the anger of the whole world. Are not the Wittenbergers my sheep? And if necessary, shouldn't I expose myself to death for their sakes?"[5]

The Power of the Word

The news soon spread through Wittenberg that Luther had returned and was to preach. The church was filled. With great wisdom and gentleness he instructed and reproved:

"The mass is a bad thing. God is opposed to it, and it ought to be abolished. . . . But we must not tear anyone from it by force. . . . God's . . . word must act, and not we. . . . We have a right to speak; we do not have the right to act. Let us preach; the rest belongs to God. If I were to use force, what would I gain? God takes hold of the heart, and when He conquers it, all is won. . . .

"I will preach, discuss, and write, but I will force none, for faith is a voluntary act. . . . I stood up against the pope, indulgences, and those who supported the papacy, but without violence or rioting. I put forward God's word; I preached and wrote—this was all I did. And yet while I was asleep, . . . the word that I had preached overthrew the papal system, so that neither prince nor emperor has done it as much harm. And yet I did nothing. The word alone did it all."[6] The Word of God broke the spell of fanatical excitement. The gospel brought misguided people back into the way of truth.

Several years later the fanaticism broke out with more terrible results. Luther said: "To them the Holy Scriptures were no more than a dead letter, and they all began to cry, 'The Spirit! the Spirit!' But most assuredly I will not follow where their spirit leads them."[7]

Thomas Münzer, the most active of the fanatics, was a man with considerable ability, but he had not learned true religion. "He was possessed with a desire to reform the world, and forgot, as all fanatics do, that the reformation should begin with himself."[8] He was unwilling to be second, even to Luther. He claimed that God Himself had commissioned him to introduce the true reform: "He who

possesses this spirit, possesses the true faith, even if he never sees the Scriptures in his life."[9]

The fanatical teachers allowed themselves to be governed by impressions, taking every thought and impulse as the voice of God. Some even burned their Bibles. Thousands of people received Münzer's doctrines. He soon declared that those who obeyed princes were trying to serve both God and Satan.

Münzer's revolutionary teachings led the people to break away from all control. Terrible scenes of conflict followed, and the fields of Germany were drenched with blood.

Luther Experiences Agony of Soul

The princes who favored the pope declared that the rebellion was the fruit of Luther's doctrines. This charge brought the Reformer great distress— that the cause of truth should be disgraced by being classed with the worst fanaticism. On the other hand, the leaders in the revolt hated Luther. He had not only denied their claims to divine inspiration, but had called them rebels against the civil authority. In retaliation they denounced him as an evil pretender.

Rome's supporters expected to see the downfall of the Reformation. And they blamed Luther even for the errors that he had tried most earnestly to correct. The fanatical party, falsely claiming to have been treated unjustly, gained sympathy. People began to regard them as martyrs. In this way the ones opposed to the Reformation received both sympathy and praise. This was the work of the same spirit of rebellion that first showed its face in heaven.

Satan is constantly trying to deceive people and lead them to call sin righteousness and righteousness sin. Counterfeit holiness, false sanctification, still exhibits the same spirit as in the days of Luther, diverting minds from Scripture and leading people to follow feelings and impressions rather than the law of God.

Fearlessly Luther defended the gospel from attack. With the Word of God he warred against the pope's usurped authority, while he stood firm as a rock against the fanaticism that tried to join itself to the Reformation.

Both of these opposing elements set aside the Holy Scriptures, exalting human wisdom as the source of truth. Rationalism idolizes reason and makes it the standard for religion. Romanism claims an unbroken line of inspiration from the apostles, giving it the opportunity to conceal extravagance and corruption under the "apostolic" commission. The inspiration that Münzer claimed came from the mists of his imagination. True Christianity receives the Word of God as the test of all inspiration.

When he returned from Wartburg, Luther completed his translation of the New Testament, and soon the gospel went to the people of Germany in their own language. Everyone who loved the truth received this translation received with great joy.

The priests were alarmed at the thought that the common people would now be able to discuss God's Word with them, which would expose their own ignorance. Rome used all her authority to prevent the Scriptures from spreading. But the more she prohibited the Bible, the more the people wanted to know what it really taught. All who could read carried it around with them and were not content until they had memorized large portions of it. Luther immediately began to translate the Old Testament.

Luther's writings found a welcome in both city and village. "What Luther and his friends composed, others circulated. Monks who were convinced that their monastic vows were unlawful, but who were too ignorant to proclaim the word of God, . . . sold the books of Luther and his friends. Germany soon swarmed with these bold book salesmen."[10]

Bible Study Everywhere

At night the teachers of the village schools read aloud to little groups gathered by the fireside. Each time, some hearts would be convicted of the truth. "The entrance of Your words gives light; it gives understanding to the simple" (Psalm 119:130).

The pope's followers who had left the study of the Scriptures to the priests and monks now called for them to disprove the new teachings. But, ignorant of the Scriptures, the priests and friars were totally defeated. "Unfortunately," said a Catholic writer, "Luther had persuaded his followers to put no faith in any other guide than the Holy Scriptures."[11] Crowds would gather to hear men with little education preach the truth. The shameful ignorance of great men became obvious as the simple teachings of God's Word refuted their arguments. Laborers, soldiers, women, and even children were better acquainted with the Bible than priests and educated scholars were.

Noble-minded youths devoted themselves to study, investigating Scripture and becoming familiar with the masterpieces of antiquity. Possessing active minds and brave hearts, these young men soon acquired knowledge so great that for a long time no one could compete with them. In the new teachings, the people had found what satisfied the desires of their hearts, and they turned away from those who had fed them for so long with the worthless husks of superstitious rites and human traditions.

When persecution broke out against the teachers of the truth, they followed the words of Christ: "When they persecute you in this city, flee to another" (Matthew 10:23). Somewhere the fugitives would find a hospitable door opened to them, and they would preach Christ, sometimes in the church or in private houses or in the open air. The truth spread with irresistible power.

Church and civil authorities resorted to imprisonment, torture, fire, and sword, but without success. Thousands of believers sealed their faith with their blood, and yet persecution served only to extend the truth. The fanaticism that Satan tried to unite with it resulted in making more clear the contrast between the work of Satan and the work of God.

---

1. J. H. Merle D'Aubigné, *History of the Reformation of the Sixteenth Century,* bk. 9, ch. 1.
2. Ibid., bk. 9, ch. 7.
3. Ibid.
4. Ibid.
5. Ibid., bk. 9, ch. 8.

6. Ibid.
7. Ibid., bk. 10, ch. 10.
8. Ibid., bk. 9, ch. 8.
8. Ibid., bk. 10, ch. 10.
10. Ibid., bk. 9, ch. 11.
11. Ibid.

The Protest of the Princes

One of the noblest testimonies ever given for the Reformation was the Protest that the Christian princes of Germany made at the Diet of Spires in 1529. The courage and firmness of those men of God resulted in liberty of conscience for succeeding generations and gave the reformed church the name of Protestant.

God's intervention had held back the forces that opposed the truth. Charles V was determined to crush the Reformation, but as often as he raised his hand to strike he had been forced to direct the blow elsewhere. Again and again at the critical moment the Turkish armies appeared on the frontier, or the king of France or even the pope himself made war on him. In this way, amid the strife and turmoil of nations, the Reformation had been left to strengthen and spread.

Finally, however, the Catholic rulers united against the Reformers. The emperor summoned a diet, or council, to convene at Spires in 1529 for the purpose of crushing heresy. If peaceful methods failed, Charles was prepared to use the sword.

Rome's loyalists at Spires openly showed their hostility toward the Reformers. Melanchthon said: "We are what the world hates and tries to sweep away. But Christ will look down on His poor people and preserve them."[1] The people of Spires thirsted for the Word of God, and despite the fact that it was forbidden, thousands flocked to services held in the chapel of the elector of Saxony. This brought on the crisis even sooner. Religious toleration had already been legally established, and the states where the Reformation was strong resolved to oppose any restriction on their rights. In Luther's place stood his coworkers and the princes God had raised up to defend His cause. Frederick of Saxony had died, but Duke John, his successor, had joyfully welcomed the Reformation and displayed great courage.

The priests demanded that the states that had accepted the Reformation submit to Rome's jurisdiction. The Reformers, on the other hand, could not consent for Rome again to control those states that had received the Word of God.

It was finally proposed that where the Reformation had not become established, the Edict of Worms should be enforced; and that "where the people could not conform to it without danger of revolt, they should at least introduce no new reform, ... they should not oppose the celebration of the mass, [and] they should permit no Roman Catholic to embrace Lutheranism." This measure passed the council, to the great satisfaction of the priests and church officials.

Mighty Issues at Stake

If this edict were enforced, "the Reformation could neither be extended . . . nor be established on solid foundations . . . where it already existed."[2] Liberty would be prohibited. No conversions would be allowed. The hopes of the world seemed about to be extinguished.

The evangelicals looked at each other in blank dismay: "What can we do?" "Should the leaders of the Reformation submit, and accept the edict? . . . The Lutheran princes were guaranteed the free exercise of their religion. The same privilege was extended to all of their subjects who had embraced the reformed views before the measure passed. Shouldn't this satisfy them? . . .

"Fortunately, they looked at the principle on which this arrangement was based, and they acted in faith. What was that principle? It was the right of Rome to force the conscience and forbid free inquiry. But weren't they and their Protestant subjects to enjoy religious freedom? Yes, as a favor specially provided in the arrangement, but not as a right. . . . If they accepted the proposed arrangement, they would virtually have been admitting that religious liberty ought to be confined to reformed Saxony; and as for all the rest of Christendom, free inquiry and the profession of the re-

formed faith were crimes and must be punished with the dungeon and the stake. Could they consent to localize religious liberty? . . . Could the Reformers have claimed that they were innocent of the blood of those hundreds and thousands who would have to yield up their lives in Catholic lands as a result of this arrangement?"[3]

"Let us reject this decree," the princes said. "In matters of conscience the majority has no power." To protect liberty of conscience is the duty of the state, and this is the limit of its authority in matters of religion.

The Catholic rulers determined to put down what they termed "daring obstinacy." The representatives of the free cities were required to declare whether they would accept the terms of the proposition. They pleaded for delay, but were refused. Nearly one half sided with the Reformers, knowing that their position marked them for future condemnation and persecution. One of them said, "We must either deny the word of God, or—be burnt."[4]

Noble Stand of the Princes

King Ferdinand, the emperor's representative, tried the art of persuasion. He "begged the princes to accept the decree, assuring them that the emperor would be greatly pleased with them." But these faithful men answered calmly: "We will obey the emperor in everything that may contribute to maintaining peace and the honor of God."

The king finally announced that "their only remaining course was to submit to the majority." Having said this, he left the chamber, giving the Reformers no opportunity to reply. "They sent representatives begging the king to return." He answered only, "It is a settled affair; submission is all that remains."[5]

The imperial party believed smugly that the cause of the emperor and the pope was strong and the Reformers' position weak. If the Reformers had depended on human aid alone, they would have been as powerless as the Catholic side supposed. But they appealed "from the report of the Diet [Council] to the word of God, and from the emperor Charles to Jesus Christ, the King of kings and Lord of lords."

Because Ferdinand had refused to honor their conscientious convictions, the princes decided not to let his absence stop them, but to bring their protest before the national council immediately. They drew up a solemn declaration and presented it to the diet:

"We protest by these words . . . that, for us and for our people, we neither consent to nor accept in any manner whatsoever the proposed decree, in anything that is contrary to God, to His holy word, to our right conscience, to the salvation of our souls. . . . For this reason we reject the yoke that is imposed on us. . . . At the same time we expect that his imperial majesty will behave toward us like a Christian prince who loves God above all things; and we declare ourselves ready to offer him, as well as to you, gracious lords, all the affection and obedience that are our just and legitimate duty."[6]

The majority were amazed and alarmed by the boldness of the protesters. Dissension, war, and bloodshed seemed inevitable. But the Reformers, relying on God's omnipotent arm, were "full of courage and firmness."

"The principles contained in this celebrated protest . . . constitute the very essence of Protestantism. . . . Protestantism sets the power of conscience above the ruler, and the authority of God's word above the visible church. . . . It . . . says with the prophets and apostles, 'We must obey God rather than man.' In the presence of the crown of Charles the Fifth, it uplifts the crown of Jesus Christ."[7] The Protest of Spires was a solemn witness against religious intolerance and an assertion of the right of all people to worship God according to their own consciences.

The experience of these noble Reformers contains a lesson for all ages to follow. Satan is still opposed to making the Scriptures the guide of life. People in our time need to return to the great Protestant principle—the Bible, and the Bible only, as the rule of faith and duty. Satan is still working to destroy religious liberty. The anti-Christian power that the protesters of Spires rejected is now seeking to reestablish its lost supremacy.

The Diet at Augsburg

King Ferdinand denied a hearing to the evangelical princes, but to quiet the dissensions that were disturbing the empire, in the year following the Protest of Spires Charles V convened a diet at Augsburg. He announced he intended to preside in person, and he summoned the Protestant leaders.

The elector of Saxony's councilors urged him not to appear at the diet: "Is it not risking everything to go and shut oneself up within the walls of a city with a powerful enemy?" But others nobly declared, "Let the princes only conduct themselves with courage, and God's cause is saved." "God is faithful; He will not abandon us," said Luther.[8]

The elector started out for Augsburg. Many went forward with gloomy faces and troubled hearts. But Luther, who accompanied them as far as Coburg, revived their faith by singing the hymn he wrote on that journey, "A Mighty Fortress Is Our God." Many a heavy heart lightened at the sound of the inspiring song.

The reformed princes had decided to have a statement of their views, with the evidence from the Scriptures, to present before the council. They committed the task of preparing it to Luther, Melanchthon, and their associates. The Protestants accepted this Confession, and they assembled to sign their names on the document.

The Reformers were careful not to mix their cause with political questions. As the Christian princes came forward to sign the Confession, Melanchthon objected, saying, "It is for the theologians and ministers to propose these things. Let us reserve the authority of the mighty ones of the earth for other matters." John of Saxony replied: "God forbid that you should exclude me. I am resolved to do what is right, without troubling myself about my crown. I want to confess the Lord. My electoral hat and my ermine are not so precious to me as the cross

of Jesus Christ." Another of the princes said as he took the pen, "If the honor of my Lord Jesus Christ requires it, I am ready . . . to leave my goods and life behind." "I would rather renounce my subjects and my states, rather leave the country of my fathers with staff in hand," he continued, "than receive any other doctrine than what is contained in this Confession."[9]

The appointed time came. Charles V, surrounded by the electors and the princes, took time to hear the Protestant Reformers. In that high and formal assembly the Reformers clearly set forth the truths of the gospel and pointed out the errors of the Catholic church. That day has been called "the greatest day of the Reformation, and one of the most glorious in the history of Christianity and of mankind."[10]

Luther had stood alone at Worms. Now in his place were the most powerful princes of the empire. "I am overjoyed," Luther wrote, "that I have lived until this hour, to see Christ publicly exalted by such illustrious confessors, and in so glorious an assembly."

What the emperor had forbidden to be preached from the pulpit was proclaimed from the palace. What many had regarded as unfit even for servants to listen to was heard with amazement by the masters and lords of the empire. Crowned princes were the preachers, and the sermon was the royal truth of God. "Since the apostolic age there has never been a greater work or a more magnificent confession."[11]

One of the principles that Luther most firmly maintained was that no one should enlist the secular power in support of the Reformation. He re-joiced that princes of the empire confessed the gospel, but when they proposed uniting in a defensive alliance, he declared that "the doctrine of the gospel would be defended by God alone. . . . In Luther's view, all the political precautions suggested came from improper fear and sinful mistrust."[12]

Later, referring to the league the reformed princes had suggested, Luther declared that the only weapon in this warfare should be "the sword of the Spirit." He wrote to the elector of Saxony: "We cannot conscientiously approve of the proposed alliance. The cross of Christ must be carried. Let your highness be without fear. We will

do more by our prayers than all our enemies can do by their boastings."[13]

From the secret place of prayer came the power that shook the world in the Reformation. At Augsburg Luther "did not pass a day without devoting at least three hours to prayer." In the privacy of his room he was heard pouring out his soul before God in words "full of adoration, fear, and hope." To Melanchthon he wrote: "If the cause is unjust, abandon it. If the cause is just, why should we dishonor the promises of Him who commands us to sleep without fear?"[14] The Protestant Reformers had built on Christ. The gates of hell could not prevail against them!

1. J. H. Merle D'Aubigné, *History of the Reformation of the Sixteenth Century,* bk. 13, ch. 5.

2. Ibid.

3. James A. Wylie, *History of Protestantism,* bk. 9, ch. 15.

4. D'Aubigné, bk. 13, ch. 5.

5. Ibid.

6. D'Aubigné, bk. 13, ch. 6.

7. Ibid.

8. Ibid., bk. 14, ch. 2.

9. Ibid., bk. 14, ch. 6.

10. Ibid., bk. 14, ch. 7.

11. Ibid.

12. D'Aubigné, London ed., bk. 10, ch. 14.

13. Ibid., bk. 14, ch. 1.

14. Ibid., bk. 14, ch. 6.

Daybreak in France

After the Protest of Spires and the Confession at Augsburg came years of conflict and darkness. Weakened by divisions, Protestantism seemed headed for destruction.

But in the moment when the emperor apparently triumphed, he was struck with defeat. He was forced at last to grant toleration to the doctrines that he had wanted most in life to destroy. He saw his armies wasted by battle, his treasuries drained, his many kingdoms threatened by revolt, while the faith he had tried to suppress was growing everywhere. Charles V had been battling against omnipotent power. God had said, "Let there be light," but the emperor had tried to keep the darkness unbroken. Worn out with the long struggle, he gave up the throne and buried himself in a monastery.

Many of Switzerland's regions, or cantons, accepted the reformed faith, but others clung to the teachings of Rome. Persecution resulted in civil war. Zwingli and many who had joined in the reform fell on the bloody field of Cappel. Rome was triumphant and in many places seemed about to recover all that she had lost. But God had not forsaken His cause or His people. In other lands He raised up workers to carry on the reform.

In France, one of the first to catch the light was Lefevre, a professor in the University of Paris. In his research into ancient literature, his attention was directed to the Bible, and he introduced some of his students to its study. He had begun to prepare a history of the saints and martyrs as given in the legends of the church, and had already made considerable progress in it, when, thinking that the Bible might help him in the project, he began to study it. Here indeed he found saints, but not the kind featured in the Roman church's calendar. In disgust he turned away from his self-appointed work and devoted himself to the Word of God.

In 1512, before either Luther or Zwingli had begun the work of reform, Lefevre wrote, "It is God who gives us, by faith, that righteousness which by grace alone justifies us to eternal life."[1] And while teaching that the glory of salvation belongs only to God, he also declared that the duty of obedience belongs to man.

Some of Lefevre's students listened eagerly to his words and continued to declare the truth long after the teacher's voice was silenced. One of these was William Farel. The son of religious parents and himself a devoted follower of Rome, he was zealous to destroy all who dared to oppose the church. "I would gnash my teeth like a furious wolf," he said later, "when I heard anyone speaking against the pope." But adoration of the saints, worshiping at the altars, and adorning the holy shrines with gifts could not bring peace to his heart. Conviction of sin came over him, and no act of penance could banish it. He listened to Lefevre's words, "Salvation is of grace." "It is the cross of Christ alone that opens the gates of heaven and shuts the gates of hell."[2]

By a conversion like Paul's, Farel turned from the slavery of tradition to the liberty of the sons of God. "Instead of having the murderous heart of a prowling wolf," he came back, he says, "quietly like a meek and harmless lamb, with his heart entirely withdrawn from the pope and given to Jesus Christ."[3]

While Lefevre spread the light among students, Farel went out to preach the truth in public. A dignitary of the church, the bishop of Meaux, soon united with them. Other teachers joined in proclaiming the gospel, and it won followers from the homes of craftsmen and peasants to the palace of the king. The sister of Francis I accepted the reformed faith. With high hopes the Reformers looked forward to the time when France would be won to the gospel.

French New Testament

But their hopes would not be fulfilled. Trial and persecution lay ahead for the disciples of Christ. However, a time of peace interrupted the flow of events, allowing them to gain strength to meet the coming storm, and the Reformation made rapid progress. Lefevre began to translate the New Testament, and at the very time when Luther's German Bible came from the press in Wittenberg, the French New Testament was published at Meaux. Soon the peasants of Meaux had the Holy Scriptures. The workers in the field, the craftsmen in the workshop, cheered their daily labors by talking about the precious truths of the Bible. Though they belonged to the humblest class—the unschooled and hardworking peasantry—the reforming, uplifting power of divine grace was visible in their lives.

The light ignited at Meaux sent its beams to distant places. Every day the number of converts was increasing. For a time the king held back the rage of the church's hierarchy, but the papal leaders finally prevailed. The stake was set up, and many witnessed for the truth in the flames.

In the lordly halls of the castle and the palace there were kingly souls who valued truth above wealth or position or even life. Louis de Berquin was of noble birth, devoted to study, polished in manners, and blameless in morals. "He crowned all his other virtues by viewing Lutheranism with a special hatred." But God guided him to the Bible, and he was amazed to find there "not the doctrines of Rome, but the doctrines of Luther." He gave himself to the cause of the gospel.

Rome's supporters in France put him in prison as a heretic, but the king freed him. For years, King Francis wavered between Rome and the Reformation. Three times the papal authorities imprisoned Berquin, only to have the king release him, refusing to sacrifice him to the hatred of the church leaders. Berquin was warned repeatedly about the danger that threatened him in France, and he was urged to follow the steps of those who had found safety in voluntary exile.

Bold Berquin

But Berquin's zeal only grew stronger. He decided to take bolder measures. He would not only stand in defense of the truth, he would attack error. The most active of his opponents were the educated monks in the theological department of the University of Paris, one of the highest church authorities in the nation. From the writings of these doctors, Berquin drew twelve propositions that he publicly declared to be "opposed to the Bible," and he appealed to the king to act as judge in the controversy.

The king was glad for an opportunity to humble the pride of these haughty monks, so he ordered the Romanists defend their cause by the Bible. They would find little help from this weapon; torture and the stake were arms that they better understood how to use. Now they saw themselves about to fall into the pit into which they had hoped to push Berquin. They looked around them for some way to escape.

"Just at that time an image of the virgin at the corner of one of the streets was mutilated." Crowds flocked to the place, grieving and angry. The king was deeply moved. "These are the fruits of Berquin's doctrines," the monks proclaimed. "Everything is about to be overthrown—religion, the laws, the throne itself—by this Lutheran conspiracy."[4]

The king withdrew from Paris, leaving the monks free to do as they wished. Berquin was tried and condemned to die. To keep Francis from intervening to save him, they carried out the sentence on the very day it was pronounced. At noon a huge crowd gathered to witness the event, and many were astonished to see that the victim had been chosen from the best and bravest of the noble families of France. Amazement, indignation, scorn, and bitter hatred darkened the faces of that surging crowd, but on one face no shadow rested. The martyr was conscious only of the presence of his Lord.

Berquin's face radiated with the light of heaven. He wore "a cloak of velvet, a jacket of satin and damask, and golden pants."[5] He was about to testify to his faith in the presence of the King of kings, and no sign of mourning should contradict his joy.

As the procession moved slowly through the crowded streets, the people noticed with amazement his look of joyous triumph. They said, "He is like someone sitting in a temple, meditating on holy things."

Berquin at the Stake

At the stake, Berquin tried to say a few words to the people, but the monks began to shout and the soldiers to strike their weapons, and their noise drowned the martyr's voice. So in 1529 the highest church authority of cultured Paris "gave the populace of revolutionary France in 1793 the detestable example of suppressing on the scaffold the sacred words of the dying."[6] Berquin was strangled, and his body was consumed in the flames.

Teachers of the reformed faith left for other fields. Lefevre made his way to Germany. Farel returned to his native town in eastern France, to spread the light in his childhood home. The truth that he taught found listeners. Soon he was banished from the city. He traveled from village to village, teaching in private homes and hidden meadows, finding shelter in the forests and among rocky caverns that he had known in boyhood.

As in the apostles' days, persecution had "actually turned out for the furtherance of the gospel" (Philippians 1:12). Driven from Paris and Meaux, "those who were scattered went everywhere preaching the word" (Acts 8:4). And so the light found its way into many remote provinces of France.

The Call of Calvin

In one of the schools of Paris was a thoughtful, quiet young man known for his blameless life, for intellectual vigor, and for religious devotion. His genius and diligence made him the pride of the college, and people confidently expected that John Calvin would become one of the most effective defenders of the church.

But a ray of divine light penetrated the walls of scholasticism and superstition that enclosed Calvin. Olivetan, a cousin of Calvin, had joined the Reformers. The two cousins discussed together the matters disturbing Christendom. "There are only two religions in the world," said Olivetan, the Protestant. "The one . . . which humans have invented, in . . . which we save ourselves by ceremonies and good works; the other is that one religion revealed in the Bible, which teaches us to look for salvation only from the free grace of God."

"I will have none of your new doctrines," exclaimed Calvin. "Do you think that I have lived in error all my life?"[7] But when he was alone in his room he thought about his cousin's words. He saw himself without an intercessor in the presence of a holy and just Judge. Prayers to saints, good works, the ceremonies of the church— all were powerless to atone for sin. Confession and penance could not reconcile the sinner to God.

Witness to a Burning

One day when he happened to visit one of the public squares, Calvin witnessed the burning of a heretic. In the tortures of that dreadful death and under the terrible condemnation of the church, the martyr displayed a faith and courage that the young student painfully contrasted with his own despair and darkness. He knew that the "heretics" rested their faith on the Bible. He determined to study it and discover the secret of their joy.

In the Bible he found Christ. "O Father," he cried, "His sacrifice has appeased Your anger, His blood has washed away my impurities, His cross has taken my curse, His death has atoned for me. . . . You have touched my heart, so that I may turn away in disgust from all other merits except those of Jesus."[8]

Now he determined to devote his life to the gospel. But he was naturally timid and wanted to devote himself to study. The earnest appeals of his friends, however, finally led him to agree to become a public teacher. His words were like dew falling to refresh the earth. He was now in a provincial town under the protection of the princess Margaret, who loved the gospel and extended her protection to its disciples. Calvin's work began with the people in their homes. Those who heard the message carried the good news to others. Calvin went forward, laying the foundation of churches that would produce fearless witnesses for the truth.

Paris would receive another invitation to accept the gospel. It had rejected the call of Lefevre and Farel, but again all classes in that great capital were to hear the message. The king had not yet fully sided with Rome against the Reformation. Margaret resolved to have the reformed faith preached in Paris. She ordered a Protestant minister to preach in the churches. When the papal dignitaries prohibited this, the princess opened up the palace. It was announced that every day a sermon would be preached, and the people were invited to attend. Thousands gathered every day.

The king then ordered that two of the churches of Paris should be opened. Never had the city been so moved by the Word of God. Temperance, purity, order, and industry were taking the place of drunkenness, immorality, strife, and idleness. While many accepted the gospel, most of the people rejected it. Leaders who favored the papacy succeeded in regaining their influence. Again the churches were closed, and the stake was set up.

Calvin was still in Paris. Finally the authorities determined to bring him to the flames. He had no idea he was in danger when friends came hurrying to his room with the news that officers were on their way to arrest him. At that instant they heard a loud knocking at the outer entrance. There was not a moment to lose. Friends delayed the officers at the door, while others helped the Reformer let himself down from a window, and he hurried to the cottage of a laborer who was a friend of the reform. He disguised himself in his host's clothes and, with a hoe over his shoulder, started on his journey. Traveling southward, he again found refuge in Princess Margaret's territory.

Calvin could not remain inactive for long. As soon as the storm had quieted a little, he set out for a new field of work in Poitiers, where some people already favored the new views. Persons from all classes gladly listened to the gospel. As the number of hearers grew, the Reformers thought it was safer to gather outside the city. For a meeting place they chose a cave where trees and overhanging rocks kept them completely hidden. In this secluded spot they read and explained the Bible. Here French Protestants celebrated the Lord's Supper for the first time. This little church sent out several faithful evangelists.

Once more Calvin returned to Paris, but he found almost every door closed to his work. He finally decided to go to Germany. He had scarcely left France when trouble burst on the Protestants. The French Reformers decided to rally the whole nation by striking a bold blow against the superstitions of Rome. Signs attacking the mass were posted all over France in one night. This zealous but unwise movement gave the Romanists a pretext for demanding the destruction of the "heretics" as agitators who were dangerous to the throne and to the peace of the nation.

One of the signs was attached to the door of the king's private chamber. The unprecedented boldness of thrusting these startling messages into the royal presence made the king angry. He expressed his rage in the terrible words: "Arrest everyone, without distinction, who is suspected of Lutheresy. I will exterminate them all."[9] The king had determined to put his influence fully on the side of Rome.

A Reign of Terror

One of those arrested was a poor man who had often called the believers to their secret gatherings. Under the threat of immediate death at the stake, he was commanded to take the papal emissary to the home of every Protestant in the city. Fear of the flames overcame him, and he agreed to betray his brethren. Morin, the royal detective, along with the traitor, slowly and silently passed through the streets of the city. When they arrived at the house of a Lutheran, the betrayer made a sign but spoke no word. The procession stopped, soldiers entered the house, dragged the family out and chained them, and the terrible company went forward in search of fresh victims. "Morin made the whole city tremble. . . . It was a reign of terror."[10]

The victims were put to death with cruel torture, on orders that the fire be lowered in order to prolong their agony. But they died as conquerors, their commitment unshaken, their peace unclouded. Their persecutors felt themselves defeated. "All Paris was able to see what kind of people the new opinions could produce. There was no pulpit like the martyr's pile. The serene joy that lighted up the faces of these Christians as they went along . . . to the place of execution . . . pleaded with irresistible eloquence on behalf of the gospel."[11]

Protestants were charged with plotting to massacre the Catholics, to overthrow the government, and to murder the king. The accusers could produce not a hint of evidence to support their allegations. Yet the cruelties done to the innocent Protestants accumulated like a huge weight of punishment that was due, and in later centuries brought about the very doom the accusers had predicted for the king, his government, and his subjects. But the ones doing it were infidels and the pope's advocates themselves. The suppression of Protestantism was to bring these terrible disasters on France.

Suspicion, distrust, and terror now extended to all classes of society. Hundreds fled from Paris, exiling themselves from their native land. In many cases their departure was the first indication that they favored the reformed faith. The officials who supported the pope looked around them in amazement at the thought of the unsuspected "heretics" that had been tolerated among them.

Printing Declared Abolished

King Francis I had delighted to gather scholars from every country to his court. But in his fresh zeal to stamp out heresy, this patron of learning issued an edict abolishing printing all over France! Francis I is one among the many examples on record showing that intellectual culture does not prevent religious intolerance and persecution.

The priests demanded blood to atone for the insult offered to High Heaven in the condemnation of the mass. January 21, 1535, was chosen for the awful ceremony. In front of every door was a lighted torch in honor of the "holy sacrament." Before daybreak the procession formed at the king's palace.

"The bishop of Paris carried the host under a magnificent canopy, . . . supported by four royal princes. . . . After the host walked the king. . . . Francis I on that day wore no crown nor robe of state."[12] At every altar he bowed in humiliation, not for the vices that defiled his soul nor the innocent blood that stained his hands, but for the "deadly sin" of his subjects who had dared to condemn the mass.

In the great hall of the bishop's palace the king appeared. In words of moving eloquence he lamented "the crime, the blasphemy, the day of sorrow and disgrace," that had come upon the nation. And he called upon every loyal subject to aid in stamping out the deadly "heresy" that threatened France with ruin. Tears choked his voice, and the whole assembly wept, all exclaiming together, "We will live and die for the Catholic religion!"[13]

"The grace that brings salvation" had appeared, but France, illuminated by its radiance, had turned away, choosing darkness rather than light. They had called evil good and good evil, till they had fallen victims to their own chosen self-deception. The light that would have saved them from deception, from staining their hearts with the guilt of innocent blood, they had deliberately rejected.

Again the procession formed. "At short distances scaffolds had been erected on which certain Protestant Christians were to be burned alive, and it was arranged that the wood should be lighted at the moment the king approached, and that the procession should stop to witness the execution."[14] There was no wavering by the victims. When he was urged to recant, one answered: "I only believe in what the prophets and the apostles preached long ago, and what all the company of saints believed. My faith has a confidence in God which will resist all the powers of hell."[15]

When they reached the palace, the crowd dispersed and the king and the church officials withdrew, congratulating themselves that the work would continue until the "heresy" had been completely destroyed.

The gospel of peace that France rejected was indeed to be rooted out, and terrible would be the results. On January 21, 1793, another procession passed through the streets of Paris. "Again the king was the chief figure, again there was uproar and shouting, again there was heard the cry for more victims, again there were black scaffolds, and again the scenes of the day closed with horrid executions. Louis XVI, struggling hand to hand with his jailers and executioners, was dragged forward to the block and held down by force till the axe had fallen and his severed head rolled on the scaffold."[16] Near the same spot twenty-eight hundred human beings died by the guillotine.

The Reformation had presented to the world an open Bible. Infinite Love had unfolded to humanity the principles of heaven. When France rejected the gift of heaven, she sowed seeds of ruin. The inevitable outworking of cause and effect resulted in the French Revolution and the Reign of Terror.

The bold and zealous Farel had been forced to flee from the land of his birth to Switzerland. Yet he continued to exert a strong influence on the reform in France. With the help of other exiles, he translated the writings of the German Reformers into French, and together with the French Bible these were printed in large quantities. Traveling book salesmen sold these works widely in France.

Farel began his work in Switzerland in the humble role of a schoolmaster, cautiously introducing the truths of the Bible. Some believed his teachings, but the priests came forward to stop the work, and they stirred up superstitious people to oppose it. "That cannot be the gospel of Christ," urged the priests, "since the preaching of it does not bring peace, but war."[17]

From village to village Farel went, enduring hunger, cold, and weariness, and everywhere risking his life. He preached in the marketplace, in the churches, and sometimes in the pulpits of the cathedrals. More than once he was beaten almost to death. Yet he kept on working. One after another he saw towns and cities that had been strongholds of Catholicism opening their gates to the gospel.

Farel had wanted to plant the Protestant banner in Geneva. If this city could be won, it would be a center for the Reformation in France, Switzerland, and Italy. Many of the surrounding towns and hamlets had already become Protestant.

With just one companion he entered Geneva. But he was permitted to preach only two sermons. The priests called him before a church council, and they came to it themselves with weapons hidden under their robes, determined to take his life. They gathered a furious mob to make sure of his death if he managed to escape the council. However, the presence of magistrates and an armed force saved him. Early the next morning he was taken across the lake to a safe place. This is how his first effort to evangelize Geneva ended.

The next attempt involved a lowlier instrument—a young man so humble in appearance that even the professed friends of reform treated him coldly. But what could someone like this do where Farel had been rejected? "God has chosen the weak things of the world to put to shame the things which are mighty" (1 Corinthians 1:27).

Froment, the Schoolmaster

Froment began his work as a schoolteacher. The truths he taught the children at school they repeated at home. Soon the parents came to hear the Bible explained. New Testaments and tracts were given out freely. After a time Froment also had to flee, but the truths he taught had taken hold of the minds of the people. The Reformation had been planted. The preachers returned, and Protestant worship became finally established in Geneva.

The city had already declared itself for the Reformation when Calvin entered its gates. He was on his way to Basel when he was forced to take a detour through Geneva.

Farel recognized the hand of God in this visit. Although Geneva had accepted the reformed faith, yet the work of regeneration must be done in the heart by the power of the Holy Spirit, not by the decrees of councils. While the people of Geneva had thrown off the authority of Rome, they were not so ready to renounce the vices that had taken firm root during her rule.

In the name of God Farel solemnly appealed to the young evangelist to remain and work there. Calvin drew back in alarm. He did not want to meet the bold and even violent spirit of the people living in Geneva. He wanted to find a quiet place for study, where he could instruct and build up the churches through printed material. But he did not dare to refuse. It seemed to him "that the hand of God was stretched down from heaven, that it had taken hold of him, and fastened him forever to the place he was so impatient to leave."[18]

The Thunder of Condemnation

The pope's condemnations thun-dered against Geneva. How could this little city resist the powerful hierarchy that had forced kings and emperors to submit?

With the first triumphs of the Reformation past, Rome called up new forces to destroy it. She created the order of the Jesuits, the most cruel, unscrupulous, and powerful of all the champions of the papal system. Dead to the claims of natural affection, and with consciences completely silenced, its members acknowledged no rule, no tie, except that of their order. (See Appendix.)

The gospel of Christ had enabled its followers to endure suffering, cold, hunger, toil, and poverty, to uphold truth in face of torture, the dungeon, and the stake. Jesuitism inspired its followers with a fanaticism that enabled them to endure similar dangers and to bring all the weapons of deception against the power of truth. There was no crime too great to commit, no deception too evil to practice, no disguise too difficult for them to assume. It was their calculated aim to overthrow Protestantism and reestablish the pope's supremacy.

They wore an appearance of holiness, visiting prisons and hospitals, ministering to the sick and the poor, and bearing the sacred name of Jesus, who went about doing good. But under this blameless exterior, they often concealed criminal and deadly intentions.

A fundamental principle of the order was that the end justifies the means. Lying, theft, perjury, and assassination were commendable when they helped the aims of the church. Under disguise the Jesuits worked their way into offices of state, climbing up to be the counselors of kings and shaping the policy of nations. They became servants in order to act as spies against their masters. They established colleges for princes and nobles, and schools for the common people. They drew the children of Protestant parents into observing Catholic rites. In this way the liberty for which the fathers had worked and bled was betrayed by the sons. Wherever the Jesuits went, a revival of Catholicism followed.

To give them greater power, the pope issued a decree reestablishing the Inquisition. Church rulers again set up this terrible tribunal, and atrocities too horrifying to bear the light of day were repeated in its secret dungeons. In many countries thousands upon thousands of the nation's best, the most intellectual and highly educated, were killed or forced to escape to other lands. (See Appendix.)

Victories for the Reformation

Rome used methods such as these to quench the light of the Reformation and to restore the ignorance and superstition of the Dark Ages. But under God's blessings and the labors of noble men whom He raised up to follow Luther, Protestantism was not overthrown. It would not owe its strength to the military might of princes. The humblest and least powerful nations became its strongholds. It was little Geneva; it was Holland, wrestling against the tyranny of Spain; it was bleak, snowy Sweden, that gained victories for the Reformation.

For nearly thirty years Calvin worked at Geneva to spread the Reformation throughout Europe. His behavior was not faultless, nor were his doctrines free from error. But he was instrumental in proclaiming especially important truths, in keeping Protestantism strong against the fast-returning tide of the papacy, and in promoting simplicity and purity of life in the reformed churches.

Publications and teachers went out from Geneva to spread the reformed doctrines. The persecuted of all lands looked to Geneva for instruction and encouragement. The city of Calvin became a refuge for the hunted Reformers of all Western Europe. Geneva welcomed and tenderly cared for them, and when they found a home here, they blessed their adopted city by their skill, their learning, and their deep faith. John Knox, the brave Scottish Reformer, many of the English Puritans, Protestants of Holland and of Spain, and the Huguenots of France all carried the torch of truth from Geneva to lighten the darkness of their native lands.

1. James A. Wylie, *History of Protestantism,* bk. 13, ch. 1.

2. Ibid., bk. 13, ch. 2.

3. J. H. Merle D'Aubigné, *History of the Reformation of the Sixteenth Century,* bk. 12, ch. 3.

4. Ibid., bk. 13, ch. 9.

5. D'Aubigné, *History of the Reformation in Europe in the Time of Calvin,* bk. 2, ch. 16.

6. Wylie, bk. 13, ch. 9.

7. Ibid., bk. 13, ch. 7.

8. W. Carlos Martyn, *The Life and Times of Martin Luther,* vol. 3, ch. 13.

9. D'Aubigné, bk. 2, ch. 30.

10. Ibid., bk. 4, ch. 10.

11. Wylie, bk. 13, ch. 20.

12. Ibid., bk. 13, ch. 21.

13. D'Aubigné, bk. 4, ch. 12.

14. Wylie, bk. 13, ch. 21.

15. D'Aubigné, bk. 4, ch. 12.

16. Wylie, bk. 13, ch. 21.

17. Ibid., bk. 14, ch. 3.

18. D'Aubigné, bk. 9. ch. 17.

The Netherlands and Scandinavia

In the Netherlands the tyranny of Rome drew a protest very early. Seven hundred years before Luther, two bishops fearlessly denounced the pope after being sent as envoys to Rome, where they had learned the true character of the "holy see": "You set up yourself in the temple of God. Instead of a pastor, you have become a wolf to the sheep. . . . While you ought to be a servant of servants, as you call yourself, you try to become a lord of lords. . . . You bring the commands of God into contempt."[1]

Over the centuries, others rose up to echo this protest. They translated the Waldensian Bible into the Dutch language. They declared "that there was great benefit in it; no jokes, no fables, no meaningless talk, no lies, but the words of truth." This is what the friends of the ancient faith wrote in the twelfth century.[2]

Then Rome's persecutions began, but the believers continued to multiply, declaring that the Bible is the only infallible authority in religion and that "no one should be forced to believe, but should be won by preaching."[3]

The teachings of Luther found earnest and faithful men in the Netherlands to preach the gospel. Menno Simons, educated as a Roman Catholic and ordained to the priesthood, was completely ignorant of the Bible and would not read it because he was afraid it was heresy. He tried to silence the voice of his conscience by ungodly living, but he did not succeed. After a while he was led to the study of the New Testament. Along with Luther's writings, this caused him to accept the reformed faith.

Soon afterward, he saw a man put to death for having been rebaptized. This led him to study the Bible regarding infant baptism. He saw that repentance and faith are required as the condition of baptism.

Menno left the Catholic Church and devoted his life to teaching the truths he had received. In both Germany and the Netherlands a class of fanatics had emerged, offending public order and decency and leading toward revolt against government. Menno strongly opposed the false teachings and wild schemes of the fanatics. For twenty-five years he traveled across the Netherlands and northern Germany, exerting a widespread influence, demonstrating in his own life the principles he taught. He was a man of integrity, humble and gentle, sincere and earnest. Many people were converted through his work.

In Germany, Emperor Charles V had banned the Reformation, but the princes restrained his tyranny. In the Netherlands his power was greater, and persecuting decrees followed one another in quick succession. To read the Bible, to hear or preach it, to pray to God in secret, to refrain from bowing to an image, to sing a psalm—all of these things were punishable by death. Thousands were killed under Charles and Philip II.

At one time a whole family was brought before the inquisitors, charged with remaining away from mass and worshiping at home. The youngest son answered: "We fall on our knees, and pray that God may enlighten our minds and pardon our sins. We pray for our king, that his reign may be prosperous and his life happy. We pray for our officials, that God may preserve them." The father and one of his sons were condemned to the stake.[4]

Not only men but women and young girls displayed unflinching courage. "Wives would stand by their husband's stake, and while he was enduring the fire they would whisper words of comfort, or sing psalms to cheer him." "Young girls, condemned to be buried alive, would lie down in their living grave as if they were going to their room for nightly sleep. Others would go out to the scaffold and the fire, dressed in their best clothes, as if they were going to their marriage."[5]

Persecution increased the number of witnesses for truth. Year after year the emperor urged on his cruel work, but he did not succeed in stamping out the Reformation. William of Orange finally brought the freedom to worship God to Holland.

Reformation in Denmark

The gospel made a peaceful entrance into the countries of the North. Students at Wittenberg returning home carried the reformed faith to Scandinavia. Luther's writings also spread the light. The hardy people of the North turned from Rome's corruption and superstitions to welcome the life-giving truths of the Bible.

Even as a child Tausen, "the Reformer of Denmark," showed that he had a bright mind, and he entered a monastery. Examination revealed that he had talent that promised to be very helpful to the church. The young student was given permission to choose a university in Germany or the Netherlands for himself, with one condition: he must not go to Wittenberg with its dangerous heresy. This is what the friars decreed.

Tausen went to Cologne, one of the strongholds of Catholicism. He soon became disgusted with the mystical teachings there. About the same time he read Luther's writings with joy, and he longed to experience the personal instruction of the Reformer. But if he did so, he would risk losing his superior's support. He soon made his decision, and before long he was a student at Wittenberg.

When Tausen returned to Denmark, he did not reveal his secret, but tried to lead his friends to a purer faith. He opened the Bible and preached Christ to them as the sinner's only hope of salvation. His supervisor at the monastery, who had high hopes for him as a defender of Rome, became very angry. He removed Tausen immediately from his own monastery, put him in another, and confined him to his cell. Through the bars of his cell Tausen shared a knowledge of the truth with his companions. If those Danish fathers had been skilled in the church's plan for dealing with heresy, Tausen would never have been heard from again. But instead of confining him in some underground dungeon, they expelled him from the monastery.

A royal decree, just issued, offered protection to the teachers of the new doctrine. Tausen found the churches open to him, and the people crowded in to listen. The New Testament in Danish was widely circulated. Efforts to overthrow the work resulted in extending it, and before long Denmark declared that it had accepted the reformed faith.

Progress in Sweden

In Sweden also, young men from Wittenberg brought the water of life to their countrymen. Two leaders in the Swedish Reformation, Olaf and Laurentius Petri, studied under Luther and Melanchthon. Like the great Reformer, Olaf captivated the people by his eloquence, while Laurentius, like Melanchthon, was thoughtful and calm. Both had unflinching courage. The Catholic priests stirred up the ignorant and superstitious people. Several times, Olaf Petri barely escaped with his life. However, these Reformers did have the protection of the king, who was committed to having a reformation and welcomed these talented helpers in the battle against Rome.

In the presence of the king and leading men of Sweden, Olaf Petri defended the reformed faith with great ability. He declared that Christians should accept the teachings of the church fathers only when they agree with Scripture, and that the Bible presents the essential doctrines of the faith in a clear manner, so that everyone can understand them.

These events show us "the sort of men that belonged to the army of the Reformers. They were not illiterate, narrow-minded, noisy people who loved to argue—far from it. They were men who had studied the word of God and knew well how to use the weapons that the Bible's armory supplied to them. They were scholars and theologians, men who thoroughly mastered the whole system of gospel truth, and who could win an easy victory over the false reasoners of the schools and the dignitaries of Rome."[6]

The king of Sweden accepted the Protestant faith, and the national assembly voted in its favor. At the request of the king, the two brothers took on the task of translating the whole Bible. The assembly ordered that throughout the kingdom, ministers should explain the Scriptures and that the children in the schools should be taught to read the Bible.

Freed from Rome's oppression, the nation achieved a strength and greatness it had never before reached. A century later, this previously feeble nation came to the deliverance of Germany in the terrible struggle of the Thirty Years' War—the only country in Europe that dared to lend a helping hand. All of Northern Europe seemed about to be brought again under Rome's tyranny. The armies of Sweden, however, enabled Germany to win toleration for Protestants and to restore liberty of conscience to those countries that had accepted the Reformation.

1. Gerard Brandt, *History of the Reformation in and About the Low Countries,* bk. 1, p. 6.

2. Ibid., p. 14.

3. W. Carlos Martyn, *The Life and Times of Martin Luther,* vol. 2, p. 87.

4. James A. Wylie, *History of Protestantism,* bk. 18, ch. 6.

5. Ibid.

6. Ibid., bk. 10, ch. 4.

Truth Advances in Britain

While Luther was opening a closed Bible to the people of Germany, the Spirit of God was leading Tyndale to do the same for England. Wycliffe had translated the Bible from the Latin text, which had many errors. The cost of manuscript copies was so great that not many were produced.

In 1516, for the first time the New Testament was printed in the original Greek language. This printing corrected many errors of former versions and conveyed the meaning more clearly. It led many of the educated people to a better knowledge of truth and gave a new energy to the work of reform. But to a great extent the common people were still shut away from God's Word. Tyndale would complete Wycliffe's work in giving the Bible to the people of England.

He preached his convictions fearlessly. To the Catholic claim that the church had given the Bible and the church alone could explain it, Tyndale responded: "Far from having given us the Scriptures, it is you who have hidden them from us. It is you who burn those who teach them, and if you could, you would burn the Scriptures themselves."[1]

Tyndale's preaching stirred up great interest. But the priests tried to destroy his work. "What can be done?" he exclaimed. "I cannot be everywhere. Oh, if Christians just possessed the Holy Scriptures in their own language, they themselves could resist these clever deceivers. Without the Bible it is impossible to establish the people in the truth."[2]

A new purpose now took hold of his mind. "Shouldn't the gospel speak the language of England among us? . . . Should the church have less light at noonday than at the dawn, when it began? . . . Christians must read the New Testament in their mother tongue."[3] Only by the Bible could people arrive at the truth.

In a dispute with Tyndale an educated Catholic exclaimed, "We would be better off without God's laws than the pope's." Tyndale replied, "I defy the pope and all his laws; and if God spares my life, in a few years I will see to it that a boy driving a plow knows more of the Bible than you do."[4]

Tyndale Translates the New Testament Into English

Driven from home by persecution, Tyndale went to London and for a while worked there undisturbed. But again the Catholic officials forced him to leave. All England seemed closed against him. In Germany he began the printing of the English New Testament. When he was forbidden to print in one city, he went to another. He finally made his way to Worms, where Luther had defended the gospel before the assembly a few years before. There were many friends of the Reformation in that city. Three thousand copies of the New Testament were soon finished, and another edition followed.

The Word of God was taken to London secretly and circulated throughout the country. Catholic officials tried to suppress the truth, but they failed. The bishop of Durham bought a bookseller's whole stock of Bibles in order to destroy them, thinking that this would harm the work. But the money this provided bought material for a new and better edition. Later, when Tyndale was taken prisoner, he was offered freedom if he would reveal the names of those who helped him with the expense of printing his Bibles. He replied that the bishop of Durham had done more than any other person by paying a large price for the books left in stock.

Tyndale finally witnessed for his faith by a martyr's death, but the weapons he prepared enabled other soldiers to do battle through the centuries, even down to our own time.

Latimer said from the pulpit that the Bible ought to be read in the language of the people. "Let us not take any side paths, but let God's word direct us. Let us not walk after . . . our forefathers, nor seek not what they did, but what they should have done."[5]

Barnes and Frith, Ridley and Cranmer, leaders in the English Reformation, were men of learning, highly regarded for zeal or piety in the Catholic religion. They opposed the papacy because they knew the errors of the "holy see."

Infallible Authority of Scripture

The grand principle that these Reformers maintained—the same that the Waldenses, Wycliffe, Huss, Luther, Zwingli, and those with them also held—was the infallible authority of Scripture. By its teaching they tested all doctrines and all claims. Faith in God's Word sustained these holy men as they yielded up their lives at the stake. "Be of good comfort," exclaimed Latimer to his fellow martyr as the flames were about to silence their voices. "Today, by God's grace, we will light such a candle in England as I believe will never be put out."[6]

For hundreds of years after the churches of England submitted to Rome, the churches in Scotland kept their freedom. In the twelfth century, however, Catholicism became established, and in no country was the darkness deeper. Still, rays of light came to pierce the gloom. The Lollards came from England with the Bible and the teachings of Wycliffe, and they did much to preserve the knowledge of the gospel. With the opening of the Reformation came Luther's writings and Tyndale's English New Testament. These messengers silently passed through the mountains and valleys, fanning into new life the torch of truth that had so nearly died out and undoing the work that four centuries of oppression had done.

Then, suddenly realizing the danger,

the Catholic leaders brought to the stake some of the noblest men in Scotland. These dying witnesses filled the hearts of the people throughout the land with an undying determination to cast off the chains of Rome.

John Knox

Hamilton and Wishart, with a long line of less prominent disciples, yielded up their lives at the stake. But from the burning pile of Wishart another man came forward whom the flames were not to silence, one who under God was to end the power of Rome in Scotland.

John Knox turned away from the traditions of the church to feed on the truths of God's Word. The teaching of Wishart confirmed his decision to forsake Rome and join the persecuted Reformers.

His companions urged him to preach, but he trembled with fear at its responsibility. Only after days of painful conflict with himself did he consent. But once he had accepted the position, he pressed ahead with unfailing courage. This truehearted Reformer had no fear of anyone. When he was brought face-to-face with the queen of Scotland, John Knox was not to be won by favors, nor did he lose courage in the face of threats. The queen said that he had taught the people to receive a religion prohibited by the state, and so he had transgressed God's command for subjects to obey their princes. Knox answered firmly: "If all the descendants of Abraham had followed the religion of Pharaoh, whose subjects they were for many years, I ask you, madam, what

religion would there have been in the world? Or if everyone in the days of the apostles had followed the religion of the Roman emperors, what religion would there have been on the face of the earth?"

Mary said, "You interpret the Scriptures in one way, and they [Roman Catholics] interpret in another; whom shall I believe, and who shall be judge?"

"You shall believe God, who plainly speaks in His word," answered the Reformer. "The word of God is plain in itself; and if any obscurity appears in one place, the Holy Spirit, who never contradicts Himself, explains it more clearly in other places."[7]

At the risk of his life and with unfailing courage, the fearless Reformer kept at his mission, until Scotland was free from Catholicism.

In England the establishment of Protestantism as the national religion reduced the persecution but did not stop it completely. Many of Rome's forms were retained. Protestants rejected the supremacy of the pope, but in his place they enthroned the king as head of the church. The religion still departed widely from the purity of the gospel. English Protestants did not yet understand religious liberty. Though the Protestant rulers rarely resorted to the horrible cruelties that Rome employed, they did not acknowledge the right of all to worship God according to their own consciences. Dissenters suffered persecution for hundreds of years.

Thousands of Pastors Expelled

In the seventeenth century, thousands of pastors were expelled, and the people were forbidden to attend any religious meetings except those that the church approved. In the sheltering depths of the forest, those persecuted children of the Lord met together to pour out their hearts in prayer and praise. Many suffered for their faith. The jails were crowded, families broken up. Yet persecution could not silence their testimony. Many were driven across the ocean to America, and there they laid the foundations of civil and religious liberty.

In a dungeon crowded with criminals, John Bunyan breathed the atmosphere of heaven and wrote his wonderful allegory of the pilgrim's journey from the land of destruction to the heavenly city. *Pilgrim's Progress* and *Grace Abounding to the Chief of Sinners* have guided many feet into the path of life.

In a time of spiritual darkness, Whitefield and the Wesleys appeared as light bearers for God. Under the established church the people had fallen into a condition that was hardly different from heathenism. The higher classes sneered at godly living; the lower classes reveled in vice. The church had no courage or faith to support the struggling cause of truth.

Justification by Faith

People had almost completely lost sight of the great doctrine of justification by faith that Luther had taught so clearly. The Catholic principle of trusting to good works for salvation had taken its place. Whitefield and the Wesleys were sincere seekers for God's favor. They had been taught that they could obtain it by living uprightly and by keeping the rules of the church.

Once when Charles Wesley became ill and expected to die soon, someone asked him on what basis he hoped to have eternal life. His answer: "I have used my best efforts to serve God." The friend did not seem fully satisfied with this answer. Wesley thought: "What! . . . Would he rob me of my efforts? I have nothing else in which to trust."[8] This was the kind of darkness that had settled on the church, turning people from their only hope of salvation—the blood of the crucified Redeemer.

Wesley and his associates came to see that God's law extends to the thoughts as well as to the words and actions. By diligent and prayerful efforts they tried to subdue the evils of the natural heart. They lived a life of self-denial and humiliation, carefully following every practice that they thought could help them become holy enough to win God's favor. But their efforts failed to free them from sin's condemnation or to break its power.

The fires of divine truth had nearly died out on the altars of Protestantism, but they were about to be relit from the ancient torch handed down by the Christians of Bohemia. Some of these, who found safety in Saxony, kept the ancient faith alive. Light came to Wesley from these Christians.

John and Charles Wesley were sent on a mission to America. A company of Moravians was also on board the ship. On the journey they encountered violent storms, and John, face to face with death, realized he did not have the assurance of peace with God. The Germans showed a calmness and trust that he didn't know. "Long before this," he said, "I had observed the great seriousness of their behavior. . . . Now there was an opportunity to see whether they were delivered from the spirit of fear, as well as from that of pride, anger, and revenge. In the middle of the psalm that began their religious service, the sea broke over the ship, split the mainsail in pieces, covered the ship, and poured in between the decks as if the great deep had already swallowed us up. A terrible screaming began among the English. The Germans calmly sang on. I asked one of them afterwards, 'Were you not afraid?' He answered, 'I thank God, no.' I asked, 'But were not your women and children afraid?' He replied calmly, 'No, our women and children are not afraid to die.' "[9]

Wesley's Heart "Strangely Warmed"

When he returned to England, Wesley gained a clearer understanding of Bible faith under the instruction of a Moravian. At a meeting of the Moravian society in London someone read a statement from Luther. As Wesley listened, faith stirred in him. "I felt my heart strangely warmed," he says. "I felt I did trust in Christ, Christ alone, for salvation, and God gave me assurance that He had taken away *my* sins, even *mine,* and saved *me* from the law of sin and death."[10]

Now he had found that the grace he had worked so hard to win by prayers and fasts and self-denial was a gift, "without money and without price." His whole heart filled with the desire to spread the glorious gospel of God's free grace everywhere. "I see all the world as my parish," he said. "In whatever part of it I am, I consider it fitting, right, and my solemn duty, to declare the glad tidings of salvation to all who are willing to hear."[11]

He continued his strict and self-denying life, but now it was not the *basis* for his faith, but the *result* of it; not the *root,* but the *fruit* of holiness. The grace of God in Christ will show itself in obedience. Wesley devoted his life to preaching the great truths he had received—justification through faith in Christ's atoning blood, and the renewing power of the Holy Spirit on the heart, which produces fruit in a life that follows Christ's example.

In their university days, George Whitefield and the Wesleys were contemptuously called "Methodists" by their ungodly fellow students—a name regarded as honorable today. The Holy Spirit urged them to preach Christ and Him crucified, and thousands were truly converted. It was necessary to protect these sheep from the prowling wolves. John Wesley had no thought of forming a new denomination, but he organized the converts under what was called the Methodist Connection.

The opposition that these preachers met from the established church was mysterious and trying, but the truth found entrance where doors would otherwise remain closed. Some of the pastors awoke from their moral stupor and became zealous preachers in their own districts.

In Wesley's time, people of different

gifts did not agree on every point of doctrine. At one point, the differences between Whitefield and the Wesleys threatened to divide them, but as they learned meekness in the school of Christ, mutual restraint and goodwill brought them back together. They had no time to dispute while error and sin were all around them.

Wesley Escapes Death

Influential people tried to stop them. Many pastors were hostile, and they closed the doors of the churches against a pure faith. The pastors who denounced the Reformers from the pulpit stirred up the elements of darkness and evil. John Wesley escaped death again and again by a miracle of God's mercy. When there seemed no way to escape, an angel in human form came to his side, the mob fell back, and the servant of Christ walked away from the danger in safety.

Speaking of one such deliverance, Wesley said: "Although many tried to take hold of my collar or clothes, to pull me down, they could not hold on at all. Only one got a firm grip on the flap of my vest, which was soon left in his hand; the other flap, covering a pocket in which was a bank note, was only half torn off. . . . A vigorous man just behind me struck at me several times with a large oak stick. If he had struck me with it once on the back of my head, it would have saved him all further trouble. But every time, the blow was turned aside, I don't know how, for I could not move to the right or the left."[12]

The Methodists of those days endured ridicule and persecution, and often violence. In some cases, people posted signs inviting those who wanted to break the windows and rob the houses of the Methodists to gather at a certain time and place. Unbelievers carried on systematic persecution against a group of people whose only fault was that they tried to turn sinners to the path of holiness.

To a great degree, the spiritual decline in England just before the time of Wesley had resulted from teaching that Christ had done away with the moral law and that Christians are under no obligation to keep it. Others declared that it was unnecessary for ministers to urge the people to obey its teachings, since those whom God had chosen for salvation would "be led to a life of piety and virtue," while those doomed to eternal damnation "did not have power to obey the divine law."

Others believed that "the ones God has chosen to save cannot fall from grace nor lose God's favor." This led them to the dreadful conclusion that "the wicked actions they commit are not really sinful, . . . and that, consequently, they have no reason either to confess their sins or to break them off by repentance."[13] So, they concluded, even one of the worst sins "that everyone considers an enormous violation of the divine law is not a sin in the sight of God" if committed by one of God's chosen ones. "They cannot do anything that is either displeasing to God or prohibited by the law."

These shocking doctrines are essentially the same as the later teaching that there is no unchangeable divine law as the standard of right, but that morality is something that society itself decides and is constantly subject to change. All these ideas are inspired by Satan, who among the sinless inhabitants of heaven began his work to break down the righteous restraints of God's law.

The doctrine that divine decrees made people's characters unchangeable had led many to reject the law of God. Wesley firmly opposed this doctrine that led to lawless living. "The grace of God that brings salvation has appeared to *all men*." "God our Savior . . . desires *all men* to be saved and to come to the knowledge of the truth. For there is one God and one Mediator between God and men, the Man Christ Jesus, who gave Himself a ransom for *all*." Christ is "the true Light which gives light to *every man* coming into the world." (Titus 2:11; 1 Timothy 2:3–6; John 1:9.) People lose out on salvation because of their own willful refusal to accept the gift of life.

In Defense of the Law of God

In answer to the claim that Christ's death had abolished the Ten Commandments along with the ceremonial law, Wesley said: "The moral law, contained in the Ten Commandments and enforced by the prophets, He did not take away. This is a law that can never be broken, which 'stands firm as the faithful witness in heaven.'"

Wesley declared that the law and the gospel were in perfect harmony. "On the one hand, the law continually makes way for the gospel and points us to it. On the other hand, the gospel continually leads us to fulfill the law more exactly. For instance, the law re-quires us to love God, to love our neighbor, to be meek, humble, or holy. We feel that we are not able to do these things. . . . But we see a promise of God to give us this love and to make us humble, meek, and holy. We lay hold of this gospel, this good news. . . . 'The righteousness of the law is fulfilled in us,' through faith in Christ Jesus. . . .

"Among the worst enemies of the gospel of Christ," said Wesley, "are people who . . . teach others to break . . . not only one commandment, whether of the least or of the greatest, but all the commandments at once. . . . They honor Him just as Judas did when he said, 'Greetings, Rabbi,' and kissed Him. . . . It is nothing less than betraying Him with a kiss, to talk of His blood and take away His crown, to make light of any part of His law under the pretense of advancing His gospel."[14]

Harmony of Law and Gospel

To those who claimed that "the preaching of the gospel fulfills all the purposes of the law," Wesley replied: "It does not fulfill the very first purpose of the law, which is to convict people of sin, awakening those who are still asleep on the brink of hell. . . . It is absurd, therefore, to offer a physician to those who are well, or who at least imagine that they are well. You must first convince them that they are sick; otherwise they will not appreciate your efforts. It is equally absurd to offer Christ to those whose hearts are whole, having never been broken."[15]

While preaching the gospel of the grace of God, Wesley, like Jesus his

Master, tried to "exalt the law and make it honorable" (Isaiah 42:21). And he lived to see glorious results. At the close of more than half a century he spent in ministry, his followers numbered more than half a million. But we will not know how many people were lifted from the degradation of sin to a higher and purer life through his efforts until the whole family of the redeemed gather in the kingdom of God. His life presents a priceless lesson to every Christian.

If only the faith, untiring zeal, self-sacrifice, and devotion of this servant of Christ were reflected in the churches of today!

1. J. H. Merle D'Aubigné, *History of the Reformation of the Sixteenth Century,* bk. 18, ch. 4.

2. Ibid.

3. Ibid.

4. Anderson, *Annals of the English Bible* (rev. ed., 1862), p. 19.

5. Hugh Latimer, "First Sermon Preached Before King Edward VI."

6. *Works of Hugh Latimer,* vol. 1, p. xiii.

7. David Laing, *The Collected Works of John Knox,* vol. 2, pp. 281, 284.

8. John Whitehead, *Life of the Rev. Charles Wesley,* p. 102.

9. Ibid., p. 10.

10. Ibid., p. 52.

11. Ibid., p. 74.

12. John Wesley, *Works,* vol. 3, pp. 297, 298.

13. McClintock & Strong, *Cyclopedia,* art. "Antinomians."

14. Wesley, Sermon 25.

15. Wesley, Sermon 35.

France's Reign of Terror: Its True Cause

Some nations welcomed the Reformation as a messenger of Heaven. Other lands excluded the light of Bible knowledge almost completely. In one country truth and error struggled for the mastery for centuries. In the end, the truth of Heaven was pushed out. The restraint of God's Spirit was removed from a people that had despised the gift of His grace. And all the world saw what happens when people willfully reject light.

The war against the Bible in France led to the Revolution, the legitimate result of Rome's having suppressed the Scriptures (see Appendix). It presented the most striking illustration the world has ever seen of the effects of the Roman Church's teaching.

In the book of Revelation, John points to the terrible results that were to come especially to France from the domination of the "man of sin":

"They will tread the holy city underfoot for forty-two months. And I will give power to my two witnesses, and they will prophesy one thousand two hundred and sixty days, clothed in sackcloth. . . . When they finish their testimony, the beast that ascends out of the bottomless pit will make war against them, overcome them, and kill them. And their dead bodies will lie in the street of the great city which spiritually is called Sodom and Egypt, where also our Lord was crucified. . . . And those who dwell on the earth will rejoice over them, make merry, and send gifts to one another, because these two prophets tormented those who dwell on the earth. Now after the three-and-a-half days the breath of life from God entered them, and they stood on their feet, and great fear fell on those who saw them" (Revelation 11:2, 3, 7, 8, 10, 11).

The "forty-two months" and "one thousand two hundred and sixty days" are the same, the time in which Rome would oppress the church of Christ. The 1,260 years began in A.D. 538 and ended in 1798 (see Appendix). At that time a French army took the pope prisoner, and he died in exile. The papal hierarchy has never since been able to wield the power it possessed before.

The persecution of the church did not continue through the entire 1,260 years. In mercy to His people, God cut short the time of their fiery trial by the influence of the Reformation.

The "two witnesses" represent the Scriptures of the Old and the New Testament, important testimonies to the origin and permanence of God's law, and also to the plan of salvation.

"They will prophesy one thousand two hundred and sixty days, clothed in sackcloth." When the Bible was forbidden and its testimony perverted, when those who dared to proclaim its truths were betrayed, tortured, martyred for their faith or compelled to run away for safety—then the faithful "witnesses" prophesied "in sackcloth." In the darkest times God gave faithful Christians wisdom and authority to declare His truth. (See Appendix.)

"And if anyone wants to harm them, fire proceeds from their mouth and devours their enemies. And if anyone wants to harm them, he must be killed in this manner" (Revelation 11:5). Trampling on the Word of God has deadly consequences!

"When they finish [are finishing] their testimony." As the two witnesses were nearing the end of their work in obscurity, "the beast that ascends out of the bottomless pit" was to make war on them. Here we see a new display of satanic power.

While professing reverence for the Bible, it had been Rome's policy to keep the Bible locked up in an unknown language, hidden from the people. Under her rule the witnesses prophesied "clothed in sackcloth." But "the beast that ascends out of the bottomless pit" was to make open, determined war on the Word of God.

"The great city" in whose streets the witnesses are killed and where their dead bodies lie is "spiritually" Egypt. Of all nations in Bible history, Egypt most boldly denied the existence of the living God and resisted His commands. No ruler ever dared to rebel against Heaven more arrogantly than did the king of Egypt, Pharaoh: "I do not know the LORD, nor will I let Israel go" (Exodus 5:2). This is atheism; and the nation represented by Egypt in the prophecy would voice a similar denial of God and reveal a similar spirit of defiance.

"The great city" of the prophecy is also compared "spiritually" to Sodom. The corruption of Sodom was especially evident in its open sexual impurity. This would also be a characteristic of the nation that would fulfill this scripture.

So according to the prophet, a little before 1798 some power of satanic character would rise to make war on the Bible. And in the land where the testimony of God's "two witnesses" would be silenced, the atheism of Pharaoh and the sexual lust of Sodom would be evident.

A Striking Fulfillment of Prophecy

This prophecy was remarkably fulfilled in the history of France during the Revolution in 1793. "France stands apart in the world's history as the single state which, by the decree of her Legislative Assembly, declared that there was no God. The entire population of the capital, and a great majority elsewhere, women as well as men, danced and sang with joy in accepting the announcement."[1]

France also revealed the characteristics that distinguished Sodom. The historian presents together the atheism and the loose sexuality of France: "Closely connected with these laws affecting religion was the law that reduced the union of marriage—the most sacred tie that human beings can form, and whose permanence contributes most strongly to the stability of society—to nothing more than a civil contract of a temporary character, which any two persons might engage in and cast aside whenever they wished. . . . Sophie Arnoult, an actress famous for saying witty things, described marriage in that era as 'the sacrament of adultery.' "[2]

Enmity Against Christ

"Where also our Lord was crucified." This was also fulfilled by France. In no other country did the truth have more cruel opposition. In the persecution heaped on those who took their stand for the gospel, France had crucified Christ in the person of His disciples.

Century after century the blood of the saints had been shed. While the Waldenses laid down their lives on the mountains of Piedmont "for the testimony of Jesus Christ," the Albigenses of France had given a similar witness. The disciples of the Reformation had been put to death with horrible tortures. King and nobles, highborn women and delicate maidens had feasted their eyes on the dying agonies of the martyrs of Jesus. The brave Huguenots had poured out their blood on many a hard-fought battlefield. Protestants had been hunted down like wild beasts.

The few descendants of the ancient Christians who remained in France in the eighteenth century, hiding away in the mountains of the south, still cherished the faith of their fathers. They were dragged away to lifelong slavery in the galleys. The most refined and intelligent of the French were chained, in horrible torture, among robbers and assassins. Others were shot down in cold blood as they fell on their knees in prayer. Their country, laid waste with the sword, the axe, and the stake, "was converted into one vast, gloomy wilderness." "These atrocities took place . . . in no dark age, but in the brilliant era of Louis XIV. Science was then cultivated, literature flourished, the clergy of the royal court and of the capital were educated and eloquent men who made a great show of the graces of meekness and charity."[3]

The Most Horrible of Crimes

But most horrible among the terrible deeds of the dreadful centuries was the St. Bartholomew Massacre. The king of France, urged on by priests and church officials, gave his permission. A bell, tolling in the middle of the night, was a signal for the slaughter. Protestants by the thousands, sleeping in their homes, trusting the honor of their king, were dragged out and murdered.

For seven days the massacre continued in Paris. By the king's order it was extended to all towns where Protestants were found. Noble and peasant, old and young, mother and child, were cut down together. Throughout France seventy thousand of the nation's best citizens died.

"When the news of the massacre reached Rome, the rejoicing among the clergy knew no limits. The cardinal of Lorraine rewarded the messenger with a thousand gold coins; the cannon of St. Angelo thundered out a joyous salute. Bells rang out from every steeple, bonfires turned night into day, and Pope Gregory XIII, accompanied by the cardinals and other church dignitaries, went in long procession to the church of St. Louis, where the cardinal of Lorraine chanted a *Te Deum*. . . . A medal was struck to commemorate the massacre. . . . A French priest . . . spoke of 'that day so full of happiness and joy, when the most holy father received the news and went in solemn state to render thanks to God and St. Louis.' "[4]

The same master spirit that urged on the St. Bartholomew Massacre led in the scenes of the Revolution. Jesus Christ was declared an impostor, and the cry of the French infidels was "Crush the Wretch," meaning Christ. Blasphemy and wickedness went hand in hand. In all this, France paid homage to Satan, while Christ, in His characteristics of truth, purity, and unselfish love, was "crucified."

"The beast that ascends out of the bottomless pit will make war against them, overcome them, and kill them" (Revelation 11:7). The atheistic power that ruled in France during the Revolution and the Reign of Terror did wage this kind of war against God and His Word. The National Assembly abolished the worship of God. Bibles were collected and publicly burned. The government abolished the institutions of the Bible. It set aside the weekly rest day, and in its place the people devoted every tenth day to unholy celebrations. Baptism and the Communion were prohibited. Announcements posted over burial places declared that death was an eternal sleep.

All religious worship was prohibited except for worship of "liberty" and the country. The "constitutional bishop of Paris was brought forward . . . to declare to the Convention that the religion which he had taught so many years was, in every respect, a piece of priestcraft that had no foundation either in history or sacred truth. In solemn and explicit terms he denied the existence of the God to whose worship he had been consecrated."[5]

"And those who dwell on the earth will rejoice over them, make merry, and send gifts to one another, because these two prophets tormented those who dwell on the earth" (Revelation 11:10). Infidel France had silenced the condemning voice of God's two witnesses. The word of truth lay "dead" in her streets, and those who hated God's law were joyful. People defied the King of heaven publicly.

Blasphemous Boldness

One of the "priests" of the new order said: "God, if You exist, avenge Your injured name. I defy You! You remain silent; You dare not launch Your thunders. After this, who will believe in Your existence?"[6] What an echo this was of Pharaoh's demand, "Who is the Lord, that I should obey His voice?" (Exodus 5:2).

"The fool has said in his heart, 'There is no God.'" And the Lord declares, "Their folly will be manifest to all." (Psalm 14:1; 2 Timothy 3:9.) After France had renounced the worship of the living God, she descended into degrading idolatry by worshiping the Goddess of Reason, an immoral woman. And this took place in the representative assembly of the nation! "One of the ceremonies of this insane time has no equal for being absurd as well as insulting to God. The doors of the Convention were thrown open. . . . The members of the city's governing body entered in solemn procession, singing a hymn in praise of liberty, and escorting, as the object of their future worship, a veiled female, whom they called the Goddess of Reason. She was brought to the front, where she was unveiled with great pageantry and placed at the right of the president. People recognized her as a dancing girl of the opera."

The Goddess of Reason

"Throughout the nation, wherever the inhabitants wanted to show themselves as having fully embraced the Revolution, the people imitated this installation of the Goddess of Reason."[7]

When the "goddess" was brought into the Convention, the speaker took her by the hand, turned to the assembly, and said: " 'Mortals, cease to tremble before the powerless thunders of a God whom your fears have created. From now on, acknowledge no god but Reason. I offer you its noblest and purest image. If you must have idols, sacrifice only to such as this. . . .'

"The goddess, after being embraced by the president, was seated on a magnificent vehicle and taken to the cathedral of Notre Dame, to take the place of God. There she was raised up on a high altar and received the adoration of all present."[8]

The church had begun the work

that atheism was completing, hurrying France on to ruin. In referring to the horrors of the Revolution, writers say that these excesses are the fault of the kings and the church. (See Appendix.) Strict justice requires them to be charged upon the church. The papal system had poisoned the minds of kings against the Reformation. The spirit of Rome inspired the cruelty and oppression that came from the throne.

Wherever people received the gospel, their minds were awakened. They began to throw off the chains that had kept them slaves of ignorance and superstition. Kings saw it and trembled for their power.

Rome was not slow to inflame their jealous fears. In 1525, the pope said to the regent of France, "This mania [Protestantism] will not only defeat and destroy religion, but all states, nobility, laws, orders, and ranks besides." A papal official warned the king: "The Protestants will upset all civil as well as religious order. . . . The throne is in as much danger as the altar."[9] Rome succeeded in turning France against the Reformation.

The teaching of the Bible would have implanted in the hearts of the people the principles of justice, temperance, and truth, which are the cornerstone of a nation's prosperity. "Righteousness exalts a nation." "A throne is established by righteousness." (Proverbs 14:34; 16:12. See Isaiah 32:17.) The person who obeys God's law is the one who will most truly respect and obey the laws of the country. But France prohibited the Bible. Century after century Christians of integrity, of intellectual and moral strength, who had the faith to suffer for truth, worked as slaves in ships' galleys, died at the stake, or rotted in dungeon cells. For 250 years after the start of the Reformation, thousands found safety only by leaving France.

"Scarcely was there a generation of Frenchmen during that long period that did not see the gospel's disciples fleeing from the insane fury of the persecutor, and taking with them the intelligence, the arts, the industry, the order, in which they were typically their country's best, to enrich the lands in which they found a refuge. . . . If France had kept all those who were driven away, what a . . . great, prosperous, and happy country—a pattern to the nations—she would have been! But a blind and unrelenting bigotry chased from her soil every teacher of virtue, every champion of order, every honest defender of the throne. . . . At the end, the ruin of the state was complete."[10] The Revolution, with all its horrors, was the result.

What Might Have Been

"With the escape of the Huguenots a general decline settled on France. Flourishing manufacturing cities fell into decay. . . . It is estimated that, at the time the Revolution began, two hundred thousand poor people in Paris claimed charity from the hands of the king. Only the Jesuits flourished in the decaying nation."[11]

The gospel would have brought France the solution to those problems that baffled her clergy, king, and legislators and that finally plunged the nation into ruin. But under Rome the people had lost the Savior's lessons of self-sacrifice and unselfish love for the good of others. The rich received no rebuke for oppressing the poor, and the poor received no help for their pitiful condition. The selfishness of the wealthy and powerful grew more and more oppressive. For centuries, the rich wronged the poor, and the poor hated the rich.

In many provinces the working classes were at the mercy of landlords and were forced to submit to exhorbitant demands. The middle and lower classes were heavily taxed by the civil authorities and clergy. "The farmers and the peasants might starve, for all their oppressors cared. . . . The lives of the agricultural workers consisted of unending work and unrelieved misery. Their complaints . . . were treated with insolent contempt. . . . Judges were notorious for accepting bribes. . . . Less than half of the taxes ever found their way into the royal or church treasury; the collectors kept the rest and squandered it in shameless self-indulgence. And the men who impoverished their fellow-subjects in this way were not required to pay taxes and were entitled by law or custom to all the privileges of the state. . . . So that these could gratify their selfish desires, millions of people were condemned to hopeless and degrading lives." (See Appendix.)

For more than half a century before the Revolution, King Louis XV occupied the throne. He was well known as a lazy, superficial, and self-indulgent monarch. With the state financially embarrassed and the people exasperated, no one needed a prophet's eye to foresee a terrible outbreak. The king's counselors urged the need for reform, but he did not listen. The doom that was coming on France was pictured in the king's selfish answer, "After me, the deluge!"

Rome had influenced the kings and ruling classes to keep the people in bondage, intending to fasten the souls of both the rulers and the people in her shackles. The moral degradation was a thousand times more terrible than the physical suffering that resulted from her policy. Deprived of the Bible, and given fully to selfishness, the people were shrouded in ignorance and sunken in vice, completely unfit to govern themselves.

Results Reaped in Blood

Instead of keeping the common people in blind submission to her teachings, Rome's work resulted in making them infidels and revolutionists. They despised Romanism as priestly deceptions. But the only god they knew was the god of Rome. They believed Rome's greed and cruelty were the fruit of the Bible, and they would have none of it.

Rome had misrepresented God's character, and now people rejected both the Bible and its Author. In the reaction, Voltaire and his associates threw God's Word completely aside and spread their anti-Christian teachings. Rome had ground the people down under her iron heel, and now the people threw off all restraint. Enraged, they rejected truth and falsehood together.

At the opening of the Revolution, the king reluctantly granted the people more political representation than that of the nobles and clergy combined. So the balance of power was in their hands, but they were not prepared to use it wisely and with moderation. The angry citizens were determined to revenge themselves. The oppressed carried out the lesson they had learned under tyranny and became the oppressors of those who had oppressed them.

France reaped a harvest in blood from her submission to Rome. Where France, under Romanism, had set up the first stake at the opening of the Reformation, there the Revolution set up its first guillotine. On the spot where the first martyrs of the Protestant faith were burned in the sixteenth century, the first victims were guillotined in the eighteenth. When the nation threw off the restraints of God's law, it swept on to revolt and anarchy. The war against the Bible stands in world history as the Reign of Terror. Whoever triumphed today was condemned tomorrow.

King, clergy, and nobles were forced to submit to the atrocities of a maddened people. Those who decreed the death of the king soon followed him to the scaffold. A general slaughter was decreed against anyone suspected of hostility to the Revolution. France became a vast field for rival masses of people, swayed by the fury of their passions. "In Paris one riot followed another, and the citizens were divided into an assortment of factions that seemed intent on nothing but exterminating each other. . . . The country was nearly bankrupt, the armies were clamoring for back pay, the people of Paris were starving, the provinces were laid waste by armed robbers, and civilization was almost extinguished in anarchy and unrestrained immorality."

All too well the people had learned the lessons of cruelty and torture that Rome had taught so diligently. This time it was not the disciples of Jesus that were dragged to the stake. Long ago these had died or been driven into exile. "The scaffolds ran red with the blood of the priests. The galleys and the prisons, once crowded with Huguenots, were now filled with their persecutors. Chained to the bench and laboring at the oar, the Roman Catholic priests experienced all the suffering that their church had inflicted so freely on the gentle heretics." (See Appendix.)

"Then came those days . . . when spies lurked in every corner, when the guillotine was at work long and hard every morning, when the jails were packed as tightly as the holds of a slave ship, when the gutters ran foaming with blood into the Seine River. . . . Long rows of captives were mowed down with grapeshot from cannons. Holes were made in the bottom of crowded barges. . . . Hundreds of young boys and of girls of seventeen were murdered by that repulsive government. Soldiers tore babies from the breast and tossed them from spear to spear along their ranks." (See Appendix.)

All this was just as Satan wanted it. His policy is deception, and his purpose is to bring wretchedness on humanity, to deface the workmanship of God, and to mar the divine purpose of love, all to cause grief in heaven. Then by his deceptive arts, he leads people to throw the blame on God, as if all this misery were the result of the Creator's plan. When the people found Romanism to be a deception, he urged them to regard all religion as a cheat and the Bible as a fable.

The Fatal Error

The fatal error that brought such misery on France was that she ignored this one great truth: true freedom lies within the limits of the law of God. "Oh, that you had heeded My commandments! Then your peace would have been like a river, and your righteousness like the waves of the sea" (Isaiah 48:18).

Those who refuse to read the lesson from the Book of God are invited to read it in history.

When Satan used the Roman Church to lead people away from obedience, he disguised his work. The Spirit of God prevented his plans from reaching their full results. The people did not trace the effect back to its cause and discover the source of their miseries. But in the Revolution the National Council openly set aside the law of God. And in the Reign of Terror which followed, everyone could see the working of cause and effect.

Breaking a just and righteous law will result in ruin. The restraining Spirit of God, which puts a limit on the cruel power of Satan, was mostly removed, and the one who delights in human wretchedness was permitted to do what he wished. Those who had chosen rebellion were left to reap its fruits. Crime filled the land. From devastated provinces and ruined cities came a terrible cry of bitter anguish. France was shaken as if by an earthquake. Religion, law, social order, the family, the state, and the church—all were struck down by the evil hand that had been lifted against the law of God.

God's two faithful witnesses, killed by the blasphemous power that "ascends out of the bottomless pit," were not to remain silent for long. "After the three-and-a-half days the breath of life from God entered them, and they stood on their feet, and great fear fell on those who saw them" (Revelation 11:11). In 1793, the decrees that set aside the Bible passed the French Assembly. Three and a half years later the same body adopted a resolution rescinding these decrees. People recognized the need for faith in God and His Word as the foundation of virtue and morality.

Concerning the "two witnesses" [the Old and New Testaments], the prophet declares further: "And they heard a loud voice from heaven saying to them, 'Come up here.' And they ascended to heaven in a cloud, and their enemies saw them" (Revelation 11:12). "God's two witnesses" have been honored as never before. In 1804, the British and Foreign Bible Society was organized, followed by similar organizations on the European continent. In 1816, the American Bible Society was founded. The Bible has since been translated into many hundreds of languages and dialects. (See Appendix.)

Before 1792, foreign missions received little attention. But toward the close of the eighteenth century a great change took place. People became dissatisfied with rationalism and realized the need for divine revelation and experiential religion. From then on, foreign missions have seen unprecedented growth. (See Appendix.)

Improvements in printing have helped to circulate the Bible. With old prejudices and national exclusiveness breaking down, and the pope's having lost secular power, the way has opened in many places for the Word of God to enter. The Bible has now gone to every part of the globe.

The infidel Voltaire said: "I am weary of hearing people repeat that twelve men established the Christian religion. I will prove that one man will be enough to overthrow it." Millions have joined in the war on the Bible. But it is far from being destroyed. Where there were a hundred copies in Voltaire's time, there are now a hundred thousand copies of the Book of God. In the words of an early Reformer, "The Bible is an anvil that has worn out many hammers."

Whatever is built on human authority will be overthrown; but things that are founded on the rock of God's Word will stand forever.

1. *Blackwood Magazine,* November 1870.

2. Sir Walter Scott, *Life of Napoleon,* vol. 1, ch. 17.

3. James A. Wylie, *History of Protestantism,* bk. 22, ch. 7.

4. Henry White, *The Massacre of St. Bartholomew,* ch. 14, par. 34.

5. Scott, vol. 1, ch. 17.

6. Lacretelle, *History,* vol. 11, p. 309; in Sir Archibald Alison, *History of Europe,* vol. 1, ch. 10.

7. Scott, vol. 1, ch. 17.

8. M. A. Thiers, *History of the French Revolution,* vol. 2, pp. 370, 371.

9. D'Aubigné, *History of the Reformation in Europe in the Time of Calvin,* bk. 2, ch. 36.

10. Wylie, bk. 13, ch. 20.

11. Ibid.

Seeking Freedom in a New World

Though the Church of England rejected the authority and creed of Rome, it welcomed into its worship many of her ceremonies. The claim circulated that things the Bible did not forbid were not evil in themselves. Observing these ceremonies tended to narrow the gulf separating the reformed churches from Rome, and some people claimed that doing so would help Catholics accept the Protestant faith.

Others did not agree. They saw these customs as badges of the slavery from which they had been delivered. They reasoned that in His Word God has established the regulations governing His worship, and that people are not free to add to these or to remove any of them. Rome began by requiring what God had not forbidden, and ended by forbidding what He had explicitly required.

Many viewed the customs of the English Church as obvious idolatry, and they could not participate in her worship. But the church, backed by civil authority, would permit no dissent. Unauthorized gatherings for worship were prohibited under penalty of imprisonment, exile, or death. The Puritans were hunted, persecuted, and imprisoned, and they could

not see any promise of better days. Some, while trying to go to Holland for refuge, were betrayed into the hands of their enemies. But their perseverance finally conquered, and they found shelter on friendly Dutch shores.

They had left their houses and their jobs. They were strangers in a strange land, forced to resort to unfamiliar occupations to earn their living. But they lost no time in idleness or complaining. They thanked God for the blessings they had and were happy that they could worship without fear.

God Overruled Events

When God's hand seemed to point them across the sea to a land where they could establish a government for themselves and leave their children the heritage of religious liberty, they went forward in the path where God was leading. Persecution and exile were opening the way to freedom.

When they first had to separate from the English Church, the Puritans made a covenant as the Lord's free people "to walk together in all His ways made known or to be made known to them."[1] This was the vital principle of Protestantism. With this intent the Pilgrims left Holland to find a home in the New World. John Robinson, their pastor, said this in his farewell address to the exiles:

"I charge you before God and His blessed angels to follow me no farther than I have followed Christ. If God should reveal anything to you by any other instrument of His, be as ready to receive it as you ever were to receive any truth from my ministry; for I am very confident the Lord has more truth and light yet to break forth out of His holy word."[2]

"For my part, I cannot feel worse over the condition of the reformed churches, who . . . now will go no farther than those who brought reformation to them. The Lutherans cannot be drawn to go beyond what Luther saw; . . . and the Calvinists, you see, stay right where they were left by that great man of God, who did not yet see all things. . . . Though these leaders were burning and shining lights in their time, yet they did not understand the whole counsel of God, but if they were living now, they would be as willing to embrace further light as the light they first received."[3]

"Remember your promise and covenant with God and with one another, to receive whatever light and truth shall come to you from His written word. But along with this, be careful, I beg you, about what you accept as truth, and compare it and weigh it with other scriptures of truth before you accept it, for it is not possible the Christian world would come so recently out of such thick anti-Christian darkness, and that full perfection of knowledge would suddenly be there."[4]

The desire for freedom of conscience inspired the Pilgrims to cross the sea, endure the hardships of the wilderness, and lay the foundation of a mighty nation. Yet the Pilgrims did not yet understand the principle of religious liberty. The freedom that they sacrificed so much to get for themselves, they were not ready to give to others. The doctrine that God has given the church the right to control the conscience and to define and punish heresy is one of the papacy's most deeply rooted errors. The Reformers were not entirely free from Rome's spirit of intolerance. The dense darkness that had enveloped Christendom had not completely vanished yet.

The colonists formed a kind of state church and authorized the government officials to suppress heresy. So secular power was in the hands of the church. This led to the inevitable result—persecution.

Roger Williams

Like the early Pilgrims, Roger Williams came to the New World for its religious freedom. But, unlike them, he saw what so few had yet seen—that this freedom was the absolute right of everyone. He was a devoted seeker for truth. Williams "was the first person in modern Christendom to establish civil government based on the doctrine of the liberty of conscience."[5] "The public or the government officials may decide," he said, "our responsibilities to each other. But when they try to decree anyone's duties to God, they are out of place, and no one is safe, for it is clear that if the official had the power, he could decree one set of opinions or beliefs today and another tomorrow. This has been done in England by different kings and queens, and by different popes and councils in the Roman Church."[6]

People were required to attend the established church under penalty of fine or imprisonment. Roger Williams believed that "to compel anyone to unite with those who believed differently was an open violation of that person's natural rights. To drag the irreligious and the unwilling to public worship seemed like simply requiring them to be hypocrites. . . . 'No one should be forced to worship, or,' he added, 'to support any kind of worship against his own will.'"[7]

People respected Roger Williams, yet they could not tolerate his demand for religious liberty. To avoid arrest he was forced to escape into the uninhabited forest during the cold and storms of winter.

"For fourteen weeks," he says, "I was in serious trouble in the bitter weather, without food or a bed." But "the ravens fed me in the wilderness," and a hollow tree often provided a shelter.[8] He continued his painful escape through snow and trackless forest until he found safety with an Indian tribe whose confidence and affection he had won.

Roger Williams laid the foundation of the first modern state to recognize the right "that all people should have liberty to worship God according to the light of their own consciences."[9] His little state, Rhode Island, increased and prospered until its foundation principles—civil and religious liberty— became the cornerstones of the American Republic.

Document of Freedom

The American Declaration of Independence stated, "We hold these truths to be self-evident, that all men are created equal; that they are endowed by their Creator with certain unalienable rights; that among these are life, liberty, and the pursuit of happiness." The Constitution guarantees that the government may not violate a person's conscience: "Congress shall make no law respecting an establishment of religion, or prohibiting the free exercise thereof."

"The framers of the Constitution recognized the eternal principle that a person's relationship to God is above human legislation, and the rights of conscience are not to be violated. . . . It is an inborn principle that nothing can eradicate."[10]

The news spread through Europe about a land where all could enjoy the fruits of their own labors and obey their own consciences. Thousands flocked to the shores of the New World. Within twenty years of the first landing at Plymouth (1620), twenty thousand Pilgrims had settled in New England.

"They asked nothing from the soil but the reasonable returns of their own labor. . . . They patiently endured the hardships of the wilderness, watering the tree of liberty with their tears and with the sweat of their brow, till it took deep root in the land."

Surest Safeguard of National Greatness

The home, school, and church all taught Bible principles. The Bible's fruits showed clearly in thrift, intelligence, purity, and temperance. For years one might "not see a drunkard, or hear a swear word, or meet a beggar."[11] Bible principles are what most surely protect a nation's greatness. The feeble colonies grew into powerful states, and the world noticed the prosperity of "a church without a pope, and a state without a king."

But increasing numbers of people were attracted to America by motives different from those of the Pilgrims. These were people who were looking only for worldly advantage.

The early colonists permitted only members of the church to vote or to hold office in the government. They accepted this measure to preserve the purity of the state. It resulted, however, in corrupting the church. Many people joined the church without a change of heart. Even in the ministry there were people who knew nothing of the renewing power of the Holy Spirit. From the days of Constantine to the present, while attempting to build up the church by the aid of the state may appear to bring the world nearer to the church, in reality it brings the church nearer to the world.

The Protestant churches of America, and those in Europe as well, failed to push forward in the path of reform. The majority, like the Jews in Christ's day or the Catholics in the time of Luther, were content to believe as their ancestors had believed. They kept their errors and superstitions. The Reformation gradually died out, until there was almost as great a need for reform in the Protestant churches as in the Roman Church in the time of Luther. The Protestant churches had the same reverence for human opinions and substitution of human theories for God's Word. People neglected to search the Scriptures, and so they continued to cling to doctrines that had no foundation in the Bible.

Pride and extravagance were encouraged under the appearance of religion, and the churches became corrupted. Traditions that would ruin millions were taking deep root. The church was upholding these traditions instead of contending earnestly for "the faith which was once for all delivered to the saints."

This is how the principles for which the Reformers had suffered so much were eroded.

1. J. Brown, *The Pilgrim Fathers,* p. 74.

2. W. Carlos Martyn, *The Life and Times of Martin Luther,* vol. 5, p. 70.

3. D. Neal, *History of Puritans,* vol. 1, p. 269.

4. Martyn, vol. 5, pp. 70, 71.

5. George Bancroft, *History of the United States of America,* pt. 1, ch. 15, par. 16.

6. Martyn, vol. 5, p. 340.

7. Bancroft, pt. 1, ch. 15, par. 2.

8. Martyn, vol. 5, pp. 349, 350.

9. Ibid., vol. 5, p. 354.

10. Congressional Documents (U.S.A.), serial no. 200, document no. 271.

11. Bancroft, pt. 1, ch. 19, par. 25.

Promises of Christ's Return

The promise of Christ's second coming to complete the great work of redemption is the main theme of the Sacred Scriptures. Since Adam and Eve left the Garden of Eden, the children of faith have waited for the coming of the Promised One to bring them to the lost Paradise again.

Enoch, the seventh generation from those who lived in Eden, who walked with God for three centuries, declared, "Behold, the Lord comes with ten thousands of His saints, to execute judgment on all" (Jude 14, 15). In the night of his suffering Job exclaimed, "I know that my Redeemer lives, and He shall stand at last on the earth; . . . in my flesh I shall see God, whom I shall see for myself, and my eyes shall behold, and not another" (Job 19:25–27).

The poets and prophets of the Bible have written about the coming of Christ in words glowing with fire. "Let the heavens rejoice, and let the earth be glad . . . before the LORD. For He is coming, for He is coming to judge the earth. He shall judge the world with righteousness, and the peoples with His truth" (Psalm 96:11–13).

Isaiah said: "It will be said in that day: 'Behold, this is our God; we have waited for Him, and He will save us. This is the LORD; we have waited for Him; we will be glad and rejoice in His salvation' " (Isaiah 25:9).

The Savior comforted His disciples with the assurance that He would come again: "In My Father's house are many mansions. . . . I go to prepare a place for you. And if I go . . . , I will come again and receive you to Myself." "When the Son of Man comes in His glory, and all the holy angels with Him, then He will sit on the throne of His glory. All the nations will be gathered before Him." (John 14:2, 3; Matthew 25:31, 32.)

Angels repeated to the disciples the promise of His return: "This same Jesus, who was taken up from you into heaven, will so come in like manner as you saw Him go into heaven" (Acts 1:11). And Paul testified: "The Lord *Himself* will descend from heaven with a shout, with the voice of an archangel, and with the trumpet of God" (1 Thessalonians 4:16). John, the prophet of Patmos, said: "Behold, He is coming with clouds, and *every eye will see Him*" (Revelation 1:7).

Then the age-long rule of evil will be broken: "The kingdoms of this world" will become "the kingdoms of our Lord and of His Christ, and He shall reign forever and ever!" (Revelation

11:15). "The Lord God will cause righteousness and praise to spring forth before all the nations" (Isaiah 61:11).

Then the peaceful kingdom of the Messiah will be established: "The Lord will comfort Zion, He will comfort all her waste places; He will make her wilderness like Eden, and her desert like the garden of the Lord" (Isaiah 51:3).

In all ages the coming of the Lord has been the hope of His true followers. In their suffering and persecution, the "appearing of our great God and Savior Jesus Christ" was the "blessed hope" (Titus 2:13). Paul pointed to the resurrection that will happen at the Savior's advent, when the dead in Christ will rise and be caught up together with the living to meet the Lord in the air. "And thus," he said, "we shall always be with the Lord. Therefore comfort one another with these words" (1 Thessalonians 4:17, 18).

On Patmos John, the beloved disciple, heard the promise, "Surely I am coming quickly," and his response is the prayer of the church, "Even so, come, Lord Jesus!" (Revelation 22:20).

From the dungeon, the stake, the scaffold, where faithful believers and martyrs witnessed for the truth, comes down through the centuries the expression of their faith and hope. Being "assured of His personal resurrection, and consequently of their own resurrection at His coming, for this reason," says one of these Christians, "they despised death, and were found to be above it."[1] The Waldenses cherished the same faith. Wycliffe, Luther, Calvin, Knox, Ridley, and Baxter looked in faith for the Lord's coming. This was the hope of the church in the apostles' time, of the "church in the wilderness," and of the Reformers.

Prophecy not only foretells the manner and purpose of Christ's second coming, but tells us how we may know when that day is near. "There will be signs in the sun, in the moon, and in the stars" (Luke 21:25). "The sun will be darkened, and the moon will not give its light; the stars of heaven will fall, and the powers in the heavens will be shaken. Then they will see the Son of Man coming in the clouds with great power and glory" (Mark 13:24–26). This is how John the revelator describes the first of the signs that come before the Second Advent: "There was a great earthquake; and the sun became black as sackcloth of hair, and the moon became like blood" (Revelation 6:12).

The Earthquake That Shook the World

This prophecy was fulfilled in 1755 in the most terrible earthquake ever recorded. (See Appendix.) Known as the Lisbon earthquake, it reached to Europe, Africa, and America. People felt it in Greenland, the West Indies, Madeira, Norway and Sweden, Great Britain and Ireland. It covered an area of at least four million square miles. In Africa the shock was almost as severe as in Europe. A major part of Algiers was destroyed. A huge wave swept over the coast of Spain and Africa, engulfing cities.

Mountains, "some of the largest in Portugal, were suddenly shaken, it seemed, from their very foundations; and some of them opened at their peaks, which were split and torn in an astonishing way, huge sections of them being thrown down into the nearby valleys. Some people say they saw flames coming from these mountains."

At Lisbon there was "a sound of thunder underground, and immediately afterwards a violent quake threw down most of that city. In only about six minutes, sixty thousand people died. The sea first drew back, and left the sandbar dry. Then it rolled in, rising fifty feet or more above its usual level."[2]

"The earthquake happened on a holy day, when the churches and convents were full of people. Very few of them escaped."[3] "The terror of the people was indescribable. No one wept; it was beyond tears. They ran here and there, frantic with horror and astonishment, beating their faces and chests, crying, 'Mercy! The world's at an end!' Mothers forgot their children and ran around loaded with crucifixed images. Unfortunately, many ran to the churches for protection; uselessly they sought to be near the bread and wine; in vain did the poor creatures embrace the altars. Images, priests, and people were buried in one common ruin."

Darkening of the Sun and Moon

Twenty-five years later the next sign appeared that was mentioned in the prophecy—the darkening of the sun and moon. In conversation with His disciples on the Mount of Olives, Jesus had clearly pointed out the time for this prophecy's fulfillment. "*In those days, after that tribulation, the* sun will be darkened, and the moon will not give its light" (Mark 13:24). The 1,260 days, or years, ended in 1798. A quarter of a century earlier, persecution had almost completely died out. Following this persecution, the sun would be darkened. On May 19, 1780, this prophecy was fulfilled.

An eyewitness in Massachusetts described the event this way: "A heavy black cloud spread over the entire sky except a narrow rim at the horizon, and it was as dark as it usually is at nine o'clock on a summer evening. . . .

"Fear, anxiety, and awe gradually filled the minds of the people. Women stood at the door, looking out at the dark landscape. Men returned from their work in the fields. The carpenter left his tools, the blacksmith his shop, the tradesman his counter. Schools were dismissed, and the children ran home in fear. Travelers asked for shelter at the nearest farmhouse. 'What is coming?' was the question on every lip and heart. It seemed as if a hurricane was about to sweep across the land, or as if it was the judgment day, the end of all things.

"People lit candles, and hearth fires glowed as brightly as they do on a moonless evening in autumn. . . . Birds flew to their roosts and went to sleep, cattle gathered at the pasture gates and lowed, frogs peeped, birds sang their evening songs, and bats flew around. But the human knew that night had not come. . . .

"Congregations came together in many . . . places. The texts for the impromptu sermons consistently were those that seemed to show that the darkness fulfilled Bible prophecy. . . . The darkness was the deepest shortly after eleven o'clock."[4]

"In most parts of the country it was so dark in the daytime that the people could not tell what time it was by either watch or clock, nor eat, nor manage their home duties, without the light of candles."[5]

Moon as Blood

"When night came, its darkness was just as odd and terrifying as the day's darkness had been. Though there was almost a full moon, no object was visible without the help of some artificial light. When people saw these lights from the neighboring houses and other places at a distance, it was as though they were looking through a kind of Egyptian darkness which seemed almost to let no light through at all."[6] "If every shining body in the universe had been wrapped in light-proof shades or struck out of existence, the darkness could not have been more complete."[7] After midnight the darkness disappeared, and the moon, when it first became visible, had the appearance of blood.

May 19, 1780, stands in history as "The Dark Day." Since the time of Moses no darkness has ever been recorded that equaled its density, extent, and duration. The description of eyewitnesses echoes the prophet Joel's words recorded twenty-five hundred years earlier: "The sun shall be turned into darkness, and the moon into blood, before the coming of the great and awesome day of the LORD" (Joel 2:31).

"When these things begin to happen," Christ said, "look up and lift up your heads, because your redemption draws near." He pointed His followers to the springtime's budding trees: "When they are already budding, you see and know for yourselves that summer is now near. So you also, when you see these things happening, know that the kingdom of God is near." (Luke 21:28, 30, 31.)

But in the church love for Christ and faith in His coming had grown cold. Those who claimed to be the people of God were blind to the Savior's instructions about the signs of His appearing. They had neglected the doctrine of the Second Advent until, to a great extent, it was ignored and forgotten, especially in America. A consuming devotion to money-making, the rush for popularity and power, led people to put off, far into the future, that solemn day when this world as we know it would pass away.

The Savior predicted the low spiritual condition of believers that would exist just before His second advent. Christ's counsel to those living at this time is: "Take heed to yourselves, lest your hearts be weighed down with carousing, drunkenness, and cares of this life, and that Day come on you unexpectedly. . . . Watch therefore, and pray always that you may be counted worthy to escape all these things that will come to pass, and to stand before the Son of Man" (Luke 21:34, 36).

It was important to alert people to prepare for the solemn events connected with the close of probation. "The day of the LORD is great and very terrible; who can endure it?" Who can stand when He appears who is "of purer eyes than to behold evil," and "cannot look on wickedness"? "I will punish the world for its evil, and the wicked for their iniquity; I will halt the arrogance of the proud, and will lay low the haughtiness of the terrible." "Neither their silver nor their gold shall be able to deliver them"; "their goods shall become booty, and their houses a desolation." (Joel 2:11; Habakkuk 1:13; Isaiah 13:11; Zephaniah 1:18, 13.)

The Call to Prepare

With that great day approaching, the Word of God calls His people to turn to Him with repentance:

"The day of the LORD is coming, for it is at hand." "Consecrate a fast, call a sacred assembly; gather the people, sanctify the congregation, assemble the elders, gather the children. . . . Let the priests, who minister to the LORD, weep between the porch and the altar." " 'Turn to Me with all your heart, with fasting, with weeping, and with mourning.' So rend your heart, and not your garments; return to the LORD your God, for He is gracious and merciful, slow to anger, and of great kindness." (Joel 2:1, 15–17, 12, 13.)

To prepare a people to stand in the day of God, there was a great work of reform to be done. In His mercy God was about to send a message to awaken those who claimed to be His people and lead them to get ready for the coming of the Lord.

We find this warning in Revelation 14. Here is a three-part message represented as proclaimed by heavenly beings and followed immediately by the Son of man's coming to reap "the harvest of the earth" (Revelation 14:15). The prophet saw an angel "flying in the midst of heaven, having the everlasting gospel to preach to those who dwell on the earth—to every nation, tribe, tongue, and people—saying with a loud voice, 'Fear God and give glory to Him, for the hour of His judgment has come; and worship Him who made heaven and earth, the sea and springs of water' " (Revelation 14:6, 7).

This message is a part of "the everlasting gospel." God has entrusted the work of preaching to us. Holy angels direct, but the servants of Christ on earth actually proclaim the gospel. Faithful men and women, obeying the urgings of God's Spirit and the teachings of His Word, were to proclaim this warning. They had been seeking the knowledge of God, regarding it as "better than the profits of silver, and her gain than fine gold." "The secret of the LORD is with those who fear Him, and He will show them His covenant." (Proverbs 3:14; Psalm 25:14.)

A Message Given by Humble Men

If scholarly theologians had been faithful watchmen, searching the Scriptures diligently and prayerfully, they would have known the time. The prophecies would have revealed to them the events about to happen. But instead, humble people gave the message. Those who neglect to seek the light when it is within their reach are left in darkness. But the Savior says, "He who follows Me shall not walk in darkness, but have the light of life" (John 8:12). God will send some star of heavenly radiance to that person to guide him into all truth.

At the time of Christ's first coming, the priests and scribes of the Holy City could have recognized "the signs of the times" and announced the coming of the Promised One. Micah identified His birthplace, and Daniel, the time of His arrival (Micah 5:2; Daniel 9:25). The Jewish leaders had no valid excuse if they did not know. Their ignorance was the result of sinful neglect.

With deepest interest the elders of Israel should have been studying the place, the time, the circumstances, of the greatest event in the world's history—the coming of the Son of God. The people should have been watching so that they could welcome the world's Redeemer. But at Bethlehem two weary travelers from Nazareth walked the length of the narrow street to the eastern edge of town without finding shelter for the night. No doors were open to receive them. In a crude stall prepared for cattle, they finally found refuge, and there the Savior of the world was born.

God appointed angels to carry the happy news to those who were ready to receive it and who would joyfully tell others. Christ had stooped to take human nature on Himself, to bear infinite agony as He made Himself an offering for sin. Yet angels wanted the Son of the Highest, even in His humiliation, to appear before the world with a dignity and glory suitable for His character. Would the great men of earth assemble at Israel's capital to greet His coming? Would angels present Him to those waiting for His arrival?

An angel visited the earth to see who were prepared to welcome Jesus. But he heard no voice of praise that the time of Messiah's coming had arrived. The angel hovered over the chosen city and temple where God's presence had appeared for ages, but even there he found the same indifference. In pomp and pride the priests offered polluted sacrifices. With loud voices the Pharisees addressed the people or made boastful prayers at the corners of the streets. Kings, philosophers, rabbis, all were ignorant of the wonderful fact that the Redeemer was about to appear.

In amazement the angel messenger was about to return to heaven with the shameful news, when he discovered a group of shepherds watching their flocks. As they gazed into the starry heavens, they thought about the prophecy of a Messiah to come, and they longed for the arrival of the world's Redeemer. Here was a group prepared to receive the heavenly message. Suddenly celestial glory flooded the entire plain, revealing an immeasurable company of angels. Then, as if the joy were too great for one messenger to bring from heaven, many voices broke out in the anthem that someday all the nations of the saved will sing: "Glory to God in the highest, and on earth peace, goodwill toward men!" (Luke 2:14).

What a lesson this wonderful story of Bethlehem is! How it rebukes our unbelief, our pride and self-sufficiency. How it warns us to watch out, so that we will not also fail to recognize the signs of the times and therefore not know our time of opportunity.

It was not just among lowly shepherds that angels found people watching for Messiah's coming. In heathen lands there were also those who looked for Him—rich, noble wise men—the philosophers of the East. From the Hebrew Scriptures they had learned about the Star that would rise out of Jacob. Eagerly they waited for the coming of the One who would be not only the "Consolation of Israel," but "a light to bring revelation to the Gentiles," and "for salvation to the ends of the earth" (Luke 2:25, 32; Acts 13:47). The Heaven-sent star guided Gentile strangers to the birthplace of the newborn King.

It is "to those who eagerly wait for Him" that Christ will "appear a second time, apart from sin, for salvation" (Hebrews 9:28). Like the news of the Savior's birth, God did not commit the message of the Second Advent to the religious leaders of the people. They had refused light from heaven, and so they were not part of the group that the apostle Paul described: "But you, brethren, are not in darkness, so that this Day should overtake you as a thief. You are all the sons of light and sons of the day. We are not of the night nor of darkness" (1 Thessalonians 5:4, 5).

The religious leaders should have been the first to catch the news of the Savior's coming, the first to announce that He was near. But they were careless and inattentive, while the people were asleep in their sins. Jesus saw His church, like the barren fig tree, covered with a show of leaves, yet without any precious fruit. They lacked the spirit of true humility, penitence, and faith. In its place they had pride, religious forms, selfishness, and oppression. A backsliding church closed their eyes to the signs of the times. They left God and separated themselves from His love. Because they refused to accept the conditions, His promises were not fulfilled to them.

Many of those who said they were followers of Christ refused to receive the light from heaven. Like the Jews of long ago, they did not know their time of opportunity. The Lord passed them by and revealed His truth to those who, like the shepherds of Bethlehem and the Eastern Magi, had followed all the light they had received.

---

1. See Daniel T. Taylor, *The Reign of Christ on Earth: Or, The Voice of the Church in All Ages,* p. 33.

2. Sir Charles Lyell, *Principles of Geology,* p. 495.

3. *Encyclopedia Americana,* art. "Lisbon" (ed. 1831).

4. *The Essex Antiquarian,* April 1899, vol. 3, no. 4, pp. 53, 54.

5. William Gordon, *History of the Rise, Progress and Establishment of the Independence of the U.S.A.,* vol. 3, p. 57.

6. Isaiah Thomas, *Massachusetts Spy; or, American Oracle of Liberty,* vol. 10, no. 472 (May 25, 1780).

7. Letter by Dr. Samuel Tenney, of Exeter, New Hampshire, December 1785, in *Massachusetts Historical Society Collections,* 1792, 1st series, vol. 1, p. 97.

New Light in
the New World

An upright, honest farmer who sincerely desired to know the truth was the man God chose to lead in proclaiming Christ's second coming. Like many other Reformers, William Miller had battled poverty and learned the lessons of self-denial.

Even as a child Miller showed more than ordinary intellectual strength. As he grew older, his mind was active and well developed, and he had a deep thirst for knowledge. He loved to study and made a habit of careful thought and keen analysis. These things made him a man of sound judgment and broad views. His moral character was excellent, and he had an enviable reputation. He performed well in the various civil and military positions he held. Wealth and honor seemed to be in his future.

In childhood he had been responsive to religious matters. In early manhood, however, he began to associate with deists,* whose influence was strong because they were mostly good citizens, humane, and benevolent. Living in the midst of a Christian society, their characters had been molded to some extent by their surroundings.

They were indebted to the Bible for the qualities that won them respect, and yet they perverted these good gifts to influence people against the Word of God. Miller adopted their views.

The interpretations of Scripture that people held then presented difficulties that seemed unsolvable to him. Yet his new belief, which set aside the Bible, offered nothing better, and he remained far from satisfied. But when Miller was thirty-four, the Holy Spirit impressed his heart that he was a sinner. He found no assurance of happiness beyond the grave. The future was dark and gloomy. Referring to his feelings at this time, he said:

"The heavens were like brass over my head, and the earth like iron under my feet. . . . The more I thought, the more scattered were my conclusions. I tried to stop thinking, but my thoughts would not be controlled. I was truly miserable, but I did not understand why. I was unhappy and complaining, but didn't know whom to blame. I knew that there was a wrong, but I did not know how or where to find the right."

---

* Deism: The belief that God exists and created the world, but thereafter assumed no control over it nor concern for the lives of people; the belief that reason is sufficient for the knowledge of truth, thus rejecting revelation.—Webster's New World Dictionary.

Miller Finds a Friend

"Suddenly," he says, "the character of a Savior came vividly to my mind. It seemed that there might be a being so good and compassionate that he would himself atone for our transgressions, and so save us from suffering the penalty of sin. . . . But the question arose, How can we prove that such a being does exist? Aside from the Bible, I found that I could get no evidence of the existence of such a Savior, or even of a future life. . . .

"I saw that the Bible did tell about just the kind of Savior I needed, and I was perplexed over how an uninspired book could develop principles so perfectly adapted to the needs of a fallen world. I was forced to admit that the Scriptures must be a revelation from God. They became my delight, and in Jesus I found a friend. The Savior became to me the Chief among ten thousand. The Scriptures, which before seemed dark and contradictory, now became the lamp to my feet and light to my path. . . . I found the Lord God to be a Rock in the midst of the ocean of life. The Bible now became my main study, and I can truly say, I searched it with great delight. . . . I wondered why I had not seen its beauty and glory before, and I was amazed that I could have ever rejected it. . . . I lost all desire for other reading and applied my heart to get wisdom from God."[1]

Miller publicly acknowledged his faith. But his unbelieving friends brought up all the arguments that he himself had often used against the Scriptures. He reasoned that if the Bible is a revelation from God, it must be consistent with itself. He decided to study the Scriptures and see whether every apparent contradiction could be harmonized.

Setting commentaries aside, he compared scripture with scripture by the aid of the marginal references and a concordance. Beginning with Genesis, reading verse by verse, when he found anything unclear he compared it with every other text that seemed to refer to the topic. He allowed every word to have its influence on the text. So whenever he came across a passage hard to understand, he found an explanation in some other part of the Scriptures. As he studied, he prayed earnestly for God to enlighten his mind, and he experienced the truth of the psalmist's words, "The entrance of Your words gives light; it gives understanding to the simple" (Psalm 119:130).

With intense interest he studied Daniel and Revelation and found that the prophetic symbols could be understood. He saw that all the various symbols, metaphors, illustrations, etc., were either explained in their immediate context or defined in other scriptures and should then be understood literally. He found link after link in the chain of truth, which rewarded his efforts. Step by step he found the meaning of the great Bible prophecies. Angels of heaven were guiding his mind.

He became satisfied that the Word of God did not teach the popular view of an earthly millennium before the end of the world. This doctrine, pointing to a thousand years of righteousness and peace before the coming of the Lord, is the opposite of the teachings of Christ and His apostles, who declared that the wheat and the tares are to grow together until the harvest, the end of the world, and that "evil men and impostors will grow worse and worse" (2 Timothy 3:13).

Personal Coming of Christ

The church in the apostles' time did not teach that the world would be converted and that Christ would reign only spiritually. Christians did not generally believe that way until about the beginning of the eighteenth century. This doctrine taught people to look far in the future for the coming of the Lord and prevented them from noticing the signs announcing His approach. It led many to neglect preparing to meet their Lord.

Miller found that the Bible plainly taught the literal, personal coming of Christ. "The Lord Himself will descend from heaven with a shout, with the voice of an archangel, and with the trumpet of God." "They will see the Son of Man coming on the clouds of heaven with power and great glory." "As the lightning comes from the east and flashes to the west, so also will the coming of the Son of Man be." "The Son of Man comes in His glory, and all the holy angels with Him." "And He will send His angels with a great sound of a trumpet, and they will gather together His elect." (1 Thessalonians 4:16; Matthew 24:30, 27; 25:31; 24:31.)

When Jesus comes, the righteous dead will be raised and the righteous living changed. "We shall not all sleep, but we shall all be changed—in a moment, in the twinkling of an eye, at the last trumpet. For the trumpet will sound, and the dead will be raised incorruptible, and we shall be changed. For this corruptible must put on incorruption, and this mortal must put on immortality." "The dead in Christ will rise first. Then we who are alive and remain shall be caught up together with them in the clouds to meet the Lord in the air. And thus we shall always be with the Lord." (1 Corinthians 15:51–53; 1 Thessalonians 4:16, 17.)

In our present condition we human beings are mortal and corruptible, but the kingdom of God will be incorruptible. Therefore in our present condition we cannot enter into the kingdom of God. When Jesus comes, He gives immortality to His people, and then He calls them to inherit the kingdom that has been theirs only by promise up to then.

Scripture and Chronology

These and other scriptures clearly proved to Miller that the universal reign of peace and God's setting up His kingdom on the earth would come after Jesus' second advent. Further, the condition of the world around Miller matched the prophetic description of the last days. He was forced to conclude that time was almost over for the earth as we know it.

"Another kind of evidence that vitally affected my mind," he says, "was the chronology of the Scriptures. . . . I found that predicted events that had been fulfilled in the past often happened within a certain stated time. . . . Events . . . that were once only a matter of prophecy, . . . were fulfilled in harmony with the predictions of time."[2]

When he found time periods in the Bible that extended to the second coming of Christ, he could not avoid seeing them as the "preappointed times" (Acts 17:26), which God had shown to His servants. "Those things which are revealed belong to us and to our children forever." The Lord declares that He "does nothing, unless He reveals His secret to His servants the prophets." (Deuteronomy 29:29; Amos 3:7.) People who study God's Word may confidently expect to find the Bible clearly pointing out the greatest event in human history.

"I was fully convinced," says Miller, "that all Scripture given by inspiration of God is profitable; that it . . . was written as holy men were moved by the Holy Spirit, and it was written for our learning, that we through the patience and comfort of the Scriptures might have hope.' . . . I therefore felt that in trying to understand what God in His mercy had seen fit to reveal to us, I had no right to ignore the prophetic periods."[3]

The prophecy that seemed to reveal the *time* of the Second Advent most clearly was Daniel 8:14: "For two thousand three hundred days; then the sanctuary shall be cleansed." Making Scripture its own interpreter, Miller learned that a day in symbolic prophecy represents a year (see Appendix). He saw that the 2,300 prophetic days, or literal years, would extend far beyond the close of the Jewish era, and so it could not refer to the sanctuary of that time.

Miller accepted the widely held view that in the Christian age the earth is the "sanctuary," so he thought that the cleansing of the sanctuary that Daniel 8:14 predicted represented the purifying of the earth by fire at the second coming of Christ. He concluded that if he could find the correct starting point for the 2,300 days, it would reveal the time of the Second Advent.

Discovering the Prophetic Timetable

Miller continued to examine the prophecies, devoting whole nights as well as days to studying what now seemed so greatly important. In the eighth chapter of Daniel he could find no clue to the starting point of the 2,300 days. The angel Gabriel, though commanded to make Daniel understand the vision, gave him only a partial explanation. As the terrible persecution to come on the church was revealed to the prophet, he could not bear it all. Daniel "fainted and was sick for days." "I was astonished by the vision," he says, "but no one understood it." (Daniel 8:27.)

Yet God had told the angel, "Make this man understand the vision." In obedience, the angel returned to Daniel, saying: "I have now come forth to give you skill to understand . . . therefore consider the matter, and understand the vision." He had left one important point in chapter 8 unexplained, specifically, the 2,300 days. So when the angel resumed his explanation, he dealt mainly with the time:

"Seventy weeks are determined for your people and for your holy city. . . . Know therefore and understand, that from the going forth of the command to restore and build Jerusalem until Messiah the Prince, there shall be seven weeks and sixty-two weeks; the street shall be built again, and the wall, even in troublesome times. And after the sixty-two weeks Messiah shall be cut off, but not for Himself. . . . Then he shall confirm a covenant with many for one week; but in the middle of the week He shall bring an end to sacrifice and offering." (Daniel 8:16; 9:22, 23, 24–27.)

God had sent the angel to Daniel to explain the point he had failed to understand—"for two thousand three hundred days; then the sanctuary shall be cleansed." The first words of the angel are, "Seventy weeks are determined for your people and for your holy city." The word translated *determined* literally means "cut off." Seventy weeks, 490 years, are to be cut off especially for the Jews.

Two Time Periods Begin Together

But from what were they cut off? Since the 2,300 days was the only period of time mentioned in chapter 8, the seventy weeks must be a part of the 2,300 days. The two periods must begin together, with the seventy weeks starting from "the going forth of the command to restore and build Jerusalem." If the date of this command could be found, then the starting point for the 2,300 days would be known.

In the seventh chapter of Ezra we find the decree, issued by Artaxerxes, king of Persia, in 457 B.C. Three kings had a part in issuing and completing the decree, bringing it to the conclusion required by the prophecy to mark the beginning of the 2,300 years. Taking 457 B.C., when the decree was completed, as the date of the "commandment," every point of the seventy-week prophecy clearly had been

fulfilled (see Appendix).

"From the going forth of the command to restore and build Jerusalem until Messiah the Prince, there shall be seven weeks and sixty-two weeks"— sixty-nine weeks, or 483 years. The decree of Artaxerxes went into effect in the autumn of 457 B.C. From this date, 483 years extend to the autumn of A.D. 27. At that time this prophecy was fulfilled. In the autumn of A.D. 27 Christ was baptized by John and received the anointing of the Spirit. After His baptism He went into Galilee, "preaching the gospel of the kingdom of God, and saying, 'The time is fulfilled'" (Mark 1:14, 15).

The Gospel Given to the World

"Then he shall confirm a covenant with many for one week"—the last seven years of the period marked off for the Jews. During this time, from A.D. 27 to A.D. 34, Christ and His disciples gave the gospel invitation especially to the Jews. The Savior's instruction to the apostles was: "Do not go into the way of the Gentiles, and do not enter a city of the Samaritans. But go rather to the lost sheep of the house of Israel" (Matthew 10:5, 6).

"In the middle of the week He shall bring an end to sacrifice and offering." In A.D. 31, three and a half years after His baptism, our Lord was crucified. With the great sacrifice offered on Calvary, symbol had met fulfillment. All the sacrifices and offerings of the ceremonial system were to end.

The 490 years given to the Jews ended in A.D. 34. At that time, through the action of the Jewish Sanhedrin, the nation sealed its rejection of the

"Unto 2,300 days; then the sanctuary shall be cleansed."

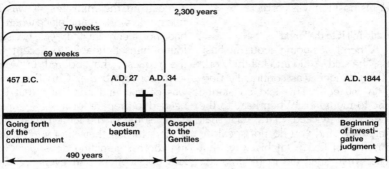

gospel by killing Stephen and persecuting the followers of Christ. Then the message of salvation went beyond the chosen people to the world. The disciples, forced to flee from Jerusalem because of persecution, "went everywhere preaching the word" (Acts 8:4).

So far every point of the prophecies was strikingly fulfilled. The beginning of the seventy weeks is established beyond question at 457 B.C., and they ended in A.D. 34. Since the seventy weeks (490 days) were cut off from the 2,300, there were 1810 days remaining. After the end of the 490 days, the 1810 days were still left to be fulfilled. From A.D. 34, 1810 years extend to 1844. So the 2,300 days of Daniel 8:14 end in 1844. At the end of this great prophetic period, "the sanctuary shall be cleansed." So the time of the cleansing of the sanctuary—which almost everyone believed would happen at the Second Advent—was pointed out. (See chart.)

Startling Conclusion

At the beginning Miller had no idea that he would reach the conclusion at which he had now arrived. He himself could hardly believe the results of his investigation. But the Scripture evidence was too clear for him to ignore.

In 1818 he reached the solemn conviction that in about twenty-five years Christ would appear to redeem His people. "I don't need to mention," says Miller, "the joy that filled my heart at this delightful prospect, nor how deeply I longed to participate in the joys of the redeemed. . . . Oh, how bright and glorious the truth appeared! . . .

"The question came home to me with mighty power about my duty to the world, in view of the evidence that had stirred up my own mind."[4] He could not help feeling that it was his duty to give to others the light he had received. He expected opposition from the ungodly, but he was confident that all Christians would rejoice in the hope of meeting the Savior. Still, he hesitated to present the hope of glorious deliverance, expected so soon, in case he might be wrong and mislead others. This led him to review the evidence and to consider carefully every objection he could think of. Five years of doing this left him convinced that his position was correct.

"Go and Tell It to the World"

"When I was going about my business," he said, " 'Go and tell the world of their danger' was continually ringing in my ears. This text constantly came to my mind: 'When I say to the wicked, "O wicked man, you shall surely die!" and you do not speak to warn the wicked from his way, that wicked man shall die in his iniquity; but his blood I will require at your hand.' I felt that if the wicked could be warned effectively, large numbers of them would repent, but that if they were not warned, their blood might be required at my hand."[5] The words kept on coming to his mind: "Go and tell it to the world; their blood will I require at your hand." For nine years he waited, and the burden got heavier on his heart, until in 1831 for the first time he publicly gave the reasons for his faith.

He was now fifty, not used to public speaking, but God blessed his labors. His first lecture sparked a religious awakening. Thirteen entire families, with the exception of two persons, were converted. People urged him to speak in other places, and in nearly every place sinners were converted. Christians were stirred to greater dedication, and deists and scoffers were led to acknowledge the truth of the Bible. His preaching awakened the public mind and obstructed the growing worldliness and immorality of the age.

In many places Protestant churches of nearly all denominations welcomed him, and invitations usually came from the ministers. It was his rule not to work in any place where he had not been invited, yet he soon found himself unable to accept half the requests that poured in. Many were convinced that Christ's coming was certain and near, and that they needed to prepare for it.

In some of the large cities, liquor dealers turned their shops into meeting rooms; gambling dens were broken up; scoffers and even the most shamelessly immoral people were reformed. The various denominations scheduled prayer meetings at almost every hour, with businessmen assembling at noon for prayer and praise. There was no extravagant excitement. Miller's work, like that of the early Reformers, tended instead to convince a person's understanding and awaken the conscience, rather than merely excite emotion.

In 1833, Miller received a license to preach from the Baptist Church. A large number of the ministers of his denomination approved his work, and he carried on his efforts with their formal endorsement. He traveled and preached without stopping, without ever receiving enough to meet the expense of travel to the places where he was invited. So his preaching put a heavy tax on his personal finances.

"The Stars Shall Fall"

In 1833, the last of the signs appeared that Jesus had promised as indications that His second advent was near: "The stars will fall from heaven." And in the book of Revelation John declared, "The stars of heaven fell to the earth, as a fig tree drops its late figs when it is shaken by a mighty wind." (Matthew 24:29; Revelation 6:13.) This prophecy was dramatically fulfilled in the great meteor shower of November 13, 1833, the most extensive and awe-inspiring display of falling stars ever recorded. "Rain never fell much thicker than the meteors fell toward the earth; east, west, north, and south, it was the same. In a word, the whole heavens seemed in motion. . . . From two o'clock until broad daylight, with the sky perfectly serene and cloudless, a constant play of dazzlingly brilliant lights continued in the whole heavens."[6] "It seemed as if the whole starry sky had come together at one point almost directly overhead, and was simultaneously shooting out, with the speed of lightning, to every part of the horizon. And yet the stars were not used up—thousands quickly followed in the tracks of thousands, as if created for the occasion."[7] "A more correct picture of a fig tree dropping its figs when blown by a mighty wind, it was not possible to see."[8]

In the New York *Journal of Commerce* of November 14, 1833, a long article appeared regarding this event: "No philosopher or scholar has told or recorded an event, I suppose, like that of yesterday morning. A prophet eighteen hundred years ago foretold it exactly, if we will take the trouble to understand stars falling to mean falling stars . . . in the only sense in which that can be literally true."

So the last of those signs of His coming happened, about which Jesus had told His disciples, "When you see all these things, know that it is near—

at the doors!" (Matthew 24:33). Many who witnessed the falling of the stars understood it as an announcement of the coming judgment.

In 1840, another remarkable fulfillment of prophecy drew widespread interest. Two years before, Josiah Litch published an explanation of Revelation 9, predicting the fall of the Ottoman Empire "in A.D. 1840, sometime in the month of August." Only a few days before it happened he wrote, "It will end on the 11th of August, 1840, when we may expect the Ottoman power in Constantinople to be broken."[9]

Prediction Fulfilled

At the very time specified, Turkey accepted the protection of the allied powers of Europe and thus placed herself under the control of Christian nations. The event exactly fulfilled the prediction. (See Appendix.) Great numbers of people were convinced that the principles of prophetic interpretation that Miller and his associates adopted were true. Men of learning and position united with Miller in preaching and publishing his views. From 1840 to 1844 the work grew rapidly.

William Miller had a strong, powerful mind, and he added to that the wisdom of heaven by connecting himself with the Source of wisdom. His life earned him respect wherever people valued integrity and moral excellence. With Christian humility, he was attentive and gracious to all, ready to listen to others and weigh their arguments. He tested all theories by the Word of God, and his sound reasoning and knowledge of Scripture made him able to refute error.

Yet, as earlier Reformers also found, the popular religious teachers did not accept the truths he presented. Since these men could not prove their position by Scripture, they resorted to human doctrines—the traditions of the Fathers. But the Word of God was the only testimony that the preachers of the advent truth would accept. Their opponents used ridicule and scoffing to discredit those who looked joyfully for the return of their Lord and were trying to live holy lives and prepare others for His appearing. The detractors made it seem like a sin to study the prophecies of the coming of Christ and the end of the world. In this way the popular ministry undermined faith in the Word of God. Their teaching made people reject God, and many felt free to indulge in ungodly desires. Then the authors of the evil charged it all upon Adventists.

While Miller was drawing crowds of intelligent hearers, the religious press seldom mentioned his name except to ridicule or condemn him. Emboldened by religious teachers, the ungodly resorted to blasphemous jokes on Miller and his work. The gray-haired man who had left a comfortable home to travel at his own expense to take to the world the solemn warning that the judgment was near was denounced as a fanatic.

Interest and Unbelief

Interest continued to increase. From dozens and hundreds, congregations had grown to many thousands. But after a time, opposition arose against these converts, and the churches started to discipline those who had accepted Miller's views. This led him to respond: "If we are wrong, please show us where we are wrong. Show us from the word of God that we are in error. We have had enough ridicule—that can never convince us that we are in the wrong. The word of God alone can change our views. We have formed our conclusions carefully and prayerfully, as we have seen the evidence in the Scriptures."[10]

When the evils of the people moved God to bring a flood on the earth, He first let them know His intentions. For 120 years they heard the warning to repent, but they did not believe it. They made fun of the messenger of God. If Noah's message were true, why did not all the world see and believe it? One man's claims against the wisdom of thousands! They would not believe the warning nor take shelter in the ark.

Scoffers pointed to the unchanging sequence of the seasons, the blue skies that had never poured out rain. In contempt they declared that Noah was a wild fanatic. They went on, more set in their evil ways than before. But at the appointed time God's judgments came down on those who rejected His mercy.

Skeptics and Unbelievers

Christ declared that as the people of Noah's day "did not know until the flood came and took them all away, so also will the coming of the Son of Man be" (Matthew 24:39). When the professed people of God are uniting with the world, when the luxury of the world becomes the luxury of the church, when everyone looks forward to many years of worldly prosperity— then, as suddenly as the lightning flashes, will come the end of their misguided hopes. Just as God sent Noah to warn the world of the coming Flood, He also sent chosen messengers to proclaim that the final judgment was near. And as Noah's contemporaries laughed scornfully at the predictions of the preacher of righteousness, so in Miller's day many of the professed people of God scoffed at the words of warning.

There can be no more convincing evidence that the churches have wandered from God than their hatred against this Heaven-sent message.

Those who accepted the advent doctrine felt that it was time to take a stand. "The things of eternity became real to them. . . . Heaven was brought near, and they felt that they were guilty before God."[11] Christians felt that time was short, that what they had to do for others must be done quickly. Eternity seemed to open before them. The Spirit of God gave power to their appeals to prepare for the day of God. Their daily life was a rebuke to lukewarm church members. These did not want to be disturbed in their pleasure, money-making, and ambition for worldly honor. This is why they opposed the advent faith.

Opposers tried to discourage investigation by teaching that the prophecies were sealed. In this way, Protestants followed in the steps of Catholics. Protestant churches claimed that an important part of the Word, that part especially meant for our time, could not be understood. Ministers declared that Daniel and the Revelation were mysteries beyond comprehension.

But Christ had pointed His disciples to the words of the prophet Daniel: "Whoever reads, let him *understand*" (Matthew 24:15). And the Revelation *is* to be understood. "The Revelation of Jesus Christ, which God gave Him to show His servants— things which must shortly take place. . . . *Blessed* is he who *reads* and those who *hear* the words of this prophecy, and *keep* those things which are written in it; for the time is near" (Revelation 1:1, 3, italics added).

"Blessed is he who reads"—there are those who will not read; "and those who hear"—there are some who refuse to hear anything concerning the prophecies; "and keep those things which are written in it"—many refuse to heed the instructions in the Revelation; none of these can claim the blessing promised.

How dare anyone teach that the Revelation is beyond human understanding? It is a mystery revealed, a book opened. Revelation directs the mind to Daniel. Both present important instruction about events at the close of world history.

John saw the dangers, conflicts, and final deliverance of the people of God. He records the closing messages that are to ripen the harvest of the earth, either for the heavenly storehouse or for the fires of destruction, so that those who turn from error to truth may learn about the dangers and conflicts ahead of them.

Why, then, is there this widespread ignorance concerning an important part of Holy Writ? It is the result of a deliberate effort by the prince of darkness to conceal from people the parts of the Bible that reveal his deceptions. For this reason, Christ the Revelator, foreseeing the warfare against the Revelation, pronounced a blessing on everyone who would read, hear, and observe the prophecy.

1. S. Bliss, *Memoirs of William Miller,* pp. 65–67.

2. Ibid., pp. 74, 75.

3. Ibid.

4. Ibid., pp. 76, 77, 81.

5. Ezekiel 33:8, 9; Bliss, p. 92.

6. R. M. Devens, *American Progress: Or, The Great Events of the Greatest Century,* ch. 28, pars. 1–5.

7. F. Reed, *Christian Advocate and Journal,* December 13, 1833.

8. "The Old Countryman," *Portland [Maine] Evening Advertiser,* November 26, 1833.

9. Josiah Litch, *Signs of the Times,* August 1, 1840.

10. Bliss, pp. 250, 252.

11. Ibid., p. 146.

Why the Great Disappointment?

From age to age, the work of God presents a striking similarity in every great reformation or religious movement. The principles of how God deals with people are always the same. The important movements of the present have their parallel in those of the past, and the church's experience in previous ages has lessons for our own time.

By His Holy Spirit God especially directs His servants on earth in advancing the work of salvation. Human beings are instruments in God's hand. He gives each one enough light to perform the work God gives him to do. But no one has ever had a full understanding of God's purpose in the work for his own time. God's representatives do not fully comprehend in all its aspects the message they speak in His name. Even the prophets did not fully understand the revelations God committed to them. He would unfold the meaning gradually, from age to age.

Peter says concerning this salvation that "the prophets have inquired and searched carefully, who prophesied of the grace that would come to you, searching *what,* or *what manner of time,* the Spirit of Christ who was in them was indicating when He testified beforehand the sufferings of Christ and the glories that would follow. To them it was revealed that, not to *themselves,* but to *us* they were ministering" (1 Peter 1:10–12, italics added). What a lesson for the people of God in the Christian age! Those holy men of God "inquired and searched carefully" concerning revelations God gave for generations that were not yet born. What a rebuke to the world-loving indifference that is content to declare that no one can understand the prophecies.

At times the minds of even God's servants are so blinded by tradition and false teaching that they only partially grasp the things revealed in His Word. Even when the Savior was with His disciples, they had the popular concept of the Messiah as an earthly prince who would exalt Israel to a universal empire. They could not understand His words predicting His suffering and death.

"The Time Is Fulfilled"

Christ had sent them out with the message: "The time is fulfilled, and the kingdom of God is at hand. Repent, and believe in the gospel" (Mark 1:15). That message was based on the prophecy of Daniel 9. The "sixty-nine weeks" were to extend to "Messiah the Prince," and the disciples looked forward to the establishment of Messiah's kingdom at

Jerusalem to rule over the whole earth.

They preached the message Jesus gave them, though they misunderstood its meaning. While their announcement was based on Daniel 9:25, they did not see in the next verse that Messiah was going to be "cut off." They had set their hearts on the glory of an earthly empire, and this blinded their understanding. At the very time when they expected to see their Lord take the throne of David, they saw Him arrested, whipped, mocked, condemned, and lifted up on the cross. What despair and anguish wrung the hearts of those disciples!

Christ had come at the exact time foretold. Scripture had been fulfilled in every detail. The Word and the Spirit of God confirmed the divine commission of His Son. And yet the disciples' minds were clouded with doubt. If Jesus had been the true Messiah, would they have been plunged into such grief and disappointment? This was the question that tortured their souls during the hopeless hours of that Sabbath between His death and resurrection.

Yet God had not forsaken them. "When I sit in darkness, the LORD will be a light to me. . . . He will bring me forth to the light; I will see His righteousness." "Unto the upright there arises light in the darkness." "I will make darkness light before them, and crooked places straight. These things I will do for them, and not forsake them." (Micah 7:8, 9; Psalm 112:4; Isaiah 42:16.)

The announcement the disciples made was correct, "The time is fulfilled, and the kingdom of God is at hand." When "the time" expired—the sixty-nine weeks of Daniel 9 that would reach to the Messiah, "the Anointed One"—Christ had received the anointing of the Spirit after His baptism by John. The "kingdom of God" was not an earthly empire, as they had been taught to believe. Nor was it that future, immortal kingdom in which "all dominions shall serve and obey Him" (Daniel 7:27).

The expression "kingdom of God" refers to both the kingdom of grace and the kingdom of glory. The apostle says, "Let us therefore come boldly to the throne of grace, that we may obtain mercy and find grace" (Hebrews 4:16). The existence of a throne implies the existence of a kingdom. Christ uses the expression "the kingdom of heaven" to designate the work of grace on human hearts. So the throne of glory represents the kingdom of glory (Matthew 25:31, 32). This kingdom is still future. It will not be set up until the second coming of Christ.

When the Savior gave up His life and cried out, "It is finished," He ratified the promise of salvation made to the sinful pair in Eden. The kingdom of grace, which had existed before by the promise of God, was then established.

In this way the death of Christ— the event the disciples saw as destroying their hope—was what actually made it secure forever. While it brought a cruel disappointment, it was the proof that their belief had been correct. The event that had filled them with despair opened the door of hope to all God's faithful ones in all ages.

Mixed in with the pure gold of the disciples' love for Jesus was the cheap metal of selfish ambitions. Their attention was fastened on the throne, the crown, and the glory. Their pride of heart, their thirst for worldly glory, had led them not to notice the Savior's words showing the true nature of His kingdom and pointing forward to His death. These errors resulted in the ordeal that God permitted to correct them. God would entrust the disciples with the glorious gospel of their risen Lord. To prepare them for this work, He permitted the experience that seemed so bitter.

After His resurrection Jesus appeared to His disciples on the road to Emmaus and "expounded to them in all the Scriptures the things concerning Himself." He wanted to fasten their faith on the "prophetic word confirmed" (Luke 24:27; 2 Peter 1:19), not just by His personal testimony, but by the prophecies of the Old Testament. And as the very first step in giving them this knowledge, Jesus directed the disciples to "Moses and all the Prophets" of the Old Testament Scriptures.

Despair to Assurance

In a more complete sense than ever before the disciples had "found Him of whom Moses in the law, and also the prophets, wrote." Assurance and unclouded faith replaced their uncertainty and despair. They had passed through the deepest trial possible for them to experience and had seen how God's Word had been fulfilled triumphantly. After this, what could shake their faith? In the deepest sorrow they had "strong consolation," a hope that was like "an anchor of the soul, both sure and steadfast" (Hebrews 6:18, 19).

The Lord says, "My people shall never be put to shame." "Weeping may endure for a night, but joy comes in the morning." (Joel 2:26; Psalm 30:5.) On His resurrection day these disciples met the Savior, and their hearts burned within them as they listened to His words. Before His ascension, Jesus instructed them, "Go into all the world and preach the gospel," adding, "Lo, I am with you always" (Mark 16:15; Matthew 28:20). On the Day of Pentecost the promised Comforter came down, and the hearts of the believers thrilled with the vivid presence of their ascended Lord.

The Disciples' Message Compared to the 1844 Message

The experience of the disciples at the first coming of Christ had its counterpart in the experience of those who announced His second coming. As the disciples preached, "The time is fulfilled, and the kingdom of God is at hand," so Miller and his associates proclaimed that the last prophetic period in the Bible was about to end, that the judgment was about to take place, and that the everlasting kingdom would soon be established. The disciples' preaching about the time was based on the seventy weeks of Daniel 9. The message that Miller and his associates gave announced the end of the 2,300 days of Daniel 8:14, of which the seventy weeks form a part. The preaching of each was based on the fulfillment of a different part of the same prophetic period.

Like the first disciples, William Miller and his associates did not fully understand the message they carried. Long established errors in the church prevented them from correctly interpreting an important point in the prophecy. So although they gave the message God had committed to them, yet because of a misunderstanding of its meaning they suffered disappointment.

Miller adopted the widely held view that the earth is the "sanctuary," and he believed that the "cleansing of the sanctuary" represented the purification of the earth by fire when Jesus would return. Therefore, he concluded, the close of the 2,300 days revealed the time of the Second Advent.

The cleansing of the sanctuary was the last service the high priest performed in the yearly cycle of worship. It was the closing work of the atonement—a removal or putting away of sin from Israel. It illustrated beforehand the closing work of our High Priest in heaven in removing or blotting out the sins of His people, which are registered in the heavenly records. This service involves investigation, a work of judgment, and it takes place just before the coming of Christ in the clouds of heaven, for when He comes, every case has been decided. Jesus says, "My reward is with Me, to give to every one according to his work" (Revelation 22:12). This is the work of judgment that the first angel's message of Revelation 14:7 announces: "Fear God and give glory to Him, for the hour of His judgment has come."

Those who proclaimed this warning gave the right message at the right time. As the disciples were mistaken about the kingdom to be set up at the end of the "seventy weeks," so Adventists were mistaken about the event to take place at the end of the "2,300 days." In both cases popular errors blinded the mind to truth. Both groups fulfilled the will of God in delivering the message He wanted given, and both experienced disappointment through misunderstanding their message.

Yet God accomplished His will in permitting the judgment warning to be given as it was. In His plan the message was to test and purify the church. Were their hearts set on this world or on Christ and heaven? Were they ready to turn away from their worldly ambitions and welcome the advent of their Lord?

The disappointment would also test the hearts of those who had claimed to receive the warning. Would they rashly give up their experience and throw away their confidence in God's Word when called to endure the scorn of the world and the test of delay and disappointment? Because they did not immediately understand God's dealings, would they reject truths that the clear testimony of His Word upheld?

This test would teach them the danger of accepting human interpretations instead of making the Bible its own interpreter. It would lead the children of faith to a closer study of the Word, to examine the foundation of their faith more carefully and to reject everything, no matter how widely accepted by the Christian world, that was not based on Scripture.

The things that seemed dark in the hour of trial would later be made plain. Despite the ordeal resulting from their errors, they would learn by a blessed experience that the Lord is "very compassionate and merciful," and that all His paths "are mercy and truth, to such as keep His covenant and His testimonies" (James 5:11; Psalm 25:10).

Love for Christ's Coming

The first angel's message of Revelation 14 predicts a great religious awakening. It portrays an angel flying "in the midst of heaven, having the everlasting gospel to preach to those who dwell on the earth—to every nation, tribe, tongue, and people." "With a loud voice," he proclaims, "Fear God and give glory to Him, for the hour of His judgment has come; and worship Him who made heaven and earth, the sea and springs of water." (Revelation 14:6, 7.)

An angel represents the high character of the work the message was to accomplish and the power and glory that would accompany it. The angel's flight "in the midst of heaven," the "loud voice," and its going "to every nation, tribe, tongue, and people" show the rapid, worldwide reach of the movement. As for the time when it is to happen, it announces the opening of the judgment.

This message is a part of the gospel which could only be proclaimed in the last days, because only then would it be true that the hour of judgment *had come*. Daniel was told to close up the part of his prophecy that related to the last days and to seal it "until the time of the end" (Daniel 12:4). Not until this time could a message about the judgment be proclaimed, based on a fulfillment of these prophecies.

Paul warned the church not to look for the coming of Christ in his day. Only after the great apostasy and the long reign of the "man of sin" can we look for the advent of our Lord. (See 2 Thessalonians 2:3.) The "man of sin"—also "the mystery of lawlessness," "the son of perdition," and "the lawless one"—represents the papacy, which was to maintain its supremacy for 1,260 years. This period ended in 1798. The coming of Christ could not take place before that time. Paul's caution covers the whole Christian era down to the year 1798. The message of Christ's second coming is to be proclaimed after that time.

No such message has ever been given in past ages. As we have seen, Paul did not preach it. He pointed into the then far-distant future for the coming of the Lord. The Reformers did not proclaim it. Martin Luther put the judgment about three hundred years into the future from his day. But since 1798 the book of Daniel has been unsealed, and many have proclaimed the message that the judgment is near.

In Different Countries Simultaneously

Like the Reformation of the sixteenth century, the Advent movement appeared in different countries at the same time. God led people of faith to study the prophecies, and they saw convincing evidence that the end was near. Isolated groups of Christians arrived at the belief that the Savior's coming was near, just by studying the Scriptures.

Three years after Miller had arrived at his understanding of the prophecies, Dr. Joseph Wolff, "the missionary to the world," began to proclaim the Lord's soon coming. Born in Germany of Hebrew parents, he was convinced while very young that the Christian religion was true. He had listened eagerly to conversations in his father's house as devout Hebrews came together to discuss the hopes of their people, the glory of the coming Messiah, and the restoration of Israel. One day, hearing Jesus of Nazareth mentioned, the boy inquired who He was. "A Jew of the greatest talent," was his father's answer; "but because He pretended to be the Messiah, the Jewish tribunal sentenced Him to death."

"Why," the boy asked, "is Jerusalem destroyed, and why are we in captivity?"

"Alas, alas!" answered his father, "because the Jews murdered the prophets." The thought immediately came to the child, "Perhaps Jesus was also a prophet, and the Jews killed Him when He was innocent." Although he was forbidden to enter a Christian church, he often lingered outside to listen to the preaching. When only seven years old, he was boasting to a Christian neighbor of Israel's future triumph when the Messi-

ah would come. The old man said kindly: "Dear boy, I will tell you who the real Messiah was. He was Jesus of Nazareth, . . . whom your ancestors have crucified. . . . Go home and read the fifty-third chapter of Isaiah, and you will be convinced that Jesus Christ is the Son of God."[1]

He went home and read the scripture, amazed to see how perfectly it had been fulfilled in Jesus of Nazareth. Were the words of the Christian true? The boy asked his father for an explanation of the prophecy but was met with silence so stern that he never again dared to refer to the subject.

When only eleven years old, he went out into the world to gain an education, to choose his religion and his lifework. Alone and with no money, he had to make his own way. He studied diligently, supporting himself by teaching Hebrew. He came to accept the Catholic faith and went to pursue his studies in the College of the Propaganda at Rome. Here he openly attacked the abuses of the church and urged reform. After a time, he was sent away from Rome. It became clear that he could never be brought to submit to the rule of Romanism. He was declared to be beyond hope and was allowed to go where he pleased. He made his way to England and joined the English Church. After two years' study, in 1821 he set out on his mission.

Wolff saw that the prophecies point to Christ's second coming with power and glory. While he tried to lead his people to Jesus of Nazareth as the Promised One, to point them to His first coming as a sacrifice for sin, he also taught them about His second coming.

Wolff believed the coming of the Lord was very near. His interpretation of the prophetic periods placed it within a few years of the time that Miller pointed out. "Did our Lord . . . not give us signs of the times, so that we may know at least the approach of His coming, as one knows the approach of the summer by the fig tree putting forth its leaves? Enough . . . shall be known by the signs of the times to persuade us to prepare for His coming, as Noah prepared the ark."[2]

Against Popular Interpretations

Concerning the popular system of interpreting the Scriptures, Wolff wrote: "Most of the Christian church have swerved from the plain sense of Scripture, and . . . suppose that when they are reading *Jews,* they must understand *Gentiles;* and when they read *Jerusalem,* they must understand the *church;* and if it says *earth,* it means *sky;* and for the coming of the Lord they must understand the progress of the *missionary societies;* and going up to the mountain of the Lord's house, signifies a *grand class meeting of Methodists.*"[3]

From 1821 to 1845, Wolff traveled in Egypt, Ethiopia, Palestine, Syria, Persia, Bokhara,* India, and the United States.

Power in the Book

Dr. Wolff traveled in the most uncivilized countries without protection, enduring hardships and surrounded with countless dangers. He was starved, sold as a slave, condemned to death three times, attacked by robbers, and sometimes nearly died of thirst. Once he was stripped of all his possessions and left to travel hundreds of miles on foot through mountains, snow beating in his face and his bare feet numbed by the frozen ground.

When people warned him against going unarmed among savage, hostile tribes, he said he was "provided with arms"—"prayer, zeal for Christ, and confidence in His help." "I am also provided with the love of God and my neighbor in my heart, and the Bible is in my hand." "I felt my power was in the Book, and that its might would sustain me."[4]

He kept on working until the message had gone to a large part of the populated world. Among Jews, Turks, Persians, Hindus, and other nationalities and races he distributed the Word of God in various languages, and everywhere he announced the Messiah's coming.

In Bokhara he found an isolated people who held the doctrine of the Lord's soon return. The Arabs of Yemen, he says, "are in possession of a book called *Seera,* which predicts the second coming of Christ and His reign in glory; and they expect great events to take place in the year 1840." "I found children of Israel, of the tribe of Dan, . . . who expect, with the children of Rechab, the speedy arrival of the Messiah in the clouds of heaven."[5]

Another missionary found a similar belief in Tatary, an area in Eastern Europe. A Tatar priest asked him

---

* *A remote region of Turkistan, between Afghanistan and Russia.*

when Christ would come the second time. When the missionary answered that he knew nothing about it, the priest seemed surprised to find such ignorance in a Bible teacher. He stated his own belief, based on prophecy, that Christ would come about 1844.

The Advent Message in England

As early as 1826 the advent message began to be preached in England. This did not usually involve teaching the exact time of the advent, but the truth of Christ's soon coming in power and glory was proclaimed extensively. An English writer states that about seven hundred ministers of the Church of England were preaching "this gospel of the kingdom."

Great Britain received the message pointing to 1844 as the time of the Lord's coming, as well. Advent publications from the United States circulated widely. In 1842, Robert Winter, an Englishman who had accepted the advent faith in America, returned to his native country to spread the news of the Lord's coming. Many joined him in the work in various parts of England.

In South America, Lacunza, a Jesuit from Spain, received the truth of Christ's speedy return. Wanting to avoid condemnation from Rome, he published his version under the assumed name of Rabbi Ben-Ezra, who claimed to be a converted Jew. About 1825 his book was translated into English. It helped to deepen the interest already awakening in England.

Revelation Unfolds to Bengel

In Germany Bengel, a Lutheran minister and Bible scholar, had taught the doctrine of Christ's soon return. While he was preparing a sermon from Revelation 21, the light of Christ's second coming broke in on his mind, and the prophecies of the Revelation opened to his understanding. The importance and glory of the prophetic scenes overwhelmed him, and he had to turn away from the subject for a time. In the pulpit it came to him again vividly. From that time he devoted himself to studying the prophecies, and soon he arrived at the belief that the coming of Christ was near. The date he established as the time of the Second Advent was within a few years of the one that Miller later held.

Bengel's writings spread in his own state of Würtemberg and to other parts of Germany. People in Germany heard the advent message at the same time that it was attracting attention in other lands.

At Geneva, Switzerland, Gaussen preached the Second Advent. When he entered the ministry he was inclined to doubt. In his youth he had become interested in prophecy. After reading Rollin's *Ancient History,* he read the second chapter of Daniel. He was struck with how the prophecy had been fulfilled exactly. Here was an indication that the Scriptures were inspired. He could not remain satisfied with rationalism, and in studying the Bible he found a positive faith.

He came to the belief that the coming of the Lord was near. Impressed that this truth was important, he wanted to present it to the people. But the popular belief that no one could understand the prophecies of Daniel was a serious obstacle. As Farel had done before him in evangelizing Geneva, he finally decided to begin with the children, and he hoped to interest the parents through them. He said, "I gather an audience of children; if the group grows, and I see that they listen, are pleased, interested, that they understand and explain the subject, I am sure to have a second circle soon, and in a while, grown people will see that it is worth their time to sit down and study. When this happens, the cause has won."[6]

As he spoke to the children, older people came to listen. The seats of his church were filled with hearers, people of rank and learning, and strangers and foreigners visiting Geneva. They, in turn, carried the message to other parts.

Encouraged by this, Gaussen published his lessons with the hope of promoting the study of the prophetic books. Later he became a teacher in a theological school, while on Sunday he continued his work of speaking to children and instructing them in the Scriptures. From the professor's chair, through the press, and as a teacher of children, for many years he was instrumental in calling people's attention to the prophecies that showed that the Lord's coming was near.

Child Preachers of Scandinavia

The advent message was also proclaimed in Scandinavia. It stirred many people to confess and forsake their sins and to ask for forgiveness in the name of Christ. But the clergy of the state church opposed the movement, and some who preached the message were thrown into prison.

In many places where officials silenced the preachers of the Lord's soon coming, God chose to send the message through little children. Since they were under age, the state could not stop them, and they were allowed to speak without interference.

In the simple homes of workers the people gathered to hear the warning. Some of the child preachers were not more than six or eight years old. While their lives testified that they loved the Savior, ordinarily they showed only the intelligence and ability that children of that age usually had. But when they stood before the people, an influence that was beyond their natural gifts moved them. Their tone and manner changed, and with solemn power they gave the warning of the judgment, "Fear God and give glory to Him, for the hour of His judgment has come."

The people heard with trembling. The Spirit of God spoke to hearts. Many began to search the Scriptures, the drunken and immoral were reformed, and a change took place so remarkable that even ministers of the state church had to admit that the hand of God was in the movement.

It was God's will to give the news of the Savior's coming in Scandinavia, and He put His Spirit on the children to accomplish the work. When Jesus came near to Jerusalem, the people, intimidated by the priests and rulers, stopped their joyful proclamation as they entered the gates of Jerusalem. But the children in the temple courtyard took up the chorus and shouted, "Hosanna to the Son of David!" (Matthew 21:8–16). As God worked through children at the time of Christ's first advent, so He worked through them in giving the message of His second advent.

The Message Spreads

America became the center of the great Advent movement. The writings of Miller and his associates went from there to distant lands, wherever missionaries had gone in all the world. The message of the everlasting gospel spread far and wide: "Fear God and give glory to Him, for the hour of His judgment has come."

The prophecies that seemed to point to the coming of Christ in the spring of 1844 took deep hold of the minds of the people. Many were convinced that the arguments from the prophetic periods were correct. Sacrificing pride of opinion, they received the truth with joy. Some ministers left their salaries and churches and joined in proclaiming the coming of Jesus. Comparatively few ministers, however, would accept this message, and so God entrusted it mostly to humble laymen. Farmers left their fields; mechanics, their tools; traders, their merchandise; professional men, their positions. They willingly endured hard work, poverty, and suffering, in order to call people to repentance and salvation. Thousands accepted the advent truth.

Simple Scripture Brings Conviction

Like John the Baptist, the preachers aimed the axe at the root of the tree and urged everyone to bear "fruits worthy of repentance." In sharp contrast to assurances of peace and safety coming from popular pulpits, the sim-

ple testimony of Scripture brought conviction few were able to resist entirely. Many came to the Lord with repentance. The affections they had set on earthly things for so long, they now fixed on heaven. With softened and subdued hearts they joined to proclaim the message, "Fear God and give glory to Him, for the hour of His judgment has come."

Sinners asked with tears, "What must I do to be saved?" Those who had been dishonest were anxious to make things right. Everyone who found peace in Christ longed to see others share the blessing. The hearts of parents turned to their children, and the hearts of children to their parents (Malachi 4:5, 6). Barriers of pride and reluctance were swept away. People made heartfelt confessions. Everywhere hearts were pleading with God. Many wrestled all night in prayer for the assurance that their sins were forgiven or for the conversion of relatives or neighbors.

All classes, rich and poor, high and low, were anxious to hear the teaching of the Second Advent. The Spirit of God gave power to His truth. People felt the presence of holy angels in these gatherings, and many more joined the believers every day. Huge crowds listened in silence to the solemn words. Heaven and earth seemed to approach each other. People went home with praises on their lips, and the glad sound rang out on the still night air. None who attended those meetings could ever forget those scenes of deepest interest.

The Message Opposed

The message of a definite time for

Christ's coming stirred up great opposition from many people in all parts of society, from the minister in the pulpit to the most Heaven-daring sinner. Many declared that they were not against the doctrine of the Second Advent, they just objected to the definite time. But God's all-seeing eye read their hearts. They did not want to hear that Christ would come to judge the world in righteousness. Their works would not pass the inspection of the heart-searching God, and they were afraid to meet their Lord. Like the Jews at the time of Christ's first advent, they were not prepared to welcome Jesus. They not only refused to listen to the clear arguments from the Bible but ridiculed those who were looking for the Lord. Satan flung the taunt in the face of Christ that His professed people had so little love for Him that they did not want Him to return.

Those who rejected the advent faith most often used the argument, "No one knows the day nor the hour." The scripture text is: "Of that day and hour no one knows, not even the angels of heaven, but My Father only" (Matthew 24:36). Those who were looking for the Lord gave a clear explanation of this text and showed plainly how their opponents were using it wrongly.

One saying of the Savior must not be made to destroy another. Though no one knows the day nor the hour of His coming, we are required to know when it is near. To refuse or neglect to know when His advent is near will be as fatal for us as it was for people in the days of Noah not to know when the Flood was coming. Christ says, "Therefore if you will not watch, I will come upon you as a thief, and you will not know what hour I will come upon you" (Revelation 3:3).

Paul speaks of those who have accepted the Savior's warning: "You, brethren, are not in darkness, so that this Day should overtake you as a thief. You are all sons of light and sons of the day" (1 Thessalonians 5:4, 5).

But those who wanted an excuse to reject truth refused to listen to this explanation, and the words "No one knows the day nor the hour" continued to echo from the scoffer and even the professed minister of Christ. As the people began to ask about the way of salvation, religious teachers stepped in between them and the truth by falsely interpreting the Word of God.

The most devoted in the churches were usually the first to accept the message. Wherever the people were not controlled by the clergy, wherever they would search the Word of God for themselves, they only needed to compare the advent doctrine with Scripture to be convinced of its divine authority.

Many were misled by husbands, wives, parents, or children and were made to believe it was a sin even to listen to such "heresies" as the Adventists taught. God sent His angels to keep faithful watch over these people, for another light was going to shine on them from His throne.

Those who had accepted the message watched for the coming of their Savior. The time when they expected to meet Him had almost arrived. They approached this hour calmly and solemnly.

None who experienced this can forget those precious hours of waiting. For some weeks before the time, for the most part they set worldly business aside. Sincere believers carefully examined their hearts as if in a few hours their earthly lives would end. There was no making of "ascension robes" (see Appendix), but all of them felt the need for inner assurance that they were prepared to meet the Savior. Their white robes were purity of heart—characters cleansed by the atoning blood of Christ. Oh, if only the people of God still had the same heart searching, the same earnest faith!

God intended to test His people. His hand covered a mistake in computing the prophetic periods. The time of expectation [that is, that Christ would come in the spring of 1844] passed, and Christ did not appear. Those who had looked for their Savior experienced a bitter disappointment. Yet God was testing the hearts of those who claimed to be waiting for His appearing. Many had acted from fear. These people declared that they had never believed that Christ would come. They were among the first to ridicule the sorrow of the true believers.

But Jesus and all of heaven looked with love and sympathy on the faithful yet disappointed ones. If the veil separating the visible from the invisible world could have been swept back, these loyal believers would have seen angels drawing near to them and shielding them from Satan's arrows.

1. *Travels and Adventures of the Rev. Joseph Wolff,* vol. 1, pp. 6, 7.

2. Joseph Wolff, *Researches and Missionary Labors,* pp. 404, 405.

3. *Journal of the Rev. Joseph Wolff,* p. 96.

4. W. H. D. Adams, *In Perils Oft,* pp. 192, 201.

5. *Journal of the Rev. Joseph Wolff,* pp. 377, 389.

6. L. Gaussen, *Daniel the Prophet,* vol. 2, preface.

Reaping the Whirlwind

William Miller and his associates had tried to help people who claimed to be religious see the true hope of the church and their need of a deeper Christian experience. They also worked to help those who were unconverted see their need to repent and be converted. "They made no attempt to convert anyone to a sect. They worked among all parties and sects." Miller said: "I wanted to benefit everyone. I thought that all Christians would rejoice that Christ's coming was near, and that those who could not see as I did would not love any less those who did embrace this doctrine. I did not imagine there would ever be any need for separate meetings. . . . The great majority of those who were converted under my preaching joined the various existing churches."[1]

But as religious leaders decided against the advent doctrine, they denied their members the privilege of going to hear preaching about the Second Advent or even speaking of their hope in the church. The believers loved their churches. But as they saw their right to investigate the prophecies taken away, they felt that loyalty to God would not allow them to submit. So they felt justified in separating. In the summer of 1844, about fifty thousand left their churches.

In most of the churches, for years people had been gradually but steadily conforming more and more to worldly practices and declining in spiritual life. But in that year there were signs of a sharp drop in nearly all the churches throughout the country. Both the press and the pulpit commented widely on this fact.

Mr. Barnes, author of a commentary and pastor of one of the leading churches in Philadelphia, "stated that . . . now there are *no awakenings, no conversions,* not much apparent growth in grace among church members, and none come to his study to talk about their salvation. . . . There is an increase of worldly-mindedness. *It is this way with all the denominations.*"[2]

In February of the same year, Professor Finney of Oberlin College said: "In general, the Protestant churches of our country were either careless or hostile to nearly all the moral reforms of the age. . . . Spiritual apathy is almost everywhere, and is fearfully deep. The religious press of the whole land testifies to this. . . . So many church members are becoming worshipers of fashion, joining hands with the ungodly in parties of pleasure, in dancing, in festivities, etc. . . . *The churches generally are becoming sadly corrupted.* They have gone very far from the Lord, and He has withdrawn Himself from them."

Rejection of Light

Spiritual darkness does not come from God's arbitrarily withdrawing His divine grace, but from men and women's rejection of light. By devotion to the world and forgetfulness of God, the Jewish people had been ignorant about Messiah's advent. In their unbelief they rejected the Redeemer. Even then God did not cut off the Jewish nation from the blessings of salvation. But those who rejected the truth had "put darkness for light, and light for darkness" (Isaiah 5:20).

After they rejected the gospel, the Jews continued their ancient rites while they admitted that the presence of God was no longer among them. The prophecy of Daniel pointed unmistakably to the time of Messiah's coming and plainly foretold His death. So they discouraged its study, and finally the rabbis pronounced a curse on anyone who would try to compute the time. In the centuries since then, the people of Israel have stood in blindness and rebellion, indifferent to God's gracious offers of salvation, neglecting the blessings of the gospel. They provide a solemn and fearful warning of how dangerous it is to reject light from heaven.

All who stifle conviction of duty because it interferes with their desires will finally lose the power to tell the difference between truth and error. They become separated from God. Where people spurn divine truth, the church will be in darkness, faith and love grow cold, and conflicts enter.

Church members focus their interests on worldly ventures, and sinners become hardened in their rebellion.

The First Angel's Message

The first angel's message of Revelation 14 was designed to separate those who claimed to be people of God from corrupting influences. In this message, God sent the church a warning which, if the people had accepted it, would have corrected the evils that were shutting them away from Him. If they had received the message, humbling their hearts and preparing to stand in His presence, the Spirit of God would have been poured out. The church would again have reached that unity, faith, and love that it had in the apostles' days, when the believers "were of one heart and one soul," and when "the Lord added to the church daily those who were being saved" (Acts 4:32; 2:47).

If God's people would receive the light from His Word, they would reach the unity that the apostle describes, "the unity of the Spirit in the bond of peace. There is," he says, "*one* body and *one* Spirit, just as you were called in *one* hope of your calling; one Lord, one faith, one baptism" (Ephesians 4:3–5).

Those who accepted the advent message came from different denominations, and their denominational barriers fell to the ground. Conflicting creeds shattered into atoms. The message corrected false views of the Second Advent. People made wrongs right, and hearts united in sweet fellowship. Love reigned supreme. This doctrine would have done the same for all, if all had accepted it.

As watchmen, ministers should have been the first to recognize the indications of Jesus' coming, but they had failed to learn the truth from the prophets or from the signs of the times. Love for God and faith in His Word had grown cold, and the advent doctrine only awakened their unbelief. As in Christ's time, people rejected the testimony of God's Word with the question, "Have any of the rulers or the Pharisees believed?" (John 7:48). Many discouraged the study of the prophecies, claiming that the prophetic books were sealed and could not be understood. Many put their trust in their pastors and refused to listen. Others were convinced of the truth, but they did not dare to announce it for fear that they would be "put out of the synagogue" (John 9:22). The message God sent to test the church revealed how many there were who had set their affections on this world rather than on Christ.

Refusing the warning of the first angel was the cause of that terrible condition of worldliness, backsliding, and spiritual death that existed in the churches in 1844.

The Second Angel's Message

In Revelation 14 a second angel follows the first, proclaiming, "Babylon is fallen, is fallen, that great city, because she has made all nations drink of the wine of the wrath of her fornication" (Revelation 14:8). The term "Babylon" comes from "Babel," and it indicates confusion. In Scripture it designates various forms of false or apostate religion. Revelation 17 portrays Babylon as a woman—a figure that the Bible uses as the symbol of a

church, a good woman representing a pure church, and an immoral woman, an apostate church.

The Bible describes the relation between Christ and His church as a marriage. The Lord declares: "I will betroth you to Me forever; yes, I will betroth you to Me in righteousness." "I am married to you." And Paul says: "I have betrothed you to one husband, that I may present you as a chaste virgin to Christ." (Hosea 2:19; Jeremiah 3:14; 2 Corinthians 11:2.)

Spiritual Adultery

When the church is unfaithful to Christ by allowing worldly things to fill the life, the Bible compares this to violation of the marriage vow. It uses this figure to represent the sin of Israel in straying from the Lord. " 'As a wife treacherously departs from her husband, so have you dealt treacherously with Me, O house of Israel,' says the LORD"; "an adulterous wife, who takes strangers instead of her husband" (Jeremiah 3:20; Ezekiel 16:32).

The apostle James says: "Adulterers and adulteresses! Do you not know that friendship with the world is enmity with God? Whoever therefore wants to be a friend of the world makes himself an enemy of God" (James 4:4).

The woman (Babylon) is "arrayed in purple and scarlet, and adorned with gold and precious stones and pearls, having in her hand a golden cup full of abominations and . . . filthiness. . . . And on her forehead a name was written: MYSTERY, BABYLON THE GREAT, THE MOTHER OF HARLOTS." The prophet says, "I saw the woman, drunk with the blood of the saints and with the blood of the martyrs of Jesus." Babylon is "that great city which reigns over the kings of the earth." (Revelation 17:4–6, 18.)

The power that ruled over the monarchs of Christendom for centuries is Rome. The purple and scarlet color, gold, precious stones, and pearls, picture the magnificence that the haughty church of Rome paraded. No other power could be so truly declared "drunk with the blood of the saints" as the church that persecuted the followers of Christ so cruelly.

Babylon is also charged with an unlawful connection with the "kings of the earth." By leaving the Lord behind and allying with the heathen, the Jewish church became a harlot, and Rome, seeking the support of worldly powers, receives the same condemnation.

Babylon is "the *mother* of harlots." Her *daughters* must be churches that cling to her teachings and follow her example of sacrificing truth in order to form an alliance with the world. The message announcing the *fall* of Babylon must apply to religious organizations that were once pure and have become corrupt. Since this message comes after the warning of the judgment, it must be given in the last days. So it cannot refer to the Roman Catholic Church alone, because that church has been in a fallen condition for centuries.

Furthermore, the people of God are called to come out of Babylon. So according to this scripture, many of God's people must still be in Babylon. And in what religious organizations do we now find the majority of the followers of Christ? In churches professing the Protestant faith. When these

churches began, they took a noble stand for truth, and God's blessing was with them. But they fell because of the same desire that ruined Israel— the desire to imitate the practices and court the friendship of the ungodly.

Union With the World

Many Protestant churches have followed Rome's example of connecting with "the kings of the earth." The state churches have done this by their relation to secular governments, and other denominations have done it by seeking the approval of the world. The term "Babylon"—confusion—applies to these groups that claim to get their doctrine from the Bible, yet are divided into nearly countless sects with conflicting beliefs.

A Roman Catholic work argues that "if the Church of Rome were ever guilty of idolatry in relation to the saints, her daughter, the Church of England, stands guilty of the same, having ten churches dedicated to Mary for one dedicated to Christ."[3]

And Dr. Hopkins declares: "There is no reason to think that the anti-Christian spirit and practices are found only in what is now called the Church of Rome. The Protestant churches have much of antichrist in them, and they are far from being completely reformed from . . . corruptions and wickedness."[4]

Concerning the separation of the Presbyterian Church from Rome, Dr. Guthrie writes: "Three hundred years ago, our church marched out from the gates of Rome with an open Bible on her banner and this motto, 'Search the Scriptures,' on her scroll." Then he asks the significant question: "Did they come *clean* out of Babylon?"[5]

First Departures From the Gospel

How did the church first move away from the simple gospel message? By making itself like paganism, so that the heathen could accept Christianity more easily. "Toward the end of the second century most of the churches took on a new form. . . . As the old disciples went to their graves, their children, along with new converts, . . . came forward and remodeled the faith." "A pagan flood flowed into the church, carrying its customs, practices, and idols with it."[6] The Christian religion obtained the favor and support of secular rulers. Thousands accepted the form of Christianity. But many of them "remained basically pagans, especially worshiping their idols in secret."[7]

Has not the same process been repeated in nearly every church that calls itself Protestant? As the founders who had the true spirit of reform pass away, their descendants "remodel the faith." Blindly refusing to accept any truth beyond what their ancestors saw, the Reformers' children depart from their example of self-denial and of turning away from the world.

It is sad how far the popular churches have strayed from the Bible standard! Speaking of money, John Wesley said: "Do not waste any part of so precious a talent . . . by needless or expensive clothing or by useless ornaments. Waste no part of it in beautifully decorating your houses, in unneeded or expensive furniture, in costly pictures, painting, gilding. . . .

As long as you are 'clothed in purple and fine linen,' and dine 'sumptuously every day' [Luke 16:19], no doubt many will applaud your elegance of taste, your generosity and hospitality. But you would do better to be content with the honor that comes from God."[8]

Rulers, politicians, lawyers, doctors, merchants, join the church as a way to advance their worldly interests. The religious organizations, reenforced by the wealth of these baptized worldlings, make an even higher bid for popularity. They build splendid, extravagant churches. They pay a high salary for a talented minister to entertain the people. His sermons must be smooth and pleasing for fashionable ears. And so they conceal fashionable sins under a show of godliness.

A writer in the New York *Independent* speaks this way about Methodism as it is: "The line of separation between the godly and the irreligious fades out into a kind of shadow, and zealous men on both sides are working to erase all difference between their varieties of action and enjoyment."

In this tide of pleasure-seeking, self-sacrifice for Christ's sake is almost entirely lost. "If funds are needed now, . . . nobody must be asked to give. Oh, no! Have a fair, a show, a mock trial, an old-time supper, or something to eat—anything to amuse the people."

Robert Atkins draws a picture of spiritual decline in England: "*Apostasy, apostasy, apostasy,* is engraved on the very front of every church; and if they only knew it, and if they felt it, there might be hope. But, no! They cry, 'We are rich, and increased in goods, and stand in need of nothing.' "[9]

Babylon's great sin is that she "made all nations drink of the wine of the wrath of her fornication." This cup represents false teachings that she has accepted as the result of her friendship with the world. In return, she exerts a corrupting influence on the world by teaching doctrines opposed to the plain statements of the Bible.

If the world were not so drunk with the wine of Babylon, large numbers of people would be convicted and converted by the plain truths of the Word of God. But religious faith appears so confused and contradictory that people do not know what to believe. The sin of the world's lack of repentance lies at the door of the church.

The second angel's message did not reach its complete fulfillment in 1844. The churches then experienced a moral fall by refusing the light of the advent message, but that fall was not complete. As they have continued to reject the special truths for this time, they have fallen lower and lower. Not yet, however, can it be said that "Babylon is fallen, . . . because she has made all nations drink of the wine of the wrath of her fornication." Protestant churches are included in the second angel's solemn denunciation. But the work of apostasy has not yet reached its height.

Before the coming of the Lord, Satan will work "with all power, signs, and lying wonders, and with all unrighteous deception"; and they that "did not receive the love of the truth, that they might be saved" will be left to receive "strong delusion, that they should believe the lie" (2 Thessalonians 2:9–11). Not until the church fully unites with the world will the fall of Babylon be complete. The change is progressive, and the ultimate fulfillment of Revelation 14:8 is still future.

In spite of the spiritual darkness in the churches that comprise Babylon, the great majority of Christ's true followers are still in those churches. Many have never seen the special truths for this time. Many are longing for clearer light. They look for the image of Christ in their churches, but they don't find it.

Revelation 18 points to the time when God will call His people who are still in Babylon to separate from her fellowship. This message, the last that the world will ever hear, will accomplish its work. The light of truth will shine on all who have hearts that are open to receive it, and all the children of the Lord in Babylon will obey the call, "Come out of her, my people" (Revelation 18:4).

1. Bliss, *Memoirs of William Miller,* p. 328.

2. *Congregational Journal,* May 23, 1844.

3. Richard Challoner, *The Catholic Christian Instructed,* preface, pp. 21, 22.

4. Samuel Hopkins, "A Treatise on the Millennium," *Works,* vol. 2, p. 328.

5. Thomas Guthrie, *The Gospel in Ezekiel,* p. 237.

6. Robert Robinson, *Ecclesiastical Researches* (ed. 1792), ch. 6, par. 17, p. 51.

7. Gavazzi, *Lectures* (ed. 1854), p. 278.

8. Wesley, *Works,* Sermon 50, "The Use of Money."

9. Second Advent Library, tract no. 39.

Prophecies Fulfilled

When the spring of 1844 passed—the time when people first expected the Lord's coming—those who had looked for His appearing experienced doubt and uncertainty. Many continued to search the Scriptures, examining again the evidence for their faith. The prophecies, clear and certain, pointed to the coming of Christ as near. The blessing of the Lord in converting and reviving Christians had testified that the message was from Heaven. Interwoven with prophecies that they thought applied to the time of the Second Advent was instruction encouraging them to wait patiently in faith that what was now unclear to them would be made plain. Among these prophecies was Habakkuk 2:1–4. No one, however, noticed that an apparent delay—a tarrying time—is in the prophecy. After the disappointment, this scripture seemed very significant: "The vision is yet for an appointed time; but at the end it will speak, and it will not lie. Though it tarries, wait for it; because it will surely come, it will not tarry. . . . The just shall live by his faith."

Ezekiel's prophecy also comforted the believers: "Thus says the Lord God: . . . 'The days are at hand, and the fulfillment of every vision. . . . I speak, and the word which I speak will come to pass; it will no more be postponed.' " "The word which I speak will be done." (Ezekiel 12:23, 25, 28.)

Those who were waiting rejoiced. God, who knows the end from the beginning, had given them hope. Without Scriptures like these, their faith would have failed.

The parable of the ten virgins in Matthew 25 also illustrates the experience of the Adventist people. Here we see the church in the last days. Their experience is illustrated by the events of an Eastern marriage:

"Then the kingdom of heaven shall be likened to ten virgins who took their lamps and went out to meet the bridegroom. Now five of them were wise, and five were foolish. Those who were foolish took their lamps and took no oil with them, but the wise took oil in their vessels with their lamps. But while the bridegroom was delayed, they all slumbered and slept. And at midnight a cry was heard: 'Behold, the bridegroom is coming; go out to meet him!' " (Matthew 25:1–6).

The coming of the bridegroom represented the coming of Christ, as announced by the first angel's message. The virgins' going out to meet the bridegroom corresponded to the widespread reformation that accompanied the message of Christ's soon coming. In this parable, all had taken their lamps, the Bible, and had gone "out to meet the bridegroom." But while the foolish "took no oil with them," "the wise took oil in their vessels with their lamps." They had studied the Scriptures to learn the truth and had a personal experience, a faith in God that disappointment and delay could not overthrow. The others responded to emotion, to their fears that the message stirred up. But they had depended on the faith of the "wise," satisfied with the flickering light of emotion, without a thorough understanding of truth or a genuine work of grace in the heart. These had gone out "to meet" the Lord, expecting an immediate reward, but they were not prepared for delay and disappointment. Their faith failed.

"While the bridegroom was delayed, they all slumbered and slept." This extended waiting for the bridegroom represents the passing of the time, the disappointment, the seeming delay. Those who based their faith on a personal knowledge of the Bible had a rock to stand on, which the waves of disappointment could not wash away. "They all slumbered and slept," one class in abandoning their faith, the other patiently waiting till clearer light would come. The superficial ones could no longer lean on the faith of the others. Each must stand or fall for himself.

Fanaticism Appears

About this time, fanaticism began to appear. Some who claimed to be believers showed a bigoted zeal. Their fanatical ideas gained no sympathy from the great majority of Adventists, yet they brought disgrace on the cause of truth.

Satan was losing his servants, and in order give the cause of God a bad reputation, he worked to deceive some who called themselves believers and drive them to extremes. Then his followers stood ready to take hold of every error, every strange or questionable act, and hold it up in the most exaggerated light to portray Adventists as a disgrace. The more people he could crowd in to profess faith in the Second Advent while his power controlled their hearts, the more advantage he would gain.

Satan is "the accuser of our brethren" (Revelation 12:10). His spirit inspires his followers to watch for defects in the Lord's people and hold them up to notice, while not mentioning their good deeds.

In all the history of the church no reformation has moved forward without meeting serious obstacles. Wherever Paul raised up a church, some who claimed to receive the faith brought in heresies. Luther also experienced distress from fanatical persons who claimed that God had spoken directly through them, who put their own ideas above Scripture. Many were deceived by the new teachers and joined Satan in tearing down what God had led Luther to build up. The Wesleys saw Satan's work in pushing unbalanced, unsanctified people into fanaticism.

William Miller had no sympathy with fanaticism. "The devil," said Miller, "has great power over the minds of some today." "I have often gotten more evidence of genuine devotion to God from an animated eye, a wet cheek, and a choked response, than from all the noise in Christendom."[1]

In the Reformation its enemies blamed the evils of fanaticism on the ones who were working most earnestly against it. Those who opposed the Advent movement followed a similar course. Not content with exaggerating the errors of fanatics, they spread reports that had not a shred of truth. Their peace was disturbed by the proclamation that Christ was almost here. They feared it might be true, yet hoped it was not. This was the secret of their warfare against Adventists.

The preaching of the first angel's message tended directly to hold fanaticism back. Those who participated in these solemn movements were in harmony. Their hearts were filled with love for one another and for Jesus, whom they expected soon to see. The one faith, the one blessed hope, proved to be a shield against Satan's assaults.

Mistake Corrected

"While the bridegroom was delayed, they all slumbered and slept. And at midnight a cry was heard, 'Behold, the bridegroom is coming; go out to meet him!' " In the summer of 1844 the believers proclaimed this message in the very words of Scripture.

The event that led to this movement was the discovery that the decree of Artaxerxes to restore Jerusalem, which was the starting point for the 2,300 days, went into effect in the autumn of 457 B.C. and not at the beginning of the year, as had been believed. Starting the calculation from the autumn of 457, the 2,300 years end in the autumn of 1844. The Old Testament symbols also pointed to the autumn as the time when the "cleansing of the sanctuary" must take place.

The killing of the Passover lamb was a shadow of the death of Christ, a symbol fulfilled, not only in relation to the event, but also to the time. On the fourteenth day of the first Jewish month, the very day and month on which for centuries the Passover lamb had been killed, Christ instituted the Lord's Supper, the feast that was to commemorate His own death as "the Lamb of God." That same night He was taken to be crucified and killed.

In the same way, the symbols that relate to the Second Advent must be fulfilled at the time indicated in the symbolic service. The cleansing of the sanctuary, or the Day of Atonement, happened on the tenth day of the seventh Jewish month. On that day the high priest, after making an atonement for all Israel and in this way removing their sins from the sanctuary, came out and blessed the people. So it was believed that Christ would appear to purify the earth by destroying sin and sinners and to bless His waiting people with immortality. The tenth day of the seventh month—the great Day of Atonement, the time of the cleansing of the sanctuary, which in 1844 fell on the twenty-second of October—was thought to be the day the Lord would come. The 2,300 days would end in the autumn, and the conclusion seemed irresistible.

"Midnight Cry"

The arguments carried strong conviction, and thousands of believers gave the "midnight cry." Like a tidal wave the movement swept from city to city, from village to village. Fanaticism disappeared like early frost in the rising sun. The work was like those times when ancient Israel returned to the Lord following messages of rebuke from His servants. There was little ecstatic joy, but instead deep searching of heart, confession of sin, and forsaking of the world. People showed full consecration to God, with nothing held back.

Of all the great religious movements since the days of the apostles, none have been more free from human imperfection and Satan's deceptions than was the Advent movement in the autumn of 1844.

In response to the call, "The bridegroom is coming," the waiting ones "arose and trimmed their lamps"; they studied the Word of God with an intensity of interest unlike anything before. The first to obey the call were not the most talented, but the most humble and devoted. Farmers left their crops in the fields, mechanics laid down their tools and happily went out to give the warning. The churches in general closed their doors against this message, and a large number of people who received it withdrew their membership. Unbelievers who flocked to the Adventist meetings felt convincing power supporting the message, "Behold, the bridegroom is coming!" Faith brought answers to prayer. Like showers of rain on the thirsty earth, the Spirit of grace descended on the earnest seekers. Those who expected soon to stand face-to-face with their Redeemer felt a solemn joy. The Holy Spirit melted their hearts.

Those who received the message came up to the time when they hoped to meet their Lord. They prayed frequently with one another. They often met in out-of-the-way places to talk with God, and the voice of intercession went up to heaven from fields and wooded groves. They wanted the assurance of the Savior's approval more than their daily food, and if a cloud darkened their minds, they did not rest until they felt the assurance of pardoning grace.

Disappointed Again

But again, the time that they expected Jesus to come passed, and their Savior did not appear. Now they felt like Mary did when she came to the Savior's tomb and found it empty, and she exclaimed with tears, "They have taken away my Lord, and I do not know where they have laid Him" (John 20:13).

The fear that the message might be true had restrained the unbelieving world. But when they saw no signs of God's anger, they recovered from their fears and began their taunts and ridicule again. A large number who had claimed to believe renounced their faith. The scoffers persuaded the weak and cowardly to join them, and they all united in declaring that the world might stay the same for thousands of years.

The earnest, sincere believers had given up everything for Christ. They believed they had given their last warning to the world. With intense desire they had prayed, "Come, Lord Jesus." But now to pick up the burden of life's perplexities again and to endure the jeers of a scoffing world was a terrible trial.

When Jesus rode triumphantly into Jerusalem, His followers believed that He was about to take the throne of David and deliver Israel from her oppressors. With high hopes, many spread their outer garments as a carpet in His path or strewed leafy palm branches before Him. The disciples were fulfilling God's intentions, yet they were doomed to a bitter disappointment. Only a few days passed before they witnessed the Savior's agonizing death and laid Him in the tomb. Their hopes died with Jesus. Not till their Lord had come out from the grave could they understand that prophecy had foretold all of this.

Messages Given at the Right Time

Similarly, Miller and his associates fulfilled prophecy and gave a message that Inspiration had foretold should go to the world. They could not have given it if they had fully understood the prophecies pointing out their disappointment and presenting another message that would have to be preached to all nations before the Lord returns. The first and second angels' messages were given at the right time and accomplished the work that God intended them to accomplish.

The world had been expecting that if Christ did not appear, people would give up their Adventism. Many did surrender their faith, but there were some who stood firm. The fruits

of the Advent movement—the spirit of heart searching, of renouncing the world and of reforming the life—testified that it was from God. They dared not deny that the Holy Spirit had blessed the preaching of the Second Advent. They could find no error in the prophetic periods. Their opponents had not succeeded in disproving their prophetic interpretation. They could not agree to renounce beliefs they had come to through earnest, prayerful study of the Scriptures, by minds enlightened by the Spirit of God and hearts burning with its living power, and which had stood firm against the arguments of educated and eloquent opponents.

Adventists believed that God had led them to give the warning of the judgment. They declared, "It has tested the hearts of all who heard it, . . . so that those who will examine their own hearts may know on which side . . . they would have been found, if the Lord had come then—whether they would have exclaimed, 'Behold, this is our God; We have waited for Him, and He will save us;' or whether they would have called to the rocks and mountains to fall on them to hide them from the face of Him who sits on the throne!"[2]

William Miller expressed the feelings of those who still believed that God had led them: "My hope in the coming of Christ is as strong as ever. I have done only what I felt it my duty to do, after years of solemn consideration." "To all human appearance, many thousands have been made to study the Scriptures by the preaching of the time; and by that means they have been reconciled to God through faith and the sprinkling of the blood of Christ."[3]

Belief Maintained

God's Spirit still stayed with those who did not rashly deny the light they had received and denounce the Advent movement. "Therefore do not cast away your confidence, which has great reward. For you have need of endurance, so that after you have done the will of God, you may receive the promise: 'For yet a little while, and He who is coming will come and will not tarry. Now the just shall live by faith; but if anyone draws back, My soul has no pleasure in him.' But we are not of those who draw back to perdition, but of those who believe to the saving of the soul" (Hebrews 10:35–39).

This counsel is addressed to the church in the last days. It plainly implies that the Lord would seem to delay His coming. The people addressed here had done the will of God by following the guidance of His Spirit and His Word, yet they could not understand His purpose in their experience. They were tempted to doubt whether God had indeed been leading them. The words, "Now the just shall live by faith," were applicable at this time. Crushed by disappointed hopes, they could stand only by faith in God and His Word. To renounce their faith and deny the power of the Holy Spirit that had accompanied the message would be to go back toward being lost. Their only safe course was to cherish the light they had already received from God, continue to search the Scriptures, and patiently wait and watch for further light.

1. Bliss, *Memoirs of William Miller,* pp. 236, 237.

2. *The Advent Herald and Signs of the Times Reporter,* vol. 8, no. 14 (November 13, 1844).

3. Bliss, pp. 256, 255, 277, 280, 281.

The Open Mystery of the Sanctuary

The scripture which above all others had been both the foundation and the central pillar of the advent faith was the statement, "For two thousand three hundred days; then the sanctuary shall be cleansed" (Daniel 8:14). These had been familiar words to everyone who believed in the Lord's soon coming. But the Lord had not come. The believers knew that God's Word could not fail; their interpretation of the prophecy must be at fault. But where was the mistake?

God had led His people in the great Advent movement. He would not permit it to end in darkness and disappointment, condemned as false and fanatical. Though many abandoned their calculation of the prophetic periods and denied the movement based on them, others were unwilling to renounce points of faith and experience that the Scriptures and the Spirit of God upheld. It was their duty to hold securely the truths they had already gained. With earnest prayer they studied the Scriptures to discover their mistake. Since they could see no error in their calculations of the prophetic periods, they examined more closely the subject of the sanctuary.

They learned that there is no Scripture evidence to support the popular view that the earth is the sanctuary. But they found a full Bible explanation of the sanctuary, its nature, location, and services:

"Then indeed, even the first covenant had ordinances of divine service and the earthly sanctuary. For a tabernacle was prepared: the first part, in which was the lampstand, the table, and the showbread, which is called the sanctuary; and behind the second veil, the part of the tabernacle which is called the Holiest of All, which had the golden censer and the ark of the covenant overlaid on all sides with gold, in which were the golden pot that had the manna, Aaron's rod that budded, and the tablets of the covenant; and above it were the cherubim of glory overshadowing the mercy seat" (Hebrews 9:1–5).

The "sanctuary" was the tabernacle that Moses built at God's command as the earthly dwelling place of the Most High. "Let them make Me a sanctuary, that I may dwell among them" (Exodus 25:8), was the direction God gave to Moses. The tabernacle was a magnificent structure. Besides the outer court, the tabernacle itself consisted of two rooms or apartments called the Holy and the Most Holy Place, separated by a beautiful curtain, or veil. A similar veil closed the entrance to the first room.

Holy and Most Holy Places

In the Holy Place was the lampstand on the south with its seven lamps giving light both day and night. On the north side stood the table of showbread. In front of the veil separating the Holy from the Most Holy was the golden altar of incense, from which the cloud of fragrance, with the prayers of Israel, ascended daily before God.

In the Most Holy Place stood the ark, a chest overlaid with gold, which held the Ten Commandments. Above the ark was the mercy seat holding two angels made of solid gold. In this apartment the divine presence appeared in the cloud of glory between the cherubim.

After the Hebrews settled in Canaan, the tabernacle was replaced by the temple of Solomon. Though it was a permanent structure and built on a larger scale, it had the same proportions and was furnished in the same way. The sanctuary existed in this form—except while it lay in ruins in Daniel's time—until the Romans destroyed it in A.D. 70. This is the only sanctuary on earth about which the Bible gives any information, the sanctuary of the first covenant. But does the new covenant have no sanctuary?

Turning again to the book of Hebrews, the seekers for truth found that a second or new covenant sanctuary was implied in the words already quoted: "Then indeed, even the first covenant had ordinances of divine service and the earthly sanctuary." Turning back to the beginning of the previous chapter, they read: "Now this is the main point of the things we are saying: We have such a High Priest, who is seated at the right hand of the throne of the Majesty in the heavens, a Minister of the sanctuary and of the true tabernacle which the Lord erected, and not man" (Hebrews 8:1, 2).

Here the Bible reveals the sanctuary of the new covenant. Moses made the sanctuary of the first covenant; this one is made by the Lord. In that sanctuary earthly priests performed their service; in this, Christ, our great High Priest, ministers at God's right hand. One sanctuary was on earth, the other is in heaven.

The tabernacle Moses built was made according to a pattern. The Lord directed, "According to all that I show you, that is, the pattern of the tabernacle and the pattern of all its furnishings, just so you shall make it." "And see to it that you make them according to the pattern which was shown you on the mountain." The first tabernacle "was symbolic for the present time in which both gifts and sacrifices are [were] offered," its Holy Places "copies of the things in the heavens." The priests served "the copy and shadow of the heavenly things." "Christ has not entered the holy places made with hands, which are copies of the true, but into heaven itself, now to appear in the presence of God for us." (Exodus 25:9, 40; Hebrews 9:9, 23; 8:5; 9:24.)

The sanctuary in heaven is the great original. The sanctuary that Moses built was a copy of it. The splendor of the earthly tabernacle reflected the glories of that heavenly temple where Christ ministers for us before the throne of God. The earthly sanctuary and its services taught important truths about the heavenly sanctuary and our redemption.

The Two Apartments

The Holy Places of the sanctuary in heaven are represented by the two apartments in the sanctuary on earth. John received a view of the temple of God in heaven. He saw there "seven lamps of fire . . . burning before the throne." He saw an angel "having a golden censer. . . . He was given much incense, that he should offer it with the prayers of all the saints upon the golden altar which was before the throne." (Revelation 4:5; 8:3.) Here the prophet saw the first apartment of the sanctuary in heaven, and he saw there the "seven lamps of fire" and the "golden altar," which the golden lampstand and the altar of incense represented in the sanctuary on earth.

Again, "The temple of God was opened," and he looked past the inner veil into the Holy of Holies. Here he saw "the ark of His covenant," represented by the chest that Moses constructed to contain the law of God. (Revelation 11:19.)

And so the believers studying the subject found proof that a sanctuary existed in heaven. John testifies that he saw it in heaven.

In the temple in heaven, in the Most Holy Place, is God's law. The ark that holds the law is covered with the mercy seat, in front of which Christ pleads His blood for sinners. These things represent the union of justice and mercy in the plan of redemption, a union that fills all heaven with amazement. This is the mystery of mercy that the angels would like to understand—that God can be just while He justifies the repenting sinner, that Christ could stoop to raise great numbers of people from ruin and clothe them with the spotless robes of His own righteousness.

Zechariah presents the work of Christ as our intercessor: "He shall build the temple of the LORD. He shall bear the glory, and shall sit and rule on His [the Father's] throne; so He shall be a priest on His throne, and the counsel of peace shall be between them both" (Zechariah 6:13).

"He shall build the temple of the LORD." By His sacrifice and mediation Christ is the foundation and builder of the church of God, "the chief cornerstone, in whom the whole building, being fitted together, grows into a holy temple in the Lord" (Ephesians 2:20, 21).

"He shall bear the glory." The song of those who are saved will be, "To Him who loved us and washed us from our sins in His own blood, . . . to Him be glory and dominion forever and ever" (Revelation 1:5, 6).

He "shall sit and rule on His throne; so He shall be a priest on His throne." The kingdom of glory has not yet arrived. Not until His work as a mediator is over will God give Him a kingdom of which "there will be no end" (Luke 1:33). As priest, Christ has now sat down with the Father in His throne. Upon the throne is the One who "has borne our griefs and carried our sorrows," "in all points tempted as we are, yet without sin," that He might be "able to aid those who are tempted" (Isaiah 53:4; Hebrews 4:15; 2:18). The wounded hands, the pierced side, the marred feet, plead for fallen humanity whose redemption Jesus purchased at such cost.

"And the counsel of peace shall be between them both." The love of the Father is the fountain of salvation for the lost race. Jesus said to His disciples, "The Father Himself loves you." God was "in Christ reconciling the world to Himself." "God so loved the world that He gave His only begotten Son." (John 16:27; 2 Corinthians 5:19; John 3:16.)

The Sanctuary Mystery Solved

The "true tabernacle" in heaven is the sanctuary of the new covenant. When Christ died, the symbolic service of the earthly sanctuary ended. Since Daniel 8:14 extends down to our era, the sanctuary to which it refers must be the sanctuary of the new covenant. So the prophecy, "For two thousand three hundred days; then the sanctuary shall be cleansed," points to the sanctuary in heaven.

But what is the cleansing of the sanctuary? Can there be anything in heaven that needs to be cleansed? Hebrews 9 plainly teaches the cleansing of both the earthly and the heavenly sanctuary: "According to the law almost all things are purified with blood, and without shedding of blood there is no remission. Therefore it was necessary that the copies of the things in the heavens should be purified with these [the blood of animals], but the heavenly things themselves with better sacrifices than these" (Hebrews 9:22, 23), even the precious blood of Christ.

The Cleansing of the Sanctuary

The cleansing in the real service in heaven must be accomplished with the blood of Christ. "Without shedding of blood there is no remission." Remission, or putting away of sin, is the work to be accomplished.

But how could there be sin connected with the sanctuary in heaven? We can find the answer by looking at the symbolic service, since the priests on earth served in "the copy and shadow of the heavenly things" (Hebrews 8:5).

The ministry of the earthly sanctuary consisted of two parts. The priests ministered each day in the Holy Place, while once a year the high priest performed a special work of atonement in the Most Holy, to cleanse the sanctuary. Day by day repentant sinners brought their offerings. They placed their hands on the victim's head, confessed their sins, symbolically transferring the sins from themselves to the innocent sacrifices. The animals were then killed. "The life of the flesh is in the blood" (Leviticus 17:11). The broken law of God demanded the life of the transgressor. The priest carried the blood, representing the life of the sinner whose guilt the victim bore, into the Holy Place and sprinkled it in front of the veil, behind which was the law that the sinner had broken. This ceremony transferred the sin symbolically to the sanctuary. In some cases the priest did not take the blood into the Holy Place, but then he ate the flesh. Both ceremonies symbolized the transfer of sin from the repentant sinner to the sanctuary.

This was the work that went on throughout the year. The sins of Israel were transferred in this way to the sanctuary, and a special work became necessary to remove them.

The Great Day of Atonement

Once a year, on the great Day of Atonement, the high priest entered the Most Holy Place for the cleansing of the sanctuary. Two young goats were brought and lots were cast, "one lot for the LORD and the other lot for the scapegoat" (Leviticus 16:8). The goat for the Lord was killed as a sin offering for the people, and the priest was to take his blood past the veil and sprinkle it in front of the mercy seat and also on the altar of incense just in front of the veil.

"Aaron shall lay both his hands on the head of the live goat, confess over it all the iniquities of the children of Israel, and all their transgressions, concerning all their sins, putting them on the head of the goat, and shall send it away into the wilderness by the hand of a suitable man. The goat shall bear on itself all their iniquities to an uninhabited land" (Leviticus 16:21, 22). The scapegoat would never again come into the camp of Israel.

The ceremony was designed to impress the Israelites with the holiness of God and His hatred of sin. Every Israelite was required to examine his own heart while this work of atonement was going on. All business was laid aside, and Israel spent the day in prayer, fasting, and searching of heart.

God accepted a substitute in the sinner's place, but the blood of the victim did not cancel the sin; rather, the sin was transferred to the sanctuary. By offering the blood the sinner acknowledged the authority of the law, confessed his sin, and expressed his faith in a Redeemer to come, but he was not yet completely free from the law's condemnation. On the Day of Atonement the high priest took an offering from the congregation and went into the Most Holy Place. He sprinkled the blood of this offering on the mercy seat, directly over the law, to satisfy its claims. Then, as mediator, he took the sins on himself and brought them out of the sanctuary. Placing his hands on the scapegoat's head, he symbolically transferred all these sins from himself to the goat. The goat then carried them away, and they were considered forever separated from the people.

Heavenly Reality

What happened symbolically in the services of the earthly sanctuary happens in reality in the heavenly sanctuary. After His ascension our Savior began His work as our High Priest: "Christ has not entered the holy places made with hands, which are copies of the true, but into heaven itself, now to appear in the presence of God for us" (Hebrews 9:24).

The service of the priest in the first apartment, "behind the veil" which separated the Holy Place from the outer court, represents the work that Christ began when He ascended. In the daily service the priest presented before God the blood of the sin offering and also the incense that went up with the prayers of Israel. Likewise, Christ pleaded His blood before the Father for sinners and presented to Him the prayers of repentant believers with the fragrance of His own righteousness. This was the ministry in the first apartment of the sanctuary in heaven.

The faith of Christ's disciples followed Him to that first apartment when He ascended. This is where their hopes centered. "This hope we have as an anchor of the soul, both sure and steadfast, and which enters the Presence behind the veil; where the forerunner has entered for us, even Jesus, having become High Priest forever." "He entered once for all into the Holy Place . . . with His own blood, thus obtaining eternal redemption." (Hebrews 6:19, 20; Hebrews 9:12, NRSV.)

For eighteen centuries this work continued in the first apartment of the sanctuary. The blood of Christ obtained pardon and acceptance with the Father for repentant believers, but their sins still remained on the books of record. As in the symbolic service there was a work of atonement at the close of the year, so before Christ's work for humanity is done there is a work of atonement to remove sin from the sanctuary. This began when the 2,300 days ended. At that time our High Priest entered the Most Holy Place to cleanse the sanctuary.

A Work of Judgment

In the new covenant the sins of the repentant believers are by faith placed on Christ and transferred in fact to the heavenly sanctuary. And as the symbolic cleansing of the earthly sanctuary was accomplished by removing the sins that had polluted it, so the actual cleansing of the heavenly is accomplished by removing, or blotting out, the sins recorded there. But before this can happen, there must be an examination of the books of record to determine who, through repentance and faith in Christ, are entitled to the benefits of His atonement. So the cleansing of the sanctuary involves a work of investigation—a work of judgment—before the coming of Christ, because when He comes, His reward is with Him to give to every one according to his works. (See Revelation 22:12).

So those who followed the light of the prophetic word saw that, instead of coming to the earth at the end of the 2,300 days in 1844, Christ entered the Most Holy Place of the heavenly sanctuary to perform the closing work of atonement in preparation for His coming.

When Christ, by the power of His blood, removes the sins of His people from the heavenly sanctuary at the close of His ministry, He will put them on Satan, who must bear the final penalty. The scapegoat was sent away into an uninhabited land, never to come again into the congregation of Israel. Likewise, Satan will be banished forever from the presence of God and His people, and he will be blotted out of existence in the final destruction of sin and sinners.

What Is Christ Doing Now?

The subject of the sanctuary unlocked the mystery of the disappointment of 1844. It revealed a complete system of truth, connected and harmonious, showing that God's hand had directed the great Advent movement. Those who had looked in faith for His second coming expected Him to appear in glory, but when their hopes were disappointed, they had lost sight of Jesus. Now in the Holy of Holies they again saw their High Priest, soon to appear as king and deliverer. Light from the sanctuary lit up the past, the present, and the future. Though they had failed to understand the message they had given, it had been correct.

The mistake had not been in calculating the prophetic periods, but in the *event* that was to take place at the end of the 2,300 days. Yet everything that the prophecy foretold had happened.

Christ had come, not to the earth, but to the Most Holy Place of the temple in heaven: "I was watching in the night visions, and behold, One like the Son of Man, coming with the clouds of heaven! He came"—not to the earth, but—"to the Ancient of Days, and they brought Him near before Him" (Daniel 7:13).

Malachi also foretold this coming: " 'The Lord, whom you seek, will suddenly come to His temple, even the Messenger of the covenant, in whom you delight. Behold, He is coming,' says the LORD of hosts" (Malachi 3:1). The coming of the Lord to His temple was "sudden," unexpected, to His people. They were not looking for Him there.

The people were not yet ready to meet their Lord. They still needed a work of preparation. As by faith they would follow their High Priest in His ministry, they would find new duties revealed. There was another message of warning and instruction to be given to the church.

Who Can Stand?

The prophet wrote: "Who can endure the day of His coming? And who can stand when He appears? . . . He will sit as a refiner and a purifier of silver; He will purify the sons of Levi, and purge them as gold and silver, that they may offer to the LORD an offering in righteousness" (Malachi 3:2, 3). Those living on earth when the intercession of Christ ends will stand in the sight of God without a mediator. Their robes must be spotless, their characters purified from sin by the sprinkled blood. Through the grace of God and their own diligent effort they must be conquerors in the battle with evil. While the investigative judgment is going forward in heaven, while the sins of repentant believers are being removed from the sanctuary, God's people on earth are to engage in a special work of putting away sin. This work is presented in the message of Revelation 14. When this work has been accomplished, the followers of Christ will be ready for His appearing. Then the church which our Lord is to receive at His coming will be "a glorious church, not having spot or wrinkle or any such thing" (Ephesians 5:27).

"Behold, the Bridegroom Is Coming"

The coming of Christ as High Priest to the Most Holy Place for the cleansing of the sanctuary (Daniel 8:14), the coming of the Son of man to the Ancient of Days (Daniel 7:13), and the coming of the Lord to His temple (Malachi 3:1) are the same event. This is also represented by the bridegroom's coming to the marriage in the parable of the ten virgins of Matthew 25.

In the parable, when the bridegroom came, "those who were ready went in with him to the wedding." This coming of the bridegroom takes place before the marriage. The marriage represents Christ's receiving of His kingdom. The Holy City, the New Jerusalem, the capital and symbol of the kingdom, is called "the bride, the Lamb's wife." The angel said to John, "Come, I will show you the bride, the Lamb's wife." "He carried me away in the Spirit," says the prophet, "and showed me the great city, the holy Je-

rusalem, descending out of heaven from God" (Revelation 21:9, 10).

The bride represents the Holy City, and the virgins that go out to meet the bridegroom are a symbol of the church. In the book of Revelation the people of God are described as guests at the marriage supper. If *guests,* they cannot be the *bride.* Christ will receive from the Ancient of Days in heaven "dominion and glory and a kingdom," the New Jerusalem, the capital of His kingdom, "prepared as a bride adorned for her husband" (Daniel 7:14; Revelation 21:2). When He has received the kingdom, He will come as King of kings and Lord of lords to redeem His people who are to eat of the marriage supper of the Lamb.

Waiting for Their Lord

The proclamation "Behold, the bridegroom is coming" led thousands to expect the Lord to come immediately. At the appointed time the Bridegroom came—not to the earth, but to the Ancient of Days in heaven, to the marriage, the reception of His kingdom. "Those who were ready went in with him to the wedding." They were not to be present in person, since they are on the earth. The followers of Christ are to "wait for their master, when he will *return from* the wedding" (Luke 12:36). But they are to understand His work and follow Him by faith. In this sense they are said to go in to the marriage.

In the parable, those who had oil in their lamps went in to the marriage. Those who, in the night of their bitter trial, had patiently waited, searching the Bible for clearer light—these saw the truth concerning the sanctuary in heaven and the Savior's change of priestly service. By faith they followed Him in His work in the sanctuary above. And all who accept the same truths, following Christ by faith as He performs the last work of mediation, go in to the marriage.

Closing Work in the Sanctuary

Similarly, in the parable of Matthew 22 the judgment takes place before the marriage. Previous to the wedding the king comes in to see if all the guests are wearing the wedding garment, the spotless robe of character washed in the blood of the Lamb (Revelation 7:14). In God's examination, all who have the wedding garment on are accepted and judged worthy of a share in God's kingdom and a seat on His throne. This work of character examination is the investigative judgment, the closing work in the sanctuary above.

When the cases of those who in all ages have professed Christ have been examined and decided, then probation will close and the door of mercy will be shut. So in one short sentence, "Those who were ready went in with him to the wedding; and the door was shut," we are carried down to the time when the great work for our salvation will be completed.

In the earthly sanctuary, when the high priest entered the Most Holy Place on the Day of Atonement, the service in the first apartment ended. Likewise, when Christ entered the Holy of Holies to perform the closing work of the atonement, He ended His ministry in the first apartment. Then the ministry in the second apartment began. Christ had completed only one part of His work as our intercessor, in order to begin another portion of the work. He still pleaded His blood before the Father in behalf of sinners.

While it is true that that door of hope and mercy was closed by which for eighteen hundred years sinners had found access to God, another door had opened. God still offered forgiveness of sins through the intercession of Christ in the Most Holy. There was still an "open door" to the heavenly sanctuary, where Christ was ministering for sinners.

Now people could see the meaning of those words of Christ in the Revelation, meant for this very time: "These things says He who is holy, He who is true, 'He who has the key of David, He who opens and no one shuts, and shuts and no one opens': . . . See, I have set before you an open door, and no one can shut it" (Revelation 3:7, 8).

Those who by faith follow Jesus in the great work of the atonement receive the benefits of His mediation, while those who reject the light get no benefit from it. The Jews who refused to believe on Christ as Savior could not receive forgiveness through Him. When Jesus ascended and entered the heavenly sanctuary to pour out on His disciples the blessings of His mediation, those Jews were left in darkness to continue their useless sacrifices and offerings. The door that before had given people access to God was no longer open. The Jews had refused to seek Him in the only way He could then be found, through the sanctuary in heaven.

The unbelieving Jews illustrate the condition of the careless and unbelieving among professed Christians who are willingly ignorant of the work of our High Priest. In the symbolic service, when the high priest went into the Most Holy Place, all of the Israelites were required to gather around the sanctuary and humble their hearts before God, so that they could receive pardon of sins and not be "cut off" from the congregation. How much more essential in this final Day of Atonement that we understand the work of our High Priest and know what duties are required of us.

Heaven sent a message to the world in Noah's day, and their salvation depended on how they treated that message (Genesis 6:6–9; Hebrews 11:7). In the time of Sodom, all but Lot with his wife and two daughters were consumed by fire sent down from heaven (Genesis 19). It was the same in the days of Christ. The Son of God declared to the unbelieving Jews of that generation, "Your house is left to you desolate" (Matthew 23:38).

Looking down to the last days, the same Infinite Power declares concerning those who "did not receive the love of the truth, that they might be saved": "For this reason God will send them strong delusion, that they should believe the lie" (2 Thessalonians 2:10, 11). As they reject the teachings of His Word, God withdraws His Spirit and leaves them to the deceptions that they love. But Christ still intercedes for humanity, and God will give light those who seek it.

The passing of the time in 1844 brought great trial to those who held the advent faith. Their only relief was the light that pointed their minds to the sanctuary above. As they waited and prayed, they saw that their great High Priest had begun another work of ministry. As they followed Him by faith, He led them to see also the closing work of the church. They had a clearer understanding of the first and second angels' messages, and were prepared to receive the solemn warning of the third angel of Revelation 14 and give it to the world.

God's Law Unchangeable

The temple of God was opened in heaven, and the ark of His covenant was seen in His temple" (Revelation 11:19). The ark of God's covenant is in the Holy of Holies, the second apartment of the sanctuary. In the services of the earthly tabernacle, which served as "the copy and shadow of the heavenly things," this section was opened only on the great Day of Atonement for the cleansing of the sanctuary. So the announcement that the temple of God was opened in heaven and the ark of His testament was seen points to the opening of the Most Holy Place of the heavenly sanctuary in 1844 as Christ entered there to perform the closing work of the atonement. Those who followed their great High Priest by faith as He began His ministry in the Most Holy Place took notice of the ark of His covenant. As they had studied the subject of the sanctuary, they had come to understand the Savior's change of ministry, and they saw that He was now officiating before the ark of God.

The ark in the tabernacle on earth contained the two tablets of stone on which God had inscribed His law. When the temple of God was opened in heaven, the ark of His covenant was seen. Within the Holy of Holies in heaven, the divine law is enshrined—the law that God Himself spoke and also wrote with His finger on the tablets of stone.

Those who came to understand this point saw, as never before, the importance of the Savior's words, "Till heaven and earth pass away, one jot or one tittle will by no means pass from the law" (Matthew 5:18). As a revelation of His will, a transcript of His character, the law of God must endure forever.

In the heart of the Ten Commandments is the Sabbath commandment. The Spirit of God impressed those students of His Word that they had ignorantly broken this law by disregarding the Creator's rest day. They began to examine the reasons for keeping the first day of the week. They could find no evidence that God had abolished the fourth commandment or changed the Sabbath. They had been honestly seeking to know and to do God's will. Now they showed their loyalty to God by keeping His Sabbath holy.

Many people tried to overthrow the faith of the believers. None could fail to see that accepting the truth about the heavenly sanctuary involved the claims of God's law and the Sabbath of the fourth commandment. Here was the secret behind the determined opposition to the harmonious explanation of Scriptures that revealed Christ's ministry in the heavenly sanctuary. People tried to close the door that God had opened and to open the door that He had closed. But Christ had opened the door to the ministry of the Most Holy Place. The fourth commandment was included in the law enshrined there.

Those who accepted the light about Christ's mediation and the law of God found that these were the truths of Revelation 14, a three-part warning to prepare the earth's inhabitants for the Lord's second coming. (See Appendix.) The announcement "The hour of His judgment has come" highlights a truth that must be proclaimed until the Savior's intercession ends and He returns to take His people to Himself. The judgment that began in 1844 must continue until the cases of all are decided, both of the living and the dead; so it will extend to the close of human probation.*

So that we may be ready to stand in the judgment, the message commands us to "fear God and give glory to Him, . . . and worship Him who made heaven and earth, the sea and springs of water." The Bible tells us the result of accepting these messages: "Here are those who keep the commandments of God and the faith of Jesus." (Revelation 14:7, 12.)

To be prepared for the judgment, we should keep the law of God, the standard of character in the judgment. Paul declares: "As many as have

sinned in the law will be judged by the law . . . in the day when God will judge the secrets of men by Jesus Christ." "The doers of the law will be justified." Faith is essential in order to keep the law of God, for "without faith it is impossible to please Him." "Whatever is not from faith is sin." (Romans 2:12, 16, 13; Hebrews 11:6; Romans 14:23.)

The first angel calls us to "fear God and give glory to Him" and to worship Him as the Creator of heaven and earth. To do this, we must obey His law. Without obedience no worship can be pleasing to God. "This is the love of God, that we keep His commandments" (1 John 5:3; see Proverbs 28:9).

A Call to Worship the Creator

The duty to worship God is based on the fact that He is the Creator. "Oh come, let us worship and bow down; let us kneel before the LORD our Maker" (Psalm 95:6; see Psalm 96:5; Psalm 100:3; Isaiah 40:25, 26; 45:18).

Revelation 14 calls people to worship the Creator and keep the commandments of God. One of these commandments points to God as the Creator: "The seventh day is the Sabbath of the LORD your God. . . . For in six days the LORD made the heavens and the earth, the sea, and all that is in them, and rested the seventh day. Therefore the LORD blessed the Sabbath day and hallowed it" (Exodus 20:10, 11). The Sabbath, the Lord says, is a "sign . . . that you may know that I am the LORD your God" (Ezekiel

----

* *That is, the end of the opportunity God extends to people to be saved.*

20:20). If everyone had kept the Sabbath, it would have led them to the Creator as the object of their worship. There would never have been an idol worshiper, atheist, or unbeliever. Keeping the Sabbath is a sign of loyalty to "Him who made heaven and earth, the sea and springs of water." The message that commands people to worship God and keep His commandments will especially call them to keep the fourth commandment.

In contrast to those who keep the commandments of God and the faith of Jesus, the third angel points to another group: "If anyone worships the beast and his image, and receives his mark on his forehead or on his hand, he himself shall also drink of the wine of the wrath of God" (Revelation 14:9, 10). What do the beast, the image, and the mark represent?

The Identity of the Dragon

The prophecy where these symbols are found begins with Revelation 12. The dragon who tried to destroy Christ at His birth is Satan (Revelation 12:9), who stirred up Herod to put the Savior to death. But the Roman Empire was the agent Satan used to make war on Christ and His people during the first centuries, and paganism was its prevailing religion. So in a secondary sense, the dragon is a symbol of pagan Rome.

Revelation 13 presents another beast, "like a leopard," to which the dragon gave "his power, his throne, and great authority." This symbol, as historically most Protestants have believed, represents the papacy, which took over the power and seat and authority that the Roman Empire once held. The Bible says about this leopardlike beast: "He was given a mouth speaking great things and blasphemies. . . . Then he opened his mouth in blasphemy against God, to blaspheme His name, His tabernacle, and those who dwell in heaven. It was granted to him to make war with the saints and to overcome them. And authority was given him over every tribe, tongue, and nation" (Revelation 13:2, 5–7). This prophecy, nearly identical with the description of the little horn of Daniel 7, unquestionably points to the papacy.

"He was given authority to continue for forty-two months"—the three years and a half, or 1,260 days, of Daniel 7—during which the papal power was to oppress God's people. This period, as stated in earlier chapters, began with the supremacy of the papacy, A.D. 538, and ended in 1798. At that time the papal power received its "deadly wound," and the prediction was fulfilled, "He who leads into captivity shall go into captivity."

The Rise of a New Power

At this point the prophecy introduces another symbol: "I saw another beast coming up out of the earth, and he had two horns like a lamb" (Revelation 13:11). This nation is unlike those presented by the preceding symbols. The great kingdoms that have ruled the world were presented to the prophet Daniel as beasts of prey, rising when "the four winds of heaven were stirring up the Great Sea" (Daniel 7:2).

But John saw the beast with lamblike horns "coming up out of the earth." Instead of overthrowing other powers to establish itself, the nation represented this way must arise in territory previously unoccupied and grow up peacefully. So it could not appear among the crowded and struggling nations of the Old World. We must look for it in the Western Continent.

What nation of the New World was rising into power in 1798, giving promise of strength, and attracting the attention of the world? One nation, and only one, meets this prophecy—the United States of America. In describing the rise of this nation, the historian unconsciously used almost the exact words of the Bible. A prominent writer speaks of *"the mystery of her coming forth from vacancy,"* and says, "Like a *silent seed* we grew into empire."[1] A European journal in 1850 spoke of the United States as "emerging" and "amid the silence of the earth daily adding to its power and pride."[2]

"And he had two horns like a lamb." The lamblike horns indicate youth, innocence, and gentleness. Among the Christian exiles who first fled to America from royal oppression and religious intolerance were many who determined to establish civil and religious liberty. The Declaration of Independence proclaims the truth that "all men are created equal" and are endowed with the inalienable right to "life, liberty, and the pursuit of happiness." The Constitution guarantees the people the right of self-government, requiring that representatives elected by popular vote shall enact and administer the laws. It also granted freedom of religion. Republicanism and Protestantism became the fundamental principles of the nation, the secret of its power and prosperity. Millions have flocked to its shores, and the United States has risen to a place among the most powerful nations of the earth.

A Striking Contradiction

But the beast with lamblike horns "spoke like a dragon. And he exercises all the authority of the first beast in his presence, and causes the earth and those who dwell in it to worship the first beast, whose deadly wound was healed. . . . Telling those who dwell on the earth to make an image to the beast who was wounded by the sword and lived" (Revelation 13:11, 12, 14).

The lamblike horns and dragon voice point to a contradiction. The prediction that it will speak "like a dragon" and exercise "all the authority of the first beast" foretells that it will develop a spirit of intolerance and persecution like those of the dragon and the leopardlike beast. And the statement that the beast with two horns "causes the earth and those who dwell in it to worship the first beast" indicates that the authority of this nation will enforce giving allegiance to the papacy.

Such action would be against the basic principles of its free institutions, against the solemn statements of the Declaration of Independence, and against the Constitution. The Constitution provides that "Congress shall make no law respecting an establishment of religion, or prohibiting the free exercise thereof," and that "no religious test shall ever be required as a qualification to any office or public trust under the United States." Yet the symbol points to flagrant violation of these safeguards to liberty. The beast with lamblike horns—professing to be pure, gentle, and harmless—speaks like a dragon.

"Telling *those who dwell on the earth* to make an image to the beast." Here the prophecy presents a form of government in which the legislative power rests with the people, a most striking evidence that the United States is the nation indicated here.

But what is the "image to the beast"? How is it to be formed?

When the early church became corrupted, she set out to get the support of secular power. The result: the papacy, a church that controlled the state, especially for the punishment of "heresy." In order for the United States to form an "image to the beast," the religious power must so control the civil government that the church will use the state to accomplish her own ends.

Protestant churches that have followed in the steps of Rome have shown a similar desire to restrict freedom of conscience. An example is the Church of England's long-running persecution of dissenters. During the sixteenth and seventeenth centuries, nonconformist pastors and people faced fines, imprisonment, torture, and martyrdom.

Apostasy led the early church to seek the help of civil government, and this prepared the way for the papacy—the beast. Said Paul: "The falling away comes . . . , and the man of sin is revealed" (2 Thessalonians 2:3). The Bible declares: "In the last days perilous times will come: For men will be *lovers of themselves,* lovers of money, boasters, proud, blasphemers, disobedient to parents, unthankful, unholy, unloving, unforgiving, slanderers, without self-control, brutal, *despisers of good,* traitors, headstrong, haughty, *lovers of pleasure rather than lovers of God, having a form of godliness* but denying its power" (2 Timothy 3:1–5). "Now the Spirit expressly says that in latter times some will depart from the faith, giving heed to deceiving spirits and doctrines of demons" (1 Timothy 4:1).

All who do "not receive the love of the truth, that they might be saved" will accept "strong delusion, that they should believe the lie" (2 Thessalonians 2:10, 11). When this happens, the same results will follow as in the first centuries.

Many think that the wide diversity of belief among Protestant churches is proof that no forced uniformity can ever happen. But for years in Protestant churches there has been a growing desire to unite. To bring about such union, they must avoid discussing subjects on which they do not all agree. In the effort to have complete uniformity, it will be only a step to resort to force.

When the leading churches of the United States unite on the points of doctrine that they hold in common and influence the state to enforce their decrees and to support their institutions, then Protestant America will have formed an image of the Roman hierarchy, and civil penalties on dissenters will inevitably follow.

The Beast and His Image

The beast with two horns "causes all, both small and great, rich and poor, free and slave, to receive a mark on their right hand or on their foreheads, and that no one may buy or sell except one who has the mark or the name of the beast, or the number of his name" (Revelation 13:16, 17). The third angel warns, "If anyone worships the beast and his image, and receives his mark on his forehead or on his hand, he himself shall also drink of the wine of the wrath of God."

"The beast" whose worship is enforced is the first, or leopardlike, beast of Revelation 13—the papacy. The "image to the beast" represents the form of apostate Protestantism that will develop when the Protestant churches seek the help of civil power to enforce their beliefs. The "mark of the beast" still remains to be defined.

Those who keep God's commandments are contrasted with those who worship the beast and his image and receive his mark. The keeping of God's law, on the one hand, and its violation, on the other, will be what distinguishes between the worshipers of God and the worshipers of the beast.

The special characteristic of the beast and of his image is the breaking of God's commandments. Daniel says that the little horn, the papacy, "shall intend to change times and law" (Daniel 7:25). Paul called the same power the "man of sin" (2 Thessalonians 2:3), who would exalt himself above God. Only by changing God's law could the papacy exalt itself above God. Whoever would knowingly keep the law in its changed form would be giving supreme honor to papal laws, a mark of allegiance to the pope in place of God.

The papacy has attempted to change the law of God. It has changed the fourth commandment in an attempt to authorize observing the first day instead of the seventh day as the Sabbath. The Bible presents this as an intentional, deliberate change: he "shall *intend* to change times and law." The change in the fourth commandment exactly fulfills the prophecy. Here the papal power openly sets itself above God.

The worshipers of God will be especially known for keeping the fourth commandment, the sign of His creative power. The worshipers of the beast will be noted for their efforts to tear down the Creator's memorial, to exalt the sabbath of Rome. It was in behalf of Sunday as "the Lord's day" that the Church of Rome first asserted its arrogant claims. (See Appendix.) But the Bible points to the seventh day as the Lord's day. Christ said, "The Son of Man is also Lord of the Sabbath" (Mark 2:28; see also Isaiah 58:13, 14; Matthew 5:17–19). His own words disprove the frequent claim that Christ changed the Sabbath.

Complete Silence of New Testament

Protestants admit that "the New Testament is completely silent about any explicit command for the Sabbath [referring here to Sunday, the first day of the week] or definite rules for its observance."[3]

"Up to the time of Christ's death, there had been no change in the day";

and, "so far as the record shows, they [the apostles] did not . . . give any explicit command to abandon the seventh day Sabbath, and observe it on the first day of the week."[4]

Roman Catholics acknowledge that their church made the change of the Sabbath, and they declare that Protestants recognize her power by observing Sunday. They claim, "During the old law, Saturday was the day sanctified; but *the Church,* instructed by Jesus Christ and directed by the Spirit of God, has substituted Sunday for Saturday; so now we sanctify the first day, not the seventh day. Sunday means, and now is, the day of the Lord."[5]

As the sign of the Roman Church's authority, Catholic writers cite "the very act of changing the Sabbath into Sunday, which Protestants accept; . . . because by keeping Sunday, they acknowledge the church's power to authorize feasts, and to command them as something that it is sinful to ignore."[6]

What then is the change of the Sabbath, but the sign, or mark, of the authority of the Roman Church—"the mark of the beast"?

The Roman Church has not given up her claim to supremacy. When the world and the Protestant churches accept a sabbath that she created while they reject the Bible Sabbath, they virtually admit her claim. In doing so they ignore the principle that separates them from Rome—that "the Bible, and the Bible only, is the religion of Protestants." As the movement to enforce Sunday gains favor, it will eventually bring the whole Protestant world under the banner of Rome.

Catholic spokesmen declare that "the observance of Sunday by the Protestants is a tribute they pay, in spite of themselves, to the authority of the [Catholic] Church."[7] If a church enforced a religious duty by secular power, this would form an image to the beast; so the enforcement of Sunday keeping in the United States would be enforcing the worship of the beast and his image.

Christians of past generations observed Sunday while thinking they were keeping the Bible Sabbath, and there are now true Christians in every church who honestly believe that God established Sunday as the day for worship. God accepts their sincerity and integrity. But when Sunday observance is enforced by law and the world is enlightened about the true Sabbath, then whoever transgresses the command of God in order to obey a teaching of Rome will, in doing so, honor the papacy above God. Such people are paying tribute to Rome. They are worshiping the beast and his image. In doing this, people will accept the sign of allegiance to Rome—"the mark of the beast." Not until the issue is plainly explained to the people and they have to choose between the commandments of God and the commandments of men, will those who continue to violate God's law receive "the mark of the beast."

The Warning of the Third Angel

The third angel's message contains the most fearful warning ever addressed to mortals. People will not be left in darkness about this important matter. The warning will be given to the world before God's judgments come, so that all may have opportunity to escape them. The first angel makes his announcement to "every nation, tribe, tongue, and people." The warning of the third angel will not be less extensive than that. It will be proclaimed with a loud voice and will command the attention of the world.

The message will divide the world's population into two great classes—those who keep the commandments of God and the faith of Jesus, and those who worship the beast and his image and receive his mark. Church and state will unite to compel "all" to receive "the mark of the beast," yet the people of God will not receive it. The prophet saw "those who have the victory over the beast, over his image and over his mark and over the number of his name, standing on the sea of glass, having harps of God" (Revelation 15:2).

---

1. G. A. Townsend, *The New World Compared With the Old,* p. 462.

2. *Dublin Nation.*

3. George Elliott, *The Abiding Sabbath,* p. 184.

4. A. E. Waffle, *The Lord's Day,* pp. 186–188.

5. *Catholic Catechism of Christian Religion.*

6. Henry Tuberville, *An Abridgement of the Christian Doctrine,* p. 58.

7. Monsignor Segur, *Plain Talk About the Protestantism of Today,* p. 213.

Champions for Truth

Isaiah predicted Sabbath reform in the last days: "Thus says the LORD, 'Keep justice, and do righteousness, for My salvation is about to come, and My righteousness to be revealed. Blessed is the man who does this, and the son of man who lays hold on it; who keeps from defiling the Sabbath, and keeps his hand from doing any evil.' . . . 'Also the sons of the foreigner who join themselves to the LORD, to serve Him, and to love the name of the LORD, to be His servants—everyone who keeps from defiling the Sabbath, and holds fast My covenant—even them I will bring to My holy mountain, and make them joyful in My house of prayer'" (Isaiah 56:1, 2, 6, 7).

These words apply in the Christian age, as the context shows: "The Lord GOD, who gathers the outcasts of Israel, says, 'Yet I will gather to him others besides those who are gathered to him'" (verse 8). This passage foreshadows the gospel's gathering in of the Gentiles, when His servants preach the good news to all nations.

The Lord commands, "Seal the law among my disciples" (Isaiah 8:16). The fourth commandment contains the seal of God's law. Only this commandment, of all the ten, includes both the name and the title of the Lawgiver. When the papal power tried to change the Sabbath, this seal was removed from the law. God calls for the disciples of Jesus to restore it by exalting the Sabbath as the Creator's memorial and sign of His authority.

God commands, "Cry aloud, spare not; lift up your voice like a trumpet; tell My people their transgression" (Isaiah 58:1). Those whom the Lord calls "My people" need to be told that they are breaking His law, even though they think that they are doing what is right in the service of God. But the solemn rebuke of the One who searches hearts shows that they are trampling on the divine commandments.

Here is how the prophet points out the law they have forsaken: "You shall raise up the foundations of many generations; and you shall be called the Repairer of the Breach, the Restorer of Streets to Dwell In. If you turn away your foot from the Sabbath, from doing your pleasure on My holy day, and call the Sabbath a delight, the holy day of the LORD honorable, and shall honor Him, not doing your own ways, nor finding your own pleasure, nor speaking your own words, then you shall delight yourself in the LORD" (Isaiah 58:12–14).

The "breach" in the law of God

was made when the Roman power changed the Sabbath. But the time has come to repair the breach.

Adam kept the Sabbath in his innocence in Eden; he still kept it when, fallen yet repentant, he was driven from the Garden. All the patriarchs from Abel to Noah, to Abraham, to Jacob kept the Sabbath. When the Lord delivered Israel from Egypt, He proclaimed His law to the emerging nation.

True Sabbath Always Kept

From that day to now the Sabbath has been kept. Though the "man of sin" succeeded in trampling God's holy day underfoot, yet faithful believers hidden in secret places paid it honor. Since the Reformation, some in every generation have kept it.

These truths found in Revelation 14 in connection with "the everlasting gospel" will distinguish the church of Christ at the time of His appearing. "Here are those who keep the commandments of God and the faith of Jesus" (Revelation 14:12).

Those who received the light about the sanctuary and the law of God were filled with joy as they saw the harmony of truth. They wanted all Christians to have the light. But many who claimed to follow Christ did not welcome truths that were out of step with the world.

When they heard the claims of the Sabbath, many said: "We have always kept Sunday, our fathers kept it, and many good Christians have died happy while keeping it. The keeping of a new Sabbath would throw us out of harmony with the world. What can a little group keeping the seventh day accomplish against all the world who are keeping Sunday?" By arguments like these the Jews justified rejecting Christ. Similarly, in the time of Luther, Romanists reasoned that true Christians had died in the Catholic faith, so that religion was sufficient. Reasoning like this would stand in the way of every move forward in faith.

Many argued that Sunday keeping had been a widespread custom of the church for centuries. Against this argument others showed that the Sabbath and its observance were older still, even as old as the world itself—established by the Ancient of Days.

When they could find no Bible support, many urged: "Why don't our great men understand this Sabbath question? Few believe as you do. It cannot be that you are right and all the educated people are wrong."

To refute arguments like these, it was enough just to quote the Scriptures and show how the Lord had dealt with His people in all ages. The reason why He does not more often choose people of learning and position to lead out in reform is that they trust to their creeds and theological systems and feel no need for God to teach them. God sometimes calls people to preach the truth who have little formal education. He chooses them, not because they are uneducated, but because they are not too self-sufficient for God to teach them. Their humility and obedience make them great.

The history of ancient Israel is a striking illustration of the Adventist believers' past experience. God led His people in the Advent movement, just as He led the people of Israel from Egypt. If all who had worked so closely together in 1844 had accepted the third angel's message and proclaimed it in the power of the Holy Spirit, years ago the earth would have been warned and Christ would have come to redeem His people.

Faith and Courage

It was not God's will for Israel to wander forty years in the wilderness. He wanted to lead them directly to Canaan and establish them there as a holy, happy people. But "they could not enter in because of unbelief" (Hebrews 3:19). In the same way, it was not God's will to delay the coming of Christ so long and to have His people remain so many years in this world of sin and sorrow. Unbelief separated them from God. In mercy to the world, Jesus delays His coming so that sinners may hear the warning and find shelter before God pours out His wrath.

Now as in earlier ages, presenting the truth will stir up opposition. With evil intent, many attack the character and motives of those who defend unpopular truth. Elijah was called a troubler in Israel, Jeremiah a traitor, Paul a polluter of the temple. From then until now, those who want to be loyal to truth have been denounced as rebellious, heretical, or divisive.

The confession of faith made by true believers and martyrs, those examples of holiness and firm integrity, inspires courage in those who are now called to stand as witnesses for God. The command comes to the servant of God today, "Lift up your voice like a trumpet; tell My people their transgression, and the house of Jacob their sins." "I have made you a watchman for the house of Israel; therefore you shall hear a word from My mouth and warn them for Me." (Isaiah 58:1; Ezekiel 33:7.)

The great obstacle to accepting truth is that it involves inconvenience and criticism. This is the only argument against the truth that those who defend truth have never been able to refute. But true followers of Christ do not wait for truth to become popular. They accept the cross, agreeing with Paul that "our light affliction, which is but for a moment, is working for us a far more exceeding and eternal weight of glory"; and with Moses, "esteeming the reproach of Christ greater riches than the treasures in Egypt" (2 Corinthians 4:17; Hebrews 11:26).

We should choose the right because it is right, and leave consequences with God. The world is indebted to people of principle, faith, and daring for its great reforms. The work of reform for this time must be carried forward by people like that.

How Successful Are Modern Revivals?

Wherever the Word of God has been faithfully preached, the results that followed demonstrated that it was from God. Sinners felt their consciences awaken. Deep conviction took hold of their minds and hearts. They had a sense of God's righteousness, and they cried out, "Who will deliver me from this body of death?" (Romans 7:24). As the cross of Jesus was revealed, they saw that nothing but the merits of Christ could atone for their sins. Through the blood of Jesus, "God had passed over the sins that were previously committed" (Romans 3:25).

These people believed and were baptized and rose to walk in newness of life. By the faith of the Son of God they would follow in His steps, reflect His character, and purify themselves even as He is pure. Things they once hated they now loved, and things they once loved they hated. The proud became meek, the vain and haughty became serious and meek. The drunken became sober, the immoral pure. Christians did not seek the outward decoration of "arranging the hair, wearing gold, or putting on fine apparel," but "the incorruptible beauty of a gentle and quiet spirit, which is very precious in the sight of God" (1 Peter 3:3, 4).

Revivals brought solemn appeals to the sinner. They bore fruit in people who did not draw back from self-denial but rejoiced that they were counted worthy to suffer for the sake of Christ. Onlookers could see a transformation in those who decided to follow Jesus. Effects like these used to follow times of religious awakening.

But many modern revivals are very different from these. It is true that many people claim to be converted, and large numbers join the churches. But the results do not support the belief that there has been an increase of real spiritual life in those who responded. The light that flames up for a while soon dies out.

Popular revivals too often excite the emotions, appealing to the love for something new and startling. People converted in this way have little desire to listen to Bible truth. Unless a religious service has something sensational in it, it does not attract them.

With every truly converted person, relating to God and to eternal things will be the great topic of life. Where in the popular churches of today is the spirit of consecration to God? Converts do not turn their backs on pride and love of the world. They are no more willing to deny self and follow the meek and lowly Jesus than they were before their conversion. Godliness has almost completely gone away from many of the churches.

True Followers of Christ

Despite the widespread decline in faith, there are true followers of Christ in these churches. Before God finally brings His judgments, among the people of the Lord there will be a revival of authentic godliness not seen since the time of the apostles. The Spirit of God will be poured out. Many will separate from those churches in which love of this world has replaced love for God and His Word. Many ministers and people will gladly accept the great truths that prepare a people for the Lord's second coming.

Satan wants to interfere with this work, and before the time for such a movement arrives, he will try to prevent it by bringing in a counterfeit. In churches that he can bring under his power, he will make it appear that God is pouring out His special blessing. Many will boast, "God is working marvelously," when the work belongs to another spirit. Under a religious disguise, Satan will try to extend his influence over the Christian world. In such revivals there is an emotional excitement, a mingling of the true with the false, well designed to mislead.

Yet in the light of God's Word it is not difficult to recognize the nature of these movements. Wherever people neglect the instruction of the Bible, turning away from those plain, heart-testing truths that require them to deny self and renounce the world, there we may be sure that God is not bestowing His blessing. And by the rule, "You will know them by their fruits" (Matthew 7:16), it is clear that these movements are not the work of the Spirit of God.

The truths of God's Word are a shield against Satan's deceptions. Neglecting these truths has opened the door to the evils that are now widespread in the world. To a great extent people have lost sight of the importance of God's law. A wrong idea about the divine law has led to errors in conversion and sanctification, lowering the standard of godly living. Here we find the reason why the Spirit of God is missing in the revivals of today.

The Law of Liberty

Many religious teachers claim that Christ abolished the law by His death. Some say it is a heavy yoke, and in contrast to the "bondage" of the law they present the "liberty" that the gospel supposedly grants us to enjoy.

But this is not the way the prophets and apostles thought of the holy law of God. David said, "I will walk at liberty, for I seek Your precepts" (Psalm 119:45). The apostle James refers to the Ten Commandments as "the perfect law of liberty" (James 1:25). John the revelator pronounces a blessing on those "who do His commandments, that they may have the right to the tree of life, and may enter through the gates into the city" (Revelation 22:14).

If it had been possible to change the law or set it aside, Christ would not have needed to die to save us from the penalty of sin. The Son of God came to "exalt the law and make it honorable" (Isaiah 42:21). He said, "Do not think that I came to destroy the Law"; "till heaven and earth pass away, one jot or one tittle will by no means pass from the law." Concerning Himself Jesus declared, "I delight to do Your will, O my God, and Your law is within my heart." (Matthew 5:17, 18; Psalm 40:8.)

The law of God is unchangeable, a revelation of its Author's character. God is love, and His law is love. "Love is the fulfillment of the law." The psalmist says, "Your law is truth"; "all Your commandments are righteousness." Paul declares, "The law is holy, and the commandment holy and just and good." (Romans 13:10; Psalm 119:142, 172; Romans 7:12.) A law like this must be as long-lasting as its Author.

It is the work of conversion and sanctification to restore people to God by leading them to obey the principles of His law. In the beginning, human beings were in perfect harmony with the law of God. But sin alienated them from their Maker. Their hearts were at war with God's law. "The carnal mind is enmity against God; for it is not subject to the law of God, nor indeed can be" (Romans 8:7). But "God so loved the world that He gave His only begotten Son," so that sinners could be reconciled to God and be brought again into harmony with their Maker. This change is the new birth, without which the sinner "cannot see the kingdom of God." (John 3:16, 3.)

Conviction of Sin

The first step in becoming right with God is the conviction of sin. "Sin is lawlessness." "By the law is the knowledge of sin." (1 John 3:4; Romans 3:20.) In order to see their guilt, sinners must test their character by God's law—a mirror that shows what a perfect righteous character looks like and enables them to recognize the defects in their own.

The law shows us our sin, but it provides no remedy. It declares that death is the reward of the transgressor. Only the gospel of Christ can free us from the condemnation or the defilement of sin. We must have repentance toward God, whose law we have broken, and faith in Christ, our atoning sacrifice. In this way we receive forgiveness for "sins that were previously committed" (Romans 3:25) and become children of God.

Are we now free to disobey God's law? Paul says: "Do we then make void the law through faith? Certainly not! On the contrary, we establish the law." "How shall we who died to sin live any longer in it?" John declares: "This is the love of God, that we keep His commandments. And His commandments are not burdensome." In the new birth the heart comes into harmony with God and His law. When this change has taken place, the sinner has passed from death into life, from law-breaking and rebellion to obedience and loyalty. The old life has ended; the new life of forgiveness, faith, and love has begun. Then "the righteous requirement of the law" will "be fulfilled in us who do not walk according to the flesh but according to the Spirit." The language of the heart will be: "Oh, how I love Your law! It is my meditation all the day." (Romans 3:31; 6:2; 1 John 5:3; Romans 8:4; Psalm 119:97.)

Without the law, people have no true conviction of sin and feel no need to repent. They do not realize how much they need the atoning blood of Christ. They accept the hope of salvation without a radical change of heart or reformation of life. So there are many superficial conversions, and many people join the church who have never been united to Christ.

What Is Sanctification?

Wrong ideas of sanctification also spring from neglecting or rejecting the divine law. These theories, involving false teachings and dangerous practical results, are often popular.

Paul wrote, "This is the will of God, your sanctification." The Bible clearly teaches what sanctification is and how we can attain it. The Savior prayed for His disciples: "Sanctify them by Your truth. Your word is truth." And Paul taught that believers are to be "sanctified by the Holy Spirit." (1 Thessalonians 4:3; John 17:17; Romans 15:16.)

What is the work of the Holy Spirit? Jesus told His disciples, "When He, the Spirit of truth, has come, He will guide you into all truth" (John 16:13). And the psalmist says, "Your law is truth." Since the law of God is "holy and just and good," a character formed by obeying that law will be holy. Christ is a perfect example of a character like this. He says: "I have kept My Father's commandments." "I always do those things that please Him." (John 15:10; 8:29.) The followers of Christ are to become like Him—by the grace of God to form characters in harmony with the principles of His holy law. This is biblical sanctification.

Only Through Faith

We can accomplish this work only through faith in Christ, by the power of the Spirit of God living within us. Christians will feel sin tempting them, but they will keep up a constant warfare against it. They need Christ's help to do this. Human weakness unites with divine strength, and faith exclaims, "Thanks be to God, who gives us the victory through our Lord Jesus Christ" (1 Corinthians 15:57).

The work of sanctification is progressive. When the sinner finds peace with God at conversion, the Christian life has just begun. Now he is to "go on to perfection," to grow up "to the measure of the stature of the fullness of Christ." "I press toward the goal for the prize of the upward call of God in Christ Jesus." (Hebrews 6:1; Ephesians 4:13; Philippians 3:14.)

Those who experience the sanctification of the Bible will be humble. They see how unworthy they are in contrast with the purity and perfection of God. The prophet Daniel was an example of true sanctification. Instead of claiming to be pure and holy, this honored prophet identified himself with the really sinful of Israel as he pleaded before God for his people. (See Daniel 9:15, 18, 20.)

Those who walk in the shadow of Calvary's cross will not exalt themselves or make boastful claims that they are free from sin. They feel that it was their sin that caused the agony that broke the heart of the Son of God, and this thought leads them to deep humility. Those who live closest to Jesus understand most clearly how frail and sinful humanity is, and their only hope is in the merit of a crucified and risen Savior.

The sanctification now gaining notice in the religious world carries a spirit of self-exaltation and a disregard for the law of God that identify it as foreign to the Bible. Those who teach it claim that sanctification happens instantly, and by this means, through "faith alone," they reach perfect holiness. "Only believe," they say, "and the blessing is yours." No further effort is supposed to be required from the receiver. At the same time they deny the authority of God's law, claiming that they are released from any obligation to keep the commandments. But is it possible to be holy without coming into harmony with the principles that express God's nature and will?

The Word of God testifies against this traplike doctrine of faith without works. It is not faith that claims God's favor without complying with the conditions on which He grants mercy. It is presumption. (See James 2:14–24.)

Let none deceive themselves that they can become holy while they willfully violate one of God's requirements. Known sin silences the witnessing voice of the Spirit and separates the heart from God. Though John dwells so much on love, he does not hesitate to reveal the true character of those who claim to be sanctified while living in violation of God's law. "He who says, 'I know Him,' and does

not keep His commandments, is a liar, and the truth is not in him. But whoever keeps His word, truly the love of God is perfected in him" (1 John 2:4, 5). Here is the test of everyone's profession. If people belittle and make light of God's law, if they break "one of the least of these commandments" and teach others to do the same (Matthew 5:19), we may know that their claims have no foundation.

The claim to be without sin is evidence that the person who makes this claim is far from holy. Such a one has no true concept of God's infinite purity and holiness, and of how hateful and evil sin is. The greater the distance between us and Christ, the more righteous we appear in our own eyes.

Biblical Sanctification

Sanctification includes the entire being—spirit, soul, and body (see 1 Thessalonians 5:23). Christians are called to present their bodies "a living sacrifice, holy, acceptable to God" (Romans 12:1). Every practice that weakens physical or mental strength unfits us for the service of our Creator. Those who love God with all their heart will constantly try to bring every power of their being into harmony with the laws that make them better able to do His will. They will not weaken or defile the offering they present to their heavenly Father by indulging their appetites or passions.

Every sinful practice tends to numb and deaden the mental and spiritual understanding; the Word or Spirit of God can make only a feeble impression on the heart. "Let us cleanse ourselves from all filthiness of the flesh and spirit, perfecting holiness in the fear of God" (2 Corinthians 7:1).

How many professed Christians are degrading their godlike manhood or womanhood by gluttony, by wine drinking, by forbidden pleasure! And the church too often encourages the evil, to fill her treasury when love for Christ is too feeble to do it. If Jesus were to enter the churches of today and see the feasting that goes on there in the name of religion, would He not drive out those who desecrate His house that way, as He banished the moneychangers from the temple?

"Do you not know that your body is the temple of the Holy Spirit who is in you, whom you have from God, and you are not your own? For you were bought at a price; therefore glorify God in your body and in your spirit, which are God's" (1 Corinthians 6:19, 20). Christians whose bodies are the temple of the Holy Spirit will not be enslaved by an evil habit. Their powers belong to Christ. Their property is the Lord's. How could they squander this treasure that He has entrusted to them?

Every year professed Christians spend an immense amount of money on harmful pleasures. They rob God in tithes and offerings, while they consume on the altar of destroying lust more than they give to relieve the poor or support the gospel. If all who claim Christ's name were truly sanctified, they would give their money generously into the Lord's treasury instead of spending it for needless and hurtful indulgences. Christians would set an example of temperance and self-sacrifice. Then they would be the light of the world.

"The lust of the flesh, the lust of the eyes, and the pride of life" (1 John 2:16) control most people. But Christ's followers have a holier calling. "Come out from among them and be separate, says the Lord. Do not touch what is unclean." To those who comply with the conditions, God promises, "'I will receive you.' 'I will be a Father to you, and you shall be my sons and daughters, says the Lord Almighty'" (2 Corinthians 6:17, 18).

Direct Access to God

Every step of faith and obedience brings the believer into closer connection with the Light of the World. The bright beams of the Sun of Righteousness shine on the servants of God, and they are to reflect His rays. The stars tell us that there is a light in heaven whose glory makes them bright. In the same way, Christians reveal to the world that there is a God on the throne whose character is worthy of praise and imitation. The holiness of His character will be visible in His witnesses.

Through the merits of Christ we have access to the throne of Infinite Power. "He who did not spare His own Son, but delivered Him up for us all, how shall He not with Him also freely give us all things?" Jesus says: "If you then, being evil, know how to give good gifts to your children, how much more will your heavenly Father give the Holy Spirit to those who ask Him!" "If you ask anything in My name, I will do it." "Ask, and you will receive, that your joy may be full." (Romans 8:32; Luke 11:13; John

14:14; 16:24.)

It is the privilege of all to live in such a way that God will approve and bless them. It is not the will of our heavenly Father for us always to live in condemnation and darkness. It is not true humility if we go around with our heads bowed down and our hearts filled with thoughts of self. We may go to Jesus and be cleansed and stand before the law without shame and remorse.

Through Jesus the fallen sons of Adam become "sons of God." "He is not ashamed to call them brethren." The Christian's life should be one of faith, victory, and joy in God. "The joy of the LORD is your strength." "Rejoice always, pray without ceasing, in everything give thanks; for this is the will of God in Christ Jesus for you." (Hebrews 2:11; Nehemiah 8:10; 1 Thessalonians 5:16–18.)

These things are the fruits of Bible conversion and sanctification. It is only because people treat the great principles of righteousness shown in the law with such indifference that these fruits are so rare. This is why we see so little of that deep, lasting work of the Spirit that used to accompany revivals.

It is by beholding that we become changed. As people have neglected those sacred commandments in which God has revealed the perfection and holiness of His character, and their minds have been attracted to human teachings and theories, a decline of holy living in the church has followed. Only when the law of God is restored to its rightful position can a revival of authentic faith and godliness take place among His professed people.

Facing Our Life Record

I watched till thrones were put in place, and the Ancient of Days was seated; His garment was white as snow, and the hair of His head was like pure wool. His throne was a fiery flame, its wheels a burning fire; a fiery stream issued and came forth from before Him. A thousand thousands ministered to Him; ten thousand times ten thousand stood before Him. The court was seated, and the books were opened" (Daniel 7:9, 10).

This is how Daniel saw the great day when the lives of all humanity pass in review before the Judge of all the earth. The Ancient of Days is God the Father. He is the source of all being, the origin of all law, and He will preside in the judgment. And holy angels will be there as ministers and witnesses.

"And behold, One like the Son of Man, coming with the clouds of heaven! He came to the Ancient of Days, and they brought Him near before Him. Then to Him was given dominion and glory and a kingdom, that all people, nations, and languages should serve Him. His dominion is an everlasting dominion, which shall not pass away" (Daniel 7:13, 14).

The coming of Christ described here is not His second coming to the earth. He comes to the Ancient of Days in heaven to receive a kingdom, which will be given Him when His work as mediator is done. It is this coming, and not His second advent to the earth, that was to take place at the end of the 2,300 days in 1844. Our great High Priest enters the Holy of Holies to carry out His last priestly service on our behalf.

In the earthly, symbolic service, only those whose sins were transferred to the sanctuary had a part in the Day of Atonement. So in the great final atonement and investigative judgment, the only cases considered are of those who profess to be the people of God. The judgment of the wicked is a separate work at a later time. Judgment must "begin at the house of God" (1 Peter 4:17).

The record books in heaven will determine the judgment's decisions. The book of life contains the names of all who have ever entered the service of God. Jesus told His disciples, "Rejoice because your names are written in heaven." Paul speaks of his fellow workers "whose names are in the Book of Life." Daniel declares that God's people will be delivered, "every one who is found written in the book." And John the revelator says that only those whose names "are written in the Lamb's Book of Life" will enter the City of God. (Luke 10:20; Philippians 4:3; Daniel 12:1; Revelation 21:27.)

In "a book of remembrance" God has recorded the good deeds of "those who fear the LORD and who meditate on His name." Every temptation resisted, every evil overcome, every word of pity expressed, every act of sacrifice, every sorrow endured for Christ's sake is recorded. "You number my wanderings; put my tears into Your bottle; are they not in Your book?" (Malachi 3:16; Psalm 56:8.)

Secret Motives

There is a record also of people's sins. "God will bring every work into judgment, including every secret thing, whether good evil." "For every idle word men may speak, they will give account of it in the day of judgment. For by your words you will be justified, and by your words you will be condemned." Secret motives appear in the record, for God "will both bring to light the hidden things of darkness and reveal the counsels of the hearts." (Ecclesiastes 12:14; Matthew 12:36, 37; 1 Corinthians 4:5.) Next to each name in the books of heaven is entered every wrong word, every selfish act, every unfulfilled duty, and every secret sin. Heaven-sent warnings or reproofs neglected, wasted moments, the influence exerted for good or for evil, with its far-reaching results, are all listed by the recording angel.

The Standard of Judgment

The law of God is the standard in the judgment. "Fear God and keep His commandments, for this is man's all. For God will bring every work into judgment." "So speak and so do as those who will be judged by the law of liberty." (Ecclesiastes 12:13, 14; James 2:12.)

Those "considered worthy" will have part in the resurrection of the just. Jesus said: "Those who are considered worthy of a place in that age and in the resurrection from the dead . . . are children of God, being children of the resurrection." "Those who have done good" will come out from the grave "to the resurrection of life." (Luke 20:35, 36, NRSV; John 5:29.) The righteous dead will not be raised until after the judgment that accounts them worthy of "the resurrection of life." So they will not be present in person when God examines their records and decides their cases.

Jesus will stand as their lawyer, to plead their cases before God. "If anyone sins, we have an Advocate with the Father, Jesus Christ the righteous." "For Christ has not entered the holy places made with hands, which are copies of the true, but into heaven itself, now to appear in the presence of God for us." "Therefore He is also able to save to the uttermost those who come to God through Him, since He always lives to make intercession for them." (1 John 2:1; Hebrews 9:24; 7:25.)

As the books of record are opened in the judgment, the lives of all who have believed on Jesus come in review before God. Beginning with those who first lived on the earth, our Advocate presents the cases of each generation after the other. Every name is mentioned, every case investigated.

Names are accepted, names rejected. When any have sins remaining on the books of record, unrepented of and unforgiven, their names will be blotted out of the book of life. The Lord declared to Moses, "Whoever has sinned against Me, I will blot him out of My book" (Exodus 32:33).

All who have truly repented and by faith have claimed the blood of Christ as their atoning sacrifice have had pardon entered in the books of heaven. Since they have become partakers of the righteousness of Christ and their characters are found to be in harmony with the law of God, their sins will be blotted out, and they will be accounted worthy of eternal life. The Lord declares: "I, even I, am He who blots out your transgressions for My own sake; and I will not remember your sins." "He who overcomes shall be clothed in white garments, and I will . . . confess his name before My Father and before His angels." "Therefore whoever confesses Me before men, him I will also confess before My Father who is in heaven. But whoever denies Me before men, him I will also deny before My Father who is in heaven." (Isaiah 43:25; Revelation 3:5; Matthew 10:32, 33.)

Jesus, the divine Intercessor, asks that all who have overcome through faith in His blood be restored to their Eden home and crowned as joint heirs with Himself to "the former dominion" (Micah 4:8). Christ now asks that God's plan in our creation be carried into effect as if we had never fallen. He asks not only for pardon and justification for His people, but for a share in His glory and a seat with Him on His throne.

While Jesus is pleading for the subjects of His grace, Satan accuses them before God. He points to the record of their lives, their defects of character, their unlikeness to Christ, and to all the sins he has tempted them to commit. Because of these he claims them as his subjects.

Jesus does not excuse their sins, but He shows their repentance and faith. Claiming forgiveness for them, He lifts His wounded hands before the Father, saying, I have graven them on the palms of My hands. "The sacrifices of God are a broken spirit, a broken and a contrite heart—these, O God, You will not despise" (Psalm 51:17).

The Lord Rebukes Satan

And to the accuser He says: "The LORD rebuke you, Satan! The LORD who has chosen Jerusalem rebuke you! Is this not a brand plucked from the fire?" (Zechariah 3:2). Christ will clothe His faithful ones with His own righteousness, that He may present them to His Father "a glorious church, not having spot or wrinkle or any such thing" (Ephesians 5:27).

This is how they will experience the complete fulfillment of the new-covenant promise: "I will forgive their iniquity, and their sin I will remember no more." " 'In those days and in that time,' says the LORD, 'the iniquity of Israel shall be sought, but there shall be none; and the sins of Judah, but they shall not be found.' " "And it shall come to pass that he who is left in Zion and remains in Jerusalem will be called holy—everyone who is recorded among the living in Jerusalem." (Jeremiah 31:34; 50:20; Isaiah 4:3.)

The Blotting Out of Sins

The work of the investigative judgment and blotting out of sins will take place before the second coming of Jesus. In the symbolic service the high priest came out and blessed the congregation. In the same way, when His work as mediator is over, Christ will appear "apart from sin, for salvation" (Hebrews 9:28).

In removing the sins from the sanctuary, the priest confessed them on the head of the scapegoat. Christ will place all these sins on Satan, the instigator of sin. The scapegoat was sent away into "the wilderness" (Leviticus 16:22). Satan, bearing the guilt of sins he has caused God's people to commit, will be confined to the ruined earth for a thousand years and then will suffer the penalty of fire that will destroy the wicked. In this way the plan of redemption will be complete when sin is finally eradicated.

At the Appointed Time

At the appointed time—the close of the 2,300 days in 1844—the work of investigation and blotting out of sins began, and continues now. Sins that we do not repent of and forsake will not be blotted out of the books of record. Angels of God witnessed each sin and registered it. We may deny our sin, hide it from father, mother, wife, children, and associates, but it is laid bare before heaven. God is not deceived by appearances. He makes no mistakes. Those who are corrupt in heart may deceive others, but God reads the inner life.

What a solemn thought! The mightiest conquerer on earth cannot call back the record of a single day. Our acts, our words, even our secret motives, though forgotten by us, will bear their testimony to justify or condemn.

The judgment will examine the use we have made of every talent. How have we used our time, our pen, our voice, our money, our influence? What have we done for Christ in the person of the poor, the afflicted, the orphan, or the widow? What have we done with the light and truth God has given us? Only the love shown by our deeds is counted genuine. In the sight of Heaven, love alone gives value to any act.

Hidden Selfishness Revealed

Hidden selfishness stands revealed in the books of heaven. How often people have given to Satan the time, thought, and strength that belonged to Christ. Professed followers of Christ are absorbed in getting worldly possessions or enjoying earthly pleasures. They sacrifice money, time, and strength for display and self-indulgence, devoting only a few moments to prayer, to searching the Scriptures, and to confessing sin.

Satan invents countless schemes to occupy our minds. The archdeceiver hates the great truths that call attention to an atoning sacrifice and an all-powerful Mediator. For Satan, everything depends on diverting minds from Jesus.

Those who want to share the benefits of the Savior's mediation for us should allow nothing to interfere with their duty to develop holiness in the fear of God. Instead of giving precious hours to pleasure or to money-making, they should devote time to the prayerful study of the Word of Truth. They should clearly understand the sanctuary and the investigative judgment. Everyone needs a knowledge of the position and work of our great High Priest. Otherwise it will be impossible to exercise the faith that is essential at this time.

The sanctuary in heaven is the center of Christ's work for humanity. It concerns every person living on earth. It opens the plan of redemption to our view, bringing us down to the close of the conflict between righteousness and sin.

The Intercession of Christ

Christ's intercession for us in the sanctuary above is as essential to the plan of salvation as was His death on the cross. By His death He began that work that He ascended to complete in heaven. We must enter by faith into the sanctuary, "where the forerunner has entered for us" (Hebrews 6:20). There the light from the cross is reflected. There we gain a clearer insight into the mysteries of redemption.

"He who covers his sins will not prosper, but whoever confesses and forsakes them will have mercy" (Proverbs 28:13). If those who excuse their faults could see how Satan taunts Christ with their behavior, they would confess their sins and put them away. Through defects in the character, Satan works to gain control of the whole mind. He knows that if we cherish any of our defects, he will succeed. Therefore he constantly seeks to deceive the followers of Christ with his fatal lie that it is impossible for them to overcome. But Jesus declared to all who would follow Him: "My grace is sufficient for you." "My yoke is easy and My burden is light." (2 Corinthians 12:9; Matthew 11:30.) None should think their character defects are incurable. God will give faith and grace to overcome them.

We are now living in the great day of atonement. While the high priest was making atonement for Israel, all were required to afflict their souls by repentance for sin. Likewise, all who want their names to be kept in the book of life should now afflict their souls before God by true repentance. There must be deep, faithful heart-searching. The frivolous spirit that so many indulge must be put away. There is earnest warfare ahead for all who want to subdue the evil tendencies that try to control the life. Every one must be found without "spot or wrinkle or any such thing" (Ephesians 5:27).

At this time above all others it is important for every person to heed the Savior's counsel, "Watch and pray; for you do not know when the time is" (Mark 13:33).

The Destiny of All Decided

Probation closes a short time before the Lord appears in the clouds of heaven. Looking forward to that time, Christ declares: " 'He who is unjust, let him be unjust still; he who is filthy, let him be filthy still; he who is righteous, let him be righteous still; he who is holy, let him be holy still.' 'And behold, I am coming quickly, and My reward is with Me, to give to every one according to his work' " (Revelation 22:11, 12.)

People will be planting and building, eating and drinking, all unaware that God has pronounced the final decision in the sanctuary above. Before the Flood, after Noah entered the ark, God shut him in and shut the ungodly out; but for seven days the people continued their pleasure-loving life and mocked the warnings of judgment. The Savior says, "So also will the coming of the Son of Man be." Silently, as unnoticed as the midnight thief, the hour will come that marks the settling of everyone's destiny. "Watch therefore, . . . lest, coming suddenly, he find you sleeping." (Matthew 24:39; Mark 13:35, 36.)

Those who grow weary of watching and turn to the attractions of the world are in a dangerous condition. While the businessman is absorbed in pursuing profit, while the pleasure-lover is seeking indulgence, while the daughter of fashion is arranging her adornments—it may be in that hour the Judge of all the earth will pronounce the sentence, "You have been weighed in the balances, and found wanting" (Daniel 5:27).

Why Was Sin Permitted?

M any see the work of evil, with its pain and loss, and question how this can exist under the rulership of One who is infinite in wisdom, power, and love. Those who are inclined to doubt quickly take this as an excuse for rejecting the words of the Bible. Tradition and wrong interpretations have clouded the Bible's teaching about God's character, the nature of His government, and the principles of how He deals with sin.

It is impossible to explain the origin of sin in a way that gives a reason for its existence. Yet we can understand enough about sin's beginning and final end to show clearly God's justice and goodness. In no way was God responsible for sin. He did not just remove His divine grace, nor was there anything lacking in the divine government, that provided a cause for the rebellion. Sin is an intruder for whose presence no one can give a reason. To excuse it is to defend it. If we could find an excuse for it, it would no longer be sin. Sin is the expression of a principle that is at war with the law of love, which is the foundation of God's government.

Before sin began, there was peace and joy everywhere in the universe. Love for God was supreme, love for one another unselfish. Christ the Only Begotten of God was one with the eternal Father in nature, in character, and in purpose—the only being who could enter into all the counsels and plans of God. "By Him all things were created that are in heaven . . . , whether thrones or dominions or principalities or powers" (Colossians 1:16).

Since the law of love is the foundation of God's government, the happiness of all created beings depended on their willing harmony with its principles of righteousness. God takes no pleasure in forced allegiance, and He grants everyone freedom of will, so that they can choose to serve Him voluntarily.

But one of God's created beings chose to misuse this freedom. Sin originated with an angel who, next to Christ, had been the being God honored the most. Before his fall, Lucifer was chief of the covering cherubs, holy and pure. "Thus says the Lord GOD: 'You were the seal of perfection, full of wisdom and perfect in beauty. You were in Eden, the garden of God; every precious stone was your covering. . . . You were the anointed cherub who covers; I established you; you were on the holy mountain of God; you walked back and forth in the midst of fiery stones. You were perfect in your ways from the day you were created, till iniquity was found in you. . . . Your heart was lifted up because of your beauty; you corrupted your wisdom for the sake of your splendor.' " "You have set your heart as the heart of a god." "You have said . . . , 'I will exalt my throne above the stars of God; I will also sit on the mount of the congregation . . . ; I will ascend above the heights of the clouds, I will be like the Most High.' " (Ezekiel 28:12–15, 17; 28:6; Isaiah 14:13, 14.)

Coveting the honor that the Father had given His Son, this prince of angels wanted the power that was Christ's alone to use. A note of discord now marred heaven's harmonies. Seeing someone exalt himself gave the other angels, who hold God's glory as supreme, a strange dread of something evil. The heavenly councils pleaded with Lucifer. The Son of God showed him the goodness and justice of the Creator and the sacred nature of His law. In rejecting it, Lucifer would dishonor his Maker and bring ruin on himself. But the warning only stirred his resistance. Lucifer allowed his jealousy of Christ to control him.

Pride fed his desire for supremacy. The high honors God had given Lucifer did not make him grateful to the Creator. He wanted to be equal with God. Yet everyone recognized that the Son of God was the Ruler of heaven, one with the Father in power and authority. Christ participated in all the councils of God, but Lucifer was not allowed to enter into the divine plans. This mighty angel questioned, "Why should Christ have the supremacy? Why is He honored like this above Lucifer?"

Discontent Among the Angels

Leaving his place in God's presence, Lucifer went out to spread discontent among the angels. With mysterious secrecy, hiding his real purpose under an appearance of reverence for God, he tried to make the angels dissatisfied with the laws that governed heavenly beings. He suggested that these laws were unnecessary and held them back. Since their natures were holy, he urged that angels should follow their own wills. God had dealt unfairly with him by giving supreme honor to Christ. He claimed he was not trying to exalt himself but was seeking to win liberty for every being in heaven, so that each one could reach a higher level of existence.

God was patient with Lucifer. He did not remove him from his honored position even when he began to make false claims to the angels. Again and again God offered him pardon if he would repent and submit. God made efforts that only infinite love could devise to convince him of his error. Discontent had never before been known in heaven. At first, Lucifer himself did not understand the real nature of his feelings. As God showed that there was no reason for his dissatisfaction, Lucifer was convinced that the divine claims were right and that he ought to acknowledge them to all heaven. If he had done this, he would have saved himself and many angels. If he had been willing to return to God, satisfied to fill the place God had given him, God would have reinstated him to his position. But pride would not let him submit. He claimed that he did not need to repent, and he fully committed himself to the great controversy against his Maker.

He now applied all the powers of his master mind to deception, to gain the sympathy of the angels. Satan claimed that God had judged him wrongly and had restricted his liberty. After misrepresenting Christ's words he moved on to telling actual lies, accusing the Son of God of plotting to humiliate him before the inhabitants of heaven.

All whom he could not win to his side he accused of being indifferent to the concerns of heavenly beings. He resorted to misrepresenting the Creator. He tried to perplex the angels with subtle arguments about God's plans. Everything simple he shrouded in mystery, and by clever perversion he made the plainest statements of God appear doubtful. His high position gave greater credibility to his claims. He persuaded many to join him in rebellion.

Disaffection Ripens Into Active Revolt

God in His wisdom allowed Satan to carry on his work, until the spirit of dissent ripened into revolt. It was necessary for God to allow him to develop his plans fully, so that anyone could see their true nature. Lucifer was greatly loved by the heavenly beings, and his influence over them was strong. God's government included not only the inhabitants of heaven, but of all the worlds He had created. Satan thought that if he could bring the angels with him in rebellion, he could

also bring the other worlds. Using false reasoning and fraud, he had great power to deceive. Even the loyal angels could not fully discern his character or see where his work was leading.

Satan had been so highly honored, and he had cloaked all his actions with so much mystery, that it was difficult to show the angels the true nature of his work. Sin would not appear to be the evil thing it was until it was fully developed. Holy beings could not recognize what would be the results of setting aside God's law. At first Satan claimed to be trying to promote God's honor and the good of all of heaven's inhabitants.

In His response to sin, God could use only righteousness and truth. Satan could use what God could not—flattery and deceit. Everyone needed to understand the true character of this angel who wanted God's position. He must have time to reveal himself by his evil works.

Satan blamed God for the discord that his own actions had caused in heaven. He declared that all evil was the result of God's government. So it was necessary that he demonstrate how his proposed changes in God's law would work out. His own acts must condemn him. The whole universe must see the deceiver unmasked.

Even after deciding that Satan could no longer remain in heaven, Infinite Wisdom did not destroy him. The loyalty of God's creatures must rest on the conviction that He is just and fair. The inhabitants of heaven and of other worlds were not prepared to understand the consequences of sin, so they could not then have seen the justice and mercy of God if He had destroyed Satan at that time. If God had blotted him out of existence immediately, they would have served God from fear rather than from love. God would not have fully destroyed the deceiver's influence nor wiped out the spirit of rebellion. For the good of the universe through eternal ages, Satan must develop his principles more fully. Then all created beings would be able to see his charges against the divine government in their true light.

Satan's rebellion was to be a testimony to the universe about the terrible results of sin. His rule would show the fruit of setting aside God's authority. The history of this terrible experiment of rebellion would be a safeguard forever to all holy beings to save them from sin and its punishment.

When the announcement came that the great usurper must be expelled from heaven with all his sympathizers, the rebel leader boldly swore his contempt for the Creator's law. He denounced the divine statutes as a restriction of liberty and declared his intention to abolish all law. Freed from this restraint, he claimed, the inhabitants of heaven could achieve a higher state of existence.

Banished From Heaven

Satan and his followers threw the blame for their rebellion on Christ. They declared that if they had not been rebuked, they would never have rebelled. Stubborn and defiant, yet blasphemously claiming to be innocent victims of oppressive power, the chief rebel and his sympathizers were banished from heaven (see Revelation 12:7–9).

Satan's spirit still inspires rebellion on earth in unrepentant people. Like him they promise liberty through violating God's law. Condemning sin still stirs up hatred. Satan leads people to justify themselves and to try to get the sympathy of others in their sin. Instead of correcting their errors, they spread resentment of the one who points out their sin, as if he were the cause of the difficulty.

Satan persuaded Adam and Eve to sin by using the same misrepresentation of God's character as he had practiced in heaven. He made them think that God was severe and tyrannical. Then he claimed that God's unjust restrictions had led to our first parents' fall, as they had led to his own rebellion.

In banishing Satan from heaven, God declared His justice and honor. But when humanity sinned, God gave evidence of His love by offering up His Son to die for the fallen race. In the atonement we see the character of God revealed. The mighty argument of the cross demonstrates that sin was in no way the fault of God's government. During the Savior's earthly ministry, the great deceiver's character was unmasked. The daring blasphemy of his demand that Christ worship him, the unsleeping evil intent that hunted Jesus from place to place, inspiring the hearts of priests and people to reject His love and to cry, "Crucify Him! Crucify Him!"—all this drew the amazement and indignation of the universe. The prince of evil exerted all his power and crafty skills to destroy

Jesus. Satan used human beings as his agents to fill the Savior's life with suffering and sorrow. And on Calvary the pent-up fires of envy and spite, hatred and revenge, burst out against the Son of God.

Now Satan's guilt stood out plainly, without excuse. He had revealed his true character. Satan's lying charges against God's character appeared as they truly were. He had accused God of seeking to exalt Himself by requiring obedience from His creatures. He had declared that while the Creator demanded self-denial from all others, He Himself practiced no self-denial and made no sacrifice. Now it was clear that the Ruler of the universe had made the greatest sacrifice that love could make, for "God was in Christ reconciling the world to Himself" (2 Corinthians 5:19). In order to destroy sin, Christ had humbled Himself and become obedient to the point of death.

An Argument in Our Behalf

All heaven saw God's justice revealed. Lucifer had claimed that the sinful race was beyond redemption. But the penalty of the law fell on Him who was equal with God. Sinners were now free to accept the righteousness of Christ and by repentance and humility triumph over Satan's power.

But Christ did not come to earth to die just so that He could redeem humanity. He came to demonstrate to all the worlds that God's law is unchangeable. The death of Christ proves that the law is permanent and demonstrates that justice and mercy are the foundation of God's government. In the final judgment it will be clear that no cause for sin exists. When the Judge of all the earth demands of Satan, "Why have you rebelled against Me?" the originator of evil will have no excuse to offer.

The Savior's dying cry, "It is finished," rang the death knell for Satan. The long-standing great controversy was then decided, the final eradication of evil made certain. When the day comes, " 'burning like an oven, . . . all the proud, yes, all who do wickedly will be stubble. And the day which is coming shall burn them up,' says the LORD of hosts, 'that will leave them neither root nor branch' " (Malachi 4:1).

Evil will never arise again. The law of God will be honored as the law of liberty. A tested and proved creation will never again turn from loyalty to Him who has demonstrated that His character is fathomless love and infinite wisdom.

Satan and Humanity at War

I will put enmity between you and the woman, and between your seed and her Seed; He shall bruise your head, and you shall bruise His heel" (Genesis 3:15). This enmity, or hostility, is not natural. When Adam and Eve broke the divine law, their natures became evil, in harmony with Satan. Fallen angels and wicked people united in desperate companionship. If God had not intervened, Satan and mankind would have formed an alliance against Heaven, and the whole human family would have been united in opposition to God.

When Satan heard that enmity would exist between himself and the woman, and between his seed and her seed, he knew that by some means human beings were going to be enabled to resist his power.

Grace from Christ

Christ implants in us resistance against Satan. Without this converting grace and renewing power, we would continue as Satan's servants, always ready to obey him. But the new principle in the heart creates conflict; the power that Christ gives enables us to resist the tyrant. To hate sin instead of loving it displays a principle that is entirely from above.

The world's reception of Jesus strikingly displayed the antagonism between Christ and Satan. The purity and holiness of Christ stirred up the hatred of the ungodly against Him. His self-denial was a constant rebuke to a proud, sensual people. Satan and evil angels joined with evil human beings against the Champion of truth. They show the same enmity toward Christ's followers. Whoever resists temptation will ignite Satan's anger. Christ and Satan cannot harmonize. "All who desire to live godly in Christ Jesus will suffer persecution" (2 Timothy 3:12).

Satan's representatives try to deceive Christ's followers and draw them away from their loyalty. They twist Scripture to achieve their goal. The spirit that put Christ to death moves the wicked to destroy His followers. All this is foreshadowed in that first prophecy: "I will put enmity between you and the woman, and between your seed and her Seed."

Why is it that Satan meets no more resistance than he does? Because the soldiers of Christ have so little real connection with Christ. Sin is not repulsive to them like it was to their Master. They do not go against it with determined resistance. They are blind to the character of the prince of darkness. So many do not know that their enemy is a mighty general, warring against Christ. Even ministers of the gospel overlook the evidences of Satan's activity. They seem to ignore the fact that he even exists.

An Alert Enemy

This alert enemy is intruding his presence into every household, every street, in the churches, in national councils, in courts of justice. He is busy perplexing, deceiving, seducing, everywhere ruining the souls and bodies of men, women, and children. He breaks up families, planting seeds of hatred, strife, rebellion, and murder. And the world seems to think that God has decreed these things and so they must exist. All who are not committed followers of Christ are servants of Satan. When Christians choose to associate with the ungodly, they expose themselves to temptation. Satan hides himself from view and draws his deceptive covering over their eyes.

Following worldly customs converts the church to the world, never the world to Christ. Familiarity with sin will cause it to seem less repulsive. When we encounter trials because we are doing what God wants, we may be sure that He will protect us. But if we place ourselves where we will be tempted, sooner or later we will fall.

The tempter often works most successfully through those whom we least suspect of being under his control. Talent and culture are gifts of God, but when these lead away from Him, they become a trap. Many people with cultured intellects and pleasant manners are polished instruments in the hands of Satan.

Never forget the inspired warning ringing down the centuries to our time: "Be sober, be vigilant; because your adversary the devil walks about like a roaring lion, seeking whom he may devour." "Put on the whole armor of God, that you may be able to stand against the wiles of the devil." (1 Peter 5:8; Ephesians 6:11.) Our great enemy is preparing for his last campaign. All who follow Jesus will have conflicts with this enemy. The more nearly Christians imitate the divine Pattern, the more surely they will make themselves a target for the attacks of Satan.

Satan attacked Christ with fierce and subtle temptations, but Jesus repulsed him in every conflict. Those victories make it possible for us to conquer. Christ will give strength to all who seek it. Satan cannot overcome any without their own consent. The tempter has no power to control the will or force the person to sin. He can cause distress, but not defilement. The fact that Christ conquered should inspire His followers with courage to fight the battle against sin and Satan.

Evil Spirits

Angels of God and evil spirits are plainly revealed in Scripture and are interwoven with human history. Many think that the holy angels who "minister for those who will inherit salvation" (Hebrews 1:14) are actually the spirits of the dead. But the Scriptures present proof that they are not disembodied spirits of the dead.

Before God created human beings, angels were in existence, for when the foundations of the earth were laid, "the morning stars sang together, and all the sons of God shouted for joy" (Job 38:7). After the fall of Adam and Eve but before any human being had died, God sent angels to guard the tree of life. Angels are superior to humans, for man was made "a little lower than the angels" (Psalm 8:5).

Says the prophet, "I heard the voice of many angels around the throne." In the presence of the King of kings they wait—"ministers of His, who do His pleasure," "heeding the voice of His word," "an innumerable company." (Revelation 5:11; Psalm 103:21, 20; Hebrews 12:22.) They go out as God's messengers, "in appearance like a flash of lightning," their flight is so swift. The angel that appeared at the Savior's tomb, with his face "like lightning," caused the soldiers to quake with fear of him, and they "became like dead men." When Sennacherib blasphemed God and threatened Israel, "the angel of the LORD went out, and killed in the camp of the Assyrians one hundred and eighty-five thousand." (Ezekiel 1:14; Matthew 28:3, 4; 2 Kings 19:35.)

God sends angels on missions of mercy to His children. To Abraham, with promises of blessing; to Lot, to rescue him from Sodom's doom; to Elijah, about to die in the desert; to Elisha, with chariots and horses of fire when he was surrounded by his enemies; to Daniel, when he was abandoned to become the lion's prey; to Peter, doomed to death in Herod's dungeon; to the apostles in Philippi's jail; to Paul in the stormy night on the sea; to open the mind of Cornelius to receive the gospel; to send Peter with the message of salvation to the Gentile stranger—in all these ways holy angels have ministered to God's people.

Guardian Angels

God has appointed a guardian angel to every follower of Christ. "The angel of the LORD encamps all around those who fear Him, and delivers them." Speaking of those who believe in Him, Jesus said, "In heaven their angels always see the face of My Father." (Psalm 34:7; Matthew 18:10.) God's people are exposed to the unsleeping hatred of the prince of darkness, but God assures them that the angels never stop guarding them. God gives them this assurance because they will have to face mighty agencies of evil—agencies that are numerous, determined, and untiring.

Evil Angels Oppose God's Plans

Evil spirits were originally created sinless. They were equal in nature, power, and glory with the holy beings that are now God's messengers. But now they are fallen because of sin, and they have joined together to dishonor God and destroy humanity. United with Satan in rebellion, they cooperate with him in warfare against divine authority.

Old Testament history mentions their existence, but during the time when Christ was on earth evil spirits showed their power in the most striking ways. Christ had come to redeem humanity, and Satan was determined to control the world. He had succeeded in establishing idol worship in every part of the earth except Palestine. Christ came to the only land not fully yielded to the tempter, stretched out His arms of love, and invited all to find pardon and peace in Him. The angels of darkness understood that if Christ's mission were successful, their rule would end soon.

The New Testament clearly states that people have been possessed with demons. Such people were not simply suffering with disease from natural causes. Christ recognized the direct presence and influence of evil spirits. The demon-possessed men at Gadara were wretched maniacs, writhing, foaming, and raging, and they were doing violence to themselves and putting everyone else in danger who came near them. Their bleeding, disfigured bodies and deranged minds made a spectacle that pleased the prince of darkness. One of the demons controlling the sufferers said, "My name is Legion; for we are many" (Mark 5:9). In the Roman army a legion consisted of from three to five thousand men. At the command of Jesus the evil spirits fled from their victims, leaving them subdued, intelligent, and gentle. But the demons swept a herd of pigs into the sea. To the people living in Gadara, the loss outweighed the blessing Christ had brought, and so they asked the divine Healer to leave. (See Matthew 8:23–34.) By blaming Jesus for their loss, Satan stirred up the selfish fears of the people and prevented them from listening to His words.

Christ allowed the evil spirits to destroy the pigs as a rebuke to Jews who were raising unclean animals for profit. If Christ had not restrained the demons, they would have plunged not only the pigs, but also their keepers and owners into the sea.

Furthermore, God permitted this event so that the disciples could witness the cruel power of Satan on both people and animals and would not be deceived by his delusions. Jesus also wanted the people to see His power to break Satan's hold and release his captives.

Though Jesus Himself went away, the men He had delivered so amazingly remained there to tell about the mercy of their Benefactor.

The Bible records other examples: The daughter of the Syro-Phoenician woman, severely afflicted with a devil whom Jesus cast out by His word (Mark 7:25–30); a youth who had a spirit who had often "thrown him both into the fire and into the water to destroy him" (Mark 9:17–27); the maniac, tormented by a spirit of an unclean devil who disturbed the Sabbath quiet at Capernaum (Luke 4:33–36)—the Savior healed them all. In nearly every instance, Christ addressed the demon as an intelligent being, commanding him not to torment his victim ever again. The worshipers at Capernaum "were all amazed and spoke among themselves, saying, 'What a word this is! For with authority and power He commands the unclean spirits, and they come out'" (Luke 4:36).

In order to get supernatural power, some welcomed the satanic influence. Of course, these people had no conflict with the demons. Included in this group were those who had the spirit of divination—Simon Magus, Elymas the sorcerer, and the slave girl who followed Paul and Silas at Philippi (see Acts 8:9, 18; 13:8; 16:16–18).

Danger

None are in greater danger than those who deny that the devil and his angels exist. Many accept their suggestions while they think they are following their own wisdom. As we approach the end of time, when Satan will work with his greatest power to deceive, he spreads everywhere the belief that he does not exist. It is his policy to conceal himself and his way of working.

The great deceiver is afraid that we will become acquainted with his deceptions. To disguise his real character he has influenced people to portray him as something to ridicule or despise. He is pleased to be painted as comical, misshapen, half animal and half human. He is pleased to hear his name used in jokes and mockery. Because he has masked himself with superb skill, many people ask, "Does such a being really exist?" Because Satan can easily control the minds of those who are unaware of his influence, the Word of God reveals to us his secret forces, and this puts us on guard.

Safety With Jesus

We may find shelter and deliverance in our Redeemer's superior power. We carefully make our houses secure with bolts and locks to protect our property and lives from evil people. But seldom do we think of the evil angels and that, in our own strength, we have no defense against their attacks. If they are allowed, they can confuse our minds, torment our bodies, and destroy our possessions and our lives. But those who follow Christ are safe under His watchful care. Angels that excel in strength are sent to protect them. The wicked one cannot break through the guard that God has stationed around His people.

How to Defeat Satan

The great controversy between Christ and Satan will close soon, and the wicked one is increasing his efforts to defeat the work of Christ for humanity. His aim is to hold people in darkness and rebellion until the Savior's sanctuary ministry is over. When people in the church are indifferent, Satan is not concerned. But when hearts inquire, "What must I do to be saved?" he is there to match his power against Christ and to counteract the Holy Spirit's influence.

On one occasion, when the angels came to present themselves before the Lord, Satan also came among them, not to bow before the Eternal King, but to carry forward his evil plans against the righteous (see Job 1:6). He is present when Christians gather for worship, working diligently to control the minds of the worshipers. As he sees the messenger of God studying the Scriptures, he notices the subject to be presented. Then he uses his subtle skills and shrewdness so that the message may not reach those whom he is deceiving on that very point. The one who most needs the warning will be urged into some business transaction or will be prevented in some other way from hearing the word.

Satan sees the Lord's servants bur-dened because of the darkness that surrounds the people. He hears their prayers for divine grace and power to break the spell of indifference and laziness. Then with renewed zeal Satan tempts people to indulge their appetites or gratify themselves, and in this way he dulls their perceptions so that they fail to hear the very things they most need to learn.

Satan knows that all who neglect to pray and read the Bible will be overcome by his attacks. So he invents every possible diversion to occupy the mind. His right-hand helpers are always active when God is at work. They will describe the most earnest, self-denying servants of Christ as deceived or deceivers. Their work is to misrepresent the motives of every noble deed, to spread doubts, and arouse suspicion in the minds of the inexperienced. But we can easily see whose children they are, whose example they follow, and whose work they do. "You will know them by their fruits" (Matthew 7:16; also see Revelation 12:10).

The Truth Sanctifies

The great deceiver has many heresies prepared to fit the different tastes of those he wants to ruin. His plan is to bring into the church insincere, unconverted people who will encourage doubt and unbelief. Many who have no real faith in God agree to a few principles of truth and pass as Christians, and in this way they are able to introduce error as Bible doctrine. Satan knows that the truth, received in love, sanctifies the life. So he tries to substitute false theories, fables, another gospel. From the beginning, servants of God have opposed false teachers, not because they considered them vicious people, but because they taught falsehoods that were fatal to the spiritual life. Elijah, Jeremiah, Paul, firmly opposed those who were turning others from the Word of God. The liberal mind-set that thinks correct faith is not important found no welcome with these holy defenders of truth.

The vague and inventive interpretations of Scripture and the conflicting religious theories in the Christian world are the work of our great adversary to confuse minds. The discord and division among the churches come mostly from twisting the Scriptures to support a favorite theory.

In order to prove false doctrines, some take hold of passages of Scripture separated from the context. They quote half a verse as proving their point, when the remaining portion shows that the meaning is the opposite. With the wily deceit of the serpent they take their position behind unrelated statements intended to please carnal desires. Others turn to figures and symbols, interpret them to suit their ideas with little care for the testimony of Scripture as its own interpreter, and then present their erratic thoughts as the teachings of the Bible.

The Whole Bible a Guide

Whenever people begin to study the Scriptures without a prayerful, teachable spirit, they will twist the plainest passages away from their true meaning. The whole Bible should be given to the people just as it reads.

God gave the sure word of prophecy. Angels and even Christ Himself came to make known to Daniel and John the things that "must shortly take place" (Revelation 1:1). God did not reveal important matters about our salvation in a way to perplex and mislead the person who is honestly seeking for truth. The Word of God is plain to all who study it with a prayerful heart.

By the cry "Open-mindedness" people are blinded to Satan's deceptions. He succeeds in displacing the Bible with human speculations. People set aside the law of God, and the churches are in slavery to sin while they claim to be free.

God has permitted a flood of light to pour over the world in scientific discoveries. But, if the Word of God is not their guide, even the greatest minds become bewildered in trying to investigate how science and revelation fit together.

Human knowledge is partial and imperfect. This is why many are unable to harmonize their ideas of science with Scripture. Many accept things that are only theories as scientific facts, and they think that they should test God's Word by "what is falsely called knowledge" (1 Timothy

6:20). Because they cannot explain the Creator and His works by natural laws, they consider Bible history as unreliable. Those who doubt the Old and New Testaments too often go a step further and doubt the existence of God. Once they let go of their anchor, they beat about on the rocks of unbelief.

It is a masterpiece of Satan's deceptions to keep people speculating about things that God has not made known. Lucifer became dissatisfied because God did not share with him all the secrets of God's purposes, and he turned his back on the things God had revealed. Now he tries to fill people with the same spirit and lead them also to ignore the direct commands of God.

Truth Rejected Because It Involves a Cross

The less spiritual and self-denying the doctrines presented, the greater the favor with which people receive them. Satan is ready to supply what people want, and he palms off deception in the place of truth. This is how the papacy gained its power over the minds of so many. And by rejecting the truth because it involves a cross, Protestants are following the same path. All who study convenience and popular opinion, so that they will not be out of step with the world, will be left to receive "destructive heresies" in place of truth (2 Peter 2:1). Those who look with horror on one deception will eagerly receive another. "For this reason God will send them strong delusion, that they should believe the lie, that they all may be condemned who did not believe the

truth but had pleasure in unrighteousness" (2 Thessalonians 2:11, 12).

Dangerous Errors

The lying wonders of spiritualism are among Satan's most successful agencies. When people reject the truth, they become easy targets for deception.

Another error is the doctrine that denies the deity of Christ, claiming that He had no existence before He was born into this world. This theory contradicts Jesus' own statements about His relationship with the Father and His preexistence. It undermines faith in the Bible as a revelation from God. If people reject the testimony of Scripture about the deity of Christ, it is useless to argue with them. No argument, however strong, could convince them. None who hold this error can have a true understanding of Christ or of God's plan for our redemption.

Still another error is the belief that Satan does not exist as a personal being, that the Bible uses that name simply to represent people's evil thoughts and desires.

Some teach that the second advent of Christ is His coming to each individual at death. This is a deception to divert minds from Jesus' personal coming in the clouds of heaven. By this means, Satan has been saying, "Behold, he is in the secret chambers" (Matthew 24:23–26, KJV), and many have been lost by accepting this deception.

Again, many scientists claim that there can be no real answer to prayer, because this would be a violation of law—a miracle, and miracles have no existence. The universe, they say, is governed by fixed laws, and God Himself does nothing against these laws. So they represent God as limited by His own laws—as if divine laws could exclude divine freedom.

Did not Christ and His apostles work miracles? The same Savior is as willing to listen to the prayer of faith today as when He walked visibly on the earth. The natural cooperates with the supernatural. It is a part of God's plan to grant us, in answer to the prayer of faith, what He would not give if we did not ask in faith.

The Landmarks of the Word

False doctrines among the churches remove landmarks that the Word of God has established. Few people stop when they have rejected just one truth. The majority set aside one after another of the principles of truth, until they reject the Christian faith altogether.

The errors of popular theology have driven many people to skepticism. It is impossible for them to accept doctrines that outrage their sense of justice, mercy, and kindness. Since the churches say that these are the teachings of the Bible, such people refuse to acknowledge it as the Word of God.

Many people look distrustfully at the Word of God because it rebukes and condemns sin. Those who are unwilling to obey try to overthrow its authority. Many reject religion in order to justify their neglect of duty. Others, who love ease too much to accomplish anything that requires self-denial, acquire a reputation for superior wisdom

by criticizing the Bible.

Many feel it is a virtue to stand on the side of unbelief, skepticism, and irreligion. But underneath an appearance of honesty they act from self-confidence and pride. Many delight in finding something in the Scriptures to puzzle the minds of others. Some at first reason on the wrong side just because they love a controversy. But once they have openly expressed unbelief, they then join with the ungodly.

Enough Evidence

In His Word God has given enough evidence of its divine character. Yet finite minds are inadequate to comprehend fully the intentions of the Infinite One. "How unsearchable are His judgments and His ways past finding out!" (Romans 11:33). We can understand His actions and motives enough to see unlimited love and mercy united to infinite power. Our Father in heaven will reveal to us as much as it is good for us to know. Beyond that we must trust the Hand that is all-powerful, the Heart that is full of love.

God will never remove all excuse for unbelief. All who look for hooks to hang their doubts on will find them. And those who refuse to obey until every objection is gone will never come to the light. The unrenewed heart is in conflict with God. But faith is inspired by the Holy Spirit and will flourish as we cherish it. No one can become strong in faith without persistent effort. If people allow themselves to raise trivial objections, they will find doubt becoming stronger.

But those who doubt and distrust the assurance of His grace dishonor

Christ. They are unproductive trees that block the sunlight from other plants, causing them to droop and die under their chilling shadow. The life-work of these people will always stand as a witness against them.

For those who honestly want to be freed from doubts, there is only one course to pursue. Instead of questioning the things they do not understand, they should pay attention to the light that already shines on them, and they will receive greater light.

Satan can produce a counterfeit that so closely resembles the truth that it deceives those who are willing to be deceived, who want to avoid the sacrifice that the truth demands. But it is impossible for him to hold even one person under his power who honestly desires to know the truth, no matter what the cost. Christ is the truth, the "Light which gives light to every man coming into the world." "If anyone wills to do His will, he shall know concerning the doctrine." (John 1:9; 7:17.)

The Lord permits His people to go through the fiery ordeal of temptation, not because He enjoys their distress, but because this is essential to their final victory. It would be inconsistent with His own glory to shield them from temptation, because the purpose of the trial is to prepare them to resist all the attractions of evil. Neither wicked people nor devils can shut God's presence away from His people if they will confess their sins, put them away, and claim His promises. Every temptation, open or secret, they may successfully resist, " 'not by might nor by power, but by My Spirit,' says the LORD of hosts" (Zechariah 4:6).

"Who is he who will harm you if you become followers of what is good?" (1 Peter 3:13). Satan is well aware that the weakest Christian who abides in Christ is more than a match for all the armies of darkness. For this reason, he tries to draw the soldiers of the cross away from their strong defenses, while he waits in ambush, ready to destroy all who step onto his ground. Only when we rely on God and obey all His commandments can we be secure.

No one is safe for a day or an hour without prayer. Plead with the Lord for wisdom to understand His Word. Satan is an expert in quoting Scripture, placing his own interpretation on passages in hopes of causing us to stumble. We should study with humility of heart. While we must constantly guard against Satan's deceptions, we should pray in faith continually, "Do not lead us into temptation" (Matthew 6:13).

What Happens After Death?

Satan, who had stirred up rebellion in heaven, wanted to bring those living on the earth to join him in his warfare against God. Adam and Eve had been perfectly happy in obeying God's law—a constant testimony against the claim Satan had made in heaven that God's law was oppressive. Satan was determined to cause their fall so that he could possess the earth and establish his kingdom here in opposition to the Most High.

God had warned Adam and Eve about this dangerous enemy, but Satan worked in the dark, hiding his intentions. Using the snake as his medium, whose appearance then was fascinating, he said to Eve, "Has God indeed said, 'You shall not eat of every tree of the garden'?" Eve dared to talk with him and became a victim of his deceptive skill: "The woman said to the serpent, 'We may eat the fruit of the trees of the garden; but of the fruit of the tree which is in the midst of the garden, God has said, "You shall not eat it, nor shall you touch it, lest you die."' Then the serpent said to the woman, 'You will not surely die. For God knows that in the day you eat of it your eyes will be opened, and you will be like God, knowing good and evil'" (Genesis 3:1–5).

Eve yielded to temptation, and through her influence Adam sinned. They accepted the words of the serpent. They distrusted their Creator and imagined that He was restricting their liberty.

But what did Adam find to be the meaning of the words, "In the day that you eat of it you shall surely die"? Was he going to be ushered into a higher existence? Adam did not find this to be the meaning of the divine sentence. God declared that as a penalty for his sin, he and his descendants would return to the ground: "Dust you are, and to dust you shall return" (Genesis 3:19). Satan's words, "Your eyes will be opened," proved to be true only in this sense: their eyes were opened to see how foolish they had been. They did know evil, and they tasted the bitter fruit of transgression.

The fruit of the tree of life had the power to sustain life forever. Adam would have continued to enjoy free access to this tree and would never have died, but when he sinned he was cut off from the tree of life and became subject to death. He had lost immortality by his sin. There could have been no hope for the fallen race if God had not brought immortality within their reach by the sacrifice of

His Son. While "death spread to all men, because all sinned," Christ has "brought life and immortality to light through the gospel." We can only receive immortality through Christ. "He who believes in the Son has everlasting life; and he who does not believe the Son shall not see life." (Romans 5:12; 2 Timothy 1:10; John 3:36.)

The Great Lie

The one who promised Adam life in disobedience was the great deceiver. And the serpent's claim in Eden—"You will not surely die"—was the first sermon ever preached on the immortality of the soul. Yet this claim, resting only on Satan's authority, echoes from pulpits today, and most people accept it as readily as our first parents did. The divine sentence, "The soul who sins shall die" (Ezekiel 18:20), is made to mean, The soul who sins shall *not* die, but live eternally. If God had allowed Adam and Eve free access to the tree of life after their fall, sin would have been immortalized. But God has not permitted even one of the family of Adam to eat of the life-giving fruit. As a result, there is no immortal sinner.

After the Fall, Satan instructed his angels to instill in people the belief that they are naturally immortal. After persuading the people to accept this error, evil angels were to lead them to conclude that sinners would live in eternal misery. Now the prince of darkness presents God as a revengeful tyrant who plunges into hell all who do not please Him and looks down on them with satisfaction while they writhe in eternal flames. In this way

the one who started all evil paints the Benefactor of the human race with his own characteristics. Cruelty is satanic. God is love. Satan is the enemy who tempts us to sin and then destroys us if he can. How offensive it is to love, mercy, and justice to teach that God torments the wicked dead in an eternally burning hell, that for the sins of a brief life on earth they suffer torture as long as God shall live! A well-educated minister said, "The sight of hell's torments will increase the happiness of the redeemed forever by making them conscious of how happy they are."

Where can anyone find such teaching in God's Word? Will the redeemed exchange feelings of common humanity for the cruelty of the savage? No, such things are not the teaching of the Book of God. " 'As I live,' says the Lord GOD, 'I have no pleasure in the death of the wicked, but that the wicked turn from his way and live. Turn, turn from your evil ways! For why should you die?' " (Ezekiel 33:11).

Does God delight in witnessing unending tortures? Is He pleased with the groans and shrieks of suffering creatures whom He holds in the flames? Can these horrid sounds be music to the ear of Infinite Love? What a terrible blasphemy! God's glory is not increased by keeping sin alive through ages without end.

The Heresy of Eternal Torment

Untold evil has come from the heresy of eternal torment. It takes the religion of the Bible, so full of love and goodness, darkens it by superstition, and clothes it with terror. Satan has painted the character of God in false colors, making people fear, dread, and even hate our merciful Creator. The repulsive views of God that have spread over the world from the teachings of the pulpit have made millions of people skeptics and unbelievers.

Eternal torment is one of the false doctrines, the wine of abomination (Revelation 14:8; 17:2), which Babylon makes all nations drink. Ministers of Christ accepted this heresy from Rome, just as they received the false sabbath. If we turn from God's Word and accept false doctrines because our ancestors taught them, we come under the condemnation that the Bible pronounces on Babylon. We are drinking from the wine of her abomination.

Many people are driven to the opposite error. They see that Scripture presents God as a being of love and compassion, and they cannot believe that He will condemn His creatures to an eternally burning hell. Since they hold the idea that the soul is naturally immortal, they conclude that all mankind will be saved. So the sinner can live in selfish pleasure, ignoring God's requirements, and still be welcomed into His favor. A doctrine like this, which presumes on God's mercy but ignores His justice, pleases the unconverted heart.

Universal Salvation Is Not Biblical

Believers in universal salvation twist the Scriptures. The professed minister of Christ repeats the lie that the serpent spoke in Eden, "You will not surely die. . . . In the day you eat of it your eyes will be opened, and you will be like God, knowing good and evil." He asserts that the worst of sinners—the murderer, the thief, the adulterer—will enter into immortal bliss after death. This is no more than a pleasing fable, designed to appeal to the unconverted heart!

If it were true that everyone went directly to heaven at death, we might well desire death rather than life. This belief has led many to commit suicide. When they are overwhelmed with trouble and disappointment, it seems easy to break the thread of life and soar into the bliss of the eternal world.

In His Word God has given decisive evidence that He will punish those who trample on His law. Is He too merciful to execute justice on the sinner? Look to the cross of Calvary. The death of God's Son testifies that "the wages of sin is death" (Romans 6:23), that every violation of God's law must receive its punishment. Christ the sinless became sin for us. He bore the guilt of sin and the hiding of His Father's face until His heart was broken and His life crushed out—all this so that sinners could be redeemed. And every person who refuses to accept the atonement provided at such a cost must bear his own guilt and the punishment for his own sins.

Conditions Are Specified

"I will give of the fountain of the water of life freely to him who thirsts." This promise is only for those who are thirsty. "He who overcomes shall inherit all things, and I will be his God and he shall be My son." (Revelation 21:6, 7.) This text also specifies conditions. To inherit all things, we must overcome sin.

"It will not be well with the wicked" (Ecclesiastes 8:13). The sinner is treasuring up for himself "wrath in the day of wrath and revelation of the righteous judgment of God, who 'will render to each one according to his deeds,'" "tribulation and anguish, on every soul of man who does evil" (Romans 2:5, 6, 9).

"No fornicator, unclean person, nor covetous man, who is an idolater, has any inheritance in the kingdom of Christ and God." "Blessed are those who do His commandments, that they may have the right to the tree of life, and may enter through the gates into the city. But outside are dogs and sorcerers and sexually immoral and murderers and idolaters, and whoever loves and practices a lie." (Ephesians 5:5; Revelation 22:14, 15.)

God has given us a clear statement of how He will deal with sin. "All the wicked He will destroy." "The transgressors shall be destroyed together; the future of the wicked shall be cut off." (Psalms 145:20; 37:38.) The authority of the divine government will put down rebellion, yet His justice in punishing sin will be consistent with the character of God as a merciful, kind being.

God does not force the will. He takes no pleasure in slavelike obedience. He wants the creatures He has made to love Him because He is worthy of love. He would like them to obey Him because they have an intelligent appreciation of His wisdom, justice, and kindness.

The principles of God's govern-ment are in harmony with the Savior's command, "Love your enemies" (Matthew 5:44). God executes justice on the wicked for the good of the universe and even for the good of those who receive His judgments. He would make them happy if He could. He surrounds them with evidences of His love and follows them with offers of mercy. But they despise His love, overturn His law, and reject His mercy. Even while they constantly receive His gifts, they dishonor the Giver. The Lord is very patient with their determined self-will, but will He chain these rebels to His side and force them to do what He wants?

Not Prepared to Enter Heaven

Those who have chosen Satan as their leader are not prepared to enter the presence of God. Pride, deception, immorality, cruelty, have become established in their characters. Can they enter heaven to live forever with those whom they hated on earth? Truth will never be agreeable to a liar. Meekness will not satisfy self-esteem. Purity is not acceptable to the corrupt. Unselfish love does not appear attractive to the selfish. What enjoyment could heaven offer those who are focused on selfish interests?

Will those whose hearts are filled with hatred of God, of truth and holiness, be able to mingle with the inhabitants of heaven and join their songs of praise? God granted them years of grace to prepare for eternity with Him, but they never trained the mind to love purity. They never learned the language of heaven. Now it is too late. A life of rebellion against God has made them unfit for heaven. Its purity and peace would be torture to them; the glory of God would be a consuming fire. They would long to escape from that holy place and would welcome destruction, just to be hidden from the face of Him who died to redeem them. It is their own choice that decides the destiny of the wicked. They voluntarily exclude themselves from heaven, and God is just and merciful in ratifying their choice. Like the waters of the Flood, the fires of the great day declare God's verdict that the wicked are incurable. They have exercised their will in revolt. When life is over, it is too late to turn their thoughts from law-breaking to obedience, from hatred to love.

Two Destinies

"The wages of sin is death, but the gift of God is eternal life in Christ Jesus our Lord" (Romans 6:23). Life is the inheritance of the righteous, and death is the destiny of the wicked. The Bible places "the second death" in contrast with everlasting life (see Revelation 20:14).

Because of Adam's sin, death came upon the whole human race. Everyone goes down into the grave. And through the plan of salvation, all will be brought up from their graves: "There will be a resurrection of the dead, both of the just and the unjust" "for as in Adam all die, even so in Christ all shall be made alive." But the Bible makes a distinction between the two classes that are resurrected: "All who are in the graves will hear His voice and come forth—those who have done good, to the resurrection of life, and those who have done evil, to the resurrection of condemnation." (Acts 24:15; 1 Corinthians 15:22; John 5:28, 29.)

The End of Suffering

They who have been "counted worthy" of the resurrection of life are "blessed and holy." "Over such the second death has no power." (Luke 20:35; Revelation 20:6.) But those who have not received pardon through repentance and faith must receive "the wages of sin," punishment "according to their works," which ends in the "second death."

Since it is impossible for God to save sinners in their sins, He deprives them of their existence, which their transgressions have forfeited and of which they have proven themselves unworthy. "Yet a little while and the wicked shall be no more; indeed, you will look carefully for his place, but it shall be no more." "They shall be as though they had never been." (Psalm 37:10; Obadiah 16.) They sink into hopeless, eternal oblivion.

And so God will make an end of sin. "You have destroyed the wicked; You have blotted out their name forever and ever. O enemy, destructions are finished forever!" (Psalm 9:5, 6). In the book of Revelation, John hears a universal anthem of praise without one note of discord. No lost souls blaspheme God as they writhe in neverending torment. No wretched beings in hell will mingle their shrieks with the songs of the saved.

The error of natural immortality is the basis for the doctrine of consciousness in death. Like eternal torment, this doctrine is opposed to Scripture, to reason, and to our feelings of humanity.

According to popular belief, the redeemed in heaven know everything that takes place on earth. But how could the dead be happy in knowing the troubles of the living, in seeing them endure the sorrows, disappointments, and anguish of life? And how revolting is the belief that as soon as the breath leaves the body, the soul of the unrepentant is sent to the flames of hell!

What do the Scriptures say? Humanity is not conscious in death: "When their breath departs, they return to the earth; on that very day their plans perish." "The living know that they will die; but the dead know nothing. . . . Their love, their hatred, and their envy have now perished; nevermore will they have a share in anything done under the sun." "Sheol [the grave] cannot thank You, death cannot praise You; those who go down to the pit cannot hope for Your truth. The living, the living man, he shall praise You, as I do this day." "In death there is no remembrance of You; in the grave who will give You thanks?" (Psalm 146:4, NRSV; Ecclesiastes 9:5, 6; Isaiah 38:18, 19; Psalm 6:5.)

On the Day of Pentecost Peter declared that David "is both dead and buried, and his tomb is with us to this day. . . . For David did not ascend into the heavens" (Acts 2:29, 34). The fact that David remains in the grave until the resurrection proves that the righteous do not go to heaven when they die.

Paul said: "If the dead do not rise, then Christ is not risen. And if Christ is not risen, your faith is futile; you are still in your sins! Then also those who have fallen asleep in Christ have perished" (1 Corinthians 15:16–18). If for four thousand years the righteous had gone directly to heaven when they died, how could Paul have said that if there is no resurrection, "those who have fallen asleep in Christ have perished"?

Resurrection to Eternal Life

When He was about to leave His disciples, Jesus did not tell them that they would soon come to Him. "I go to prepare a place for you," He said. "And if I go and prepare a place for you, I will come again and receive you to Myself" (John 14:2, 3). Paul tells us further that "the Lord Himself will descend from heaven with a shout, with the voice of an archangel, and with the trumpet of God. And the dead in Christ will rise first. Then we who are alive and remain shall be caught up together with them in the clouds to meet the Lord in the air. And thus we shall always be with the Lord." And he adds, "Comfort one another with these words." (1 Thessalonians 4:16–18.) When the Lord comes, He will break the chains of death and will raise the "dead in Christ" to eternal life.

God will judge everyone by the things written in the books and reward them as their works have been. This judgment does not take place at death. "He has appointed a day on which He will judge the world in righteousness." "Behold, the Lord comes with ten thousands of His saints, to execute judgment on all." (Acts 17:31; Jude 14, 15.)

But if the dead are already enjoying heaven or writhing in the flames of hell, what need is there for a future judgment? Ordinary minds can understand God's Word on these points. But what unbiased mind can see either wisdom or justice in the current theory? Will the righteous receive God's approving words, "Well done, good and faithful servant. . . . Enter into the joy of your lord," when they have already been living in His presence for long ages? Are the wicked called from torment to receive the Judge's sentence, "Depart from Me, you cursed, into the everlasting fire"? (Matthew 25:21, 41.)

The theory that the soul is immortal was one of those false doctrines that Rome borrowed from paganism. Luther classed it with the "monstrous fables that form part of the Roman dunghill of decrees."[1] The Bible teaches that the dead sleep until the resurrection.

---

1. E. Petavel, *The Problem of Immortality*, p. 255.

Immortality When Jesus Returns

Sweet rest for the weary righteous! Time, whether it is long or short, is only a moment to them. They sleep, and then the trumpet of God awakens them to a glorious immortality. "For the trumpet will sound, and the dead will be raised incorruptible. . . . So when this corruptible has put on incorruption, and this mortal has put on immortality, then shall be brought to pass the saying that is written, 'Death is swallowed up in victory' " (1 Corinthians 15:52, 54).

Called to arise from their sleep, they begin to think just where they had stopped. The last sensation was the stroke of death; the last thought, that they were falling beneath the power of the grave. When they come out from the tomb, their first glad thought will be echoed in the triumphant shout, "O death, where is your sting? O Hades, where is your victory?" (1 Corinthians 15:55).

Who Are the "Spirits" in Spiritualism?

The doctrine that we are naturally immortal came from pagan philosophy. In the darkness of the great apostasy it became a part of the Christian faith, where it has now replaced the truth that "the dead know nothing" (Ecclesiastes 9:5). Many people believe that the spirits of the dead are the "ministering spirits sent forth to minister for those who will inherit salvation" (Hebrews 1:14).

The belief that spirits of the dead return to help the living has prepared the way for modern spiritualism. If the dead are entrusted with knowledge far beyond what they had before, why not return to earth and instruct the living? If spirits of the dead hover around their friends on earth, why not communicate with them? How can those who believe in human consciousness in death reject "divine light" that comes through glorified spirits? Here is a channel that people think is sacred but which Satan uses. Fallen angels appear as messengers from the spirit world.

The prince of evil has power to bring before people the appearance of departed friends. The counterfeit is perfect, reproduced with amazing exactness. Many take comfort in the assurance that their loved ones are enjoying heaven. Without suspecting danger, they open their lives "to deceiving spirits and doctrines of demons" (1 Timothy 4:1).

Those who went into the grave unprepared claim to be happy and to occupy high positions in heaven. Pretended visitors from the world of spirits sometimes give warnings that prove to be correct. Then, as they win people's confidence, they present doctrines that undermine the Scriptures. The fact that they speak some truths and at times foretell future events makes them appear reliable, and people accept their false teachings. The law of God is set aside, the Spirit of grace despised. The spirits deny the deity of Christ and place the Creator on a level with themselves.

While it is true that the results of trickery have often been presented as genuine manifestations, there have also been clear exhibitions of supernatural power, the direct work of evil angels. Many believe that spiritualism is nothing more than human fraud. When they come face to face with happenings that they cannot explain as anything but supernatural, they will be deceived and will accept them as the great power of God.

With help from Satan, Pharaoh's

magicians counterfeited the work of God (see Exodus 7:10–12). Paul testifies that before the coming of the Lord we will see "the working of Satan, with all power, signs, and lying wonders, and with all unrighteous deception" (2 Thessalonians 2:9, 10). And John declares: "He performs great signs, so that he even makes fire come down from heaven on the earth in the sight of men. And he deceives those who dwell on the earth by those signs which he was granted to do" (Revelation 13:13, 14). This is not predicting mere tricks. People are deceived by the miracles that Satan's agents actually do, not that they only pretend to do.

Satan's Appeal to Intellectuals

To cultured and refined people, the prince of darkness presents the more refined and intellectual aspects of spiritualism. He delights the imagination with entrancing scenes and eloquent portrayals of love and charity. He leads people to take such great pride in their own wisdom that in their hearts they despise the Eternal One.

Satan deceives people now as he deceived Eve in Eden, by stirring up their ambition to exalt themselves. "You will be like God," he says, "knowing good and evil" (Genesis 3:5). Spiritualism teaches "that a human being is the creature of progression . . . toward the Godhead." It claims, "The judgment will be right, because it is the judgment of self. . . . The throne is within you." "Any just and perfect being is Christ."

In this way Satan has substituted a person's own sinful human nature for the law of God as the only rule of judgment. This is progress, not upward, but downward. Men and women will never rise higher than their standard of purity or goodness. If self is their highest ideal, they will never reach anything higher. The grace of God alone has power to exalt them. Left to themselves, their path will be downward.

Appeal to the Pleasure-loving

To people who are self-indulgent, pleasure-loving, and sensual, spiritualism appears in a less subtle disguise. In its grosser forms they find what agrees with their inclinations. Satan notes the sins each individual is inclined to commit and then makes sure that opportunities come along to gratify the tendency. He tempts people through intemperance, leading them to weaken their physical, mental, and moral power. He destroys thousands through indulgence of passion, brutalizing the entire nature. And to complete his work, the spirits declare that "true knowledge places a person above all law," that "whatever is, is right," that "God does not condemn," and that "all sins . . . are innocent." When people believe that desire is the highest law, that liberty is license, that they are accountable only to themselves, who can be surprised that corruption flourishes everywhere? Great numbers of people eagerly accept the urgings of lust. Satan sweeps thousands into his net who profess to follow Christ.

But God has given enough light to detect the snare. The very foundation of spiritualism is at war with Scripture. The Bible declares that the dead know nothing, that their thoughts have perished. They have no part in the joys or sorrows of those on earth.

Forbidden Fellowship

Furthermore, God has forbidden all pretended communication with departed spirits. The Bible says that "familiar spirits," as these visitors from other worlds were called, are "the spirits of demons" (see Numbers 25:1–3; Psalm 106:28; 1 Corinthians 10:20; Revelation 16:14). God prohibited dealing with them under penalty of death (Leviticus 19:31; 20:27). But spiritualism has made its way into scientific circles, invaded churches, and found a welcome in legislative bodies, even in the courts of kings. This mammoth deception is a revival in a new disguise of the witchcraft condemned long ago.

By representing the most evil of sinners as in heaven, Satan says to the world: "No matter whether you believe or disbelieve God and the Bible, live as you please. Heaven is your home." But the Word of God says, "Woe to those who call evil good, and good evil; who put darkness for light, and light for darkness" (Isaiah 5:20).

Bible Represented as Fiction

Lying spirits impersonate the apostles, making them contradict what they wrote when on earth. Satan is making the world believe that the Bible is fiction, a book suited to the infancy of the race but obsolete today. The Book that is to judge him and his followers he puts in the shadows. The Savior of the world he makes to be no more than a common man. And believers in spirit appearances try to make it seem that there is nothing miraculous in our Savior's life. They declare that their own miracles are far greater than the works of Christ.

Spiritualism is now adopting a Christian appearance. But it cannot deny or hide its teachings. In its present form it is a more dangerous and more subtle deception. It now professes to accept Christ and the Bible, but it interprets the Bible in a way that is pleasing to the unrenewed heart. It dwells on love as the chief attribute of God, but it degrades this love to a weak sentimentalism. God's condemnations of sin, the requirements of His holy law, are kept out of sight. Fables lead men and women to reject the Bible as the foundation of their faith. Christ is denied as surely as before, but most people do not recognize the deception.

Few have a proper understanding of spiritualism's deceptive power. Many tamper with it merely out of curiosity. They would be horrified at the thought of yielding to the spirits' control. But they dare to go onto forbidden ground, and the destroyer exercises his power on them against their will. If he can get them to submit their minds to his direction just once, he will hold them captive. Nothing but the power of God, in answer to earnest prayer, can deliver them.

All who willfully cherish known sin are inviting Satan's temptations. They separate themselves from God and the watchcare of His angels, leaving themselves without defense.

"When they say to you, 'Seek those who are mediums and wizards, who whisper and mutter,' should not a people seek their God? Should they seek the dead on behalf of the living? To the law and to the testimony! If they do not speak according to this word, it is because there is no light in them" (Isaiah 8:19, 20).

If people had been willing to accept the Bible truth concerning our human nature and the condition of the dead, they would see in spiritualism Satan's power and lying wonders. But so many close their eyes to the light, and Satan weaves his snares around them. "Because they did not receive the love of the truth, that they might be saved," therefore "God will send them strong delusion, that they should believe the lie" (2 Thessalonians 2:10, 11).

Those who oppose spiritualism attack Satan and his angels. Satan will not yield one inch of ground except as the heavenly messengers drive him back. He can quote Scripture and will twist its teachings. Those who intend to stand in this time of danger must understand for themselves what the Bible teaches.

Understanding the Scriptures

Spirits of devils impersonating relatives or friends will appeal to our tender sympathies and will work miracles. We must resist them with the Bible truth that the dead know nothing and that they who appear this way are the spirits of devils.

All whose faith is not established on the Word of God will be deceived and overcome. Satan works "with all unrighteous deception," and his deceptions will increase. But those who are looking for a knowledge of the truth and who purify their lives through obedience will find a sure defense in the God of truth. The Savior would sooner send every angel out of heaven to protect His people than leave one person who trusts in Him to be overcome by Satan. Those who comfort themselves with the assurance that there is no punishment for the sinner, who reject the truths that Heaven has provided as a defense for the day of trouble, will accept the lies that Satan offers, the deceptive claims of spiritualism.

Scoffers ridicule what Scripture says about the plan of salvation and the punishment that will fall on those who reject truth. They pretend to have great pity for minds so narrow, weak, and superstitious as to obey the requirements of God's law. They have yielded themselves to the tempter so fully, united with him so closely, and drunk so deeply of his spirit that they have no desire to break away from his snare.

Satan laid the foundation of his work in the assurance he gave to Eve in Eden: "You will not surely die. . . . In the day you eat of it your eyes will be opened, and you will be like God, knowing good and evil" (Genesis 3:4, 5). He will reach his masterpiece of deception at the very end of time. Says the prophet: "I saw three unclean spirits like frogs. . . . For they are spirits of demons, performing signs, which go out to the kings of the earth and of the whole world, to gather them to the battle of that great day of God Almighty" (Revelation 16:13, 14).

Except for those whom God's power keeps through faith in His

Word, the whole world will be swept into the ranks of this deception. The people are quickly being lulled into a fatal security, and only the outpouring of God's wrath will awaken them.

Liberty of Conscience Threatened

Protestants now regard Catholicism far more favorably than they did years ago. In those countries where Catholicism takes a peaceful course to gain influence, the opinion is gaining ground that we do not differ so widely on vital points as we had supposed, and that a little concession on our part will bring us into better understanding with Rome. Some time ago, Protestants taught their children that to seek harmony with Rome would be disloyalty to God. But how different are the sentiments people express now!

Defenders of the papacy claim that the church has been misrepresented, and that it is unfair to judge the church of today by her reign during the centuries of ignorance and darkness. They excuse the church's horrible cruelty as the harsh customs of the times.

Have these people forgotten the claim of infallibility coming from this power? Rome asserts that the "church *never erred; nor will it, according to* the Scriptures, *ever err.*"[1]

The papal church will never give up her claim to infallibility. If secular governments remove their current restraints and Rome regains her former power, there would quickly be a revival of the church's tyranny and persecution.

It is true that there are real Christians in the Roman Catholic faith. Thousands in that church are serving God according to the best light they have. God looks with pitying tenderness upon these souls who have been educated in a faith that is delusive and unsatisfying. He will cause rays of light to penetrate the darkness, and many will yet join with His people.

But Romanism as a system is no more in harmony with the gospel of Christ now than at any time before. The Roman Church is using every means available to regain control of the world, to re-establish persecution, and to undo everything that Protestantism has done. Catholicism is gaining ground on every side. See the increasing number of her churches. Look at the popularity of her colleges and seminaries, so widely attended by Protestants. Look at the growth of ritualism in England and the frequent defections to the ranks of the Catholics.

Compromises and Concessions

Protestants have supported Catholicism. They have made compromises and concessions that Catholics themselves are surprised to see. People are closing their eyes to the real character of Romanism. They need to resist the advances of this dangerous opponent of civil and religious liberty.

While Catholicism is based on deception, it is not coarse and clumsy. The religious service of the Roman Church is a most impressive ceremony. Its gorgeous display and solemn rites fascinate the people and silence the voice of reason and conscience. It charms the eye. Magnificent churches, stately processions, golden altars, jeweled shrines, choice paintings, and superb sculpture appeal to the love of beauty. The music is of the finest quality. The rich notes of the deep-toned organ blend with the melody of many voices as the music swells through the soaring domes and pillared aisles of her grand cathedrals, impressing the mind with awe and reverence.

This outward splendor and ceremony mocks the longings of the sin-sick soul. The religion of Christ does not need attractions like this. The light that shines from the cross is so pure and lovely that no external decorations can add to its true worth.

Satan often uses high concepts of art and delicate refinement of taste to lead people to forget the real needs of the heart and to live for this world alone.

The pomp and ceremony of Catholic worship has a seductive, bewitching power that deceives many. They begin to see the Roman Church as the gate of heaven. Only those whose feet stand firmly on the foundation of truth and whose hearts are renewed by the Spirit of God are secure against her influence. The form of godliness without the power is what most people want.

The church claims the right to pardon, and this leads its people to feel free to sin. The rite of confession also tends to open the way to evil. Those who kneel before fallen man and open the secret imaginations of their hearts in confession are degrading their spiritual natures. In unfolding their sins to a priest—an imperfect mortal—they lower their standard of character and corrupt themselves. Their idea of God is degraded to the image of fallen humanity, because the priest stands as a representative of God. This degrading confession of human to human is the secret spring from which has flowed much of the evil that is defiling the world. Yet to those who love to follow their own desires, it is more pleasing to confess to a fellow mortal than to open the heart to God. Human nature finds it more agreeable to do penance than to turn away from sin. It is easier to punish the flesh by sackcloth than to crucify fleshly lusts.

A Striking Similarity

When Christ lived on earth, the Jews were secretly trampling on God's law while outwardly they kept its requirements strictly, loading it down with additional duties that made obedience a burden. As the Jews professed to revere the law, so do Romanists claim to reverence the cross.

They place crosses on their churches, their altars, and their clothing. Everywhere the symbol of the cross is outwardly honored and exalted. But the teachings of Christ are buried beneath senseless traditions and rigorous requirements. Church teachings keep conscientious people in fear of the wrath of an offended God, while many officials of the

church live in luxury and sensual pleasure.

Satan constantly tries to misrepresent the character of God, the nature
of sin, and the real issues at stake in
the great controversy. His false arguments give people permission to sin.
At the same time he implants false
ideas of God so that they think of Him
with fear and hate rather than with
love. By such perverted ideas of God's
character, Satan led heathen nations
to believe that human sacrifices were
necessary to secure God's favor. People have carried out horrible cruelties
under the various forms of idolatry.

Union of Paganism and Christianity

The Roman Catholic Church has
united paganism and Christianity and,
like paganism, has misrepresented the
character of God and resorted to practices that are just as cruel. Instruments
of torture compelled people to accept
her doctrines. Officials of the church
studied to invent ways to cause the
greatest possible torture and not end
the life of those who would not give in
to the church's claims. In many cases
the sufferer welcomed death as a
sweet release.

For those who followed Rome's
teachings, the church had the discipline of the whip, of hunger, and of
denying the body's normal needs. To
gain Heaven's approval, repentant
people were taught to break the ties of
family and friendship which God has
formed to bless and gladden our
earthly journey. The churchyard contains millions of victims who spent
their lives trying unsuccessfully to repress every thought and feeling of
sympathy with their fellow creatures,
as though these were offensive to
God.

God does not put these heavy bur-
dens on us. Christ's life provides no
example for men and women to shut
themselves in monasteries in order to
become fit for heaven. He has never
taught us to repress our human love
and sympathy.

Doctrines From the Dark Ages

The pope claims to be the vicar, or
representative, of Christ. But was
Christ ever known to put people in
prison because they did not worship
Him as the King of heaven? Was His
voice heard condemning to death
those who did not accept Him?

The Roman Church now presents
a pleasing front to the world, covering
with apologies her record of horrible
cruelties. She has clothed herself in
Christlike garments, but she is unchanged. Every principle of the papacy in past ages exists today. The
church still holds the doctrines devised
in the Dark Ages. The papacy that
Protestants now honor is the same that
ruled in the days of the Reformation,
when men of God stood up at the risk
of their lives to expose her evils.

The papacy is just what prophecy
declared that she would be, the apostasy of the end times. (See 2 Thessalonians 2:3, 4.) Under the changeable
appearance of the chameleon she
conceals the changeless venom of the
serpent. Shall we now acknowledge
this power, whose record for a thousand years is written in the blood of
the saints, as a part of the church of
Christ?

A Change in Protestantism

In Protestant countries we hear the claim that Catholicism differs less from Protestantism than it did before. There has been a change, but the change is not in the papacy. Catholicism does in fact resemble much Protestantism that now exists because Protestantism has degenerated so greatly since the days of Reformers.

The Protestant churches are seeking the approval of the world, and so they believe good of all evil. As a result, they will finally believe evil of all good. They are now, as it were, apologizing to Rome for their unkind opinion of her, begging pardon for their "bigotry." Many claim that the intellectual and moral darkness that ruled during the Middle Ages helped to spread Rome's superstitions and oppression. They say that the greater intelligence of modern times and the increasing liberality in matters of religion will prevent any revival of intolerance. They ridicule the idea that such a state of things will exist in this enlightened age. But we should remember that the greater the light that is given, the greater the darkness of those who pervert and reject it.

An era of great intellectual darkness has been favorable to the papacy's success. We will yet see that an era of great intellectual light is equally favorable. In past ages when people did not have the knowledge of the truth, thousands were caught in the snare, not seeing the net spread for their feet. In this generation also, many do not see the net and walk into it as readily as if they were blindfolded. When people place their own theories above the Word of God, intelligence can do even more harm than ignorance. So today's false science will prove successful in preparing people to accept the papacy, just as the withholding of knowledge did in the Dark Ages.

Sunday Observance

Sunday observance is a custom that originated with Rome, and she claims it as the sign of her authority. The spirit of the papacy—of following worldly customs and honoring human traditions above the commandments of God—is seeping into the Protestant churches and leading them to the same work of exalting Sunday that the papacy has done before them.

Royal edicts, general councils, and church ordinances backed by secular power were the steps by which the pagan festival reached its position of honor in the Christian world. The first legal effort to enforce Sunday observance was the law that Constantine enacted. Though it was basically a heathen statute, the emperor enforced it after he accepted the forms of Christianity.

Eusebius, a bishop who tried to gain the favor of princes and who was the special friend of Constantine, claimed that Christ had transferred the Sabbath to Sunday. He offered no proof from Scripture. Eusebius himself unwittingly admits that this claim was false. "All things," he says, "that it was our duty to do on the Sabbath, these we have transferred to the Lord's Day."[2]

As the papacy became established, it continued to exalt Sunday.

For a time people still regarded the seventh day as the Sabbath, but steadily a change came in. Later the pope directed the parish priests to warn violators of Sunday that their behavior could bring some great calamity on themselves and their neighbors.

When the decrees of church councils were not enough, the church called on the secular authorities to issue a decree that would strike terror to the hearts of the people and force them to stop working on Sunday. A synod held in Rome reaffirmed all previous decisions and incorporated them into church law. The civil authorities in nearly all Christian countries enforced them.[3]

Still the lack of scriptural authority for Sunday keeping was embarrassing. The people questioned the right of their teachers to set aside the declaration, "The seventh day is the Sabbath of the LORD your God," in order to honor the day of the sun. To make up for the lack of Bible testimony, the church had to resort to other proofs.

About the close of the twelfth century, a zealous advocate of Sunday visited the churches of England. Faithful witnesses for the truth resisted him, and his efforts were so fruitless that he left the country for a time. When he returned, he brought with him a document that claimed to be from God Himself. It contained the needed command to observe Sunday, with awful threats to terrify the disobedient. This precious document, he claimed, had fallen from heaven and was found in Jerusalem on the altar of St. Simeon, in Golgotha. But in fact, the pope's palace at Rome was the source. In all ages, the papal hierarchy has regarded frauds and forgeries as acceptable. (See Appendix, note for page 27.)

But despite all efforts to establish Sunday sacredness, Catholics themselves publicly admitted the divine authority of the Sabbath. In the sixteenth century, a papal council declared: "Let all Christians remember that the seventh day was consecrated by God, and has been received and observed not only by the Jews, but by all others who claim to worship God, though we Christians have changed their Sabbath into the Lord's Day."[4] Those who were tampering with God's law were not ignorant of what they were doing.

Severe Penalties

An impressive illustration of Rome's policy is found in the long and bloody persecution of the Waldenses, some of whom kept the Sabbath. (See Appendix.) Also, the history of the churches of Ethiopia and Abyssinia is especially significant. Amid the gloom of the Dark Ages, the world lost sight of the Christians of Central Africa and forgot them. For many centuries, then, they enjoyed freedom in their faith. Finally Rome learned that they existed and tricked the emperor of Abyssinia into acknowledging the pope as the vicar of Christ. Then the church issued an edict forbidding people to observe the Sabbath under severe penalties.[5] But Roman tyranny soon became a yoke so bitter that the Abyssinians determined to break it. They banished the Romanists from their territory and restored the ancient faith.

While the churches of Africa kept the seventh day in obedience to the commandment of God, they also refrained from work on Sunday in keeping with the custom of the church. Rome trampled on the Sabbath of God to exalt her own, but the churches of Africa, hidden for nearly a thousand years, did not share this apostasy. When brought under Rome's control, they were forced to set aside the true and exalt the false sabbath. But no sooner had they regained their independence than they returned to obedience to the fourth commandment. (See Appendix.)

These records clearly reveal the hatred of Rome toward the true Sabbath and its defenders. The Word of God teaches that these scenes will be repeated as Catholics and Protestants unite to exalt Sunday.

The Beast With Lamblike Horns

The prophecy of Revelation 13 declares that the beast with lamblike horns will cause "the earth and those who dwell in it" to worship the papacy—symbolized by the beast "like a leopard." The beast with two horns will also tell "those who dwell on the earth to make an image to the beast." Furthermore, it will command all, "both small and great, rich and poor, free and slave," to receive the mark of the beast. (Revelation 13:11–16.) The United States is the power that the beast with lamblike horns represents. This prophecy will be fulfilled when the United States enforces Sunday observance, which Rome claims as the special acknowledgment of her supremacy.

"I saw one of his heads as if it had been mortally wounded, and his deadly wound was healed. And all the world marveled and followed the beast" (Revelation 13:3). The deadly wound points to the downfall of the papacy in 1798. After this, says the prophet, "his deadly wound was healed. And all the world marveled and followed the beast." Paul states that the "man of sin" will carry on his work of deception to the very end of time (2 Thessalonians 2:3–8). And "all who dwell on the earth will worship him, whose names have not been written in the Book of Life" (Revelation 13:8). In both the Old and the New World, the papacy will receive worship in the honor paid to Sunday.

Since the middle of the nineteenth century, students of prophecy have presented this message of Revelation 13 to the world. Now we see events rapidly moving toward the fulfillment of the prediction. Protestant teachers make the same claim of divine authority for Sunday keeping with the same lack of Bible evidence as do Catholic leaders. The assertion that God sends His judgments on people for violating the Sunday-sabbath will be repeated; already it is beginning to be heard.

The Roman Church is amazingly shrewd. She can read what is happening and what will come—that Protestant churches are recognizing her superiority by accepting the false Sabbath, and that they are preparing to enforce it in the same way that she herself did in ages past. It is not hard to guess how quickly she will come to the help of Protestants in this work.

The Roman Catholic Church

forms one vast organization under the control of the papal see. Its millions of members in every country are bound in loyalty to the pope, whatever their nationality or their government. Though they may take the oath pledging loyalty to the state, yet behind this lies the vow of obedience to Rome.

History tells of her sly and persistent efforts to insert herself into the affairs of nations, and having gained a foothold, to advance her own aims, even if it means the ruin of princes and people.[6]

Rome boasts that she never changes. Protestants do not understand what they are doing when they propose to accept Rome's help in the work of exalting Sunday. While they are focused on their purpose, Rome is aiming to re-establish her power, to recover her lost supremacy. Once the principle is established that the church may control the power of the state, that religious observances may be enforced by secular laws—in short, that the authority of church and state is to dominate the conscience—Rome's triumph is assured.

The Protestant world will learn what Rome's intentions are only when it is too late to escape the snare. She is silently growing in power. Her doctrines are exerting their influence in legislative halls, in the churches, and in people's hearts. She is strengthening her forces to gain the advantage when the time comes to strike. All that she wants is favorable ground, which she is already receiving. Soon, whoever believes and obeys the Word of God will face censure and persecution.

1. John L. von Mosheim, *Institutes of Ecclesiastical History,* bk. 3, cent. 11, pt. 2, ch. 2, sec. 9, n. 17.

2. Robert Cox, *Sabbath Laws and Sabbath Duties,* p. 538.

3. See Heylyn, *History of the Sabbath,* pt. 2, ch. 5, sec. 7.

4. Thomas Morer, *Discourse in Six Dialogues on the Name, Notion, and Observation of the Lord's Day,* pp. 281, 282.

5. See Michael Geddes, *Church History of Ethiopia,* pp. 311, 312.

6. See, for example, John Dowling, *The History of Romanism,* bk. 5, ch. 6, sec. 55; and Mosheim, bk. 3, cent. 11, pt. 2, ch. 2, sec. 9, n. 17.

The Approaching Conflict

From the very beginning of the great controversy in heaven, Satan has been trying to overthrow the law of God. Whether he can get people to discard the law altogether or to reject just one of its commandments, the result will be the same. The person who offends "in one point" shows contempt for the whole law. His influence and example are on the side of law-breaking; he becomes "guilty of all" (James 2:10).

Satan has perverted the doctrines of the Bible, and as a result errors have become a part of the faith of thousands. The last great conflict between truth and error is over the law of God. It is a battle between the Bible and the religion of fable and tradition. The Bible is within the reach of all, but few accept it as the guide of life. In the church many deny the pillars of the Christian faith. They reject Creation, the fall of man, the atonement, and the law of God either completely or in part. Thousands consider it a sign of weakness to place complete confidence in the Bible.

It is as easy to make an idol of false theories as it is to create an idol of wood or stone. By misrepresenting God, Satan leads people to think of Him in a false light. They put a philo-

sophical idol on the throne in the place of the living God as He is revealed in His Word, in Christ, and in the works of creation. The god of many philosophers, poets, politicians, journalists—the god of many universities, even of some theological institutions—is little better than Baal, the sun-god of Phoenicia in the days of Elijah.

No error strikes more boldly against the authority of Heaven or brings more harmful results than the doctrine that God's law is no longer binding. Suppose that prominent ministers were to teach publicly that the laws governing their land were not necessary, that they restricted the liberties of the people and should not be obeyed. How long would such preachers be allowed in the pulpit?

It would be more consistent for nations to abolish their statutes than for the Ruler of the universe to annul His law. France tried the experiment of making God's law void when atheism became the controlling power. This demonstrated that to throw off the God-given restraints is to accept the prince of evil as ruler.

Setting Aside the Law of God

Those who teach the people to

treat the commandments of God carelessly are sowing disobedience to reap disobedience. When people completely throw aside the restraints of God's law, they will soon disregard human laws. The results of banishing God's commandments would be like nothing they anticipate. Property would no longer be safe. People would take their neighbors' possessions by force, and the strongest would become the richest. Life itself would not be respected. The marriage vow would no longer stand as a defensive wall to protect the family. Whoever had the power would take his neighbor's wife by violence. The fifth commandment would be ignored with the fourth. Children would not hesitate to take the life of their parents if doing so would get them what their corrupt hearts want. The civilized world would become a mob of robbers and assassins, and peace and happiness would be banished from the earth.

Already this doctrine has opened the floodgates of evil on the world. Lawlessness and corruption sweep in like an overwhelming tide. Even in households that claim to be Christian there is hypocrisy, damaged relationships, betrayal of sacred trusts, indulgence of lust. Religious principle, which should be the foundation of social life, seems to be swaying and ready to fall. Depraved criminals often receive attention as if they had done some great thing. Their crimes get wide publicity. The press publishes revolting details of evil, instructing others in fraud, robbery, and murder. The fascination with evil, the terrible intemperance and iniquity of every kind,

should awaken everyone. What can be done to stop the tide of evil?

Intemperance Has Beclouded Many

Courts are corrupt, rulers are driven by desire for money and by love of sensual pleasure. Intemperance has beclouded the minds of many so that Satan has almost complete control of them. Judges are corrupted, bribed, deluded. Drunkenness and partying, dishonesty of every sort, are found among those who administer the laws. Now that Satan can no longer keep the world under control by denying people the Scriptures, he resorts to other ways to accomplish the same objective. To destroy faith in the Bible serves just as well as to destroy the Bible itself.

As in past ages, Satan has worked through the churches to move his plans forward. In combating unpopular truths in the Scriptures, they adopt interpretations that sow the seeds of unbelief far and wide. Clinging to the Catholic error of natural immortality and human consciousness in death, they reject the only defense against the false teachings of spiritualism. The doctrine of eternal torment has led many to reject the Bible. As the claims of the fourth commandment are presented, people see that it calls for them to keep the seventh-day Sabbath. Seeing no other way to free themselves from a duty they are not willing to perform, popular teachers throw out the law of God and the Sabbath together. As Sabbath reform extends, this rejection of God's law to avoid the fourth commandment will become nearly universal. Religious leaders open the door to unbelief, spiritualism, and contempt for God's holy law—a fearful responsibility for the evils that exist in the Christian world.

Yet these very people claim that enforcing Sunday observance would improve the morals of society. It is one of Satan's deceptions to combine falsehood with just enough truth to make it believable. The leaders of the Sunday movement may campaign for reforms that the people need, principles in harmony with the Bible. But while they combine these with a requirement contrary to God's law, His servants cannot join with them. Nothing can justify setting aside the commandments of God for human laws.

Through the two great errors, the immortality of the soul and Sunday sacredness, Satan will bring the people under his deceptions. While the immortality of the soul lays the foundation of spiritualism, Sunday sacredness creates ties of sympathy with Rome. The Protestants of the United States will take the lead in stretching their hands across the gulf to grasp the hand of spiritualism; they will also reach over the abyss to clasp hands with the Roman power; and under the influence of this three-part union, this country will follow in the steps of Rome in trampling on the rights of conscience.

As spiritualism imitates the popular Christianity of the day, it has great power to deceive. Satan himself seems "converted." He will appear as an angel of light. Through spiritualism, miracles will take place, the sick will be healed, and many undeniable wonders will be performed.

Catholics who boast of miracles as a sign of the true church will be easily deceived by this wonder-working power, and Protestants, who have thrown away the shield of truth, will also be deluded. Catholics, Protestants, and secular people will all see in this union a grand movement for the conversion of the world.

Through spiritualism, Satan appears to be someone who blesses humanity, healing diseases and presenting a new system of religious faith, but at the same time he leads many people to ruin. Alcohol use overcomes reason; sensual indulgence, conflict, and bloodshed follow. War stirs up the worst passions of the heart and sweeps its victims into eternity, covered in vice and blood. It is Satan's goal to prod the nations to war, because in this way he can divert people from preparing for the judgment and eternity.

Satan has studied the secrets of nature, and he uses all his power to control the elements as far as God allows. It is God who shields His creatures from the destroyer. But the Christian world has shown contempt for His law, and the Lord will do what He said He would—remove His protecting care from those who rebel against His law and who force others to do the same. Satan has control of everyone whom God does not especially guard. He will favor and prosper some in order to advance his own plans, and he will bring trouble on others and lead them to believe that God is the one who is mistreating them.

While appearing to be a great

physician who can heal all their ill- nesses, Satan will bring disease and disaster until crowded cities are re- duced to ruin. In accidents by sea and land, in great fires, in fierce tornadoes and hailstorms, in gales, floods, hurri- canes, tidal waves, and earthquakes, in a thousand forms, Satan is exerting his power. He sweeps away the ripen- ing harvest, and famine and misery follow. He gives the air a deadly taint, and thousands die.

And then the great deceiver will persuade people to blame all their troubles on the believers whose obedi- ence to God's commandments is a constant rebuke to those who break God's law. They will say that these people are offending God by violating Sunday, and that this sin has brought disasters that will not stop until Sun- day observance is strictly enforced. They will claim that those who destroy reverence for Sunday are preventing their restoration to God's favor and material prosperity. They will repeat the accusation urged long ago against the servant of God: "When Ahab saw Elijah, Ahab said to him, 'Is it you, you troubler of Israel?'" (1 Kings 18:17, 18, NRSV).

Satan will use miracle-working power against those who obey God rather than human laws. The "spirits" will declare that God has sent them to convince those who reject Sunday that they are wrong. They will act sad over the great wickedness in the world, and they will support the testimony of reli- gious teachers that the low state of morals is the result of desecrating Sunday.

Under Rome's rule, people said

that those who suffered for the gospel were evildoers in partnership with Sa- tan. It will be the same way now. Sa- tan will cause those who honor God's law to be accused as people who are bringing judgments on the world. He uses fear to try to rule the conscience, persuading religious and secular au- thorities to enforce human laws and defy the law of God.

Those who honor the Bible Sab- bath will be blamed as enemies of law and order, breaking down the moral restraints of society, causing lawless- ness and corruption, and calling down the judgments of God on the earth. They will be accused of undermining the government. Ministers who deny that people need to keep God's law will preach about the duty of obeying the civil authorities. In legislative halls and courts of justice, commandment- keepers will be condemned. People will put a false slant on their words and the worst construction on their motives.

Leaders of church and state will unite to persuade or force everyone to honor Sunday. Even in free America rulers and legislators will give in to the popular demand for a law enforcing Sunday observance. Liberty of con- science, which has cost so great a sac- rifice, will no longer be respected. In the soon-coming conflict we will see the prophet's words fulfilled: "The dragon was enraged with the woman, and he went to make war with the rest of her offspring, who keep the com- mandments of God and have the testi- mony of Jesus Christ" (Revelation 12:17).

Our Only Safeguard

God points His followers to the Bible as their safeguard against the deceptive power of evil spirits. Satan uses every possible way to prevent people from gaining a knowledge of the Bible. At every revival of God's work, his activity becomes more intense. We will soon see a final struggle begin against Christ and His followers. The counterfeit will resemble the true so closely that it will be impossible to tell the difference between them except by the Scriptures.

Those who try to obey all of God's commandments will be opposed and mocked. To endure the trial, they must understand the will of God as revealed in His Word. They can honor Him only as they correctly understand His character, government, and goals, and act in harmony with them. Only those who have fortified their minds with the truths of the Bible will stand firmly through the last great struggle.

Before His crucifixion the Savior explained to His disciples that He was going to be killed and would rise again. Angels were there to impress His words on their minds and hearts. But they forgot the very words they needed to remember. When the trouble came, the death of Jesus destroyed their hopes as completely as if He had not warned them beforehand. Similarly, the prophecies open the future before us as clearly as Christ opened it to the disciples. But most people have no more understanding of these important truths than if God had never revealed them.

When God sends warnings, He requires every sound-minded person to obey the message. The fearful judgments against worshiping the beast and his image (Revelation 14:9–11) should lead everyone to learn what the mark of the beast is and how to avoid receiving it. But the great majority of people do not want Bible truth, because it goes against the desires of the sinful heart. Satan supplies them with the deceptions they love.

But God will have a people who hold the Bible, and the Bible only, as the standard of all doctrines and the basis of all reforms. The opinions of educated men, the conclusions of science, the decisions of church councils, the voice of the majority—not one nor all of these should we take as evidence for or against any doctrine. We should demand a plain "Thus says the Lord." Satan leads the people to look to pastors, to professors of theology, as their guides instead of searching the Scriptures for themselves. By controlling these leaders, he can influence most people.

When Christ came, the common people heard Him gladly. But the chief priests and the nation's leaders wrapped themselves in prejudice, rejecting the evidence that He was the Messiah. "How is it," the people asked, "that our rulers and enlightened scribes do not believe on Jesus?" Teachers like this led the Jewish nation to reject their Redeemer.

Exalting Human Authority

Christ foresaw that people would exalt human authority to rule over the conscience. In all ages this has been a terrible a curse. As an appeal to future generations, the Bible recorded His warnings not to follow blind leaders.

The Roman Church teaches that only her clergy have the right to interpret the Scriptures. Though the Reformation gave the Scriptures to everyone, yet the same principle that Rome held prevents multitudes in Protestant churches from searching the Bible for themselves. They are taught to accept its teachings *as interpreted by the church.* Thousands do not dare to accept anything, no matter how plain it is in Scripture, that is contrary to their creed.

Many are ready to commit their eternal destiny to the clergy. They pay almost no attention to the Savior's teachings. But are ministers infallible? How can we trust them to guide us unless we know from God's Word that they are light-bearers? A lack of moral courage leads many to follow educated people, and they become hopelessly attached to error. They see the truth for this time in the Bible and feel the power of the Holy Spirit accompany the giving of it, yet they allow the clergy to turn them from the light.

Satan keeps many of his followers by attaching them with silken cords of affection to those who are enemies of the cross of Christ. This attachment may be to parents, brothers or sisters, husband or wife, or friends. Under their influence, many people do not have the courage to obey their convictions of what is right.

Many claim that it makes no difference what one believes, if that person lives the right life. But the life is molded by the faith. If truth is within reach and we neglect it, we are really rejecting it, choosing darkness rather than light.

Ignorance is no excuse for error or sin when we have every opportunity to know the will of God. A man who is traveling comes to a place where there are several roads and a signpost telling where each one leads. If he ignores the sign and takes whatever road seems to be right, he may be sincere, but he is likely to find himself on the wrong road.

The First and Highest Duty

It is not enough to have good intentions, to do what we think is right or what the minister tells us is right. We should search the Scriptures for ourselves. We have a map pointing out every key point on the journey to heaven, and we should not guess at anything.

It is the first and highest duty of every rational person to learn from the Scriptures what is truth, and then to walk in the light and encourage others to do the same. In our study, with God's help we are to form our opinions for ourselves, since we are to answer for ourselves before God.

Educated people, with a show of great wisdom, teach that the Scriptures have a secret, spiritual meaning that is not easily seen in the language used. They are false teachers. We should explain the language of the Bible by its obvious meaning, unless it uses a symbol or figure. If people would only take the Bible as it reads, it would accomplish a work that would bring thousands into the fold of Christ who now are wandering in error.

Many a Scripture which scholars ignore as unimportant is full of comfort to those who have been learning in the school of Christ. To understand Bible truth, we do not so much need the power of intellect for the search. Rather, we need a thirst for Bible truth more than anything else and an earnest longing for righteousness.

Results of Neglecting Prayer and Bible Study

We should never study the Bible without prayer. Only the Holy Spirit can cause us to feel the importance of things we understand easily or prevent us from twisting difficult truths. Heavenly angels prepare the heart to comprehend God's Word. We will be charmed with its beauty and strengthened by its promises. Temptations often seem irresistible because the tempted one cannot quickly remember God's promises and oppose Satan with the Scripture weapons. But angels are close to those willing to be taught, and they will bring to their memory the truths they need.

"He will teach you all things, and bring to your remembrance all things that I said to you" (John 14:26). But we must first store the teachings of Christ in the mind in order for the Spirit of God to bring them to our remembrance in the time of danger.

The destiny of all people on earth is about to be decided. Every follower of Christ should ask earnestly, "Lord, what do You want me to do?" (Acts 9:6). We should now seek a deep and living experience in the things of God. We have no time to lose. We are on Satan's territory. Sentinels of God, don't be caught sleeping!

Many congratulate themselves for the wrong acts that they do not commit. But it is not enough for them to be trees in the garden of God. They are to bear fruit. In the books of heaven they are registered as those who use up the ground. Yet God's heart of long-suffering love still pleads with those who have despised His mercy and abused His grace.

In the summer there is no noticeable difference between evergreens and other trees. But when the storms of winter come, the evergreens remain unchanged while other trees lose their leaves. If opposition arises, intolerance again prevails, and persecution is kindled, the halfhearted and hypocritical will give up the faith. But the true Christians will stand firm, their faith stronger, their hope brighter, than in times of prosperity.

"He shall be like a tree planted by the waters, which spreads out its roots by the river, and will not fear when heat comes; but its leaf will be green, and will not be anxious in the year of drought, nor will cease from yielding fruit" (Jeremiah 17:8).

God's Final Message

I saw another angel coming down from heaven, having great authority, and the earth was illuminated with his glory. And he cried mightily with a loud voice, saying, 'Babylon the great is fallen, is fallen, and has become a dwelling place of demons, a prison for every foul spirit, and a cage for every unclean and hated bird!' . . . And I heard another voice from heaven saying, 'Come out of her, my people, lest you share in her sins, and lest you receive of her plagues'" (Revelation 18:1, 2, 4).

The second angel's announcement in Revelation 14:8 is going to be repeated, but with the additional mention of the corruptions that have been entering Babylon since that message was first given.

This new message describes a terrible condition. Every time people reject truth, their minds become darker, their hearts more stubborn. They will continue to trample on one of the Ten Commandments until they persecute those who hold God's law as sacred. They reject Christ by the contempt they show for His Word and His followers.

People will claim to be religious, but their religion will become a cover for the worst evils. A belief in spiritualism opens the door to doctrines of devils, and in this way evil angels will influence the churches. Babylon has filled up the measure of her guilt, and destruction is about to fall.

But God still has people in Babylon, and He must call these faithful ones out so that they will not share in her sins and "receive of her plagues." The angel comes down from heaven, lighting up the earth with his glory and announcing the sins of Babylon. The call goes out, "Come out of her, my people." These announcements are the final warning that goes to the inhabitants of the earth.

The powers of earth will unite in warring against the commandments of God. They will decree that "all, both small and great, rich and poor, free and slave" (Revelation 13:16) must conform to the customs of the church by observing the false sabbath. All who refuse will finally be judged as deserving death. On the other hand, the law of God calls for people to honor the Creator's rest day, and it threatens God's punishment against all who break its requirements.

When circumstances like these bring the issue clearly before them, all who trample on God's law to obey a human law receive the mark of the beast, the sign of allegiance to the power they choose to obey instead of God. "If anyone worships the beast and his image, and receives his mark on his forehead or on his hand, he himself shall also drink of the wine of the wrath of God, which is poured out full strength into the cup of His indignation" (Revelation 14:9, 10).

Not one experiences the wrath of God until the truth has been brought home to his mind and conscience and he has rejected it. Many have never had opportunity to hear the special truths for this time. The God who reads every heart will allow none to be deceived about the issues of the controversy if they want to know the truth. Everyone will have enough light to make an intelligent decision.

The Great Test of Loyalty

The Sabbath, the great test of loyalty, is the truth especially under attack. While observing the false sabbath will be a pledge of allegiance to a power who opposes God, keeping the true Sabbath is an evidence of loyalty to the Creator. While one group receives the mark of the beast, the other receives the seal of God.

Many say that it is groundless and ridiculous to predict that religious intolerance will gain control, that church and state will persecute those who keep the commandments of God. But when Sunday observance is widely agitated, people will see that the event they have doubted so long is actually approaching, and the message will produce an effect it could not have had before.

In every generation God has sent His servants to rebuke sin in the world and in the church. Many Reformers started their work determined to exercise great restraint in attacking the sins of the church and the nation. By the example of a pure Christian life, they hoped to lead the people back to the Bible. But the Spirit of God came over them. Fearless of consequences, they could not hold back from preaching the plain doctrines of the Bible.

That is just how the message will be proclaimed. The Lord will work through humble instruments who consecrate themselves to His service. The workers will be qualified by the anointing of His Spirit rather than by training in schools. They will feel compelled to go out with holy zeal, declaring the message that God gives. The sins of Babylon will be laid open. The solemn warnings will stir the people. Thousands have never heard words like these. They learn that Babylon is the church, fallen because of her sins, because of her rejection of truth. As the people go to their teachers to ask, "Are these things so?" the ministers present fables to quiet the awakened conscience. But since many demand a plain "Thus says the Lord," the popular ministry will stir up the sin-loving crowds to accuse and persecute those who proclaim the message.

The clergy will put forth almost superhuman efforts to shut away the light, to keep people from discussing these vital questions. The church appeals to the strong arm of civil power, and, in this work, Catholics and Protestants unite. As the movement for Sunday enforcement becomes more bold, commandment-keepers will be threatened with fines and imprisonment. Some will be offered positions of influence and other rewards to give up their faith. But their answer is, "Show us our error from the Word of God." Those accused before courts make a strong defense of truth, and some who hear them are led to make their decision to keep all the commandments of God. In this way light comes to thousands who otherwise would know nothing of these truths.

Obedience to God will be treated as rebellion. Parents will treat their believing children harshly. They will disinherit them and drive them from home. "All who desire to live godly in Christ Jesus will suffer persecution" (2 Timothy 3:12). As the defenders of truth refuse to honor Sunday, some will be put in prison, some will be exiled, some will be treated as slaves. When God withdraws His Spirit from people, there will be strange developments. The heart can be very cruel when God's fear and love are removed.

The Storm Approaches

As the storm approaches, many who have claimed to believe in the third angel's message, but have not been sanctified through obeying the truth, abandon their position and join the opposition. By uniting with the world they have come to see things nearly as the world does, and they choose the popular side. People who once were enthusiastic about the truth use their talents and speaking ability to mislead others. They become bitter enemies of the believers who used to be their friends in the faith. These apostates are efficient agents of Satan to misrepresent and accuse Sabbath-keepers and stir up the authorities against them.

The Lord's servants have given the warning. God's Spirit has impelled them. They have not been concerned about their wealth or their reputations or their lives. The work seems far greater than they can accomplish. Yet they cannot turn back. Feeling helpless, they turn to the Mighty One for strength.

Different periods in history have been notable for the development of some special truth that exactly met the needs of God's people at that time. Every new truth has made its way against opposition. Christ's ambassadors must perform their duty and leave the results with God.

Opposition Rises to New Intensity

The opposition rises to a fierce intensity. The servants of God are perplexed again, because it seems to them that they have caused the crisis. But conscience and the Word of God assure them that their course is right. Their faith and courage rise with the emergency. Their testimony is, "Christ has conquered the powers of earth, and are we going to be afraid of a world already conquered?"

No one can serve God without drawing opposition from the powers of darkness. Evil angels will assail such faithful ones, alarmed that their influence is taking the prey away from them. Evil people will try to separate them from God with attractive temptations. When these things do not succeed, they will use power to force the conscience.

But so long as Jesus remains our

intercessor in the sanctuary above, rulers and people feel the restraining influence of the Holy Spirit. While many of our rulers are active agents of Satan, God also has His agents among the leaders of the nation. A few God-fearing statesmen will hold back a powerful current of evil. The opposition from the enemies of truth will be restrained so that the third angel's message may do its work. The final warning will capture the attention of these leaders, and some will accept it and stand with the people of God during the time of trouble.

The Latter Rain and the Loud Cry

The angel who unites with the third angel is to illuminate the whole earth with his glory. The first angel's message went to every mission station in the world, and in some countries there was the greatest religious interest ever seen since the Reformation. But the last warning of the third angel will exceed these demonstrations of God's power.

The work will be similar to what happened on the Day of Pentecost. God gave the "former rain" at the opening of the gospel to cause the precious seed to spring up. Likewise He will give the "latter rain" at its close to ripen the harvest. (Hosea 6:3; Joel 2:23). The great work of the gospel will not close with less demonstration of God's power than its opening had. The prophecies that were fulfilled with the outpouring of the former rain at the opening of the gospel will be fulfilled again with the latter rain at its close. Here are the "times of refreshing" to which the apostle Peter looked forward (Acts 3:19, 20).

Servants of God, their faces shining with holy devotion, will hurry from place to place to tell the message from heaven. Miracles will take place, the sick will be healed. Satan also works with deceptive miracles, even bringing down fire from heaven (Revelation 13:13). These things will move the inhabitants of the earth to choose sides.

The message will succeed not so much by argument as by the deep conviction of the Spirit of God. The arguments have been presented, publications have exerted their influence, yet Satan has kept many from fully understanding the truth. Now they see the truth in its clearness. Family relationships and church connections are powerless to stop the honest children of God now. Regardless of the forces combined against the truth, a large number take their stand on the Lord's side.

The Time of Trouble

At that time Michael shall stand up, the great prince who stands watch over the sons of your people; and there shall be a time of trouble, such as never was since there was a nation, even to that time. And at that time your people shall be delivered, every one who is found written in the book" (Daniel 12:1).

When the third angel's message closes, the people of God have finished their work. They have received "the latter rain" and are prepared for the difficult time ahead of them. The final test has come on the world, and all who have proved loyal to the divine law have received "the seal of the living God." Then Jesus ends His ministry in the sanctuary in heaven and with a loud voice says, "It is done!" "He who is unjust, let him be unjust still; he who is filthy, let him be filthy still; he who is righteous, let him be righteous still; he who is holy, let him be holy still" (Revelation 22:11). Christ has made the atonement for His people and blotted out their sins. "The kingdom and dominion, and the greatness of the kingdoms under the whole heaven" (Daniel 7:27) is about to be given to the heirs of salvation, and Jesus is to reign as King of kings and Lord of lords.

When He leaves the sanctuary, darkness covers those living on the earth. The righteous must live in the sight of a holy God without an intercessor. The restraint on the wicked is removed, and Satan has entire control of the unrepentant. They have resisted the Spirit of God persistently, and He has been finally withdrawn. Then Satan will plunge the earth's population into one great, final trouble. Angels of God stop holding back the fierce winds of human evil. The whole world will be involved in ruin more terrible than that which ancient Jerusalem experienced. There are forces now ready, only waiting the divine permission, to spread destruction everywhere.

People will think that those who honor the law of God are the cause of the fearful conflict and bloodshed that fill the earth with misery. The power that accompanies the last warning has enraged the wicked, and Satan will stir up the spirit of hatred and persecution against all who have received the message.

When God withdrew His presence from the Jewish nation, priests and people still thought of themselves as the chosen of God. The services in the temple continued, and every day the priests pronounced the divine blessing on those who were guilty of the blood of God's Son. Similarly, when the final decision of the heavenly sanctuary has been pronounced and the destiny of the world has been decided permanently, the inhabitants of the earth will not know it. People from whom the Spirit of God has been withdrawn will continue the forms of religion. The prince of evil will inspire them to accomplish his wicked plans.

As the Sabbath becomes the special point of controversy throughout the Christian world, people will claim that the few who stand in opposition to the church and the state should not be tolerated, that it is better for them to suffer than for whole nations to be thrown into confusion and lawlessness. The same argument was brought against Christ. Caiaphas said, "It is expedient for us that one man should die for the people, and not that the whole nation should perish" (John 11:50). This argument will appear conclusive. A decree will finally be issued against those who honor the Sabbath of the fourth commandment, denouncing them and giving the people permission after a certain time to kill them. Romanism in the Old World and apostate Protestantism in the New will pursue a similar course toward those who keep all of God's commandments. The people of God will then be plunged into those scenes of distress that the Bible calls "the time of Jacob's trouble" (Jeremiah 30:5-7; see Genesis 32:24-30).

The Time of Jacob's Trouble

Because Jacob had deceived his father in order to get the blessing intended for Esau, he had to flee for his life to escape his brother's deadly threats. After remaining an exile for many years, he had set out to return to his native country. When he reached the border, he was filled with terror at the news that Esau was coming, no doubt intending to get revenge. Jacob's only hope was in the mercy of God; his only defense must be prayer.

Alone with God, he confessed his sin with deep repentance. The crisis in his life had come. In the darkness he continued praying. Suddenly he felt a hand on his shoulder. He thought an enemy was going to kill him. With all the energy of despair he wrestled with his attacker. When the day began to break, the stranger used his superhuman power. Jacob seemed paralyzed. He fell, helpless and weeping, on the neck of his mysterious enemy. He knew then that it was the Angel of the covenant with whom he had been struggling. For years he had endured remorse for his sin; now he must have the assurance that it was forgiven. The Angel urged him, "Let Me go, for the day breaks," but Jacob exclaimed, "I will not let You go unless You bless me!" Jacob confessed his weakness and unworthiness, yet he trusted the mercy of a covenant-keeping God. Through repentance and self-surrender, this sinful mortal received what he wanted most from the Majesty of heaven.

Satan had accused Jacob to God because of his sin, and he had moved Esau to march against him. During Jacob's night of wrestling, Satan tried to discourage him and break his hold on God. Jacob was driven almost to despair, but he had sincerely repented of his sin. He held the Angel tightly and urged his request with earnest cries until he prevailed.

Just as Satan accused Jacob, he will bring his accusations against the people of God, but those who keep the commandments of God resist his supremacy. He sees that holy angels are guarding them, and he concludes that their sins have been pardoned. He has an accurate knowledge of the sins he has tempted them to commit, and he declares that it is unjust for the Lord to forgive their sins and yet destroy him and his angels. He demands that God give these people into his hands to destroy.

The Lord permits him to test them to the limit. Their confidence in God, their faith, will be severely tested. Satan tries to terrify them. He hopes to destroy their faith so that they will yield to temptation and turn from their loyalty to God.

Anguish That God Will Be Dishonored

Yet the anguish that God's people suffer is not because they dread persecution. They fear that through some fault in themselves they will fail to experience the Savior's promise: I "will keep you from the hour of trial which shall come upon the whole world" (Revelation 3:10). If they prove to be unworthy because of their own defects of character, then God's holy name would be dishonored.

They point to their past repentance for their many sins and plead the Savior's promise, "Let him take hold of My strength, that he may make peace with Me; and he shall make peace with Me" (Isaiah 27:5). Though they are suffering anxiety and distress, they do not stop their earnest praying. They lay hold of God as Jacob laid hold of the Angel, and the language of their souls is, "I will not let You go unless You bless me!"

Sins Blotted Out

In the time of trouble, if the people of God had unconfessed sins to appear before them while they were tortured with fear and anguish, they would be overwhelmed. Despair would cut off their faith, and they could not plead with God to deliver them. But they have no concealed wrongs to reveal. Their sins have gone beforehand to judgment and have been blotted out, and they cannot bring them to mind.

In His dealings with Jacob, the Lord shows that He will not tolerate evil. Satan will overcome all who excuse or conceal their sins and allow them to remain on the books of heaven unconfessed and unforgiven. The more honorable the position they hold, the more sure is their adversary's triumph. Those who delay their preparation cannot get it in the time of trouble, or at any later time. Their case is hopeless.

Jacob's history is also an assurance that God will not reject those who, lured into sin, have returned to Him with true repentance. God will send angels to comfort them in danger. The Lord's eye is on His people. The flames of the furnace seem about to consume them, but the Refiner will bring them through as gold tried in the fire.

A Faith That Endures

The time of distress and anguish ahead of us will require a faith that can endure weariness, delay, and hunger, a faith that will not crumble even though it is tested severely. Jacob's victory is an evidence of the power of persistent prayer. All who will lay hold of God's promises, as Jacob did, will succeed as he succeeded. Wrestling with God—how few know what it is! When waves of despair sweep over the needy, praying ones, how few cling with faith to the promises of God.

Those who exercise very little faith now are in the greatest danger of falling under the power of Satan's delusions. And even if they endure the test, they will be plunged into deeper distress because they have never made it a habit to trust in God. We should gain experience now in relying on His promises.

Often we anticipate worse trouble than what actually comes, but this is not true of the crisis ahead of us. The most vivid description cannot reach the level of the ordeal. In that time of trial every believer must stand for himself before God.

Now, while our High Priest is making the atonement for us, we should seek to become perfect in Christ. Not even by a thought could our Savior be brought to yield to the power of temptation. Satan finds some point in human hearts where he can gain a foothold. People cherish some sinful desire, and his temptations use that desire to assert their power. But Christ declared about Himself, "The ruler of this world is coming, and he has noth-ing in Me" (John 14:30). Satan could find nothing in the Son of God that would enable him to gain the victory. There was no sin in Him that Satan could use to his advantage. This is the condition needed by those who will stand in the time of trouble.

It is in this life that we are to separate sin from us, through faith in the atoning blood of Christ. Our precious Savior invites us to join ourselves to Him, to unite our weakness to His strength, our unworthiness to His merits. It is up to us to cooperate with Heaven in the work of conforming our characters to the divine model.

Fearful sights of a supernatural kind will soon appear in the heavens, in support of the power of miracle-working demons. Spirits of demons will go out to the "kings of the earth" and to the whole world, to urge them to unite with Satan in his last struggle against the government of heaven. People will come forward, pretending to be Christ Himself. They will perform miracles of healing and profess to have revelations from heaven that contradict the Scriptures.

The Crowning Act

As the crowning act in the great drama of deception, Satan himself will appear as if he were Christ. The church has long looked for the Savior's coming as the fulfillment of her hopes. Now the great deceiver will make it appear that Christ has come. Satan will show himself as a majestic being of dazzling brightness, resembling the description of the Son of God in the book of Revelation (Revelation 1:13–15).

The glory that surrounds him is greater than anything that mortal eyes have yet seen. The shout of triumph rings out, "Christ has come!" The people bow down before him. He lifts up his hands and blesses them. His voice is soft, yet full of melody. In compassionate tones he presents some of the same heavenly truths the Savior spoke. He heals diseases, and then, in his assumed character of Christ, claims to have changed the Sabbath to Sunday. He declares that those who keep holy the seventh day are showing contempt for him. This is the strong, almost overpowering delusion. Vast numbers believe his sorceries, saying, This is "the great power of God" (Acts 8:10).

God's People Not Misled

But the people of God will not be misled. The teachings of this false christ are not in harmony with the Scriptures. He pronounces his blessing on the worshipers of the beast and his image, the very class on whom the Bible says that God will pour out His undiluted wrath.

Furthermore, God does not permit Satan to counterfeit the manner of Christ's coming. The Savior warned His people against being deceived on this point. "False christs and false prophets will rise and show great signs and wonders to deceive, if possible, even the elect. . . . Therefore if they say to you, 'Look, He is in the desert!' do not go out; or 'Look, He is in the inner rooms!' do not believe it. For as the lightning comes from the east and flashes to the west, so also will the coming of the Son of Man be" (Matthew 24:24, 26, 27; see also Matthew 25:31; Revelation 1:7; 1 Thessalonians 4:16, 17). This coming is impossible to counterfeit. The whole world will witness it.

Only those who have studied the Scriptures diligently and have received the love of the truth will be shielded from the powerful deception that takes the world captive. By the Bible testimony, they will detect the deceiver in his disguise. Are the people of God now so firmly established on His Word that they would not give in to the evidence of their senses? In such a crisis, would they cling to the Bible, and the Bible only?

The decree from the various Christian rulers against commandment keepers withdraws the protection of government and abandons them to those who want their destruction. At that time, the people of God will flee from the cities and villages and associate together in small groups, living in the most desolate and lonely places. Many will find safety in the strongholds of the mountains, like the Christians of the Piedmont valleys (see chapter 4). But many of all nations and of all classes, high and low, rich and poor, black and white, will be thrown into the most unjust and cruel bondage. Those whom God loves pass weary days shut in by prison bars, sentenced to be killed, apparently left to die in dark, disgusting dungeons.

Will the Lord forget His people in this difficult hour? Did He forget faithful Noah, Lot, Joseph, Elijah, Jeremiah, or Daniel? Though enemies may put them into prison, yet dungeon walls cannot cut off communication between their hearts and Christ. Angels will come to them in lonely cells. The prison will be like a palace, and the gloomy walls will be lighted up as when Paul and Silas sang at midnight in the Philippian dungeon.

God Sends His Plagues

God's judgments will fall on those who are trying to destroy His people. To God, punishment is a "strange act" (Isaiah 28:21, KJV; see also Ezekiel 33:11). The Lord is "merciful and gracious, longsuffering, and abounding in goodness and truth, . . . forgiving iniquity and transgression and sin," yet "by no means clearing the guilty" (Exodus 34:6, 7; see also Nahum 1:3). He bears long with the nations, but when they have filled up their measure of iniquity, they will finally drink the cup of wrath unmixed with mercy.

When Christ ends His ministry in the sanctuary, God will pour out the unmingled wrath threatened against those who worship the beast. The plagues on Egypt were similar to the more widespread judgments that will fall on the world just before the final deliverance of God's people. John the revelator says: "A foul and loathsome sore came upon the men who had the mark of the beast and those who worshiped his image." The sea "became blood as of a dead man." And "the rivers and springs of water . . . became blood." The angel declares: "You are righteous, O Lord, . . . because You have judged these things. For they have shed the blood of saints and prophets, and You have given them blood to drink. For it is their just due." (Revelation 16:2–6.) By condemning

the people of God to death, they have become guilty of their blood as truly as if they had shed it with their own hands. Christ declared the Jews of His time guilty of all the blood of holy men shed since the days of Abel (Matthew 23:34–36), for they possessed the same spirit as those murderers of the prophets.

In the plague that follows, God gives power to the sun "to scorch men with fire." The prophets describe this fearful time: "The harvest of the field has perished. . . . All the trees of the field are withered; surely joy has withered away from the sons of men." "How the animals groan! The herds of cattle are restless, because they have no pasture. . . . The water brooks are dried up, and fire has devoured the open pastures." (Joel 1:11, 12, 18, 20.)

These plagues are not universal, yet they will be the most awful afflictions ever known. All judgments before the close of probation have been mingled with mercy. The blood of Christ has shielded the sinner from the full impact of his guilt. But in the final judgment, wrath is unmixed with mercy. Many will want the shelter of God's mercy which they have despised.

While the people of God will be persecuted and distressed and will suffer for lack of food, God will not leave them to die. Angels will supply their needs. "Bread will be given him, his water will be sure." "I, the LORD, will hear them; I, the God of Israel, will not forsake them." (Isaiah 33:16; 41:17.)

Yet to human sight it will seem that the people of God must soon die for their faith, as the martyrs did before them. It is a time of dreadful agony. The wicked boast, "Where now is your faith? Why does not God deliver you out of our hands if you are indeed His people?" But the waiting ones remember Jesus dying on Calvary's cross. Like Jacob, all are wrestling with God.

Companies of Angels Watch

God stations angels around those who have kept Christ's command to persevere. They have witnessed the faithful ones' distress and heard their prayers. They wait for word from their Commander to snatch them from their danger. But they must wait a little longer. The people of God must drink of the cup and be baptized with the baptism (Matthew 20:20–23). Yet for their sake the time of trouble will be shortened. The end will come more quickly than people expect.

Though a general decree has set the time when commandment-keepers may be killed, in some cases their enemies will rush ahead of the decree and try to take their lives. But none can pass the guardians stationed around every faithful believer. Some are attacked as they flee from the cities, but the weapons raised against them break like straw. Others are defended by angels in the form of soldiers.

In all ages heavenly beings have taken an active part in human affairs. They have accepted hospitality in people's homes, acted as guides to confused travelers, opened prison doors and set free the servants of the Lord. They came to roll away the stone from the Savior's tomb.

Angels visit the assemblies of the wicked for the same reason that they went to Sodom, to determine whether they have passed the boundary of God's leniency. For the sake of a few who really serve Him, the Lord restrains disasters and prolongs the peace of the population. Little do sinners realize that they are indebted for their lives to the faithful few whom they love to oppress.

Often in the councils of this world, angels have spoken out. Human ears have listened to their appeals, human lips have ridiculed their counsels. These heavenly messengers have proved themselves better able to plead the cause of the oppressed than their most eloquent defenders. They have defeated and stopped evils that would have caused great suffering to God's people.

With earnest longing, God's people wait for the approach of their coming King. As the wrestling ones plead with God, the heavens glow with the dawn of eternal day. Like the melody of angel songs the words fall on the ear, "Help is coming." Christ's voice comes from the gates ajar: "Lo, I am with you. Do not be afraid. I have fought the battle on your behalf, and in My name you are more than conquerors."

The precious Savior will send help just when we need it. The time of trouble is a fearful ordeal for God's people, but by faith every true believer may see the rainbow of promise encircling him. "The ransomed of the LORD shall return, and come to Zion with singing, with everlasting joy on their heads. They shall obtain joy and gladness;

sorrow and sighing shall flee away" (Isaiah 51:11).

If the blood of Christ's witnesses were shed at this time, their faithfulness would not be a witness to convince others of the truth, because the stubborn heart has beaten back the waves of mercy until they do not come any more. If the righteous were now to be killed by their enemies, it would be a triumph for the prince of darkness. Christ has spoken: "Come, my people, enter your chambers, and shut your doors behind you; hide yourself, as it were, for a little moment, until the indignation is past. For behold, the LORD comes out of His place to punish the inhabitants of the earth for their iniquity" (Isaiah 26:20, 21).

How glorious will be the deliverance of those who have patiently waited for His coming and whose names are written in the book of life!

God's People Delivered

When the protection of human laws is withdrawn from those who honor the law of God, in different lands there will be a simultaneous movement to destroy them. As the time set in the decree approaches, the people will conspire to strike in one night a decisive blow that will silence dissent and reproof.

The people of God—some in prison cells, some in forests and mountains—plead for divine protection. Armed men, urged on by evil angels, are preparing for the work of death. Now, in the hour of greatest extremity, God will step in: "You shall have a song as in the night when a holy festival is kept, and gladness of heart as when one goes . . . to come into the mountain of the LORD, to the Mighty One of Israel. The LORD will cause His glorious voice to be heard, and show the descent of His arm, with the indignation of His anger and the flame of a devouring fire, with scattering, tempest, and hailstones" (Isaiah 30:29, 30).

Mobs of evil men are about to rush upon their prey, when a dense blackness, deeper than night, falls on the earth. Then a rainbow spans the sky and seems to encircle each praying group. The angry crowds are stopped. They forget the objects of their rage. They gaze on the symbol of God's covenant, and they long to be shielded from its brightness.

The people of God hear a voice saying, "Look up." Like Stephen they look up and see the glory of God and the Son of man on His throne (see Acts 7:55, 56). They recognize the marks of His humiliation, and they hear His request, "I desire that they also whom You gave Me may be with Me where I am" (John 17:24). They hear a voice saying, "They come, holy, harmless, and undefiled! They have kept My command to persevere."

Deliverance Comes

At midnight God unveils His power to deliver His people. The sun appears shining in its strength. Signs and wonders follow. The wicked look with terror on the scene, while the righteous see the indications of their deliverance. In the midst of the angry sky is one clear space of indescribable glory. The voice of God comes from there like the sound of many waters, saying, "It is done!" (Revelation 16:17).

That voice shakes the heavens and the earth. There is a mighty earthquake, "such a mighty and great earthquake as had not occurred since men were on the earth" (Revelation 16:18). Ragged rocks are scattered on every side. The sea is lashed into fury. There is the shriek of a hurricane like the voice of demons. The earth's surface is breaking up. Its very foundations seem to be giving way. Seaports that have become like Sodom for wickedness are swallowed up by the angry waters. "Babylon the great" is "remembered before God, to give her the cup of the wine of the fierceness of His wrath" (Revelation 16:19). Great hailstones do their work of destruction. Proud cities are laid low. Grand palaces on which people have lavished their wealth crumble before their eyes. Prison walls are torn apart, and God's people are set free.

Graves are opened, and "many of those who sleep in the dust of the earth . . . awake, some to everlasting life, some to shame and everlasting contempt." "Even they who pierced Him," those who mocked Christ's dying agonies, and the most violent opposers of His truth, are raised to see the honor placed on the loyal and obedient. (Daniel 12:2; Revelation 1:7.)

Fierce lightnings wrap the earth in a sheet of flame. Above the thunder, voices—mysterious and awful—declare the doom of the wicked. Those who were boastful and defiant, cruel to God's commandment-keeping people, now shudder in fear. Demons tremble while men and women beg for mercy.

The Day of the Lord

The prophet Isaiah said: "In that day a man will cast away his idols of silver and his idols of gold, which they made, each for himself to worship, to the moles and bats, to go into the clefts of the rocks, and into the crags of the rugged rocks, from the terror of the LORD and the glory of His majesty, when He arises to shake the earth mightily" (Isaiah 2:20, 21).

Those who have sacrificed everything for Christ are now safe. Before the world and in the face of death they have demonstrated their loyalty to Him who died for them. Their faces, so recently pale and gaunt, are now aglow with awe. Their voices rise in triumphant song: "God is our refuge and strength, a very present help in trouble. Therefore we will not fear, even though the earth be removed, and though the mountains be carried into the midst of the sea; though its waters roar and be troubled, though the mountains shake with its swelling" (Psalm 46:1–3).

While these words of holy trust ascend to God, the glory of the celestial city streams from heaven's open gates. Then, against the sky, a hand appears, holding two tablets of stone. That holy law, which God spoke from Sinai, is now revealed as the rule of judgment. The words are so plain that everyone can read them, and they awaken memories that sweep the darkness of superstition and heresy from every mind.

It is impossible to describe the horror and despair of those who have trampled on God's law. To gain the approval of the world, they set aside the law's requirements and taught others to disobey it. Now that law which they have despised condemns them. They see that they are without excuse.

The enemies of God's law have a new understanding of truth and duty. Too late they see that the Sabbath is the seal of the living God. Too late they see the sandy foundation on which they have been building. They have been fighting against God. Religious teachers have led people to destruction while claiming to guide them to Paradise. How great is the responsibility of those in holy office, how terrible the results of their unfaithfulness!

The King of Kings Appears

The voice of God is heard declaring the day and hour of Jesus' coming. The people of God stand listening, their faces lighted up with His glory. Soon in the east a small black cloud appears. It is the cloud that surrounds the Savior. In solemn silence the people of God gaze at it as it comes nearer, until it is a great white cloud, its base a glory like consuming fire, and above it the rainbow of the covenant. Not now a "Man of sorrows," Jesus rides forward as a mighty conqueror. Holy angels, a vast crowd of them too many to count, come with Him, "ten thousand times ten thousand, and thousands of thousands." Every eye sees the Prince of life. A crown of glory rests on His brow. His face is brighter than the noonday sun. "And He has on His robe and on His thigh a name written: KING OF KINGS AND LORD OF LORDS" (Revelation 19:16).

The King of kings descends on the cloud, wrapped in flaming fire. The earth trembles before Him: "Our God shall come, and shall not keep silent; a fire shall devour before Him, and it shall be very tempestuous all around

Him. He shall call to the heavens from above, and to the earth, that He may judge His people" (Psalm 50:3, 4).

"And the kings of the earth, the great men, the rich men, the commanders, the mighty men, every slave and every free man, hid themselves in the caves and in the rocks of the mountains, and said to the mountains and rocks, 'Fall on us and hide us from the face of Him who sits on the throne and from the wrath of the Lamb! For the great day of His wrath has come, and who is able to stand?' " (Revelation 6:15–17).

Mocking jokes have ended; lying lips are hushed. Nothing is heard except the voice of prayer and the sound of weeping. The wicked pray to be buried beneath the rocks rather than have to face Him whom they have despised. That voice which penetrates the ear of the dead, they know. How often its tender tones have called them to repentance! How often they have heard it in the appeals of a friend, a brother, a Redeemer. Oh, if only it were the voice of a stranger to them! That voice awakens memories of warnings they despised and invitations they refused.

Those who mocked Christ in His humiliation are there. He declared, "Hereafter you will see the Son of Man sitting at the right hand of the Power, and coming on the clouds of heaven" (Matthew 26:64). Now they look at Him in His glory; they are yet to see Him sitting at the right hand of power. There is the haughty Herod who jeered at His royal title. There are the men who placed the thorny crown on His brow and the mimic scepter in

His hand—those who bowed before Him in blasphemous mockery, who spat on the Prince of life. They try to run from His presence. Those who drove the nails through His hands and feet gaze at these marks with terror and remorse.

With terrible clarity priests and rulers remember the events of Calvary, how, wagging their heads in satanic gloating, they exclaimed, "He saved others; Himself He cannot save" (Matthew 27:42). Louder than the shout, "Crucify Him, crucify Him!" which rang through Jerusalem, swells the despairing wail, "He is the Son of God!" They try to run from the presence of the King of kings.

In the lives of all who reject truth there are moments when conscience wakes up, when the mind is troubled with vain regrets. But what are these compared with the remorse of that day! In the midst of their terror they hear the voices of the redeemed exclaiming, "Behold, this is our God; we have waited for Him, and He will save us" (Isaiah 25:9).

Resurrection of God's People

The voice of the Son of God calls the sleeping saints from their graves. Throughout the earth the dead will hear that voice, and they that hear will live, a great army of every nation, tribe, tongue, and people. From the prison house of death they come, clothed with immortal glory, crying out: "O death, where is your sting? O Hades, where is your victory?" (1 Corinthians 15:55).

All come out from their graves the same height as when they entered the tomb. But all arise with the freshness and vigor of eternal youth. Christ came to restore what was lost. He will change our lowly bodies and conform them to His glorious body. The mortal, corruptible form, once polluted with sin, becomes perfect, beautiful and immortal. Blemishes and deformities are left in the grave. The redeemed will "grow up" (Malachi 4:2, KJV) to the full stature of the race in its original glory. The last lingering traces of the curse of sin will be removed. In mind and soul and body, Christ's faithful ones will reflect the perfect image of their Lord.

The living righteous are changed "in a moment, in the twinkling of an eye." At the voice of God they are made immortal, and with the risen redeemed they are caught up to meet their Lord in the air. Angels "gather together His elect from the four winds, from one end of heaven to the other" (Matthew 24:31). They carry little children to their mothers' arms. Friends long separated by death are united, never to part again, and with songs of gladness they ascend together to the city of God.

Into the Holy City

Throughout the countless numbers of the redeemed every gaze is fastened on Jesus. Every eye beholds the glory of Him whose "visage was marred more than any man, and His form more than the sons of men" (Isaiah 52:14). Jesus places the crown of glory on the heads of the overcomers. For each there is a crown bearing his own "new name" (Revelation 2:17) and the inscription, "Holiness to the

Lord." Every hand receives the victor's palm and the shining harp. Then, as the commanding angels strike the note, all the redeemed sweep the strings with skillful touch in rich, melodious tones. Each voice is raised in grateful praise: "To Him who loved us and washed us from our sins in His own blood, and has made us kings and priests to His God and Father, to Him be glory and dominion forever and ever" (Revelation 1:5, 6).

Just ahead of the assembled redeemed is the Holy City. Jesus opens the gates, and the people from all nations who have kept the truth enter in. Then He says, "Come, you blessed of My Father, inherit the kingdom prepared for you from the foundation of the world" (Matthew 25:34). Christ presents to the Father those His blood has purchased, declaring: "Here am I and the children whom God has given Me." "Those whom You gave Me I have kept." (Hebrews 2:13; John 17:12.) Oh, the joy of that moment when the infinite Father, looking at the ransomed, will see His image, sin's decay removed, and the human once more in harmony with the divine!

The Savior's joy is in seeing, in the kingdom of glory, the people who have been saved by His agony and humiliation. The redeemed will share in His joy, as they see others who were won through their prayers, labors, and loving sacrifice. Gladness will fill their hearts when they see that one has brought others, and these still others.

The Two Adams Meet

As the ransomed are welcomed to the city of God, a triumphant cry rings out. The two Adams are about to meet. The Son of God will receive the father of our race—whom He created, who sinned, and for whose sin the marks of the crucifixion are on the Savior's body. As Adam sees the prints of the nails, in humiliation he throws himself at Christ's feet. The Savior lifts him up and invites him to look once more on the Eden home from which he was exiled so long ago.

Adam's life was filled with sorrow. Every dying leaf, every animal sacrifice, every stain on mankind's purity, was a reminder of his sin. His agony of remorse was terrible as he was blamed for being the cause of sin. Faithfully he repented of his sin, and he died in the hope of a resurrection. Now, through the atonement, Adam is reinstated in his Eden home.

Filled with joy, he sees the trees that were once his delight, whose fruit he himself had gathered in the days of his innocence. He sees the vines his own hands trained, the very flowers he once loved to care for. This is truly Eden restored!

The Savior leads him to the tree of life and invites him to eat. He sees so many of his family redeemed. Then he throws his crown at the feet of Jesus and embraces the Redeemer. He touches the harp, and heaven echoes the triumphant song, "Worthy is the Lamb who was slain" (Revelation 5:12). The family of Adam throw their crowns at the Savior's feet as they bow in adoration. Angels wept when Adam sinned, and they rejoiced when Jesus opened the grave for all who would believe on His name. Now they see the work of redemption accomplished, and they unite their voices in praise.

On the "sea of glass mingled with fire" are gathered those who have gotten "the victory over the beast, over his image and over his mark and over the number of his name." The one hundred forty-four thousand were redeemed from among humanity, and they sing a new song, the song of Moses and the Lamb. (Revelation 15:2, 3.) None but the hundred forty-four thousand can learn that song, because it is the song of an experience that no other group ever had. "These are the ones who follow the Lamb wherever He goes." These, having been taken to heaven from among the living, are the "firstfruits to God and to the Lamb." (Revelation 14:4, 5.) They passed through the time of trouble such as never was since there was a nation. They endured the anguish of the time of Jacob's trouble. They stood without an intercessor through the final outpouring of God's judgments. They "washed their robes and made them white in the blood of the Lamb." "In their mouth was found no deceit, for they are without fault" before God. "They shall neither hunger anymore nor thirst anymore; the sun shall not strike them, nor any heat; for the Lamb who is in the midst of the throne shall shepherd them and lead them to living fountains of waters. And God will wipe away every tear from their eyes." (Revelation 7:14; 14:5; 7:16, 17.)

The Redeemed in Glory

In all ages the Savior's chosen ones have walked in narrow paths. They were purified in the fires of afflic-tion. For Jesus' sake they endured hatred, slander, self-denial, and bitter disappointments. They learned the evil of sin, its power, its guilt, its misery. They abhor it now. A sense of Jesus' infinite sacrifice for its cure humbles them and fills their hearts with gratitude. They love much because they have been forgiven much (see Luke 7:47). Partakers of Christ's sufferings, they are prepared to be partakers of His glory.

The heirs of God come from attics, hovels, dungeons, scaffolds, mountains, deserts, caves. They were "destitute, afflicted, tormented." Millions went to the grave dishonored by nearly everyone because they refused to yield to Satan. But now they are no longer afflicted, scattered, and oppressed. From this point onward they stand dressed in richer robes than the most honored of the earth have worn, wearing crowns more glorious than were ever placed on the head of earthly rulers. The King of glory has wiped the tears from all faces. They join in a song of praise, clear, sweet, and harmonious. The anthem swells throughout heaven, "Salvation belongs to our God who sits on the throne, and to the Lamb!" And all respond, "Amen! Blessing and glory and wisdom, thanksgiving and honor and power and might, be to our God forever and ever." (Revelation 7:10, 12.)

In this life we can only begin to understand the wonderful theme of redemption. With our limited comprehension we may consider very earnestly the shame and the glory, the life and the death, the justice and the mercy, that meet in the cross. Yet even with the greatest stretch of our mental powers, we fail to grasp its full significance. The length and the breadth, the depth and the height, of redeeming love we only dimly comprehend. The plan of redemption will not be fully understood even when the ransomed see as they are seen and know as they are known, but through the eternal ages new truth will continually unfold to their amazed and delighted minds. Though the griefs and pains and temptations of earth are over and their cause removed, the people of God will always have a distinct, intelligent knowledge of what their salvation has cost.

The cross will be the song of the redeemed through all eternity. In Christ glorified they see Christ crucified. They will never forget that the Majesty of heaven humbled Himself to uplift fallen men and women, that He bore the guilt and shame of sin and the hiding of His Father's face till the anguish of a lost world broke His heart and crushed out His life. The Maker of all worlds laid aside His glory from love to humanity—this will forever inspire the awe of the universe. As the nations of the saved look on their Redeemer and know that His kingdom will have no end, they break out in song: "Worthy is the Lamb that was slain, and has redeemed us to God by His own most precious blood!"

The mystery of the cross explains all mysteries. It will be clear that God who is infinite in wisdom could invent no plan for our salvation except by the sacrifice of His Son. His compensation for this sacrifice is the joy of peopling the earth with ransomed beings, holy, happy, and immortal. So great is the value of each person that the Father is satisfied with the price paid. And Christ Himself, seeing the fruits of His great sacrifice, is satisfied.

The Earth in Ruins

When the voice of God brings the captivity of His people to an end, a terrible awakening takes place among those who have lost everything in the great conflict of life. Blinded by Satan's deceptions, the rich prided themselves that they were better than those less favored. But they had neglected to feed the hungry, clothe the naked, deal justly, and love mercy. Now they have lost everything that made them great, and they are left with nothing. They watch in terror as their idols are destroyed. They have sold their souls for earthly enjoyments and have not become rich toward God. Their lives are a failure, their pleasures turned bitter. The gain of a lifetime is swept away in a moment. The rich mourn the destruction of their grand houses, the scattering of their gold and silver, and the fear that they themselves will perish with their idols. The wicked are sorry that the result is what it is, but they do not repent of their wickedness.

The minister who has sacrificed truth to gain people's approval now recognizes the influence of his teachings. Every line written, every word uttered that led others to rest secure in falsehood has been sowing seed, and now he sees the harvest of lost people around him. Says the Lord: "Woe to the shepherds who destroy and scatter the sheep of My pasture! . . . Behold, I will attend to you for the evil of your doings." "With lies you have made the heart of the righteous sad, whom I have not made sad; and you have strengthened the hands of the wicked, so that he does not turn from his wicked way to save his life." (Jeremiah 23:1, 2; Ezekiel 13:22.)

Ministers and people see that they have rebelled against the Author of all righteous law. Setting aside God's laws opened the way to thousands of springs of evil, until the earth became one vast pit of corruption. No language can express the longing the disloyal feel for what they have lost forever—eternal life.

The people accuse one another of having led them to destruction, but they all unite in heaping their bitterest condemnation on the unfaithful pastors who prophesied "smooth things" (Isaiah 30:10), who led their hearers to make void the law of God and persecute those who wanted to keep it holy. "We are lost," they cry, "and you are the cause." The same people who once heaped honor and praise on them will turn against them to destroy them. Everywhere there is conflict and bloodshed.

The Son of God and heavenly messengers have been in conflict with the evil one to warn, enlighten, and save the lost. Now all have made their decisions; the wicked have fully united with Satan in his warfare against God. The controversy is not just with Satan, but with human beings. "The LORD has a controversy with the nations" (Jeremiah 25:31).

The Angel of Death

Now the angel of death goes out, represented in Ezekiel's vision by the men with the slaughtering weapons, to whom the command is given: "Utterly slay old and young men, maidens and little children and women; but do not come near anyone on whom is the mark; and begin at My sanctuary." "They began with the elders who were before the temple," those who professed to be the spiritual guardians of the people. (Ezekiel 9:6.)

False watchmen are the first to fall. "The LORD comes out of His place to punish the inhabitants of the earth for their iniquity; the earth will also disclose her blood, and will no more cover her slain." "A great panic from the LORD will be among them. Everyone will seize the hand of his neighbor, and raise his hand against his neighbor's hand." (Isaiah 26:21; Zechariah 14:13.)

In the wild strife of their own fierce passions and by the pouring out of God's unmingled wrath, wicked priests, rulers, and people fall. "At that day the slain of the LORD shall be from one end of the earth even to the other" (Jeremiah 25:33).

At the coming of Christ the wicked are destroyed by the brightness of His glory. Christ takes His people to the city of God, and the earth has no more inhabitants. "Behold, the LORD makes the earth empty and makes it waste, distorts its surface and scatters abroad its inhabitants. . . . The land shall be entirely emptied and utterly plundered, for the LORD has spoken this word. . . . Because they have transgressed the laws, changed the ordinance, broken the everlasting covenant. Therefore the curse has devoured the earth, and those who dwell in it are desolate. Therefore the inhabitants of the earth are burned" (Isaiah 24:1, 3, 5, 6).

The earth looks like a desolate wilderness. Cities destroyed by the earthquake, uprooted trees, ragged rocks torn out of the earth, are scattered over its surface. Vast caverns mark the spot where the mountains have been torn from their foundations.

The Banishment of Satan

Now the event takes place that was foreshadowed in the last solemn service of the Day of Atonement. When the sins of Israel had been removed from the sanctuary through the blood of the sin offering, the scapegoat was presented alive before the Lord. The high priest confessed over him "all the iniquities of the children of Israel, . . . putting them on the head of the goat" (Leviticus 16:21). Similarly, when Jesus has completed the work of atonement in the heavenly sanctuary, then, in the presence of God and heavenly angels and the legions of the redeemed, the sins of God's people will be placed on Satan.

He will be declared guilty of all the evil that he has caused them to commit. As the scapegoat was sent away into an uninhabited land, so Satan will be banished to the desolate earth.

After presenting scenes of the Lord's coming, John continues: "I saw an angel coming down from heaven, having the key to the bottomless pit and a great chain in his hand. He laid hold of the dragon, that serpent of old, who is the Devil and Satan, and bound him for a thousand years; and he cast him into the bottomless pit, and shut him up, and set a seal on him, so that he should deceive the nations no more till the thousand years were finished. But after these things he must be released for a little while" (Revelation 20:1-3).

The "bottomless pit" represents the earth in confusion and darkness. Looking forward to the great day of God, Jeremiah declares: "I beheld the earth, and indeed it was without form, and void;* and the heavens, they had no light. I beheld the mountains, and indeed they trembled, and all the hills moved back and forth. I beheld, and indeed there was no man, and all the birds of the heavens had fled. I beheld, and indeed the fruitful land was a wilderness, and all its cities were broken down" (Jeremiah 4:23-26).

This earth is to be the home of Satan with his evil angels for a thousand years. Limited to the earth, he will not have access to other worlds to tempt and annoy those who have never fall-

en. In this sense he is "bound." No one is left on whom he can exercise his power. He is cut off from the work of deception and ruin that has been his one delight.

Looking forward to Satan's overthrow, Isaiah exclaimed: "How you are fallen from heaven, O Lucifer, son of the morning! How you are cut down to the ground, you who weakened the nations! For you have said in your heart: 'I will ascend into heaven, I will exalt my throne above the stars of God; . . . I will be like the Most High.' Yet you shall be brought down to Sheol, to the lowest depths of the Pit. Those who see you will gaze at you, and consider you, saying: 'Is this the man who made the earth tremble, who shook kingdoms, who made the world as a wilderness and destroyed its cities, who did not *open the house of his prisoners?*'" (Isaiah 14:12-17).

For six thousand years, Satan's prison house has received God's people, but Christ has broken his chains and set the prisoners free. Alone with his evil angels Satan realizes the effect of sin: "The kings of the nations, all of them, sleep in glory, everyone in his own house [the grave]; but you are cast out of your grave like an abominable branch. . . . You will not be joined with them in burial, because you have destroyed your land and slain your people" (Isaiah 14:18-20).

For a thousand years, Satan will gaze on the results of his rebellion against the law of God. He suffers

---

* The word for "deep" in Genesis 1:2 in the Greek translation of the Old Testament is abyssos, which also appears here in Jeremiah. This same word is found in the Greek text of Revelation 20:1, rendered in the New King James Version as "bottomless pit."

intensely. He is now left to think about the part he has acted since he rebelled and to look forward with terror to the dreadful future when he must be punished.

During the thousand years between the first and second resurrections, the judgment of the wicked takes place. Paul points to this as an event that follows the Second Advent (1 Corinthians 4:5). The righteous reign as kings and priests. John says: "I saw thrones, and they sat on them, and judgment was committed to them. . . . They shall be priests of God and of Christ, and shall reign with Him a thousand years" (Revelation 20:4, 6).

At this time "the saints will judge the world" (1 Corinthians 6:2). In union with Christ they judge the wicked, deciding every case according to the deeds done in the body. Then the punishment the wicked must suffer is set, according to their works, and it is recorded against their names in the book of death.

Christ and His people judge Satan and the evil angels. Paul says, "Do you not know that we shall judge angels?" (1 Corinthians 6:3). Jude declares, "The angels who did not keep their proper domain, but left their own abode, He has reserved in everlasting chains under darkness for the judgment of the great day" (Jude 6).

At the close of the thousand years, the second resurrection will take place. Then the wicked will be raised from the dead and appear before God for the execution of "the written judgment" (Psalm 149:9). So John says: "The rest of the dead did not live again until the thousand years were finished" (Revelation 20:5). And Isaiah declares concerning the wicked, "They will be gathered together, as prisoners are gathered in the pit, and will be shut up in the prison; *after many days they will be punished*" (Isaiah 24:22).

Eternal Peace: The Controversy Ended

At the close of the thousand years, Christ returns to the earth accompanied by the redeemed and by legions of angels. He commands the wicked dead to arise to receive their doom. They come out, numberless as the sands of the sea, bearing the traces of disease and death. What a contrast to those raised in the first resurrection!

Every eye turns to see the glory of the Son of God. With one voice the vast army of the wicked exclaims, "Blessed is He who comes in the name of the LORD!" (Matthew 23:39). It is not love that inspires this utterance. The force of truth urges the words from unwilling lips. As the wicked went into the graves, so they come out with the same hatred of Christ and the same spirit of rebellion. They will have no new probation in which to remedy their past lives.

Says the prophet, "In that day His feet will stand on the Mount of Olives, . . . and the Mount of Olives shall be split in two" (Zechariah 14:4). As the New Jerusalem comes down out of heaven, it rests on the place made ready for it, and Christ, with His people and the angels, enters the Holy City.

While he was cut off from his work of deception, the prince of evil was miserable and dejected, but when the wicked dead are raised and he sees the vast forces on his side, his hopes revive. He determines not to give up the great controversy. He will rally the lost under his banner. In rejecting Christ they have accepted the rule of the rebel leader, and they are ready to do his bidding. Yet, true to his early practice, he does not acknowledge himself to be Satan. He claims to be the rightful owner of the world whose inheritance has been taken from him unlawfully. He represents himself as a redeemer, assuring his deluded subjects that it is his power that has brought them from their graves. Satan makes the weak strong and inspires all with his own energy. He proposes to lead them in battle to take possession of the city of God. He points to the unnumbered millions who have been raised from the dead, and he declares that as their leader he is well able to regain his throne and kingdom.

In the vast assembly are many from the long-lived race that existed before the Flood, people of tall stature and giant intellect, whose amazing works led the world to idolize their genius, but whose cruelty and evil practices caused God to blot them from

His creation. There are kings and generals who never lost a battle. In death these leaders experienced no change. As they come up from the grave, they are driven by the same desire to conquer that ruled them when they died.

The Final Assault Against God

Satan consults with these mighty men. They declare that the army within the city is small in comparison with theirs and can be overcome. Skillful craftsmen construct weapons of war. Military leaders marshal warlike men into companies and divisions.

At last the order to advance is given, and the countless horde moves on, an army that the combined forces of all ages could never equal. Satan leads the procession, kings and warriors following. With military precision the densely packed ranks advance over the earth's broken surface to the City of God. By command of Jesus, the gates of the New Jerusalem are closed, and the armies of Satan prepare for the attack.

Now Christ appears in view of His enemies. Far above the city, on a foundation of burnished gold, is a throne. The Son of God sits on this throne, and around Him are the subjects of His kingdom. The glory of the Eternal Father enfolds His Son. The brightness of His presence flows out beyond the gates, flooding the earth with radiance.

Nearest the throne are those who were once zealous in Satan's cause, but who, plucked like brands from the fire, have followed their Savior with intense devotion. Next are those who perfected character while surrounded by falsehood and unbelief, who honored the law of God when the world declared it void, and the millions from all ages who were martyred for their faith. Beyond is the "great multitude which no one could number, of all nations, tribes, peoples, and tongues, . . . clothed with white robes, with palm branches in their hands" (Revelation 7:9). Their warfare is over, their victory won. The palm branch is a symbol of triumph, the white robe an emblem of the righteousness of Christ, which is now theirs.

In all that vast crowd there are none who credit salvation to themselves by their own goodness. Nothing is said of what they have suffered. The keynote of every anthem is, Salvation to our God and to the Lamb.

Sentence Pronounced Against the Rebels

In the presence of the assembled inhabitants of earth and heaven the coronation of the Son of God takes place. And now, acknowledged as having supreme majesty and power, the King of kings pronounces sentence on the rebels who have broken His law and oppressed His people. "I saw a great white throne and Him who sat on it, from whose face the earth and the heaven fled away. And there was found no place for them. And I saw the dead, small and great, standing before God, and books were opened. And another book was opened, which is the Book of Life. And the dead were judged according to their works, by the things which were written in the books" (Revelation 20:11, 12).

As the eye of Jesus looks upon the wicked, they are conscious of every sin they have ever committed. They see where their feet left the path of holiness. The alluring temptations that they encouraged by indulging in sin, the messengers of God they despised, the warnings they rejected, the waves of mercy that their stubborn, unrepentant hearts beat back—all appear as if written in letters of fire.

Above the throne they see the cross. Like a panoramic view they watch the scenes of Adam's fall and the steps that followed it in the plan of redemption. The Savior's humble birth; His life of simplicity; His baptism in the Jordan; His fasting and temptation in the wilderness; His ministry bringing heaven's blessings to humanity; the days crowded with acts of mercy, the nights of prayer in the mountains; the plottings of envy and meanness that repaid His benefits; His mysterious agony in Gethsemane beneath the weight of the sins of the world; His betrayal to the murderous mob; the events of that night of horror—the unresisting prisoner abandoned by His disciples, put on trial in the high priest's palace, in the judgment hall of Pilate, before the cowardly Herod, mocked, insulted, tortured, and condemned to die—these events are all vividly portrayed.

And now the swaying crowd watches the final scenes: the patient Sufferer treading the path to Calvary; the Prince of heaven hanging on the cross; the priests and rabbis mocking His dying agony; the supernatural darkness marking the moment when the world's Redeemer yielded up His life.

The awful spectacle appears just as it was. Satan and his subjects have no power to turn away from the picture. Each actor remembers the part he performed. Herod, who killed the innocent children of Bethlehem; the evil Herodias, guilty of the blood of John the Baptist; the weak, political Pilate; the mocking soldiers; the raging crowd who shouted, "His blood be on us and on our children!"—all try but fail to hide from the divine majesty of His face, while the redeemed throw their crowns at the Savior's feet, exclaiming, "He died for me!"

There is Nero, monster of cruelty and vice, watching the exaltation of those Christians in whose dying anguish he found satanic delight. His mother witnesses her own work, how the passions that her influence and example encouraged have borne fruit in crimes that made the world shudder.

There are Catholic priests and officials who claimed to be Christ's ambassadors, yet used the rack, the dungeon, and the stake to control His people. There are the proud popes who exalted themselves above God and dared to try to change the law of the Most High. Those pretended fathers have an account to settle with God. Too late they are made to see that the All-knowing One is particular about His law. They learn now that Christ identifies His interests with His suffering people.

The whole wicked world stands arraigned on the charge of high treason against the government of heaven. The lost have no one to plead their cause. They are without excuse, and God pronounces the sentence of eternal death against them.

The wicked see what they have forfeited by their rebellion. "All this," cries the lost sinner, "I might have had. Why was I so blind! I have exchanged peace, happiness, and honor for wretchedness, disgrace, and despair." All see that God is just in excluding them from heaven. By their lives they have declared, "We will not have this man [Jesus] to reign over us" (see Luke 19:14).

Satan Defeated

As if hypnotized, the wicked watch the coronation of the Son of God. They see in His hands the tablets of the divine law they have despised. They witness the outburst of adoration from the saved; and as the wave of melody sweeps over the crowds outside the city, all exclaim, "Just and true are Your ways, O King of the saints!" (Revelation 15:3). Falling face down, they worship the Prince of life.

Satan seems paralyzed. He had once been a covering cherub, and he remembers how much he has lost. He is forever excluded from the council where he once was honored. He sees another now standing near to the Father, an angel of majestic presence. He knows that the exalted position of this angel might have been his.

Memory recalls what heaven was like to him in his innocence, the peace and contentment that were his until his rebellion. He reviews his work among humanity and its results—the hostility of one person or group toward another, the terrible destruction of life, the overturning of thrones, the riots, conflicts, and revolutions. He recalls his constant efforts to oppose the work of Christ. As he looks at the fruit of his work, he sees only failure. Again and again in the progress of the great controversy he has been defeated and forced to yield.

The aim of the great rebel has always been to prove that God's government was responsible for the rebellion. He has led vast multitudes to accept his version of the great controversy. For thousands of years, this chief of conspiracy has sold falsehood for truth. But the time has now come when everyone will see the history and character of Satan. In his last effort to dethrone Christ, destroy His people, and take possession of the City of God, the archdeceiver has been fully unmasked. Those who united with him see the total failure of his cause.

Satan sees that his voluntary rebellion has made him unfit for heaven. He has trained his powers to war against God. The purity and harmony of heaven would be supreme torture to him. He bows down and admits the justice of his sentence.

Every question of truth and error in the long-standing controversy has now been fully answered. The whole universe has seen the results of setting aside God's law. For all eternity, the history of sin will stand as a witness that the happiness of all the beings God has created depends on the existence of His law. The whole universe, loyal and rebellious, with one voice declares, "Just and true are Your ways, O King of the saints!"

The hour has come when Christ is glorified above every name that is named. For the joy set before Him—

that He might bring many sons and daughters to glory—He endured the cross. He gazes on the redeemed, renewed in His own image. He sees in them the result of the labor of His soul, and He is satisfied (Isaiah 53:11). In a voice that reaches everyone, righteous and wicked, He declares: "See the purchase of My blood! For these I suffered, for these I died."

Violent End of the Wicked

Satan's character remains unchanged. Rebellion bursts out again like a raging flood. He determines not to give up the last desperate struggle against the King of heaven. But of all the countless millions whom he has drawn into rebellion, none now follow him as leader. The same hatred of God that inspires Satan fills the wicked, but they see that their case is hopeless. "Because you have set your heart as the heart of a god, behold, therefore, I will bring strangers against you, the most terrible of the nations; and they shall draw their swords against the beauty of your wisdom, and defile your splendor. They shall throw you down into the Pit." "I will destroy thee, O covering cherub, from the midst of the stones of fire. . . . I will cast thee to the ground, I will lay thee before kings, that they may behold thee. . . . I will bring thee to ashes upon the earth in the sight of all them that behold thee. . . . Thou shalt be a terror, and never shalt thou be any more." (Ezekiel 28:6–8; verses 16–19, KJV.)

"The indignation of the LORD is against all nations." "Upon the wicked He will rain coals; fire and brimstone and a burning wind shall be the portion of their cup." (Isaiah 34:2; Psalm 11:6.) Fire comes down from God out of heaven. The earth is broken up. Devouring flames burst from every yawning chasm. The very rocks are on fire. The elements melt with fervent heat, the earth also, and the works that are in it are burned up (2 Peter 3:10). The earth's surface seems one molten mass—a vast, boiling lake of fire. "It is the day of the LORD's vengeance, the year of recompense for the cause of Zion" (Isaiah 34:8).

The wicked are punished "according to their deeds." Satan is made to suffer not only for his own rebellion, but for all the sins that he has caused God's people to commit. In the flames the wicked are finally destroyed, root and branch—Satan the root, his followers the branches. Evildoers have received the full penalty of the law; the demands of justice have been met. Satan's work of ruin is ended forever. Now God's creatures are forever delivered from his temptations.

While the earth is wrapped in fire, the righteous are safe in the Holy City. To the wicked, God is a consuming fire, but to His people He is a shield. (See Revelation 20:6; Psalm 84:11.)

Our Final Home

"I saw a new heaven and a new earth, for the first heaven and the first earth had passed away" (Revelation 21:1). The fire that consumes the wicked purifies the earth. Every trace of the curse is swept away. No eternally burning hell will keep the ransomed thinking about sin's fearful consequences.

Reminder of Sin's Results

One reminder alone remains: our Redeemer will always carry the marks of His crucifixion, the only traces of the cruel work that sin has done. Through eternal ages the wounds of Calvary will reveal His praise and declare His power.

Christ assured His disciples that He went to prepare homes for them in the Father's house. Human language cannot describe the reward of the righteous. Only those who see it will truly know it. No finite mind can comprehend the glory of the Paradise of God!

The Bible calls the inheritance of the saved "a country" (Hebrews 11:14–16). There the heavenly Shepherd leads His flock to fountains of living waters. There are ever-flowing streams, clear as crystal, and beside them waving trees cast their shadows on the paths God has prepared for the ransomed of the Lord. Wide-spreading plains rise into beautiful hills, and the mountains of God lift their high summits. On those peaceful plains, beside those living streams, God's people, who have been pilgrims and wanderers for so long, will find a home.

"They shall build houses and inhabit them; they shall plant vineyards and eat their fruit. They shall not build and another inhabit; they shall not plant and another eat; . . . My elect shall long enjoy the work of their hands." "The wilderness and the wasteland shall be glad for them, and the desert shall rejoice and blossom as the rose." "The wolf also shall dwell with the lamb, the leopard shall lie down with the young goat, . . . and a little child shall lead them. . . . They shall not hurt nor destroy in all My holy mountain." (Isaiah 65:21, 22; 35:1; 11:6, 9.)

Pain cannot exist in heaven. There will be no more tears, no funeral processions. "There shall be no more death, nor sorrow, nor crying. . . . For the former things have passed away." "The inhabitant will not say, 'I am sick'; the people who dwell in it will be forgiven their iniquity." (Revelation 21:4; Isaiah 33:24.)

There is the New Jerusalem, the capital city of the glorified new earth. "Her light was like a most precious stone, like a jasper stone, clear as crystal." "The nations of those who are saved shall walk in its light, and the kings of the earth bring their glory and honor into it." "The tabernacle of God is with men, and He will dwell with them, and they shall be His people. God Himself will be with them and be their God." (Revelation 21:11, 24, 3.)

In the City of God "there shall be no night" (Revelation 22:5). There will be no tiredness. We will always feel the freshness of the morning and always be far from its close. The light of the sun will be surpassed by a radiance that is not painfully dazzling, yet immeasurably exceeds the brightness of our noonday. The redeemed walk in the glory of perpetual day.

"I saw no temple in it, for the Lord God Almighty and the Lamb are its temple" (Revelation 21:22). The people of God are privileged to interact freely with the Father and the Son. Now we see the image of God like something in a mirror, but then we will see Him face to face, without a dimming veil between.

The Triumph of God's Love

God Himself has planted the loves and sympathies in human hearts, and in heaven they will find their truest and sweetest expression. The pure fellowship with holy beings and the faithful of all the ages, the sacred ties that bind together "the whole family in heaven and earth" (Ephesians 3:15)—these help to make up the happiness of the redeemed.

There, with delight that has no end, immortal minds will study the wonders of creative power, the mysteries of redeeming love. Every aspect of mind will be developed, every capacity increased. Learning will not exhaust the energies. The redeemed may carry on the grandest enterprises, reach their highest aims, fulfill their noblest ambitions. And still they will find new heights to conquer, new wonders to admire, new truths to comprehend, fresh objects to draw out the powers of mind and soul and body.

All the treasures of the universe will be open to God's redeemed. Not limited by mortality, they fly tirelessly to far-off worlds. The children of earth enter into the joy and wisdom of unfallen beings and share treasures of knowledge that these have gained through ages upon ages. With undimmed vision they gaze on the glory of creation—suns and stars and systems, all in their appointed order circling the throne of God.

And the years of eternity, as they roll, will bring still more glorious revelations of God and of Christ. The more we learn about God, the more we will admire His character. As Jesus opens before the redeemed the riches of redemption and the amazing achievements in the great controversy with Satan, their hearts thrill with devotion, and ten thousand times ten thousand voices unite to swell the mighty chorus of praise.

"And every creature which is in heaven and on the earth and under the earth and such as are in the sea, and all that are in them, I heard saying: 'Blessing and honor and glory and power be to Him who sits on the throne, and to the Lamb, forever and ever!' " (Revelation 5:13).

The great controversy is ended. Sin and sinners are no more. The entire universe is clean. One pulse of harmony and gladness beats through the vast creation. From Him who created all, life and light and gladness flow throughout the realms of limitless space. From the smallest atom to the greatest world, all things, animate and inanimate, in their unshadowed beauty and perfect joy, declare that God is love.

Appendix

Page 24. TITLES. Pope Innocent III declared that the Roman pope is "the vicegerent [administrative deputy] on earth, not of a mere man, but of very God." See *Decretals of the Lord Pope Gregory IX,* liber 1, title 7, ch. 3. *Corp. Jur. Canon.* (2nd Leipzig ed., 1881), col. 99.

For the title "Lord God the Pope," see a gloss on the *Extravagantes* of Pope John XXII, title 14, ch. 4, *Declaramus.* In an Antwerp edition of the *Extravagantes,* dated 1584, the words *"Dominum Deum nostrum Papam"* ("Our Lord God the Pope") occur in column 153.

Page 24. INFALLIBILITY. See Philip Schaff, *The Creeds of Christendom,* vol. II, *Dogmatic Decrees of the Vatican Council,* pp. 234–271; *The Catholic Encyclopedia,* vol. VII, art. "Infallibility"; James Cardinal Gibbons, *The Faith of Our Fathers* (Baltimore: John Murphy Co., 110th ed., 1917), chs. 7, 11.

Page 25. IMAGE WORSHIP. "The worship of images . . . was one of those corruptions of Christianity that crept into the church stealthily and almost without notice or observation. . . . So gradually was one practice af-ter another introduced in connection with it, that the church had become deeply steeped in practical idolatry, . . . almost without any firm objection; and when finally there was an attempt to root it out, the evil was found too deeply fixed to allow removal." —J. Mendham, *The Seventh General Council, the Second of Nicaea,* introduction, pages iii–vi.

For a record of the proceedings and decisions of the Second Council of Nicea, A.D. 787, called to establish the worship of images, see *A Select Library of Nicene and Post-Nicene Fathers,* 2nd series, vol. XIV, pp. 521–587 (New York, 1900); C. J. Hefele, *A History of the Councils of the Church, From the Original Documents,* bk. 18, ch. 1, secs. 332, 333; ch. 2, secs. 345–352 (T. and T. Clark, 1896 ed.), vol. 5, pp. 260–304, 342–372.

Page 25. THE SUNDAY LAW OF CONSTANTINE. The law is given in Latin and in English translation in Philip Schaff's *History of the Christian Church,* vol. III, 3rd period, ch. 7, sec. 75, p. 380, n. 1. See discussion in Albert Henry Newman, *A Manual of Church History* (Philadelphia: The American Baptist Publication Society,

1933), rev. ed., vol. 1, pp. 305–307; and in L. E. Froom, *The Prophetic Faith of Our Fathers* (Washington, D.C.: Review and Herald Publishing Assn., 1950), vol. 1, pp. 376–381.

Page 26. PROPHETIC DATES. An important principle of interpreting time prophecies is the year-day principle—under which a day of prophetic time equals a year of calendar time. These are some of the Bible reasons for this principle: (1) The year-day principle is in harmony with the principle of symbolically interpreting beasts as kingdoms, horns as powers, oceans as peoples, etc. (2) The Lord, speaking in Numbers 14:34 and Ezekiel 4:6, upholds the principle. (3) The 2,300 days (years) of Daniel 8:14 cover the history of the Medo-Persian, Grecian, and Roman empires, as the angel explains in verses 19–26 ("the vision refers to the time of the end," verse 17). These empires lasted many times longer than 2,300 literal days. Nothing can fit except the year-day principle. (4) Daniel 11 is an expansion of the prophecy of Daniel 8, yet Daniel 11 is not symbolic. Three times it speaks of "years" (verses 6, 8, 13) as a parallel of "days" in Daniel 8:14. (5) The angel explained to Daniel that these prophecies concerned the time of the end (8:19, 26; 10:13, 14). If the "days" were literal, the prophecies would not continue long enough to make sense. (6) A day for a year was a common way of speaking in Old Testament Hebrew. See Leviticus 25:8; Genesis 29:27. (7) The book of Revelation unlocks the prophecies of Daniel, showing that their fulfillment was still future in the time of the apostles. Further, many careful Bible students have recognized and accepted the year-day principle as a valid biblical principle. Among them are Joachim of Floris, Wycliffe, Joseph Mede, Sir Isaac Newton, Bishop Thomas Newton, Alexander Keith, and many others.

Page 27. FORGED WRITINGS. Among the documents generally admitted to be forgeries, the Donation of Constantine and the Pseudo-Isidorian Decretals are of major importance. See *The New Schaff-Herzog Encyclopedia of Religious Knowledge,* vol. III, art. "Donation of Constantine."

The "false writings" referred to in the text also include the "Pseudo-Isidorian Decretals"—fictitious letters ascribed to early popes from Clement (A.D. 100) to Gregory the Great (A.D. 600) and later incorporated in a ninth-century collection claiming to have been made by "Isidore Mercator." The falsity of the Pseudo-Isidorian fabrications is now admitted.

Page 28. PURGATORY. Dr. Joseph Faa Di Bruno thus defines purgatory this way: "Purgatory is a state of suffering after this life, in which those souls are detained for a time, who die after their deadly sins have been forgiven as to the stain and guilt, and as to the everlasting pain that was due to them, but who still have some debt of temporal punishment to pay because of those sins. It is the same for those souls who leave this world guilty only of venial sins."—*Catholic Belief,* p. 196 (ed. 1884; imprimatur Archbishop of New York).

See *The Catholic Encyclopedia*, vol. 12, art. "Purgatory."

Page 28. INDULGENCES. For a detailed history of the doctrine of indulgences, see *The Catholic Encyclopedia*, art. "Indulgences," vol. 7; A. H. Newman, *A Manual of Church History* (Philadelphia: The American Baptist Publication Society, 1953), vol. 2, pp. 53, 54, 62.

Page 32. THE SABBATH AMONG THE WALDENSES. Historical evidence exists for some observance of the seventh-day Sabbath among the Waldenses. A report of an inquisition before whom were brought some Waldenses of Moravia in the middle of the fifteenth century declares that among the Waldenses "not a few indeed celebrate the Sabbath with the Jews."—Johann Joseph Ignaz von Dollinger, *Beitrage zur Sektengeschichte des Mittelalters* (Contributions to the History of the Sects of the Middle Ages), Munich, 1890, pt. 2, p. 661. This source clearly indicates the observance of the seventh-day Sabbath.

Page 35. EDICT AGAINST THE WALDENSES. A portion of the papal bull or edict (from Innocent VIII, 1487) against the Waldenses is given in an English translation in Dowling's *History of Romanism*, bk. 6, ch. 5, sec. 62 (ed. 1871).

Page 38. INDULGENCES. See note for page 28.

Pages 38, 39. WYCLIFFE. For the text of the papal bulls (edicts) issued against Wycliffe with English translation, see John Foxe, *Acts and Monuments of the Church* (London: Pratt Townsend, 1870), vol. 3, pp. 4–13; see also summaries in Merle D'Aubigné, *The History of the Reformation in the Sixteenth Century* (London: Blackie and Son, 1885), vol. 4, div. 7, p. 93; Philip Schaff, *History of the Christian Church* (New York: Chas. Scribner's Sons, 1915), vol. 5, pt. 2, p. 317.

Page 39. INFALLIBILITY. See note for page 24.

Page 46. INDULGENCES. See note for page 28.

Page 46. COUNCIL OF CONSTANCE. Publications on the Council include K. Zahringer, *Das Kardinal Kollegium auf dem Konstanzer Konzil* (Munster, 1935); Th. F. Grogau, *The Conciliar Theory as It Manifested Itself at the Council of Constance* (Washington, 1949); Fred A. Kremple, *Cultural Aspects of the Council of Constance and Basel* (Ann Arbor, 1955).

See John Hus, *Letters*, 1904; E. J. Kitts, *Pope John XXIII and Master John Hus* (London, 1910); D. A. Schaff, *John Hus* (1915); and Matthew Spinka, *John Hus and the Czech Reform* (1941).

Page 57. INDULGENCES. See note for page 28.

Page 98. JESUITISM. See *Concerning Jesuits*, edited by the Rev.

John Gerard, S. J. (London: Catholic Truth Society, 1902). In this work it is said that "the mainspring of the whole organization of the Society is a spirit of entire obedience: 'Let each one,' writes St. Ignatius, 'persuade himself that those who live under obedience ought to allow themselves to be moved and directed by divine Providence through their superiors, just as though they were a dead body, which allows itself to be carried anywhere and to be treated in any manner whatever, or as an old man's staff, which serves him who holds it in his hand in whatsoever way he will.'"—p. 6.

Page 99. THE INQUISITION. See *The Catholic Encyclopedia,* vol. 8, art. "Inquisition"; and E. Vacandard, *The Inquisition: A Critical and Historical Study of the Coercive Power of the Church* (New York: Longmans, Green, and Company, 1908).

For the non-Catholic view, see Philip van Limborch, *History of the Inquisition;* Henry C. Lea, *A History of the Inquisition in the Middle Ages,* 3 vols.

Page 113. CAUSES OF THE FRENCH REVOLUTION. See H. von Sybel, *History of the French Revolution,* bk. 5, ch. 1, pars. 3–7; H. T. Buckle, *History of Civilization in England,* chs. 8, 12, 14 (New York, ed. 1895), vol. 1, pp. 364–366, 369–371, 437, 540, 541, 550; *Blackwood's Magazine,* vol. 34, no. 215 (November 1833), p. 739; J. G. Lorimer, *An Historical Sketch of the Protestant Church in France,* ch. 8, pars. 6, 7.

Page 113. PROPHETIC DATES. See note for page 26.

Page 114. EFFORTS TO SUPPRESS AND DESTROY THE BIBLE. The Council of Toulouse ruled: "We prohibit laymen possessing copies of the Old and New Testament. . . . We forbid them most severely to have the above books in the popular language." "The lords of the districts shall carefully seek out the heretics in homes, the humblest shacks, and forests, and even their underground retreats shall be entirely wiped out."—*Concil. Tolosanum, Pope Gregory IX, Anno chr. 1229.* Canons 14, 2. This council sat at the time of the crusade against the Albigenses.

"This pest [the Bible] had gone to such an extreme that some people had appointed priests of their own, and even some evangelists who distorted and destroyed the truth of the gospel and made new gospels for their own purpose, . . . [they know that] the preaching and explanation of the Bible is absolutely forbidden to the lay members."—*Acts of Inquisition,* Philip van Limborch, *History of the Inquisition,* ch. 8.

At the Council of Constance in 1415, Wycliffe was condemned after his death as "that dangerous wretch of damnable heresy who invented a new translation of the Scriptures in his mother tongue."

Opposition to the Bible by the Roman Catholic Church increased because of the success of the Bible societies. On December 8, 1864, in his proclamation *Quanta cura,* Pope Pius IX issued a list of eighty errors under ten different headings. Under heading 4 we find listed: "Socialism, communism, clandestine societies, Bible societies. . . . Pests of this sort must be destroyed by all possible means."

In recent years a dramatic and positive change has occurred in the Roman Catholic Church. On the one hand, the church has approved several Bible versions prepared on the basis of the original languages; on the other, it has promoted the study of the Holy Scriptures by means of free distribution and Bible institutes. The church, however, continues to reserve for herself the exclusive right to interpret the Bible in the light of her own tradition. In this way she justifies those doctrines that do not harmonize with biblical teachings.

Page 117. THE REIGN OF TERROR. For a reliable introduction to the history of the French Revolution, see L. Gershoy, *The French Revolution* (1932); G. Lefebvre, *The Coming of the French Revolution* (Princeton, 1947); and H. von Sybel, *History of the French Revolution,* 4 vols. (1869).

See also A. Aulard, *Christianity and the French Revolution* (London, 1927), which carries the account through 1802—an excellent study.

Page 118. THE MASSES AND THE PRIVILEGED CLASSES. See H. von Hoist, *Lowell Lectures on the French Revolution,* lecture 1; also Taine, *Ancient Regime;* and A. Young, *Travels in France.*

Page 120. RETRIBUTION. See Thos. H. Gill, *The Papal Drama,* bk. 10; Edmond de Pressense, *The Church and the French Revolution,* bk. 3, ch. 1.

Page 120. THE ATROCITIES OF THE REIGN OF TERROR. See M. A. Thiers, *History of the French Revolution* (New York, ed. 1890, tr. by F. Shoberl), vol. 3, pp. 42–44, 62–74, 106; F. A. Mignet, *History of the French Revolution* (Bohn, ed. 1894), ch. 9, par. 1; Sir Archibald Alison, *History of Europe From the Commencement of the French Revolution to the Restoration of the Bourbons in 1815,* vol. 1, ch. 14 (New York, ed. 1872), vol. 1, pp. 293–312.

Page 121. THE CIRCULATION OF THE SCRIPTURES. In 1804, according to Mr. William Canton of the British and Foreign Bible Society, "all the Bibles extant in the world, in manuscript or in print, counting every version in every land, were computed at not many more than four millions."

From 1816 to 2010, the American Bible Society (ABS) alone published more than 3.8 billion copies of the whole Bible and over 1.1 billion copies of portions of the Bible. In just the year 2010 the ABS published 4.2 million copies of the whole Bible. Other Bible societies would add many millions more copies to these figures.

The United Bible Societies reported that while the Bible was available in only sixty-eight languages at the beginning of the nineteenth century, by 2008 it was available in 2,479 languages, with at least 451 of them having the complete Bible.

Page 121. FOREIGN MISSIONS. The missionary activity of the early Christian church had virtually died out by the year 1000, and was followed by the military campaigns of the Crusades. The Reformation era saw little foreign mission work. The pietistic revival produced some missionaries. In the eighteenth century, the work of the Moravian Church was remarkable, and the British formed some missionary societies to work in colonized North America. But the great revival of foreign missionary activity began around the year 1800, at "the time of the end" (Daniel 12:4). In 1792 the Baptist Missionary Society sent William Carey to India. In 1795 the London Missionary Society was organized, and another society in 1799, which in 1812 became the Church Missionary Society. Shortly afterward the Wesleyan Methodist Missionary Society was founded. In the United States, the American Board of Commissioners for Foreign Missions was formed in 1812, and Adoniram Judson was sent out that year to Calcutta. He established himself in Burma the next year. In 1814 the American Baptist Missionary Union was formed. The Presbyterian Board of Foreign Missions was formed in 1837.

"In A.D. 1800 . . . the overwhelming majority of Christians were the descendants of those who had been won before A.D. 1500. . . . Now, in the nineteenth century, came a further expansion of Christianity. . . . Never in any similar length of time had Christianity given rise to so many new movements. It had never had quite so great an effect on Western European peoples. From this great vigor came the missionary efforts that so greatly increased the numerical strength and the influence of Christianity during the nineteenth century."—Kenneth Scott Latourette, *A History of the Expansion of Christianity,* vol. IV, The Great Century, A.D. 1800–A.D. 1914 (New York: Harper and Bros., 1914), pp. 2–4.

Page 128. LISBON EARTHQUAKE. In the time since the author first wrote these words in 1888, other earthquakes have been recorded with greater loss of life and perhaps higher magnitudes. (Scientific measurement of earthquakes was not yet in existence in 1755.) Still, the Lisbon earthquake ranks as one of the most important in modern history, not merely for its physical devastation, but because of the profound philosophical, theological, and cultural changes that resulted from this disaster.

Page 137. A DAY FOR A YEAR. See note for page 26.

Page 138. THE YEAR 457 B.C. For the certainty of the date 457 B.C. being the seventh year of Artaxerxes, see S. H. Horn and L. H. Wood, *The Chronology of Ezra 7* (Washington, D.C.: Review and Herald Publishing Assn., 1953); E. G. Kraeling, *The Brooklyn Museum Aramaic Papyri* (New Haven or London, 1953), pp. 191–193; *The Seventh-day Adventist Bible Commentary* (Washington, D.C.: Review and Herald Publishing Assn., 1954), vol. 3, pp. 97–110.

Page 141. FALL OF THE OTTO-

MAN EMPIRE. Throughout the Reformation era Turkey was a continual threat to European Christendom; the writings of the Reformers often condemn the Ottoman power. Christian writers since have been concerned with the role of Turkey in future events, and commentators on prophecy have seen Turkish power and its decline forecast in Scripture.

For the "hour, day, month, year" prophecy, as part of the sixth trumpet, Josiah Litch worked out an application of the time prophecy, ending Turkish independence in August 1840.

A book by Uriah Smith, *Thoughts on Daniel and the Revelation,* rev. ed. of 1944, discusses the prophetic timing of this prophecy on pp. 506–517.

Page 156. ASCENSION ROBES. The story that the Adventists made robes with which to ascend "to meet the Lord in the air" was invented by those who wished to discredit the advent preaching. Careful investigation has shown that it was false.

For a thorough refuting of the legend of ascension robes, see Francis D. Nichol, *The Midnight Cry* (Washington, D.C.: Review and Herald Publishing Assn., 1944), chs. 25–27, and Appendices H–J. See also L. E. Froom, *The Prophetic Faith of Our Fathers* (Washington, D.C.: Review and Herald Publishing Assn., 1954), vol. 4, pp. 822–826.

Page 180. A THREEFOLD MESSAGE. Revelation 14:6, 7 foretells the proclamation of the first angel's message. Then the prophet continues:

"Another angel followed, saying, 'Babylon is fallen, is fallen.' . . . Then a third angel followed them." The word here rendered "followed" means "to go along with," "to follow one," "go with him." It also means "to accompany." The idea intended is that of "going together," "in company with." The idea in Revelation 14:8, 9 is not simply that the second and third angels followed the first in point of time, but that they went with him. They are *three* only in the order of their rise. But having risen, they go on together.

Page 184. SUPREMACY OF THE BISHOPS OF ROME. See James Cardinal Gibbons, *The Faith of Our Fathers* (Baltimore: John Murphy Co., 110th ed., 1917), chs. 5, 9, 10, 12.

Page 234. THE SABBATH AMONG THE WALDENSES. See note for page 32.

Page 235. THE ETHIOPIAN CHURCH AND THE SABBATH. Until rather recent years the Coptic Church of Ethiopia observed the seventh-day Sabbath. The Ethiopians also kept Sunday. The observance of the seventh-day Sabbath, however, has virtually ceased in modern Ethiopia. For eyewitness accounts of religious days in Ethiopia, see Pero Gomes de Teixeira, *The Discovery of Abyssinia by the Portuguese in 1520* (translated into English in London: British Museum, 1938), p. 79; Father Francisco Alvarez, *Narrative of the Portuguese Embassy to Abyssinia During the Years 1520–1527,* in *Records of the Hakluyt Society* (London, 1881), vol. 64, pp. 22–49.